The Politics of Child Sexual Abuse

THE POLITICS OF CHILD SEXUAL ABUSE

Emotion, Social Movements, and the State

Nancy Whittier

OXFORD
UNIVERSITY PRESS

UNIVERSITY PRESS

Oxford University Press, Inc., publishes works that further
Oxford University's objective of excellence
in research, scholarship, and education.

Oxford   New York
Auckland   Cape Town   Dar es Salaam   Hong Kong   Karachi
Kuala Lumpur   Madrid   Melbourne   Mexico City   Nairobi
New Delhi   Shanghai   Taipei   Toronto

With offices in
Argentina   Austria   Brazil   Chile   Czech Republic   France   Greece
Guatemala   Hungary   Italy   Japan   Poland   Portugal   Singapore
South Korea   Switzerland   Thailand   Turkey   Ukraine   Vietnam

Copyright © 2009 by Oxford University Press, Inc.

Published by Oxford University Press, Inc.
198 Madison Avenue, New York, New York 10016

www.oup.com

First issued as an Oxford University Press paperback, 2011

Oxford is a registered trademark of Oxford University Press

All rights reserved. No part of this publication may be reproduced,
stored in a retrieval system, or transmitted, in any form or by any means,
electronic, mechanical, photocopying, recording, or otherwise,
without the prior permission of Oxford University Press.

Library of Congress Cataloging-in-Publication Data
Whittier, Nancy, 1966–
The politics of child sexual abuse : emotions, social movements, and
the state / Nancy Whittier.
   p. cm.
Includes bibliographical references and index.
ISBN 978-0-19-978331-1
1. Child sexual abuse. 2. Child sexual abuse—Government policy.
I. Title.
HV6570.W55 2009
362.76—dc22   2008053887

Printed in the United States of America

For Sally A. Kennedy

Acknowledgments

I am grateful for the communities of scholars, students, and activists who have provided feedback and a sounding board as I have worked on this research. My students at Smith College have been a source of inspiration; their questions and comments have enriched my thinking about gender, sexuality, social movements, and politics. My friends and colleagues at Smith and elsewhere have shaped my analysis through countless conversations about this project and the conceptual and political issues it raises. The activists whom I interviewed for this book gave generously of their time and insight and shared their recollections and impressions freely. Their courage and persistence are inspiring, and I am grateful that writing this book allowed me to get to know them.

I have been fortunate to have many excellent student research assistants at Smith. Allyson Mount did the initial literature sources, searched the archives for early feminist documents, transcribed interviews, and provided many useful comments and suggestions. Carolyn Gillis transcribed many interviews; Meg Chilton collected data on federal legislation; Laura Braunstein assisted with coding organizational documents; and Meg Nicoll located information on federal grants. Morgan Lynn collected and sorted a daunting amount of data on state and federal legislation, and was a fantastic sounding board; she also read and commented on parts of the manuscript. Adrienne Mathews intrepidly sought answers to my diverse queries on everything from public policy to media coverage to movement history. Smith's Committee on Faculty Compensation and Development provided the funding for these assistants. Also at Smith, reference librarian Sika Berger was a helpful resource for my research assistants and for me, as were the reference staff in the Sophia Smith Collection. The student activists in Smith's SAFE (Survivors and Friends for Education) and AWARE (Activist Women Advocating Rape Education) were an inspiration.

Martha Ackelsberg, Francesca Cancian, Rick Fantasia, Sally Kennedy, Morgan Lynn, Robin Maltz, Greg Maney, Jo Reger, Kim Voss, Kate Weigand, and participants in the Smith College Kahn Institute for Liberal Arts project on "From Local to Global: Community Activism in the New Millennium" commented on parts of the manuscript or related papers. Donna Jenson helped me talk through several thorny issues. Elaine Westerlund, Kathy Morrissey, and Maggie Jochild generously provided access to their personal archives. Tricia Bruce provided useful information about clergy abuse. The cover image is from a quilt made by Michelle Harris, Frances Grossman, K.L., Kathy Morrissey, and Elaine Westerlund. I am grateful to them for allowing me to reproduce it. Several hardy souls read and commented on the whole thing in its much-longer original form: Leila Rupp, Ross Cheit, Janice Irvine, Debra Minkoff, and several anonymous reviewers for OUP. James Cook, my editor at OUP, had many useful comments and suggestions. I am grateful for these comments, and the book is better as a result. Writing about child sexual abuse can be difficult and depressing, and I am especially grateful to Jo Reger for her support throughout the research and writing.

Two respondents for whom I used pseudonyms in the hardcover printing of the book, Maggie Jochild and Staci Haines, are referred to by name in this edition because of their importance to the historical record of this movement. I am especially grateful to both of them for giving me permission to name them, and for their assistance in this project.

This project has been with me through the birth and early childhood of three children, my own health problems and those of family members, one major move, two terms as Chair of my department, three computers, numerous smaller writing projects, and many other disruptions major and minor. It might have been done more quickly without all of these, but it would probably not have been done as well, and I certainly would have enjoyed the doing less. I particularly appreciate my partner, Kate Weigand, my oldest son, Jonah, who was two when I began the research, and my twins, Eva and Isaac, who were born in the midst of it. Thank you for the distraction and the support.

This book is dedicated to my late mother, Sally A. Kennedy. While she did not live to see it published, her influence is on every page, in my attempt to write precisely and to understand the complexities of human interaction.

Contents

Acronyms   xi

Introduction   3

1 From Rare Perversion to Patriarchal Crime: Feminist
   Challenges to Knowledge about Incest in the 1970s   21

2 The Politics of the "Therapeutic Turn": Self-Help and
   Internalized Oppression   40

3 Social Services, Social Control, and Social Change:
   The State and Public Policy in the 1970s and 1980s   70

4 Going Mainstream: Self-Help Activism During the 1980s   95

5 Diffusion and Dilution: Mass Culture Discovers Child
   Sexual Abuse   111

6 Turning Tides: Countermovement Organizing,
   "False Memory Syndrome," and the Struggle over
   Scientific Knowledge   133

7 The Politics of Visibility: Coming Out, Activist Art,
  and Emotional Change   167

8 The Paradoxical Consequences of Success   182

Conclusion   208

Notes   215

References   237

Index   253

Acronyms

CAP (Child Assault Prevention Project)

CAPTA/CAPTARA (Child Abuse Prevention and Treatment Act/ Child Abuse Prevention and Treatment and Adoption Reform Act)

CPS (Child Protective Services)

FMSF (False Memory Syndrome Foundation)

IAF (Incest Awareness Foundation)

ISA (Incest Survivors Anonymous)

ISRNI (Incest Survivors' Resource Network International)

NCCAN (National Center on Child Abuse and Neglect)

NY-WAR (New York Women Against Rape)

SIA (Survivors of Incest Anonymous)

SSBGs (Social Service Block Grants)

VAWA (Violence Against Women Act)

VOCA (Victims of Crime Act)

VOCAL (Victims of Child Abuse Laws)

VOICES, AKA VOICES in Action (loosely translated as "Voices of Incest Survivors")

Errata

In the first printing, two individuals were given pseudonyms whose real names should have been used. Elaine Westerlund was referred to as Leanne and Kathy Morrissey was referred to as Maureen.

On page 45, the final paragraph stated that Incest Resources operated into the 2000s. Incest Resources has been an active organization from 1980 to the present.

On page 51, the second paragraph stated that several members of Incest Resources drew on Re-evaluation Counseling techniques in their self-help groups, and on page 62, the final paragraph, which continues to page 63, stated that the women who organized Incest Resources had a background in co-counseling. Only one of the women who organized Incest Resources had a background in co-counseling and she was never involved with their self-help groups.

On page 60, the second paragraph identified Elaine Westerlund as white, and on page 61 she is referred to as a white feminist. She is of mixed racial identity.

On page 193, the fourth paragraph referred to Kathy Morrissey as an activist inside a state agency and stated that she formed an advisory group with local advocates and professionals in 1994. Kathy worked as an advocate inside a state agency and did not form an advisory group.

We apologize for these errors, which have been changed in the second printing.

The Politics of Child Sexual Abuse

Introduction

1950s: *Growing up in the 1940s, Barbara never talked about having been raped by a family member. As a young adult, she went to a psychiatrist who told her that people generally weren't bothered by incest, and, despite her distress, she let the matter drop.*

1982: *Several women in their twenties met through a local feminist anti-violence group. Discovering their shared experiences of childhood sexual abuse, they began meeting to support each other, theorize about child sexual abuse, and work to make the issue more visible.*

1995: *A man in his thirties confronted his parents with accusations of child sexual abuse. Denying his account, they argued that his memories were false, implanted by a therapist's suggestive techniques. They referred to literature from the False Memory Syndrome Foundation, and implored him to see a new therapist.*

1998: *The stickers read "Proud Survivor" and "The Abuse Stops Here." Fluorescent green and orange, plastered to marchers' bodies, they caught the eye of onlookers, who often cheered or mouthed, "Me, too," as Run Riot, a survivors' activist group, chanted and sang its way along the route of the San Francisco Gay Pride Parade.*

1999: *In her thirties, Susan understood the silence around her sexual abuse by a family member as the result of racism, fueled by the idea that an African-American woman speaking up about incest supported the* *demonization of Black men. In response, she proclaimed, "That fear has allowed the death of Black women and girls. At some point, I think we have to say that we are worth...speaking out about it and we are worth our brothers, Black men...to stand with us and say, 'We will not allow this to continue. We will not sanction this silence.'"*

1999: *A longtime activist I interviewed explained, "I have gone from never having seen a survivor in the early 1980s to having worked with hundreds of women by the end of the 1980s. I've gone from thinking I was the only one to being crystal-clear about how condoned sexual assault is and the implications that it has for women and children."*

2002/2003: *At a meeting with the National Centers for Disease Control and Prevention, the child sexual abuse prevention organization Stop It Now! helped outline a new approach to preventing child sexual abuse that built on successful public health campaigns against smoking and drunk driving. Impressed, the CDC funded programs by Stop It Now! and similar groups. At the same time, the Ms. Foundation convened a meeting of organizations from around the country to discuss how to jumpstart a social movement against child sexual abuse.*

Nearly everything about the cultural and political response to child sexual abuse has changed, sometimes more than once, since 1970. This book tells the story of how we got from there to here and explores what that journey tells us about child sexual abuse, gender politics, and how social change happens. The changes that these vignettes illustrate are due to the efforts of a social movement of child sexual abuse survivors, feminists, professionals, and other advocates, in tension with an opposing movement of parents accused of child sexual abuse and researchers who dispute the reliability of memory. Many of the changes are readily visible, but others occurred out of view in the arcane world of federal policy and state bureaucracy or took place within activist groups and were well known only in those circles. The connections between the actions of the government bureaucrats, local social workers, grassroots activists, and their opponents, have remained hidden until now.

This book is about those connections and how sometimes-competing groups of activists achieved a revolution in attitudes and policies toward child sexual abuse. I tell the collective story of activists and their groups alongside the story of how media portrayals and public policy around child sexual abuse evolved. I paint the first comprehensive picture of how activism on this issue emerged from the women's movement in the early 1970s, changed over time as it entered the mainstream, and ultimately transformed the political and cultural landscape. In doing so, I also examine the transformations in feminist politics more broadly, the role of emotions and the self in social change, and the sometimes unexpected ways that activists influence mainstream culture and institutions.

Until the early 1970s, the prevailing view was that child sexual abuse was extremely rare and mostly confined to the economically disadvantaged or to particular ethnic or racial groups. Seductive children were thought to provoke sexual contact with adults, and incest was often believed to be the result of controlling mothers who drove their husbands into their daughters' arms (Brownmiller 1975; Butler 1985; Rush 1980). The issue was rarely discussed, and those who had been sexually abused often disclosed their experiences to no one. While some of these ideas remain in circulation today, the scope and speed of change are remarkable.

Child sexual abuse is an unlikely political battleground. It has few advocates, and most people find it easy to condemn. And yet, there have been numerous struggles over it: Can the claims of adult survivors, the testimony of children, or the denials of those accused of offenses be believed? What is the nature of memory? Should offenders receive psychological treatment, or should they be punished? Does reducing child sexual abuse require fundamental change in the patriarchal family, or in institutions such as the Catholic Church where it occurs, or is it an aberration within otherwise functional institutions? Should government fund programs to prevent or remediate child sexual abuse, or should it stay out of the private business of families? These battles have played out in the arenas of federal and state policy, scientific research and professional therapeutic knowledge, mass culture, grassroots politics, and people's daily lives.

In the pages that follow, I tell the stories of these battles. They are instructive not just for understanding responses to child sexual abuse, but for understanding social change more generally. Activism for social change, I will suggest, takes many different forms, beyond protest demonstrations or letter-writing campaigns. It includes "bearing witness" or making new identities and experiences visible, the creation and dissemination of new knowledge, and the actions focused on changing individuals' emotions and sense of self that have often been dismissed as merely therapeutic. Correspondingly, the state, institutions, and opposing social movements, use the same range of strategies for their own ends. The broad range of activist and state actions, in concert with cultural representations, are what define and redefine the meanings, policies, and individual experiences associated with child sexual abuse—and, indeed, with most issues.

Child sexual abuse is an issue that cuts across political lines. Feminists brought it to public attention in the 1970s, but they could not maintain ownership of the issue. Indeed, their very efforts to bring attention, money, and serious societal response to child sexual abuse promoted the involvement of individuals and institutions from decidedly nonfeminist positions. Politicians of all stripes stood to gain support from their constituencies by claiming opposition to child abuse (Nelson 1984). Physicians and mental health practitioners brought their own professional priorities to the table (Davis 2005). And because child sexual abuse occurs in all social groups—across political allegiances, as well as race, class, and culture—women and men from diverse perspectives identified as survivors. In some cases, this diversity led to surprising alliances across political lines; at other times, it led to uneasy truces or episodic issue-based alliances.

Yet while the movement became extremely varied in composition, its feminist origins continued to influence how even conservative groups framed and sought to remedy child sexual abuse. The changes in policy, culture, and individual experiences around child sexual abuse reflect both the goals of feminists, and those of nonfeminist survivor activists, opponents, medical professionals, law enforcement, and elected officials. These changes, influenced by other actors, illustrate the complex long-term outcomes of the women's movement of the 1960s and 1970s.

Activism against child sexual abuse exemplifies post-Sixties politics. It was shaped by the movements of the 1960s and 1970s, entered the mainstream in watered-down form like so many other offspring of the 1960s, gradually reshaped how we see the issue and how institutions respond to it, and spawned multiple new forms and sites of activism. These new forms of activism, heavily influenced by the feminist notion of the personal as political, politicized emotion and the effects of inequality on individuals, targeting them for social change (Meyer and Whittier 1994). The movement against child sexual abuse is a microcosm of these politics of emotion and internalized oppression. In its attempts to change how people think and feel, it illustrates the politicization of emotion and identity. In its engagement with public policy, it illustrates the limits and leverage of that form of politics within the state. It therefore helps us understand the rise of a mass self-help culture, as well as debates over the political implications of public policy and social services oriented toward managing individuals' emotions and identities.

The history of the movement against child sexual abuse is not how any of the players in the polarized debates over the issue would tell it. It is not a history that fits ideas about social movements as unified, coherent challenges based in formal organizations and consistent goals. It is a history of neither failure nor triumph, neither purity of purpose nor sell-out. It is not solely a story of feminism and anti-feminism, or of individual healing from trauma, or of institutional change. It is a story of how a vibrant social movement achieved major change on an issue, but often in ways that activists could not predict or control. Precisely for these reasons, this movement sheds light on how social change—partial and contradictory—occurs.

Large numbers of people, in this movement and in others, have remained concerned with challenging the social forces that shape their lives. Paradoxically, they use the language of psychotherapy and personal growth to discuss these forces and to try to change them. They do so at a time when powerful institutions, including the government, also use these same languages in an effort to sway the populace to their own ends (Rose 1990, 1999). In other words, both activists and their targets have taken a "therapeutic turn." Activists' use of therapeutic ideas and language is not inevitably apolitical, however, but can be a means of taking the fight to the enemy, combating attempts by the powerful to affect how individuals see themselves by creating alternate models of individuals' identities and interior lives. Even as activists use therapeutic language and practices to do so, they challenge the power and control that those same practices seek to perpetuate.

A Short History of Activism and Social Change around Child Sexual Abuse

Whether child sexual abuse occurs, and how often, has been debated for centuries. Public concern and intervention have peaked and declined multiple times, sometimes springing from feminist activism and sometimes growing from other medical or political frameworks (Gordon 1988; Herman 1992; Jenkins 1998).[1] The most sizeable of the previous efforts, the child protective movement of the late 1800s, was populated by feminists (Gordon 1988). While very different from the later movements against child sexual abuse described in this book, it is evidence of a longstanding connection between feminism and activism against child abuse. Nevertheless, these previous efforts had slipped out of view by the time feminists took up the issue again nearly 100 years later.

I have divided the more recent movement against child sexual abuse into five overlapping phases, each dominated by a distinct wing or approach and corresponding to shifts in public policy and media representations of the issue: a *feminist* phase, from the early 1970s–1980, a *feminist self-help* phase from about 1980–1982, a *single-issue self-help* phase, from about 1981–1992, a *countermovement* phase from about 1992–2000, and an overlapping *post-countermovement* phase, from the late 1990s to the present. All five phases of the movement used different strategies to target overlapping arenas of personal transformation, cultural change, public policy, law enforcement, and psychotherapy.

The first phase brought child sexual abuse to public attention through the efforts of *feminists* working within the anti-rape movement in the 1970s. They saw sexual violence against children as a product of patriarchy in which fathers were granted control and access over all members of their families. Emphasizing its frequency and political roots, they were key in bringing child sexual abuse to the attention of media, psychotherapists, and the state. They sought cultural change through the creation of new knowledge about child sexual abuse and emphasized the need for institutions of law enforcement and treatment to change fundamentally in response.

The early feminist organizations spawned the second phase, the *feminist self-help movement*, around 1980. These activists created new ways of understanding child sexual abuse through grassroots and experiential research and developed new techniques for dealing with its effects on individuals based on practices of lay therapy, also known as "self-help." They saw child sexual abuse as both societal, requiring social sanction and prevention and rooted in the lack of these protections, and individual, originating and reverberating within the selves of both perpetrator and victim. They elaborated a model of "internalized oppression," arguing that societal inequalities echoed within individuals' psyches. Through self-help, they mounted a challenge to the structure and organizational dominance of professional therapy.

As their ideas reached a broader audience, and as professionals and government officials confronted child sexual abuse, a larger movement of survivors emerged. This *single-issue survivors' movement* focused on self-help, but also worked to bring greater public awareness and understanding about child sexual abuse. These activists, both men and women, thought of themselves as "non-political," and analyzed the causes and effects of child sexual abuse more narrowly, without promoting a feminist or other larger political analysis. They encouraged survivors of abuse to speak out, seek help, and help others. They achieved considerable visibility and influence, and self-help groups spread rapidly around the country during the 1980s. Like their predecessors, they sought societal change as well as personal transformation, but they placed great hope in mass media for achieving public education.

Activists from all three wings were often part of government efforts to combat abuse. The often-invisible ties that emerged between this highly decentralized grassroots movement and state bureaucracies contradict the received wisdom about what kind of social movements influence the state, how the state affects activists, and the boundary between state and challenger. As the federal government expanded mandates for state services for child sexual abuse in the late 1970s and the 1980s (Nelson 1984), government agencies funded numerous research and treatment projects and unintentionally created an infrastructure that helped to support activists who, in turn, were often unaware of how their fates rose and fell with governmental mandates and dollars. Many of the local organizations who took advantage of these monies had ties to the emerging movement. For example, feminist anti-rape organizations developed prevention programs for schoolchildren, and self-help groups provided speakers to train courtroom child advocates. But other activists and professionals also influenced the state's approach, arguing for increased law enforcement and shaping a government discourse that saw both the causes and effects of child sexual abuse in medical and criminal, rather than societal, terms. Movement influence melded with the state's agenda, leading to policies that amalgamated feminist, therapeutic, and social control approaches.

Similarly, activist efforts to bring the issue to public attention through the media paid off partially and imperfectly. Activists and authors in all three wings worked tirelessly to bring public attention to the issue and contributed to a huge increase in discussion of child sexual abuse in major magazines, self-help books, and television during the 1980s. The increased publicity was a mixed blessing. Although activists brought the issue to public attention, they could not control how the media portrayed child sexual abuse; as movement ideas were popularized, the overtly political elements dropped out. Media coverage was shaped by preexisting understandings of child sexual abuse and the conventions of journalistic story-telling and access, even as it drew on movement sources. In the end, mass media framed child sexual abuse as widespread and not the child's fault, but as a medical or criminal problem rather than a political one. The prescribed solution, thus, was treatment or incarceration of offenders rather than an increase in the social power of children or of women.

By the early 1990s, the gains of the first three phases of the movement sparked an energetic and influential *countermovement,* led by the False Memory Syndrome Foundation (FMSF). Made up of parents accused by their grown children of abuse and professionals who supported their cause, the countermovement challenged the veracity of "recovered memories," recollections of previously forgotten abuse. The countermovement defended adults charged with sexually abusing their now grown children, and also raised questions about children's testimony and adults' guilt in other child sexual abuse cases. It reshaped public opinion about memory and child sexual abuse by mustering scholarly evidence for the unreliability of childhood memories and defining its approach to the issue as based in science. The struggle between the opposing movements centered around both the social construction of knowledge and the policy gains of the movement, and ultimately led to unexpected alliances on both sides. Prevailing beliefs about child sexual abuse and recovered memory resulted from the activism of opposing movements and the cultural and political environments in which they operated. By analyzing knowledge as socially constructed, I shift the question from the veracity of opposing claims about memory to sociological questions about the conditions under which particular points of view gain credence.

When the dust from the "memory wars" settled in the mid-1990s, the political and cultural landscape around child sexual abuse was dramatically changed. A cultural climate in which accounts of child sexual abuse were greeted with belief and sympathy gave way to a climate of suspicion and doubt about the claims of both children and adults. A judicial climate in which child witnesses were treated with special care and recovered memories could lead to civil suits gave way to the discrediting of child witnesses and courts that refused to admit testimony based on recovered memories. The state, meanwhile, proceeded to incorporate child sexual abuse into the expansion and retrenchment of the prison system, proposing and implementing ever harsher laws requiring sex offenders to register with police, requiring community notification about local sex offenders, and permitting indefinite detention for offenders judged to be incurable sexual predators, even after their sentences expired.

By the turn of the century, the result was a paradoxical world in which best-selling books proclaiming fabrications in memory coexisted with those encouraging survivors to trust their memories, in which a highly educated Left largely disbelieved recovered memories and decried excessive state intervention into child welfare, seeing them as examples of victimology and state control run amok, while a self-help movement, largely made up of lower-middle and working-class white women, continued to practice lay therapy much as it had ten years earlier. It was a world in which the state defined child sexual abuse primarily as a criminal issue, and simultaneously used the discourse of trauma and recovery in many arenas, from foreign policy to domestic welfare reform. It was a world where sex offenders were depicted in the media as evil and untreatable and yet called hotlines to turn themselves in and seek treatment.

In this strange, changed climate, an active social movement against child sexual abuse continued. This *fifth phase* of the movement had two main wings, each of which focused simultaneously on individual, cultural, and policy change. One wing developed a *politics of visibility* that encompassed self-help groups for survivors, public "coming out," and activist art. The other wing entered into direct *relationship with the state*, providing services to survivors, working with crime victims' compensation programs, and developing an innovative public health approach to reducing the incidence of child sexual abuse. Politically eclectic, both wings made alliances with law enforcement and professionals in social services and medicine as easily as they did with feminists who remained active on the issue. While neither was explicitly or exclusively feminist, both modeled a politics that descended from the women's movement and blurred the lines between individuals' selves and societal institutions. They sought cultural change through visibility and targeted institutions of the state, medicine, law enforcement, and psychotherapy through direct engagement.

Most recently, public attention to abuse by clergy has brought the issue of child sexual abuse squarely into the public eye. In fact, there were many earlier accusations of sexual abuse by clergy throughout the 1980s and the Catholic Church paid out millions of dollars in settlements during that time (Castelli 1993; Investigative Staff 2002). The cases have received public attention only now because of the cultural and policy changes rendered by the survivors' movement and because of effective advocacy organizations of survivors of clergy abuse, many with roots in the earlier movement. Yet the priest cases have been framed in a way that is consistent with dominant discourses about pedophilia, a medical and sexual problem, not as a matter violence or power, and cases of clergy abuse of girls, while relatively common, have received very little press attention.[2] Whether we consider these social changes as evidence of a successful social movement depends on our definition of success and our view of the value of something less than complete social transformation.

Social Movements, Social Construction, and Social Control

The case of child sexual abuse illuminates key questions about how activists contribute to social change, how the state and mainstream culture constrain and enable those changes, and how individuals' identities and sense of self are connected to cultural representations and government policies. Scholars understand the debates over child sexual abuse from several angles. Some see them as an example of how the public identifies new social problems, either as the result of "moral panics" in which media hype arouses intense emotional response (Jenkins 1988), or through the actions of interest groups and the narratives they promote (Davis 2005). Some see the politics of child sexual abuse as a cautionary tale about how progressive and feminist movements took an apolitical "therapeutic turn," encouraged by the state's promotion of individualistic and therapeutic approaches that offer rights based on victimization (Brown 1995). In this vein, activism against child sexual abuse and the "recovery movement" have become a lightning rod for claims that feminism no longer deals with important issues but simply encourages women to revel in their victimization. This view, I suggest, misses the complexity of these movements, which sought not simply to affirm victimization, but to cast off its emotional effects and to reposition its subjects within the state and culture.

By focusing on the activists and organizations that sought to change society's response to child sexual abuse, I cast these questions in a new light. My key theoretical arguments are linked to the central questions of the meaning of the growth in therapeutic forms of activism, and the interplay between movement gains and the agendas of the state and mainstream culture in social change. I argue, first, that therapeutic activism was not inherently apolitical, but was a response to the forms of social control used by the therapeutic state. Therapeutic politics arose in tandem with the state's use of therapeutic language and individualism for social control, but they challenged the state's agendas in these areas as often as they conformed to it. In doing so, they sought to attack oppression as it resided in individual psyches as well as external society. Second, I show that the rise of medical and criminal interpretations of sexual abuse resulted from selection processes in the state and mainstream culture that submerged feminist interpretations, not from movements' own depoliticization or poor strategic choices. A detailed study of the social movement, mass media responses, and shifting governmental funding and intervention shows how activists were able to make change, but also how government, major institutions, and mass media favored the approaches and goals most consistent with their own agendas. These selection processes gave some movement organizations and approaches to the issue more influence than others, and thus shed light on processes of social change in the contemporary era. Third,

I argue that periods of rising concern about sexual abuse were not "moral panics," but the outcome of social movements.

In each case, I bring a social movements perspective to bear on questions that have been addressed predominantly through the lenses of political theory, cultural studies, and social problems. A social movements perspective entails focusing on how activists understood the issue, the full range of their actions, and the opportunities and limits they encountered as they attempted to influence culture and public policy. I seek to shift the terms of these debates, to emphasize the complexity and contradictions of politics on the ground, and to take seriously the aims and understandings of the activists involved in these social changes (Apostolidis 2008: 546).

Therapeutic Politics and the Therapeutic State

Because inequality operates at the levels of individual subjectivity, culture, and policy, social change entails changing individuals' feelings and identities, changing the culture, and changing policy (Collins 1990; Polletta 2002; Rupp and Taylor 2003; Taylor 1996; Whittier 1995, 2002). Understanding therapeutic politics requires considering the connections between the forms that social movements take and the forms of the state; thinking about the political significance of emotion and the self; and considering the implications of politics that seek to remedy trauma or injury and that interact with the state and mainstream culture in doing so. In an era when the state and major institutions attempt to shape individuals' identities and feelings, attempts to change identity and emotion entail challenges to the state and to the institutions of medicine, psychotherapy, and law enforcement. When the state allows access to rights based on identity category or experience of victimization (Brown 1995, 2005: Chap. 6), efforts to organize around those identities and to reduce or reconceptualize trauma or injury may simultaneously challenge and capitulate to the logic and agenda of the state.

An extensive literature argues that the *therapeutic state* exercises social control over people's interior worlds as well as their exterior actions. Such efforts attempt to shape how individuals identify themselves, how they feel, and how they choose to behave, using techniques such as allowing individuals access to state benefits by virtue of defined identity categories, and promulgating discourses that prescribe feelings or thought processes for particular situations (Nolan 1998; Polsky 1991; Rose 1990, 1999). Access to programs or to protection of rights rests in essentialized identity categories (such as race or gender) and claims of victimization or vulnerability (Brown 1995, 2005; Butler 1990; Smith 1987; Zerilli 2005). When government promotes intervention into individuals' selves through social work, psychotherapy, "job readiness training," mandated participation in addiction treatment programs, self-esteem promotion, and the like, it does so not just to promote the social good, but to make citizens more docile and less troublesome (Rose 1990). The addict who is required by a drug court to enter treatment will, if successful, improve her own life and those of people close to her; she will also be less likely to commit crime, reside on city streets, or contract diseases that the public health system will have to deal with (Nolan 1998). The welfare recipient who goes through job readiness training will, if successful, change how she thinks about herself and the world in ways that prepare her for her role as a low-paid cog in the capitalist economy. It is the range of technologies for molding and managing people's internal lives—their feelings, their identities, their beliefs about what is important and how the world works—that make up the therapeutic state (Polsky 1991).

A similarly influential line of argument about social movements suggests that they take shape partly in response to the forms of domination and state structures they encounter. Tarrow (1994) argues that the social movement as a particular form of organization emerged in response to the characteristics of the modern state. The consolidation of the nation-state meant that diverse, previously unlinked communities were treated as one population under national policies of conscription, taxation, and regulation, while industrialization and urbanization solidified constituencies. State regulation of relations between groups created a legal frameworks and specialized roles and identities that, in turn, provided the basis for groups to organize in a particular form, the association, which provided the model for social movement organizations for the next century. In short, citizens, constituted into constituencies by their common treatment, used the frameworks the state provided to construct challenges to the state (Tarrow 1994, 53–58).

Just as the nation state created new constituencies when it subjected people to common taxation and regulation, so too the therapeutic techniques used by authorities create constituencies with new ways of understanding themselves. The paradox is similar: the rise of the nation state simultaneously made possible greater regulation and exploitation of the population, and created the circumstances and frameworks under which challenging groups would emerge. Likewise, state regulation of daily life, emotion, and the self subjects the population to further surveillance and control, and yet creates the circumstances and frameworks under which new kinds of challenges emerge. State use of therapeutic discourse as a means of social control over daily life and interiority produced social movements that use therapeutic techniques to reconstruct feelings and identity at the same time that they advocate institutional social change.[3]

Activists against child sexual abuse organized in forms that are linked with daily life and adopted strategies to redefine the discourses used to define them. They challenged the construction of their subjectivity directly, focusing on collective identity and emotion as both strategy and goal. In doing so, they have not moved away from confrontation with the state; rather, they moved to confronting the state in its therapeutic arenas of domination. As Tarrow argues, they use the frameworks provided by the state—in this case therapeutic discourse and practice—to mount their challenge. They do so not because they are dupes who unwittingly submit to their own subjugation, but in an attempt to challenge the influence of the state and dominant culture over individuals' inner lives and to reconstruct identities, emotions, and beliefs according to their own goals. Activists have used a variety of techniques, including some that resemble psychotherapy and others that resemble more conventional collective action, to combat state authority within the self and daily life. In practice, they succeed and fail in the same mixture as movements that use nontherapeutic strategies.

Organizations took *hybrid* forms that incorporated both therapeutic and institutionally oriented efforts. Organizations in other social movements also took hybrid forms, combining advocacy with service provision (Matthews 1994; Minkoff 2002) or self-help (Taylor 1996). Like these, organizations in the movement against child sexual abuse combined advocacy with service provision and self-help, and also were ideological hybrids that combined therapeutic and institutional politics. They mirrored the therapeutic state's use of discourses of individual emotional healing and institutional transformation, but with a collective rather than individual emphasis and a critical edge. Hybridization carries advantages for organizations, allowing them access to resources from diverse sources, broadening their base of support, and helping them to survive hostile political times by offering services that seem politically neutral (Minkoff 2002).

Organizations and institutions in the political field of child sexual abuse used—or disclaimed—therapeutic politics in various ways. Whether organizations focused on therapeutic change did not predict whether they emphasized an individual or collective orientation, as table I–1 shows. Organizations in both categories sought external change in the state and mainstream culture as well as in emotions and beliefs about child sexual abuse.

Table I.1. Organizational Typology

	Therapeutic Focus	Nontherapeutic Focus
Individual Orientation	MEDICAL Treatment organizations (Phases 3, 5) Advocacy and nonprofits (Phases 1, 3, 5) Child advocacy centers (Phase 3, 5)	CRIMINAL Criminal justice reforms (Phases 1, 3, 4, 5) Offender registries; community notification (Phase 5)
Collective Orientation	HYBRIDS Feminist self-help groups (Phase 2) Single-issue self-help groups (Phase 3) Visibility politics (Phase 5) Public health groups (Phase 5)	KNOWLEDGE PRODUCERS Initial feminist activists (Phase 1) Countermovement (Phase 4)

Phases refer to the movement phases outlined on p. 7.

Thinking about Success: Selection Processes and Mainstream Influence

Activists' influence is delimited by the structure, priorities, and assumptions of the state and mainstream culture. Political opportunities—state structures, policies, balance of power and competing interests, and preexisting agendas of elected officials and various state agencies—shape movements' direction and effects, but do not determine them (Jenkins and Eckert 1986; McAdam, McCarthy, and Zald 1996; Meyer and Minkoff 2004; Tarrow 1994). The political opportunities available to movement groups depend on their position in the political process and the extent to which their goals and discourses support or conflict with existing interests. Ties to policymakers, major institutions, sources of funding, and knowledge-producers affect activists' ability to form organizations and make social change. Similarly, the existing culture shapes activists' ability to change accepted meanings or representations of their issue.[4] The kinds of access activists have to popular and academic means of disseminating their points of view are important, as is the cultural resonance of activists' frames, or their interpretations and presentations of the issue (Rochon 1998). When the interpretations that activists promote make sense within mainstream beliefs, their ideas are more likely to gain media coverage and to be persuasive to others (Rochon 1998; Snow et al.1986; Williams 1995, 2004).

In a heterogeneous movement, the organizations, frames, and identities that are most influential are those that are the most consistent with how the state and mainstream culture understand the issue. I conceptualize this as a *selection process* in which funding, media access, the workings of government bureaucracy and public policy, and internal organizational dynamics result in greater visibility and influence for some approaches than for others (Koopmans 2004). I use the term "selection process" as a metaphor to suggest the weeding out or elevating of particular positions from among a range of existing positions.[5]

Like many social movements, the movement against child sexual abuse was large and diverse, containing activists who defined being a survivor and the problem of child sexual abuse in different ways and called for drastically different solutions. They were not equal in their access to mainstream culture and the state. Those that were most consistent with prevailing cultural views and the state's preexisting priorities and institutions were the most likely to affect cultural representations and legislation and public policy. In particular, approaches that defined child sexual abuse as a crime deserving of law enforcement and punishment or a psychological issue requiring professional treatment were the most successful in influencing policy change. Organizations that understood themselves in those terms, or were able to frame part of their mission as being about reducing crime or treating pathology, fitted most easily into the state and treatment institutions, where they flourished. Their understanding of

Table I.2. Selection Processes for Movement Goals

	Entered the Mainstream	Did Not Enter the Mainstream
Therapeutic Focus	Professional therapy Victims' blamelessness Public disclosure and personal narratives	Nonprofessional self-help Internalized oppression Collective visibility, identity, solidarity
Institutional Critique	Reform of prosecution and treatment of victims/witnesses Multidisciplinary teams to address child sexual abuse cases Improved hospital procedures Increased professional treatment Prevention programs for children	Critique of patriarchy and family Critique of collusive institutions (e.g., Church, education) Alternatives to penal system

the issue and its solutions and their collective identity (or definition of what survivors are like) became more visible and influential, while other collective identities and goals receded. But the segments of the movement that moved into closer relationship with the state risked falling into a subordinate relationship, while those that packaged their message for mainstream culture risked muting their own systemic analysis of child sexual abuse.

One might expect, in line with the narrative about the women's movement's depoliticizing therapeutic turn, that organizations' service and therapeutic elements would become mainstreamed and split off from advocacy and institutional critique. In fact, the split did not occur along therapeutic/institutional lines. Instead, as activists sought change, both their therapeutic and institutional critiques were subject to selection processes, as shown in table I.2. For both therapeutic and institutional approaches, the less challenging elements of the movement's agenda entered policy or media, while the more challenging elements did not. These outcomes reflected the agendas of some groups more fully than others. Chapters 3, 5, and 8 explore these selection processes in detail.

Social Movements and Moral Panics: Child Sexual Abuse as a Social Problem

Most sociological analyses of responses to child sexual abuse take a social constructionist or social problems approach to the issue (Best 1990; Davis 2005; Hacking 1991; Jenkins 1998, 2001).[6] A social problems analysis seeks to explain how and why child sexual abuse comes to be understood at certain times as a distinct issue that is problematic. This is based on the premise that the ways we understand the phenomena we refer to as child sexual abuse—and whether, in fact, we see them as problems—change over time due to social forces (Davis 2005). To see an issue as socially constructed is to see its meaning not as intrinsic or transparent, but rather as one among many possible meanings. For example, which phenomena are considered to be part of the category "child sexual abuse"? Is it part of the same or a separate category from the rape of adults? What theories are used to explain its incidence, effects, treatment, and legal remedies? The analytical thrust of social problems analyses is to explain how the answers to these questions have changed over time.

These works provide useful historical analyses of some of the causes of changing views of child sexual abuse. They are hampered, however, by their "moral panic" theoretical framework. Most such works see child sexual abuse as generally infrequent and best defined narrowly, and thus try to explain how it has become seen as common, defined broadly, and subject to public concern and state intervention through criminal prosecution and child protective services.[7] In this view, periods of increased concern are "moral panics," led by overly zealous and ideological "child savers." A moral panic is defined as a wave of public "fear that is wildly exaggerated and wrongly directed" (Jenkins 1998: 7) in response to "beliefs about a threat from moral deviants" (Victor 1998: 541). These fears are seen as irrational and out of proportion to the actual threat (Goode and Ben Yehuda 1994; Hall et al. 1978). Analyses in this vein take public concern over satanic ritual abuse as the paradigmatic case, and show that concern ran high as a result of sensationalist media coverage and the claims of gullible or self-promoting "experts," rather than as a result of real danger (Best 1990; Jenkins 1998, 2001; Victor 1993, 1998).

Seeking to understand widespread concern about an issue as a form of collective behavior, the moral panic framework builds on earlier sociological work suggesting that people in groups or crowds adopt irrational behaviors or beliefs, in a kind of mass hysteria in which their usual behaviors and norms fall by the wayside under the influence of the group. The moral panic approach to social problems similarly assumes that people adopt irrational beliefs and feelings about an issue because they are swept up in a collective process of media hype and false information and subjected to "conformity pressures that enforce consensual beliefs" (Victor 1998: 560).[8] Writing for a popular source about the "moral panic" over sexual abuse by clergy, one sociologist described this as a "kind of fever—characterized by heightened emotion, fear, dread, anxiety, hostility, and a strong feeling of righteousness" (Hendershott 2002, cited in "Sexual Abuse by Clergy"). The panic analysis has been largely discredited in studies of crowd behavior, tramplings at soccer matches or rock concerts, or efforts to escape from burning buildings. Such studies show that tragedies such as trampling deaths in crowds occur as a result of poor engineering of facilities and queues, not "mass hysteria" (Clarke 2002). Panic or mass hysteria theories are even less applicable to cases of social movements, which are generally the outgrowth of groups' deliberate efforts to bring about social change, not individuals' possession by some kind of irrational conviction.

At issue here is not whether particular claims about child sexual abuse are accurate or not. Clearly, understandings of the issue change over time as a result of larger social forces, and it is reasonable to assume that such understandings might overplay or underplay the frequency and ramifications of what we call "child sexual abuse." However, framing a wave of concern as "moral panic" downplays social movements' influence over policy and popular understanding of an issue.[9] In contrast, I highlight how all parties to the debates—including movement actors—attempt to define and publicize child sexual abuse, and I view public silence about child sexual abuse or the belief that its impact is minimal as socially constructed, similar to public concern over the issue. Contrary to the vast majority of writing on social responses to child sexual abuse, I do not emphasize recovered memory or professional therapy for survivors as the central phenomena, although they are undeniably important. Instead, to understand social change around child sexual abuse, I focus on social movements, the state and public policy, and media representations, analyzing how these intersect in a political field (Ray 1998).

Studying Activism Against Child Sexual Abuse and Social Change

This is a book about social movements, but it is also a book about public policy and cultural representations. As a result, I have drawn on eclectic sources of information. My data on the feminist, self-help, public health, visibility, and wings of the movement are drawn from interviews with forty activists representing all of the movement wings. I sought interviewees from a range of organizations and perspectives, attempted to interview as many people of color as possible, and focused extra effort on finding interviewees who had been part of the earliest groups, about which less documentation exists. Interviews were in-depth, semistructured, and ranged from one and a half to eight hours in length. Respondents resided in all regions of the United States, with an overrepresentation of the west and east coasts. Eighty percent were white, approximately 10 percent African-American, and the remaining were Asian American, Latino/a, and Native American. Eighty-five percent were female, and ages ranged from 23 to 79. Demographically, they typify the movement against child sexual abuse.

In addition to the interviews, I draw on extensive documents from numerous movement organizations. These include newsletters, minutes of meetings, conference programs, and Web sites.[10] I also attended three conferences of adult survivor organizations, a demonstration organized by a movement organization, and several smaller events and meetings. I verified respondents' descriptions of movement activities whenever possible, by relying on multiple accounts and written documents when available. My data about the countermovement rely on documentary sources, including email notices, newsletters, and Web sites. I collected data about legislation and public policy using a wide range of governmental and nongovernmental sources. The analysis of federal funding is based on data on all federal grants disbursed by the National Center on Child Abuse and Neglect (NCCAN) between 1975–2000, as well as information on social service funding funneled through other channels. My discussion of popular culture is based on an analysis of all articles about child sexual abuse[11] indexed in the *Readers' Guide to Periodical Literature* from 1960 to 2000.

I have assigned pseudonyms to most respondents. I use the real names of a few respondents when discussing organizations they founded, for the sake of the historical record. Most respondents gave me permission to use their names, and some preferred that I do so, citing their desire to speak publicly and proudly about their experiences. Nevertheless, issues of liability and differences among respondents in their preferences have led me to use pseudonyms. Some respondents were well known within movement circles, and their identities may be apparent to participants despite my attempt to conceal identities. When I discuss actions that were public information, such as writing a book, I have used that person's real name, even though I retain the pseudonym elsewhere. In no cases have I changed identifying details, although I have sometimes omitted them to permit anonymity.

I attempt throughout the book to use the terms that participants used to describe themselves. This means that I refer to "survivors" of incest or child sexual abuse, because this was the term of choice through all the waves of the movement. The same is true for the terms "survivor movement," "false memory syndrome," "falsely accused parents," "healing," "recover," and many others. In addition to respecting participants' perspectives, I hope that my use of their terminology will help the reader to gain a sense of these movements from the inside, as participants perceived them. I make no attempt to judge the veracity of any individuals' accounts of their own experiences of abuse, nor of accused individuals' accounts of their own innocence.

Organization of the Book

The book is organized both chronologically and theoretically. Chapter 1 describes the earliest feminist exploration of child sexual abuse as a political issue, showing how that concern emerged from anti-rape organizations and began to spread through the feminist movement. Chapter 2 discusses the hybrid political and therapeutic approach of feminist self-help groups of the very early 1980s, which developed an analysis of internalized oppression that linked the political and the personal. Like the activists in chapter 1, these women constructed influential new knowledge about child sexual abuse, expanding on the politics and techniques of self-help. Chapter 3 focuses on the state and policy from the 1970s through the early 1990s, showing that the state apparatus dealing with child sexual abuse was a location of both opportunity and constraint for activists. Tracing legislation and funding, I show how professionals in the field and grass-roots activists benefited, and analyze the selection processes that pulled them toward medical and criminal approaches. Chapter 4 recounts the rise of single-issue self-help groups during the 1980s, showing how they both reflected and transformed the approach of their forebears and helped popularize a modified analysis of child sexual abuse as widespread, but not as a result of gender inequality. Chapter 5 shows how mass media portrayals of child sexual abuse during the 1970s and 1980s reflected a contradictory mixture of meanings drawn both from movement organizations and mainstream culture. Like policy gains, media selection processes favored movement messages that resonated with mainstream beliefs. Chapter 6 looks at counter-movement organizing, highlighting the struggles over the social construction of knowledge that came with the rise of the FMSF and its allies, and analyzing the political and cultural reasons for its success. Chapter 7 traces the development of a repoliticized self-help movement focused on visibility politics in the wake of the countermovement. Chapter 8 returns to the question of activists' engagement with the state, examining the different forms that movement organizations' relationships with state authorities took during the 1990s and 2000s, when the therapeutic state dealing with child sexual abuse was well developed, and shows the kind of access and compromise these relationships brought.

In the concluding chapter, I suggest that the ways that the movement against child sexual abuse sought to achieve change, and the ways that the external context shaped those changes and the movement itself, shed light on social movements more broadly. Activists against child sexual abuse did not achieve the changes they expected, but they contributed to dramatic changes in how people think and feel about child sexual abuse, how those who experience it cope and respond, how children who report it are treated, how it is represented in the mass media, and how government and public policy address it. In doing so, they also helped shape a politics that infused other social movements, blending emotion and policy, and changing both individuals' inner worlds and the larger social world.

1

From Rare Perversion to Patriarchal Crime

Feminist Challenges to Knowledge about Incest in the 1970s

In 1962, pediatrician Henry Kempe published what was to become a paradigm-shifting paper, "The Battered Child Syndrome." Based on his clinical experience with children with physical and emotional injuries, Kempe outlined the medical consequences of child abuse and argued that it was far more widespread than anyone had realized. Kempe's evidence was widely seen as indisputable since it rested on documented physical injuries. Although Kempe's focus was primarily on physical rather than sexual abuse, his work laid the groundwork for the recognition of sexual abuse by showing that parental abuse of children, far from unthinkable, was more common than previously believed, paving the way for medical and governmental intervention to detect and treat abuse. Solid and empirical, this approach began to reshape how medical professionals responded to injured children. Kempe's initial impact was on approaches to physical abuse. Professionals and policymakers continued to understand sexual abuse as the rare result of seductive children, distant wives, or deviant fathers. Responses to child sexual abuse first changed, not as a result of Kempe's groundbreaking work, but as a result of the efforts of feminist activists beginning around 1971. In rethinking rape, some of these activists also began to rethink child sexual abuse. They planted the seeds for a profound change in how laypeople, policymakers, and psychotherapists came to view child sexual abuse.

In the early 1970s, feminists active against rape began targeting child sexual abuse as a political issue and one of the many forms of violence they argued affected women. The first feminist activists on the issue broke new ground, analyzing child sexual abuse as a social and political problem rather than as individual pathology, and arguing that it was relatively common. Their new paradigm for understanding incest and child sexual abuse laid the foundation for widespread changes in public policy and mainstream culture. These first activists were scattered around the country, often with almost no connection to each other. Individuals and groups working on the issue sometimes knew about each others' existence, but more often they relied on vague rumors ("I heard there were some people working on the issue in New York") rather than actual connections. They gained a broader perspective on their own work through a handful of feminist analyses of child sexual abuse that circulated informally before being published in the late 1970s (Butler 1978; Herman 1981; Rush 1974, 1977, 1980). Their organizational networks were with other feminists, especially those working against rape. Radically decentralized, with groups in different places that were often almost totally disconnected from each other, these early challenges to child sexual abuse require us to think about social movements as something other than organizationally defined, consistent, and ongoing phenomena. In this chapter, I piece together a history of these challenges that documents the sources and contributions of the earliest activism on the issue.

"Women and Girls": The Anti-Rape Movement, Patriarchy, and Incest

In 1970, radical feminist Shulamith Firestone argued that "We must include the oppression of children in any program for feminist revolution or we will be subject to the same failing of which we have often accused men; of not having gone deep enough in our analysis" (Firestone 1970: 117, 118). As Andrea Dworkin later paraphrased Firestone, she argued that "women and children are not united by biology, we are united by politics, a shared powerlessness" (Dworkin 1988: 134). This perspective spurred some feminists to explore commonalities between the positions of women and children, and women in consciousness-raising (CR) groups discussed their childhood, including sexual experiences and assaults. For example, an undated flier from the early 1970s titled "An Introduction to the New York Radical Feminists" suggested topics for CR groups including "Early Childhood Sexual Experiences. Brothers/boys your age/older men traumas."[1] As with many topics that women discussed in CR, a political understanding of child sexual abuse coalesced gradually as participants realized that their own experiences were not uncommon.

The anti-rape movement challenged the notion that rape was about individual men's sexual perversion or criminality and argued instead that it was the exercise of men's power over women under patriarchy. It did not take long before anti-rape activists extended this analysis to the sexual abuse of children. The first analyses of patriarchal power and women's subordination as they played out in child sexual abuse were constructed by Susan Brownmiller and Florence Rush. Brownmiller, in her ground-breaking 1975 book on rape, *Against Our Will,* analyzed incest and child molestation as part of a seamless web of sexual assault against women. She used the term "father-rape" to emphasize both the similarity between rape of adults and children and the cultural legitimation of fathers' sexual access to their daughters.

Florence Rush elaborated a feminist analysis of the issue that was enormously influential. At an April 17, 1971, conference sponsored by the New York Radical Feminists, attended by 250 women,[2] Rush put forward the first extensive feminist analysis of incest.[3] Rush, a psychiatric social worker, had joined a consciousness-raising group in New York in 1971. Another member, who was part of New York Radical Feminists, told the CR group about an upcoming conference on rape. Rush explained:

> They needed someone to present a paper on incest and the sexual abuse of children, and...I just mentioned casually that as a social worker I had come across a lot [of sexual abuse], and what I noticed is that the abuser of children, or the person who was performing incest, was usually the male, and the victims were female. And she said, "Well, then, you have to do the presentation." And I said, "Are you kidding? There is no way I would do anything like that." She kept pressuring me.... I said I'd do it. So I got busy and I began researching, and I did a presentation. And it was very, very well received.

Rush's presentation, titled "The Sexual Abuse of Children: A Feminist Point of View," was indeed very, very well received. In the speech, which formed the basis for an article she published under the same title in 1974 in *Rape: A Sourcebook for Woman*, Rush argued that sexual objectification and victimization of female children by men was widespread and promoted by the patriarchal society. "The sexual abuse of children is an early manifestation of male power and oppression of the female," she said. "[T]he sexual abuse of children, who are overwhelmingly female, by sexual offenders who are overwhelmingly male adults, is part and parcel of the male-dominated society which overtly and covertly subjugates women" (Rush 1974: 66, 73). Linking incest with phenomena like public groping on subways and in theaters, flashing, ogling, and street harassment, Rush painted a picture of growing up female in which being molested was virtually universal. Such childhood experiences, she argued, were a form of the sexual objectification, assault, and subordination of women. Male sexual access to girls—daughters and strangers alike—was supported legally, religiously, and culturally, Rush argued. Far from being an unspeakable taboo, incest and child sexual abuse were the norm under patriarchy. "[T]he sexual molestation and abuse of female children is not regarded seriously by society, is winked at, rationalized, and allowed to continue through a complex of customs and mores that applauds the male's sexual aggression and denies the female's pain, humiliation, and outrage.... [S]exual abuse of children is permitted because it is an unspoken but prominent factor in socializing and preparing the female to accept a subordinate role; to feel guilty, ashamed, and to tolerate, through fear, the power exercised over her by men.... [T]he female's early sexual experiences prepare her to submit in later life to the adult forms of sexual abuse heaped on her by her boyfriend, her lover, and her husband. In short, the sexual abuse of female children is a process of education that prepares them to become the wives and mothers of America" (Rush 1974: 73–74).

Rush issued a profound challenge to the view that incest and child sexual abuse were rare, both because she linked the rape and incest of children with other types of sexual assault and because she blasted open the silence and secrecy surrounding the issue. Her approach dovetailed with the broader feminist anti-rape movement, which argued that rape was common, and that it only appeared rare because of the sanctions and stigma that kept victims from speaking about their experiences. But Rush also grounded her insistence on the widespread nature of incest in a critique of Freudian theory.[4] The view that incest was rare, she argued, stemmed from Freud's now-infamous retraction of his initial belief that many of his patients had been sexually assaulted as children. Freud's movement from his 1886 "seduction theory," which argued that hysteria resulted from actual childhood sexual experiences with the father (1953), to his 1933 repudiation of this position in favor of an emphasis on *fantasies* of sexual attraction and liaisons with the father (1966) is by now common knowledge. Rush's analysis of this shift was followed a decade later by Jeffrey Masson's (1984) more widely publicized version. In their view, Freud was forced to shift his position because it was socially unacceptable to believe his patients' reports that their prominent, respectable fathers had engaged in sex with them. Rush argued that Freud's denial of women's reports of abuse both grew from and supported the larger culture's denial of incest and of women's realities.

From all reports, Rush's speech electrified the NYRF conference. Paradigm-shifting, it conceptualized child sexual abuse, like rape, in terms of power and gender, rather than pathology or consent. The speech led to an influential book, *The Best Kept Secret: Sexual Abuse of Children*, published in 1980.

In the interim between Rush's speech and the initial publication of her work in 1974, some feminists around the country heard about Rush's analysis, while others came to similar conclusions independently. Their emerging concern with incest was grounded in experience with victims through rape crisis work. Generally organized by activists rather than professionals, rape crisis centers typically provided a telephone hotline, staffed by volunteers, and usually also offered self-defense training and public speaking. Volunteers accompanied rape victims to hospitals, police departments, and court appearances, and pressured hospitals and police to develop sensitive and appropriate procedures for dealing with rape. They saw their mission as ending rape by both empowering women to resist and changing societal attitudes. In the meantime, they sought to help victims by ending the stigma attached to rape, giving them a place to talk about it, and supporting them through whatever process of reporting and prosecution they chose. These were radical acts. Over time, rape crisis centers became absorbed by mainstream institutions, such as hospitals, mental health centers, and universities. But at the time, they were movement organizations through and through, and often targeted for change the very organizations that later absorbed them (Matthews 1994; Martin 2005).

Rape crisis centers around the country received calls from adults who had been raped or assaulted as children, children and teenagers who were currently being sexually abused, and parents or teachers of sexually abused children. Caught largely unprepared, these feminist activists extended their analysis of the rape of adult women to that of children.[5] For example, Christine Courtois (1988: xxiii), later a well-known feminist therapist and author on issues of child sexual abuse, described how, in 1972:

> I co-founded a campus rape crisis center at the University of Maryland. Although the mission of the center was to provide assistance to women immediately after a rape, it was not long before we started to get calls from women who had been raped in the past and had never told anyone before. Some of these callers confided that they had been assaulted not by strangers on the street but by men they knew and by family members.... We didn't know how to help these women. Mostly, we applied the techniques that we had learned to use with rape victims: We accepted these women's stories, told them they were not to blame, and urged them to keep trying to disclose the experience and to find someone who would help them escape if their situation were ongoing. We realized that we were dealing with another type of rape, one even more taboo than stranger rape, one that was harder to talk about and harder to recover from. We began to conceptualize incest as a compounded form of rape.

The view of incest as rape—the product of a patriarchal society, compounded by the powerless position of children—became ubiquitous in the discussions of the issue in feminist organizations and publications in the early and mid-1970s. Many articles in feminist newspapers made no distinction between adult women and girls. For example, at a 1973 speak-out on rape in Seattle, one speaker explained that "most cases she knew involved women being raped by an acquaintance or a friend, or a child raped by a parent or relative"; another "she had been raped when she was 19 but had told no one"; another "had been raped at 12 by her father, and never told anybody"; and a mother had a "14-year-old daughter [who] had been raped."[6] We see the use of the term "rape" to describe assaults, regardless of the age of the victim.

A lengthy article in the Seattle feminist newspaper *Pandora* in 1974 provides another example of the equation of child sexual abuse with adult rape in feminist analyses. The article reports on a sex-offender treatment program for almost exclusively male offenders who had assaulted either adults or children.[7] The article reported that, "In the period from July 1972 to June 1973, the program received 14 men convicted of rape and 46 convicted of indecent liberties with children" (p. 1). Despite the overwhelming majority of men who had assaulted children, the article emphasized lessons for thinking about rape, quoting a counselor that, "Male culture views *women* as objects, and these men pick that cultural interpretation and act on it, where other men are more subtle" (p. 10, emphasis added). It concluded with a call for social change that again framed adult women and girls as victims of the same social problem while recognizing the particular forms of inequality that children face:

> After receiving treatment, these men will return to a society which still considers *women and children as a class* to be victimized and exploited. Women are still advised to play the passive role rather than fight, and children are kept too ignorant to protect themselves in the name of the "innocence of childhood." (p. 11, emphasis added)

These early feminist documents mentioned the sexual assault of girls most often in the context of self-defense programs, a mainstay of rape prevention programs beginning in the early 1970s. For example, *Pandora* newspaper reported that the Feminist Karate Union in Seattle "offers self-defense classes to all women over seven years of age."[8] Many self defense programs offered special classes for girls. For example, *On Our Way*, from Waterbury, Connecticut, listed a girls' karate class for ages 8–14 in 1974[9], and the Washington, D.C., Rape Crisis Center offered "presentations to junior and senior high school female students and gives programs for girls and boys in elementary school" along with services to "*women of all ages* who are sexually assaulted [emphasis added]."[10] From the New Orleans Southern Female Rights Union came a "Program for Female Liberation," including this demand:

> We demand free self-defense instruction for females of all ages in the public schools.... Through miseducation and the lack of physical training for young females, women become weak and unable to defend themselves or another person in trouble.[11]

Overall, feminist groups were talking about *rape*, and it was clear to them that this was not a problem unique to adult women. They did not ignore the particular position of girls—in fact, they regularly called for prevention and self-defense training for girls and noted that the "protection" provided to children actually made them particularly vulnerable to assault. But any insights into the special difficulties faced by girls who were raped stemmed from the essential insights of feminist analyses of rape: that it was an abuse of power, that the chivalrous protection provided to women and children was a ruse to keep them vulnerable and weak, and that patriarchy granted power and access to men over females of any age. If anything, feminists sometimes highlighted the rape of children as a means of buttressing their redefinition of rape as a crime of power rather than sex. If babies and old women were raped, not just attractive young women, surely rapists were motivated by hatred of women and the desire to degrade and dominate them, rather than by uncontrollable lust.

Even as the issue of incest came to the forefront of some anti-rape organizers' experiences, and while Rush and Butler and others were developing their analyses, the issue did not spread to the women's movement as a whole. Newsletters and documents from feminist organizations of the early 1970s rarely referred to incest or child abuse of any kind, even when the issues addressed would seem to lend themselves to a consideration of child sexual abuse. For example, a 1972 New Haven Women's Liberation newsletter devoted to "children's issues" contains pieces about nonsexist child-raising, children's books, and the like, but no mention of sexual abuse.[12] An extensive resource directory put out in 1973 by the Women's Action Alliance contains only one relevant entry, for the Child Herald Newsletter, whose content, the directory notes, includes child abuse.[13] *Ms.* magazine did not cover child sexual abuse until 1977.

These omissions, striking from our current vantage point, illustrate the marginality of the issue to feminist agendas in the early 1970s. Activists understood sexual assault of children using the same conceptual tools that they brought to bear on rape in general, as part of a problem facing "women and girls." When Florence Rush's speech to the New York Radical Feminists conference was published in 1974, her analysis—that child sexual abuse was the extension of patriarchal control of women—mirrored the "women and children" approach of anti-rape activists, not just because Rush's perspective had been disseminated by then, but because others were developing along parallel paths.

Incest as a Feminist Issue: The Beginnings of Movementwide Attention in the Mid- to Late 1970s

Within a few years, the relatively disconnected rumblings in rape crisis centers, conferences, and newspapers in various cities began to come together, as the larger grass-roots women's movement was developing national and international institutions. In the mid-1970s, feminist presses were growing, feminist music recording labels began promoting feminist and lesbian musicians, women's studies programs began at many colleges and universities, and some feminist publications achieved a national circulation. Feminist bookstores sprang up in most cities. Large organizations such as the National Organization for Women and others had moved beyond their shaky beginnings, although they were still far from the political insiders they would become over the next decade. Feminist anti-rape groups were ubiquitous.

Most major cities and college towns had a rape crisis hotline and many sponsored rape prevention programs as well, such as self-defense training, educational programs and speakers' bureaus, and training sessions for police, medical personnel, and mental health providers (Barasko 2004; Ferree and Hess 1994; Ferree and Martin 1995; Matthews 1995; Whittier 1995).

Although the women's movement remained relatively grass-roots-oriented and decentralized, activists from different locales had more contact with each other through the growing feminist press, national and international conferences, and nascent professional networks in academia, professional associations, and government. Not surprisingly, this helped bring together activists working on child sexual abuse. Several events and organizations were key in this networking process: (1) the International Tribunal on Crimes Against Women, held in Brussels in 1975; (2) the Child Assault Prevention Project, established in Columbus, Ohio, in 1976, and promulgated to other cities over the next few years; (3) the International Women's Year conference, held in Houston in 1977; (4) the emergence of feminist therapy within rape crisis centers; and (5) the publication of key writings on incest and child sexual abuse.

Feminists continued to cast child sexual abuse as a crime against women and an example of the pervasiveness and violence of men's control of women. Some anti-violence feminists used the notion of a continuum of violence against women that included both various forms of violence and degradation (from rape and murder, to street harassment, to demeaning images of women) and female victims from infancy through old age.[14] This "women-and-children" discourse brought the issue of child sexual abuse to activists' attention without focusing on it as a unique issue. As activists in various locations began to expand their analysis of and work against child sexual abuse, and as the growing national women's movement brought them into increasing contact with each, the events and institutions in the late 1970s laid the groundwork for a broader movement against abuse in the 1980s.

The International Tribunal on Crimes Against Women

The International Tribunal on Crimes Against Women, held in March, 1976, was organized by an international group of feminists in response to the United Nations Year of the Woman in 1975. Organizers "were highly mistrustful of what would be organized during this year by people unrelated to the women's liberation movement," and opposed "the espoused IWY [International Women's Year] goal of giving women equality with men in the system as it exists today—a system that requires radical restructuring, not the integration of women into its patriarchal structures" (Russell and Van de Ven 1976: 218). Influenced by the Bertrand Russell Tribunal on Crimes Committed by the U.S. in Vietnam, the organizers argued that "*all man-made forms of women's oppression* were . . . crimes against women" (Russell and Van de Ven 1976: 219; emphasis in original). Held in Brussels at the Palais des Congrès, the use of which was granted by the Belgian government at no charge, the Tribunal was funded by donations from countries' delegations and individuals and by sales and fees at the Tribunal itself (ibid., p. 233). According to organizers, more than 2,000 women from more than 40 countries attended the five-day Tribunal, described as a "global speak out" (ibid., p. xiii).

The Tribunal consisted of testimony from women about their experiences and workshops oriented toward theoretical analysis and political action. The emphasis on women's testimony was based on the feminist belief that the personal was political, and signaled the shift toward greater emphasis on personal experience in the women's movement by the late 1970s. The editors extolled "the power of personal testimony to educate, politicize, and motivate" (ibid., p. 219). They linked this approach to consciousness-raising and speak-outs on abortion and on rape, which were important in the women's movement of the late 1960s and 1970s, and saw direct testimony as the most valid form of knowledge, writing, "let us hear from a woman who has suffered the experience, not just a researcher who can give us an abstract description and analysis of the problem" (ibid., p. 220).

In the proceedings of the Tribunal, editors Diana Russell and Nicole Van de Ven placed sexual assault against young women and girls in the chapter on violence against women. The introduction to the section on rape included mention of girls as rape victims: "Every woman is a potential victim of rape: little girls, adolescents, single women, married women, middle-aged women—and even dead women.... Women live in terror of rape from the most tender age. An incredible number of children are victims of sexual aggression even in their own families or from relatives. The climate of terror thus formed continues into adulthood and pushes women to look for "'protection'" just where it cannot be secured: from men. On the other hand, from childhood on, every woman, as a potential rape victim, is made to feel guilty and is accused of provocation" (ibid., pp. 110–111). The testimony that followed included a French woman who had been raped by a friend of her father at 14, and a 15-year-old raped by her psychiatrist in Portugal; the other reports were of rape of adults. The chapter also noted the Tribunal's "lack of a single testimony on child molestation and incest, most of which (need it be said?) involve[s] females as victims and males as aggressors." (ibid., p. 171). The Tribunal's approach illustrates how sexual assault against girls was simultaneously viewed as distinct from rape of adult women (thus the note about the lack of coverage of the issue), and as connected to rape (thus the inclusion of rape of minors with that of adult women). Child sexual abuse, in short, was conceptualized as a specific form of violence against women.

Because it brought together activists from around the world and from organizations that had previously been disconnected from each other, the Tribunal had the potential to influence these disparate groups to include child sexual abuse in their agenda for disclosing and ending violence against women. In addition, the Tribunal both represented and solidified the growing emphasis on personal testimony as a form of social change. The unadorned, un-theorized testimony by women about their own experiences was not just raw material to be analyzed and acted upon. Organizers saw the speaking of women's truths as constituting social change in itself. Breaking silence, they believed, permitted women to unite and ended the invisibility under which "crimes against women" flourished. This approach, which was growing in many segments of the women's movement, was to prove central in the survivors' movement a few years later. The fact that more than 2000 women from around the world experienced it in an intense and memorable setting could only have helped to lay the groundwork for its diffusion in the next couple of years.

The International Women's Year National Conference, Houston, 1977

The United Nations organized several international conferences on the status of women, beginning with the 1975 International Women's Year conference in Mexico City to which the International Tribunal on Crimes Against Women responded.[15] One outcome of the Mexico City conference was a number of national conferences on the status of women. The United States organized a national conference in Houston in 1977, preceded by state and regional conferences to elect delegates to the Houston meeting and vote on the conference platform."[16] Despite conflict between feminists and anti-feminists, Houston delegates endorsed a platform that was overwhelmingly in favor of women's rights (Irvine 2002; Rossi 1982; Whittier 1995).

That platform contained a statement opposing child abuse (defined as "pornographic exploitation, sexual abuse, battering, and neglect"), supporting the Child Abuse Prevention and Treatment Act of 1974 (see Chap. 3), and calling for stronger services at the state level, including counseling for victims and abusers, public education, and improved response by "police, courts, and social workers" (Rossi 1982: 389). The story of how that statement entered the platform is a story of the right person in the right place at the right time; without Fran Henry, it might easily have been omitted, since child abuse was not widely viewed as a women's issue at the time. Henry, now the founder and former executive director of STOP IT NOW!, a Massachusetts organization dedicated to prevention of child sexual abuse, worked for the National Commission for International Women's Year in 1977 as the coordinator of the state conferences in the Northeastern quadrant of the country. Sexually abused as a child by her father, Henry was in her late twenties at the time. Initially, she said, "sexual abuse was in no way on the list of issues" that the Commission gave states to vote on. "But," she said, "I wanted it to be.... As I saw all these issues go forward, it really left out this one that was so important to me. And I just started feeling, you know, clutchy, like none of these other things meant anything to me compared to this issue.... I could just feel like, do I really want to work here if something I care about so much is so completely left out?" Henry decided to try to get child sexual abuse included on the IWY agenda, explaining that "I wasn't strong enough, personally, to be out there ... publicly on this issue, but I did some behind the scenes work with a couple of staffers and with Gloria Steinem, who was on this commission.... I got the commission in a place, with Gloria's help, to address... not child sexual abuse alone, but child abuse, as a women's issue."

According to Henry, some commissioners said, "This is a children's issue, not a women's issue; we've got too many issues to deal with, we don't need to deal with this one." But ultimately they did. This was crucial because it put child abuse on the agenda for discussion at the state and national conferences. As Henry noted, "It had a lot of effect, in terms of all these women in all these state meetings having to take a position on this issue and seeing it defined as a women's issue." At least one ad hoc group took advantage of the IWY conference to bring further attention to the issue of child sexual abuse, distributing a flier that included a typical analysis of child abuse:

> One out of every four women in the United States experiences some form of sexual abuse before she reaches the age of 18, and in 34% of these cases the abuse takes place in their own homes. All children are, of course, comparatively powerless relative to adults. A young girl who is a victim of incest usually has no recourse against a father on whom she is legally as well as economically dependent.... Social control of women through violence will end only when each woman has the social and economic power necessary to control the institutions affecting her.[17]

One woman I interviewed reported going to a workshop on child abuse and neglect at her state's IWY conference, prompted by the inclusion of the issue on the platform. For her, the workshop provided a place to meet other interested activists and lent the issue legitimacy within the women's movement.

We will never know the full impact—large or small—of the state and local discussions about child abuse and its place in the women's movement, and we will never know how many women read fliers like that above by the Lucy Parsons Women's Coalition, or how many wrote similar statements themselves. However, the IWY activities brought together feminists from all over the country and from groups and factions that were usually separate—local consciousness-raising groups, radical feminist action groups, lesbian feminists, feminists of color and white feminists, members of the National Organization for Women, and women working in government. As a result, they provided a unique and important opportunity for work and theorizing on child sexual abuse to be disseminated across geographic and political divisions.

The Child Assault Prevention Project

In the early twenty-first century, elementary and secondary school curricula aimed at preventing child sexual abuse are fairly common, although of decidedly mixed quality. But in the 1970s, such curricula were virtually unknown. It was the feminist anti-rape movement that changed that, and the Child Assault Prevention Project led the way, first in Columbus, Ohio, and then nationally. Columbus, Ohio, was a center of radical feminist activism in the 1970s, with a range of flourishing groups, many of which were part of the Women's Action Collective: including a feminist newspaper, a women's car repair group, consciousness-raising groups, and a single mothers' group (Whittier 1995). The largest of these was Women Against Rape (WAR). In 1976 WAR received a grant from the National Institutes of Mental Health (NIMH) to do rape prevention. They were one of two community-based organizations nationally to receive the grant, which totaled a quarter-million dollars over four years.[18] The grant supported office space, and paid for staff and programs for rape crisis, self-defense, community education, and training for police, hospital, and mental health workers. WAR became nationally known as a center of feminist rape prevention efforts and, for the Columbus community, a likely resource on issues of rape.

One day, a nun from a local parochial school called for advice. A second-grader at her school had been raped. Other children had heard about the rape and were distressed, and teachers didn't know what to do. Would Women Against Rape be willing to come and talk to the class? Judy, who joined the group later, recounted how WAR responded. "Of course they did what most nonprofits do," she said. "They said that yes, they would come out, and then they got off the phone and went, 'Oh my god, what have I done?'" As they tried to figure out what to say to the children, they drew on their feminist approach to rape, as Judy described:

> They began to pick apart the theory [feminist analysis of rape] and try to apply it to children's vulnerability to sexual abuse and to see where it fit and where it didn't fit. I think the great light bulb that went on in the minds of those women was that women really occupy a very child-like status in our community. And while the very specific ways that vulnerability looks in kids might be different, it was based on the same assumption, and it was based on some of the very same things: women being smaller and weaker—children are smaller and weaker, often, than their attackers....Women often had a child-like relationship with adult men, where they were financially dependent, psychologically dependent....Where kids and women really differ was that women were adults and they were developmentally mature, and many children were not going to be capable of carefully analyzing a situation, or of being developmentally mature enough to understand what was happening to them, and to choose a course [of action].

Their feminist perspective allowed the women of WAR to recognize children's structural vulnerability and to see that vulnerability as something that could and should be challenged. The analogy to the ways that adult women are structurally vulnerable to rape enabled WAR to envision interventions with children similar to those they employed to help prevent rape for adults.

It is difficult to overstate how radical a departure this was from mainstream attitudes toward the position of children and women. Judy tried to convey this:

> These ideas and thoughts were wholly apart from what most people thought about women's place in society and children's place in society.... I remember thinking back in those days how radical it was to say to a woman, "You have a right not to be raped in your marriage."... I remember talking to women about saying no to men in dating relationships, and setting limits, and being brave enough and strong enough to do that.... When I saw how fearful women were of that, it was very difficult to think about suggesting to a kindergartner that he or she do the same with an adult.

But they did. The call from the nun sparked a new project in WAR: the Child Assault Prevention Project. The group soon received a grant to develop a pilot project in the Columbus public schools; in 1976, they began doing workshops with elementary school children and, separately, with parents, teachers, and staff.

The Child Assault Prevention Project workshops differed from the conventional approach to keeping children safe, which was to caution children to stay away from strangers. CAP assumed that children were at risk of sexual assault from family members and familiar adults as well as strangers. A few years earlier, this assumption might not have come so easily, but by 1976 information about women's experiences from consciousness-raising groups, and the work of pioneering thinkers like Florence Rush and Susan Brownmiller, had seeped into feminist consciousness. They assumed not only that children—like adult women—were assaulted by family and friends more often than by strangers, but also that the experiences were part of the same phenomenon: rape, which grew from patriarchy. Most radical of all, just as WAR was unwilling to tell women that the only way to protect themselves from rape was to limit their own mobility and freedom—to avoid going out alone after dark, to seek protection from a husband— CAP was unwilling to tell children that their safety depended primarily on precautions like refusing to take candy from strangers. Instead, as Judy explained, CAP used "a feminist analysis of sexual abuse," that focused on "why children are vulnerable to sexual abuse and how we might create a society where they are not vulnerable and they are not victims of sexual abuse." Reducing vulnerability, in this view, was not just about changing individual actions, but about increasing children's social power.

The CAP curriculum, developed in 1978, was titled "Safe, Strong, and Free" and aimed to teach children that they were in charge of their own bodies, that adults did not have the right to touch them in ways they didn't want, and that they should tell someone if an adult touched them in an uncomfortable or sexual way. Beginning in 1976, CAP members went into classrooms and performed three skits, each illustrating a different situation and how the child might respond to intrusive touch or inappropriate requests from an uncle, a stranger, or an older child. In the skits, the children said no, yelled, ran away, told a parent or teacher. Children practiced these skills in CAP's workshops. They role-played saying no, yelled loudly (a particularly popular activity!), and pretended to tell an adult.

Some children really did tell an adult in the course of the workshop, reporting to their teachers or CAP facilitators that they had been sexually abused. Such disclosures were risky for both children and CAP. Judy described the typical aftermath of a child's disclosure:

> A child would disclose after a workshop that he or she was having experiences at home that were sexually abusive. I remember one little girl in particular who caused this great concern.... What she told us ... was that her father "humped" her at night, and when we went a little further with that, you know, she wasn't wearing any pajama bottoms, he wasn't wearing any pajama bottoms. And this is the information we gave [Child] Protective Services in order to conduct an investigation. Within two weeks of that the father's lawyer was calling our office and threatening us. And that was pretty scary in those days, because we were on pretty loose ground. You know, what right did we have to talk to children?

Even aside from children's disclosures, the CAP project was not uncontroversial. Parents sometimes objected on the grounds that the schools were usurping a function better left to the family.

But within the women's movement, CAP was golden. The "Safe, Strong, and Free" curriculum spread to other programs around the country during the late 1970s and early 1980s, and staff traveled to train them. As a result, CAP shaped understandings of the issue nationally and began to establish networks. Within a few years, other organizations, such as Girls Clubs of America, developed child assault prevention curricula that, while similar in many respects, were not grounded in a feminist perspective (Rondon 1986). CAP, however, had far and away more influence and currency within the feminist prevention movement, and it was very influential elsewhere as well. For example, three key activists I interviewed, in different locations, attended workshops with CAP staff, found their approach exciting, and felt for the first time that they had found a connection with like-minded activists outside their own community. Because it was backed by both the sizeable grant to WAR from NIMH and funding from contracts with school systems,

CAP was able to establish and sustain considerable visibility and to spread itself nationally. Thus it was one of the vectors in the late 1970s that contributed to the mushrooming of feminist awareness and work against child sexual abuse.

Rape Crisis and the Emergence of Feminist Therapy

During the mid- to late 1970s, rape crisis centers in several cities began organizing support groups for various constituencies. Facilitated by laypeople or professional therapists, the support groups were modeled on consciousness-raising groups, but were oriented toward addressing particular experiences. Groups for women who had been raped emerged first, not surprisingly. Within a few years, support groups for incest survivors and other women who had been sexually abused as children formed, building on the same model. Feminist therapy was beginning to emerge as a field and the increasingly specialized support at rape crisis centers drew on its insights and resources. At the same time, many newly minted feminist therapists had been involved with the rape crisis movement and built on the redefinitions of rape and child sexual abuse that came from the consciousness-raising process.

New York Women Against Rape exemplifies these processes, and may have been the first anti-rape group to develop groups specifically for incest survivors. This is not surprising, since, as we have seen, much groundbreaking work on child sexual abuse emerged in New York City. The New York Radical Feminists conference on rape, at which Florence Rush spoke, was the tip of the iceberg of a community of feminist theorists and writers on the issue, including, besides Rush, Susan Brownmiller, Louise Armstrong, and others. New York Women Against Rape began running support groups for incest survivors in 1976 with the help of a therapist, Robbie Stuart. Members Janet O'Hare and Katy Taylor (1983: 215) described how they began to address incest:

> When we first began to receive calls from children who were the victims of incest or from adult survivors, we had little understanding of the problem. We quickly learned that the existing literature was limited and damaging.... We realized that the only way we could learn about incest and how to help its victims was to listen to the survivors themselves.

The women at NYWAR developed feminist definitions of incest based on the experiences of incest survivors, just as they had redefined rape based on women's experiences. O'Hare and Taylor (ibid., p. 215) dispelled a number of myths about incest, including "incest is a child's fantasy rather than an adult's behavior," "a 'bad mommy' is responsible for the abuse," and the notion that the incest has a positive side because it provides children with affection. Christine Courtois (1988: 16) described similar definitions of incest and rape that emerged from the feminist rape crisis center in Maryland that she was part of:

> The similarities [between incest and rape] also become quite obvious when a feminist (but generally non-legal) definition of rape is used. As so defined, rape is viewed primarily as an act of power exercised through sexual use or violation of the individual. It is an assault on the woman's body, but more importantly on her psyche (Brownmiller 1975 [cited in original]).

The NYWAR support groups were a hybrid of consciousness-raising, rape crisis counseling, and professional therapy. Advised by a professional, the group facilitators included women with a range of experience and formal credentials. At least some facilitators later went on to acquire professional counseling credentials. When O'Hare and Taylor wrote up their experiences in 1983 for the feminist journal *Women and Therapy*, they did so using the language of feminist therapy, focusing on the implications of the NYWAR groups for therapeutic work with survivors. This hybrid of grass-roots feminism and professional therapy was to become much more common in the 1980s; the NYWAR example suggests that it grew in part from rape crisis, as crisis counselors transformed their services to something more closely resembling professional therapy in their efforts to serve specialized constituencies.

Published Work

Several feminist analyses of child sexual abuse were published in the mid to late 1970s, contributing to the growing percolation of the issue within the women's movement. The first was Florence Rush's 1971 speech, published in 1974. Susan Brownmiller's book *Against Our Will: Men, Women, and Rape* followed in 1975, with a short section on "the sexual abuse of children" that drew on Rush's work and framed child sexual abuse, like all rape, as a common experience that enhances men's control over women through threats, intimidation, and fear as well as actual assault. In 1977, the feminist journal *Chrysalis* published Rush's article on Freud's recantation of the seduction theory of hysteria and his subsequent claim that his patients' stories of childhood sexual abuse were fantasies. Also in 1977, a remarkable booklet entitled "Frances Ann Speaks Out: My Father Raped Me" appeared. Published by a small, independent feminist press in Berkeley, New Seed Press, with no stated author, the book is the transcript of a conversation between Frances Ann and her grandmother about Frances's rape by her father. The book makes many of the basic points of the feminist anti-rape movement: that it was not Frances Ann's fault, and that her mother stayed with the rapist because she was financially dependent on him. Frances Ann ends by saying that she hates the word "victim," "'cause I'm not goin' to be anybody's victim anymore" (ibid., p. 19). The book contains nothing but the transcript—no analysis, no resource list, no call for therapy for Frances Ann. In this, it is typical of late 1970s publications, and quite different from those published a few years later.

Also in 1977, the widely circulated feminist magazine *Ms.* published its first article about incest (Weber 1977). The article laid out the same basic facts about child sexual abuse as the feminist works that preceded it: that sexual assault by strangers is rare, that incest does indeed occur, that girls are the most common victims, that they are disbelieved and mistreated in the criminal justice system. But it made little reference to patriarchy, and no reference at all to the writing or activism on the issue within the women's movement. Framed instead in the language of treatment and child protective services, the article cited experts associated with the Humane Association, the Los Angeles Police Department, and the Santa Clara Child Sexual Abuse Treatment Program in San Jose, California, run by Hank Giarretto.[19] A sidebar accompanying the article described the experience of a girl raped by her father, who also beat her mother, and the mother's alcoholic fogs that prevented her awareness of the daughter's abuse (Stucker 1977). Although the sidebar aptly portrayed the problems the daughter confronted in the social service and criminal justice systems, and made it clear that she was not to blame for the incest, it also confirmed the stereotype that incest occurs primarily in families that are alcoholic and otherwise violent. While certainly incest does occur in such families, the feminist emphasis at the time was on the wide range of "respectable," "normal"—appearing families in which incest exists. In short, the article drew on treatment discourse, not feminist discourse. The lack of reference to a feminist analysis of child sexual abuse in an article in the premiere feminist publication is testimony to the fragmentation of the nascent movement against child sexual abuse that kept activists in different areas ignorant of each others' efforts. Nevertheless, the article helped raise awareness of the issue among its far-flung feminist readership.

A flurry of books followed, including *Betrayal of Innocence* (Susan Forward and Craig Buck 1978), *Conspiracy of Silence* (Sandra Butler 1978); *Father-Daughter Incest* (Judith Herman 1981), *Incest* (Karin Meiselman 1978), *Sexually Victimized Children* (David Finkelhor 1979), *The Broken Taboo* (Blair Justice and Rita Justice 1979), and *Voices in the Night* (Toni McNaron and Yarrow Morgan 1982). Florence Rush's long-awaited book, *The Best Kept Secret: Sexual Abuse of Children*, appeared in 1980. But at the same time, Mary Daly's 1978 groundbreaking radical feminist analysis of women's violent subordination, *Gyn/Ecology*, barely mentioned the rape of girls, illustrating the degree to which feminist work on child sexual abuse remained compartmentalized.[20]

In 1978, Louise Armstrong published *Kiss Daddy Goodnight*, a collection of women's stories of being sexually abused by their fathers, based on Armstrong's interviews with 183 women. Written in Armstrong's trademark biting style, the book intersperses letters from women describing their experiences with Armstrong's pointed commentary. It exemplifies the claims made by many of the feminist books published around the same time, emphasizing the wide range of victims' ages, the various meanings they made of their abuse, and the after effects. Far from being taboo, Armstrong maintained, incest is frighteningly common, the result of men's sexualization and domination of all females. The book departed somewhat from the "women-and-children" discourse as Armstrong argued for the essential powerlessness of girls in a society that dominates them based both on gender and on age. But Armstrong's argument was firmly grounded in the notion that male domination is responsible for, and made evident in, incest.

Rush, Brownmiller, Butler, Armstrong, and others had an impact, not just through their written work, but through their travels. On book tours and speaking engagements, they spoke before audiences of activists, social workers, and physicians, made appearances on radio, and granted interviews to newspaper reporters. Sandra Butler, for example, traveled nationally speaking about child sexual abuse for several years after *Conspiracy of Silence* was published in 1978. In the 1980s, speaking tours, traveling workshops, and conferences were to become major venues for the diffusion of ideas in the movement against child sexual abuse, but in the late 1970s, they were just beginning to promote awareness and networking and to bring the insights of feminist thinkers to the larger public.

Activists working on crisis services and assault prevention drew on these published works as they struggled to develop frameworks for understanding and addressing child sexual abuse. All the early activists I interviewed, and most of those who entered the movement later, mentioned these books as influential. Most cited *Conspiracy of Silence* and *The Best Kept Secret*, and the majority also cited *Kiss Daddy Goodnight*. Many also mentioned *Daddy's Girl*, and all of the other books summarized here were mentioned by at least one activist. Their testimonials show the books' importance for overcoming the isolation that many faced both as survivors of sexual abuse and as participants in a movement with very little infrastructure to link individuals in different locations. As Elaine said, "I had read Louise Armstrong's book, *Kiss Daddy Goodnight*, so I knew there were other survivors." Another activist noted that "The first thing I ever read on incest was Sandra Butler's book, *Conspiracy of Silence*," followed by Armstrong, Butler, and Rush.... Thank God that's what we read in the beginning.... In all of them, it's all a matter of feminist analysis."

Conclusion

Feminist activism against incest was boosted by other social trends. The youth movements of the 1960s contributed to the increased willingness to take children's narratives seriously, and the human potential movement of the 1970s increased attention to the emotional well-being of individuals and their recovery from trauma (Herman 1992). The growth in welfare and social services and the relatively generous funding to service providers during the 1970s provided a location where social workers, feminists, and others focused on the common experiences of injury that women and children encountered. The same funding also permitted women's movement organizations to support their efforts, through grants like the NIMH grant that funded the Child Assault Prevention Project in Columbus, CETA workers who helped staff many rape crisis centers and battered women's shelters, and contracts with social service agencies who were themselves flush with federal and state funding.

Most of all, the thriving women's movement incubated a movement of survivors that ultimately became independent of feminism. Activists in the 1970s echoed and extended the feminist anti-rape movement. In their view, child sexual abuse was a form of rape, supported by men's sexual access to women under patriarchy, which underscored the shared oppression of women and children. They were concerned with the psychological effects of sexual abuse on individuals, but also with material conditions and institutions—the shortcomings of the criminal justice system, mental health care, and foster care. They produced reams of new knowledge about child sexual abuse that influenced both later activists and the larger culture. They saw incest and child sexual abuse primarily as *social* problems rather than as mental health problems. The solutions they advocated were, therefore, social: criminal and social service interventions that did not require the removal of the daughter from her family; strengthening the structural position of women so that mothers could support their daughters against their fathers, financially and emotionally; rooting out justifications of incest from religious discourse; and breaking silence about child sexual abuse so that victims felt neither alone nor that their abuse was justified.

None of these foci disappeared in the early 1980s. But the model of child sexual abuse's emotional consequences became considerably more complex and central as writings, workshops, and mental health specialists increased. And the focus on changing institutions took a back seat for awhile. Was this because "therapeutic feminism" replaced "political feminism"? Was it because feminist therapy, come of age, had a more robust understanding of the effects of trauma (Davis 2005)? Was it because the state was so uniformly hostile to feminism that the prospect of changing how the court system and other authorities responded to incest cases seemed impossible? Was it because the funding that had supported women's movement organizations and provided a rich environment for thinking and fomenting revolution dried up? It was, on some levels, all of these. Yet throughout the 1980s, while the focus on emotional healing grew and the mainstream self-help and recovery movements adopted feminist insights, some of the most sweeping institutional gains on child sexual abuse also occurred. For both activists and policymakers, emotional change remained tied to institutional change.

2

The Politics of the "Therapeutic Turn"
Self-Help and Internalized Oppression

Organizing around child sexual abuse mushroomed during the 1980s even as the larger women's movement declined. The earliest wave of this activism consisted of feminist self-help groups, heirs to the organizing of the 1970s. They created an extensive body of knowledge about child sexual abuse between 1980 and 1982, with a particular emphasis on how child sexual abuse affected individuals and how victims could recover emotionally. They combined externally oriented activism with self-help activities aimed at reducing the effects of their childhood experiences on their emotions and daily lives, which they saw as profoundly political. The influence of these groups far exceeds their size or their brief duration. Their theory and practice about the effects and treatment of child sexual abuse influenced both non-feminist self-helpers and the practice of professional psychotherapy.

Feminist self-help groups were *hybrid organizations*. Hybrid organizations combined a focus on self-help and other techniques by which survivors could heal from the effects of child sexual abuse with ideology and strategies aimed at changing the larger world. They engaged in lay psychotherapy, produced knowledge about incest and child sexual abuse, developed an analysis of internalized oppression and identity politics, and worked to change external institutions, including psychotherapy. Activists defined emotional, psychologically oriented activities in political terms as a means to wider social change and as an end in themselves. Developing an analysis of internalized oppression, or how systemic inequality affects individuals on an internal and emotional level, they argued that social change depended on fostering solidarity among members of oppressed groups and helping each other transcend the psychological limits they imposed on themselves. Their efforts to bring these activities to others who had been sexually abused as children were a central component of their activism. At the same time, they engaged in more conventional forms of social change work aimed at improving societal responses to child sexual abuse.

These organizations were the leading edge of what critics call the *therapeutic turn* in feminism, an ostensible shift away from collective efforts to change the world and toward individualized efforts to improve one's own life. Feminist theorists have critiqued the focus on individual transformation from a variety of perspectives. Foremost among these critics is Wendy Brown (1995), who argues that when movements organize around identity categories based on victimization and call for state protection, they evacuate power from individuals and challenging groups, ultimately increasing state power and intervention into the lives of individuals and communities. Brown views resistance, in the Foucauldian sense as inevitably arising wherever power operates, as insufficient to achieve political change. She is similarly critical of the notion of empowerment for overemphasizing the self and emotion at the expense of challenging "social and political power," and sees a focus on the individual as grounded in liberalism and as detracting from an understanding of the "power of the regime" (ibid., p. 22–23). Brown calls instead for a politics of "freedom" that eschews any engagement with, apology for, or attempt to reform the welfare state (ibid., p. 15).

Most of the post-1960s movements ("black, feminist, gay," ACT UP) come in for criticism in Brown's formulation for focusing on "rights and minimalist economic redistribution" or for "eschew[ing] the project of freedom in favor of various kinds of culturalisms and nationalisms—queer, Afrocentric, Islamic, feminist" (ibid., pp. 9–10). The upshot of all these misguided politics is what Brown, drawing on Nietzsche's concept of *ressentiment*, terms "a cultural ethos and politics of reproach, rancor, moralism, and guilt" (ibid., p. 26). Brown's critique, then, focuses, first, on the construction of what she calls "wounded identities" that produce a politics of *ressentiment*, make claims to rights based on victimization, and reify existing categories; second, on the Left's engagement with the state, particularly the welfare state; and, third, activists' focus on subjectivity rather than capital and the state. Joining Brown in this general critique are popular writers such as Louise Armstrong (1990), Wendy Kaminer (1992), Katie Roiphe (1993), Carol Tavris (1993), and academic analysts of feminism such as Alice Echols (1990) and Elayne Rapping (1996), many of whom wrote for magazines that popularized the critique to the Left outside academia.

Activism by survivors of child sexual abuse seems, on first glance, to hew closely to the characteristics Brown and others decry. It focuses on changing subjectivity and emotion; it engages with the welfare state in attempts to change child protective services, criminal justice, and medical treatment; and it organizes around a shared experience of childhood sexual victimization. A closer examination, however, suggests that these formulations do not capture the complexity of the movement's identities, goals, or engagement with the state. The "therapeutic politics" of this movement differ substantially from the therapeutic politics that are under criticism. These differences suggest, not that this particular movement is atypical, but that the critique—and its underlying theories of politics—is overly simplistic (Rose 1990). These departures suggest both a different empirical account and the need for a more nuanced understanding of therapeutic politics.

The feminist survivors' organizations were political in their goals, were collective in their orientation, and sought to achieve social change. In their focus on combating internalized oppression, they challenged the therapeutic state's efforts to achieve social control by manipulating and constructing individuals' sense of self, emotions, values, and beliefs about the self. Their activism was an effort to wrest control of the self away from dominant institutions and culture. In their construction of experiential knowledge about child sexual abuse, they countered and often preceded expert knowledge about the topic, which is a key weapon in the arsenal of the therapeutic state. Activists' challenges to expert knowledge were both substantive and epistemological, challenging the authority of experts to define reality. On both theoretical and substantive levels, then, the "therapeutic turn" cannot be considered apolitical.

These developments occurred in a feminist self-help movement that, despite its influence, was highly decentralized. Small groups organized in many cities around the country, but many never knew about each other. Grounded in an explicitly feminist—and often lesbian feminist—perspective, these groups influenced both feminists and an emerging mainstream self-help movement, and helped shape a new model of politics in social movements more broadly that incorporated the ideas of internalized oppression and psychological change. In this chapter, I focus on two organizations, Incest Resources in the Boston area and the Pleiades in the San Francisco Bay Area, which were active and influential, represent the major trends of the period, and are well documented.[1] Like groups elsewhere in the country, they broke new ground by dealing simultaneously with healing from the effects of child sexual abuse and with other forms of social change. After an overview of both groups, I discuss the self-help practices and experiential knowledge about child sexual abuse that they developed, their coalescence around a collective identity as survivors, their analysis of internalization, and their efforts to change the institution of psychotherapy.

Incest Resources

Incest Resources began in the Boston area in 1980 when a few women who had been sexually abused as children found each other. It is important to remember how isolated most incest survivors were and how little visibility the issue had, even as late as 1980. As Kathy Morrissey, one of the founders of Incest Resources, described when she looked for a support group, "I was sort of aghast that there were not many groups for incest survivors.... I actually really was not looking to do any [activist] work. My momentum was finding a group, and I became so incensed that there weren't a lot of resources. *At that point, I had never met another survivor*" [emphasis added]. She eventually found a support group listed in the local women's newspaper and called the leader, Karen, who asked if she would be interested in "getting together to organize or do anything." Kathy recounted:

> We got together and started talking.... It was such a pleasure to finally meet another survivor, have someone to have a conversation with and put words on the feelings, that we got together in the beginning, I think, once a week.... We just had a sense of cohesion and validation and sort of excitement that there were people out there you could actually talk to.

Elaine Westerlund, who along with Kathy was one of the prime movers of Incest Resources, heard Karen interviewed on public radio in 1980 and responded, "Oh, my God! I'm not the only person!" She contacted Karen, and the three women began to organize a group. Because her own experience of meeting another survivor was so significant, Kathy wanted Incest Resources to help other survivors "to break the isolation. We knew what it was like to finally find other survivors, and we knew that there must be hundreds and hundreds of other women out there who just didn't have the connections.... We knew how hard it was." "Right," agreed Elaine. "It was just a total void. We used to read literature [about incest] and sort of scream laughing as well as get outraged.... It seems ridiculous now that as late as 1980 that's what it was like, to read things and feel like there was so much victim-blaming and so much talk of provocative children."

Incest Resources (IR) set out to change all that.[2] Along with similar groups in other cities, it did. It became a large and multifaceted organization, drew in hundreds of participants, and ultimately became known for its combination of public advocacy with support and services to survivors. Like a surprising number of social change organizations, IR began as a small group, with four members who also made up the officers and—with the addition of Boston-area feminist psychiatrist Judith Herman—the board of directors.[3] They chose the name "Incest Resources" because they wanted the word "incest" in the name, so that they would be visible and accessible to people who looked them up in the phone book.

After meeting for a few months, IR incorporated in January, 1981.[4] The group met often during its first years, with board or members' meetings at least weekly and usually more often.[5] Over the next couple of years, IR applied for and received funding from several organizations, most reliably the Women in Crisis Committee of the Episcopal Diocese of Massachusetts, which funded it from 1981 through at least 1987.[6] The Cambridge Women's Center provided space for support groups and meetings.

Incest Resources' activities were varied. Members did public speaking, facilitated support groups for survivors as well as (informally) for mothers of incest survivors, and made referrals to therapists. The group produced literature about incest, including short informational articles on incest and guidelines for professionals working with survivors, as well as resource lists and brochures, and distributed other available literature.[7] Members attended conferences on child sexual abuse, helped organized a television program on incest, provided support services after another documentary on incest was aired, participated in the Boston Area Sexual Assault Coalition, and facilitated "a supervision/support group" for therapists working with incest survivors." Over time, they added support groups for deaf survivors and survivors with disabilities and an aerobics class called "I.R*obics."[8] The support groups, open to drop-in attendees, were the most visible activity and were quite large during the organization's peak.

IR was embedded in a larger women's movement whose center was the Cambridge Women's Center. Boston area feminists knew IR through its public face, both the "huge drop-in groups" and events like a fund-raiser concert by lesbian feminist songwriter Meg Christian. Other ad hoc groups also brought in speakers and organized workshops dealing with incest that drew a somewhat overlapping crowd.[9] In short, the area had a considerable amount of activity percolating on the issue, and activists felt optimistic. Andrea recalled, "It really felt like an unstoppable movement.... It really felt like just person-by-person we could do it [end incest]."

In those early years, the Boston area activists expanded the notion of political practice to include a wide range of actions, from support groups to aerobics. They defined incest survivors as a constituency, like others emerging within the women's movement, that had its own voice. The support groups helped participants both deal with their experiences of sexual abuse and find a political place. As one participant put it, the groups were "how I stumbled into connecting my own memories [of child sexual abuse] with some of the stuff that I knew about politically about violence against women." Unbeknownst to activists on either coast, a similar series of events was unfolding in San Francisco.

The Pleiades

In the fall of 1980, a group of women who had been sexually abused as children met at the West Coast Women's Music Festival, one of a number of emerging lesbian and feminist music and cultural festivals. When they returned home to San Francisco, a shifting group continued meeting as a combination support and political action group. By early 1981, seven women were meeting weekly. Members came from the lesbian, feminist, and anti-violence movements that flourished in San Francisco at the time.[10] They focused on both dealing with the emotional effects of their own abuse and doing public education to try to make the issue of incest more visible and induce more women to speak out and confront their own experiences of abuse. They adopted the name "Pleiades" and began actively "taking it back to the community," disseminating their emerging theoretical and political view of incest through workshops for lesbian feminist audiences.[11]

The Pleiades' main public activity was workshops, which attracted hundreds of women. The first workshop they led was at the Michigan Womyn's Music Festival in August, 1981, a several-days-long event with music by feminist performers, workshops on various topics, and a general celebration of lesbian feminist culture. The Pleiades' workshop, "Surviving Childhood Sexual Abuse," sought "to offer support for survivors of childhood sexual abuse, especially incest; to discuss networking among support groups nationwide; and to give ideas for forming and maintaining support groups with a woman-identified focus for survivors of childhood sexual abuse."[12] In addition to the workshop, they had hoped for an announcement from the stage about child sexual abuse, and suggested that they "would at that time like to ask for all wimmin in the audience who are survivors of such abuse to stand up (and we would expect that at least one third to one half of the wimmin present will arise) and to approach the womon standing nearest them, put their arms around each other and tell each other, 'It's not your fault.'"[13] Although the second request was turned down, it illustrates the group's signature approach, which merged visibility and mass self-help.

The workshop at Michigan was more successful than organizers had imagined, attracting more than 70 women. As Pleiades co-founder Maggie Jochild described, "We had never seen that many women at a Michigan workshop.... For me what was hitting me was there can't be this many of us." After the Michigan Festival, they presented a similar workshop at the West Coast Women's Music Festival in September of 1981. Again, turnout was enormous.[14] The next month, they conducted a similar workshop at the San Francisco women's bookstore Old Wives' Tales[15]. Once again, "it was overflowing. I mean, there were so many women it was standing room only," said Maggie. They broke the audience into small groups in which women told their stories and, as Maggie put it, did "the affirmation thing," telling each other that the abuse was not their fault. At a workshop at the Berkeley Women's Center, they covered topics focused on feelings associated with child sexual abuse, such as "feeling arousal during molestation; recent memories; alienation," effects on "sexuality, trust, intimacy, family relationships,... coming out as an incest survivor; guilt and protective feelings towards the molester; depression; discussing with kids; sexual feelings for kids."[16] Through these events, the members of the Pleiades became known as resources on child sexual abuse.

Unlike Incest Resources, which has continued to the present time, the Pleiades broke up after only a little more than a year, because of internal conflicts and burnout they attributed to the activism's emotional intensity and the stress of being visible as incest survivors. Most of the activists

I interviewed reported similar difficulties in their own groups. Organizing around child sexual abuse and incest is challenging because of the stigma of the issue and how difficult it is for survivors to spend much time focusing directly on it. The Pleiades had trouble mobilizing people at the level they envisioned and found this demoralizing. Maggie explained, "We were devastated by how it slowly became clear that we were doing something that nobody else wanted to touch, you know [laugh]?" Incest Resources encountered similar problems with burnout and mobilizing participants, but their more formal organizational structure allowed them to survive even when they cycled through periods of lower membership and activity (Staggenborg 1988, 1989). Their incorporation, their institutional home in the Cambridge Women's Center, and their body of published work endured, to be picked up again when new activists joined the exhausted longtime members.

It is likely that there were other groups like the Pleiades and Incest Resources around the country, but most left little trace. By the mid- to late 1980s, many cities had twelve-step groups for incest survivors, and national feminist events included twelve-step meetings, suggesting that attendees from various locales wanted them. Most likely, twelve-step incest survivors' groups were preceded by other forms of organizing around child sexual abuse in at least some cities. In Burlington, Vermont, for example, an activist organized self-help and public education using a lesbian feminist approach similar to the Pleiades'.[17] The evidence of such organizing is spotty, however, and although the Pleiades and IR both had connections to other activists and survivors, they were not aware of much of the other work going on around the country.[18]

At least for awhile, the Pleiades were famous in movement circles. It is hard to trace their direct influences, partly because of the diffuse and overlapping nature of lesbian feminist groups and activists, and partly because cultural norms discouraged claiming authorship of ideas or documents. It is clear, however, that they both shaped and rode a wave of therapeutic/recovery-influenced lesbian feminism that merged self-help, direct action, and coming out. Such activism changed how the women's movement conceptualized the connections between internal and external oppression, developing a distinctive hybrid approach to self-help and politics. By working to define their own subjectivity and linking it to collective identity and collective action, the Pleiades, IR, and similar groups responded—mostly unknowingly—to authorities' hybrid techniques of control.

Hybrid Organizations

The Pleiades, IR, and similar groups combined efforts to transform their own emotions and daily lives with efforts to transform the larger world through education, knowledge production, and direct confrontation. Other organizations, such as rape crisis centers or domestic violence shelters, also hybridize service delivery and advocacy (Hyde 1992, 1995; Matthews 1994; Minkoff 2002). Like these groups, the Pleiades and IR juggled dual foci, but they differed in the extent of their focus on lay therapy and their view that changing subjectivity and emotion were crucial to larger social change. The hybrid approach was evident in most aspects of IR and the Pleiades, beginning with their statements of purpose.

Incest Resources' first organizational statement, at the end of 1980, emphasized the broad goal of eliminating child sexual abuse, while highlighting the tactics of breaking silence and providing services for adult survivors:

> We are women with histories of incest, and our allies, who decided it was time for us to break the silence that surrounds the incest experience and to become active in working to eliminate incest.... Our overall goal is to eliminate the sexual abuse of young people within their families and to provide counseling and referral services for women who are incest survivors/victims.[19]

A short time later, a list of the group's "services" emphasized social change and public awareness through breaking silence and support for survivors:

1. Increasing public and professional awareness of the frequency, trauma, and implications of incest.
2. Encouraging women with histories of incest to break their silence and to speak out about the devastating effects the incest experience has had on their lives.
3. Developing new and flexible nonsexist theory in regard to incest.
4. Co-coordinating self-help groups for women with histories of incest.
5. Individual and group therapy for women with histories of incest.
6. A counseling referral service for incest victims/survivors.
7. Consultation for counselors concerned with incest....
8. Compiling and distributing a list of nonsexist Boston area resources for individuals and families concerned with incest.[20]

Similarly, a brochure for IR stated, "Because of the high incidence of incest in our society, we consider it a social as well as an individual problem."[21]

The Pleiades also hybridized therapeutic and externally oriented tactics. Their workshops sought to change how large numbers of women viewed the issue, and they also attempted to organize therapy referrals, work with social services, and prevention with children.[22] Maggie contrasted the Pleiades with apolitical therapy. "We thought if you're not being political with this stuff you're not really working for the revolution," she explained. "It wasn't enough to try and figure out what happened to you, you had to stop it." Both groups shared the feminist notion that incest was a result of male domination, and that to oppose one was to oppose the other. As Maggie put it, "We had the opinion that this was the product of societal evil, specifically male domination."

For both groups, "naming the issue," telling the truth about *both* their own experiences and societal oppression, was necessary to ending child sexual abuse. They believed that speaking out required breaking the shame that held most adult survivors in silence, and that it was impossible to tell the truth about child sexual abuse as a societal issue without also telling the truth about it as a personal issue. Conversely, they believed that individual women could not recover from the effects of incest unless the larger society changed: with greater visibility and awareness, a new understanding of the nature of child sexual abuse, improved responses by police and mental health providers, and, ultimately, women's liberation. They thought their work could facilitate sweeping social change since, as Maggie put it, many saw child abuse as "the way we first get smashed and learn to accept all the other oppressions of the world."[23]

The discerning reader may notice a disjunction between the goal—ending child sexual abuse—and the means, which are oriented toward counseling, support, and public visibility. Activists believed that it was important for adult survivors to be publicly visible and heal from their abuse not just for their own sake, but because their visibility raised awareness and increased the likelihood that ongoing abuse of children could be stopped. At the same time, counseling was a more tangible goal than eliminating child sexual abuse altogether, and consequently drew the members' day-to-day focus.

Many feminist groups that merged service provision with social change during the 1980s found that the day-to-day exigencies of meeting clients' needs and finding funding gradually supplanted their social-change goals (Hyde 1995; Matthews 1994; Reinelt 1995). While some such organizations gave up their movement ties, others, like many survivor organizations, redefined politics with emotional change as the linchpin to social change in general.

Self-Help Practices

The feminist survivors' groups of the early 1980s developed sophisticated approaches for doing nonprofessional counseling. These techniques emphasized peer connections to foster the emotional and cognitive shifts entailed in identifying as a survivor rather than a victim. They rejected, not only the myths and stigma associated with child sexual abuse, but also the dominant discourse of psychotherapy that had created these myths. They were thus inextricably linked to the political perspective and goals of the larger movement, particularly the critique of medicine fostered by the feminist health movement (Morgen 2002). As deliberate attempts to develop new ways of healing from the effects of child sexual abuse, they were a form of grassroots psychotherapy (see Taylor 1996).

Self-help facilitators drew on a range of counseling techniques, not all of which were distinct from professional therapeutic techniques.[24] Nevertheless, they saw their approach as quite different from the psychotherapeutic establishment, especially in the early days when feminist therapy was in its infancy (Davis 2005). In a presentation to the American Psychiatric Association, IR member Kathy Morrissey provided a practical outline of IR's self-help approach, implicitly contrasting it with professional treatment:

> The task for those of us working in self-help is essentially this: (1) To look at the ways in which the incest is still hard now. (2) To see the incest survivor as a whole person, and not just as a victim. (3) To hold out that the abuse is over. (4) To hold out that the world can be safe, and that they can be safe in it. (5) To make the world safer by raising the consciousness of laypeople and the therapeutic community alike about both the problems and strengths of incest survivors.

But she went on to emphasize that "Certainly we are not suggesting that self-help preclude [professional] treatment, but rather that self-help and treatment need to work hand-in-hand for a successful recovery." Her advocacy of professional treatment was both a concession to her audience and a reminder that they therefore needed to address incest seriously in their practice. Furthermore, she assumed that self-help worked in conjunction with "mak[ing] the world safer." Individuals could not recover without broader social change; in this case, "raising the consciousness of laypeople and the therapeutic community."

Both groups used a variety of self-help and counseling techniques to try to address the emotional residue of their experiences. As Maggie described, Pleaides' members' approaches included "a traditional therapeutic model, where you talk a lot, and the other person makes notes and then they sort of tell you what they think is wrong... a witch [who] was really into ritual.... affirmations and things like that... and RC" [Re-evaluation Counseling: see below]. Maggie's account of her first experience with the group that would become the Pleiades illustrates their process. She attended at the urging of friends, who were concerned that she seemed overwhelmed and out of control. Maggie had continuous recall of childhood sexual abuse but, like most survivors at the time, had never sought professional therapy. The group employed an assortment of counseling techniques, as she described:

> Because I was the new person, they suggested that I tell my story. And I couldn't. And so___ suggested that if I couldn't tell what had happened to me, maybe I could act it out. Now I'm appalled at our process, but it was all we had, you know?... So I said ok. So, she said, "So tell me what to do." Somebody turned the lights down a little, 'cause I said it was too bright... and I said, "Well, I'm in the bathtub." So I sat down on the floor like I was sitting in a bathtub. And___ said, "Is there someone in the room with you?" and I said yes. And so she sat like a little distance away, and then she said, "Does this person get near the tub?" And I said yes. And so she got to where she was sitting next to the tub, and she was absolutely acting out what happened.... And so

she said, "What are you doing?" and I said, "I'm looking at the water, I'm sitting here looking at the water." And so she just reached her arm like she was reaching over the side of a tub, and started reaching toward my leg.... And there it was—it was [my assailant]. And so, I just snapped. And the next thing I remember is that I had her up against the wall and I was choking her, as hard as I could.... The rest of them were standing around screaming at me, "Let her go, let her go," which wasn't working, and they weren't able to pull me off. But___ had the presence of mind—she was in my face, she was shouting at me, "I'm not him, I'm not him." And that got through. And I let go. And I was horrified. And everybody else was horrified. But___ was pretty calm. I mean, she was mad, but she was pretty calm. And she sort of rubbed at her neck, and she said, "You have a fucking problem. And you have to keep coming back until that would never happen again." And I said ok.

Many meetings took this approach, with one or more members having time to talk about and work through feelings, although usually in less dramatic fashion.

Similarly, at IR's groups for survivors, attendees talked about their experiences and expressed their feelings, led by facilitators trained by IR. Both groups thought one main reason self-help worked was that it allowed survivors to build connections with each other, and they viewed solidarity between survivors as personally transformative, as Morrissey explained in her talk to the American Psychiatric Association. Self-help, Morrissey said, was uniquely effective because of the presence of other survivors, which "proves untrue almost immediately that it only happened to her.... Here, at last, a survivor is given emotional permission to share her secret and tell the story. Because of the common bond of experience, there is an immediate sense of understanding and acceptance."

The Pleiades developed techniques that took those connections a step beyond the small self-help group. The Pleiades' signature public action was a sort of mass self-help, in which large groups of women told their stories of abuse and repeated the affirmations they had devised. They improvised this format at the first workshop they did, at the Michigan Womyn's Music Festival. They had expected a small crowd, which they could divide up into groups that could operate the way the Pleiades themselves did. When they found a crowd of more than 70 women, they re-thought the plan. Instead, Maggie recounted, "We decided to have every woman go around and say her name and where she was from and to say how she was molested. Like a one or two sentence thing to break the silence for the whole group. That took an hour, at least. For... many of the women there, it was the first time they had ever told anybody.... So then we broke them down into smaller groups and... we had them say these affirmations. "It's not my fault. I'm completely loveable. I can heal this up. I'm a survivor, not a victim." Although at some events they also made more formal presentations, the Pleiades always stressed "breaking silence" and the use of affirmations in groups.

Self-help groups or group therapy are now widely accepted in psychotherapeutic contexts as helpful to incest survivors, but they were not then. Morrissey appeared on the APA panel with professional feminist therapists because her knowledge and perspective were respected and original in the barely congealing field of therapy for child sexual abuse. That these ideas now are commonplace in professional therapy is a testimony to the ability of grassroots self-help groups to change institutions.

Co-Counseling

The Pleiades had a number of members with a background in co-counseling, also known as Re-Evaluation Counseling (RC), a widespread form of peer counseling during the 1980s, with a national network of leaders and teachers, regular local and national workshops, and several publications. The RC approach was similar enough to other therapeutic approaches and assumptions that it conflicted relatively little with these as members developed their eclectic self-help techniques. People who were involved with RC shared a belief that nonprofessionals could provide counseling for each other, and shared access to a training process to do so. They also saw internalized oppression as important and were unlikely to separate political from individual change. It is therefore not surprising that a number of the founders of the Pleiades (and other organizations around that time) had a background in RC. They drew on RC techniques in their self-help groups. As Maggie wrote in an article for a co-counseling publication, "RC was the process of choice, although we did other things as well."[25]

Networks of those involved with co-counseling were pervasive. Maggie, for example, said that in early 1980s San Francisco, "almost every lesbian I knew had either been in RC or was in RC, and these are political dykes who are out there spreading the word," and other respondents told me that co-counseling was similarly pervasive in activist networks in their own cities. About half the respondents who were involved in the movement prior to the mid-1980s had either already participated in RC or were exposed to it as they entered the survivors' movement. It is impossible to quantify their influence, but it seems likely that they helped to shift the feminist focus to merge personal and political change.

During the early 1980s, activists also were organizing around incest and child sexual abuse within RC itself, attending workshops on child sexual abuse and "early sexual memories" on both coasts.[26] After attending a workshop, Maggie and two other co-counselors started an RC support group for incest survivors in the Bay Area that lasted for years. That group developed specific techniques for co-counseling about incest, particularly "counseling lightly" on sexual abuse, an "irreverent" approach that avoided constant direct confrontation with the worst experiences, and published an article in the major RC journal that shaped how other such groups dealt with sexual abuse.[27] By the mid-1980s a critical mass developed within RC, developing theory on incest and child sexual abuse was influential beyond the "RC community" itself.[28]

RC drew in many progressive activists during this period and, consequently, was influential in a variety of movements, from feminism to peace activism. It also connected feminist activists to a broader demographic, including male survivors. Thus it was one of the conduits through which issues of incest and child sexual abuse appeared on the horizon of many progressive activists and, equally important, through which the analysis of internalized oppression became influential in progressive movements.

Writing Workshops

Self-help and co-counseling groups were not the only lay-led sources of new methods for working through traumatic experiences. Feminist writing workshops began with a more general focus on writing to tell one's own story and workshops specifically for survivors, based on the idea that writing about one's experiences could aid emotional healing, emerged nationally beginning in 1982 or 1983. Ellen Bass, who later co-wrote the best-selling book on child sexual abuse, *The Courage to Heal*, was one of the first to travel around the country leading writing workshops for survivors that tapped existing activist networks. Boston area activist Leslie asked Bass to do a workshop. Leslie described how even publicizing the workshop entailed a kind of activism because it required speaking openly about child sexual abuse:

> At that point—this was in '83—every time I would put those words [child sexual abuse] up in a public place, it felt like this incredible little action. I would get so moved thinking some woman was going to...walk by and change her life. Because it was still so silenced at that point....It felt like getting those fliers out was going to help bring about some kind of social change, some kind of awareness.

The workshop did serve as a catalyst, as Leslie recounted: "People were calling me up who had literally—I mean, the name of the workshop was 'I Never Told Anyone.' Literally, they had never told anyone." Over the next few years, hundreds of women went through such workshops. Participants wrote about their own experiences, read their writings out loud, and listened to the writings of others.

Another respondent also conducted workshops around the country, and explained that she saw them as addressing political and healing goals simultaneously:

> I made up my way of doing my work, which I call "writing as healing." ...It was the most basic Feminism 101 stuff...which was basically, you're the expert of your experience. You want a place where you can hear the sound of your own life come through your own throat, where you won't be challenged.

Although this respondent was a professional, she, like others, reported finding no assistance from professional literature on how to work with survivors. Like other activists, she "made it up."

In the introduction to *I Never Told Anyone*, an anthology of the workshop writings, the editors explain how they thought writing was related to healing and social change:

> We sincerely hope that this anthology will help prevent further child sexual abuse.... The women in these pages have transformed themselves, like phoenixes rising from the ashes, through their own words. Ideally this anthology will unlock the power of the spoken or written word for the thousands of additional women who never told anyone (Bass and Thornton 1983: 17, 19, 22).

Leslie believed that the workshops were effective because participants supported each other and because they provided a public space in which to disclose abuse. Bass's approach, she said, "was very much [to say], 'I'm here as a witness'.... She completely saw what she was doing as activism and politics and not as, she didn't see herself as a therapist. She was just [saying], 'Women speaking their truth will crack the world open.'"

Like self-help groups, writing workshops were therapeutic for participants. Their effectiveness came, not from the intervention of experts, but from breaking the mandated silence—telling secrets—in the company of others. But they were more than therapy: they were part of a social movement. They built networks among survivors of child sexual abuse[29] and helped disseminate a view of survivors that grew from feminist self-help groups and writings.

Many of the techniques and understandings of how child sexual abuse affected survivors that developed in the feminist self-help groups, writing workshops, and co-counseling made their way into the broader culture. It is difficult to disentangle the influence of the feminist survivors' movement from co-counseling or the emerging professional feminist therapy, all of which overlapped and influenced each other (Davis 2005). Several assumptions that emerged from the intersection of these forces later became widely accepted. Both self-help and RC groups, for example, believed that physical ailments could be a result of experiences of sexual abuse.[30] The notion of psychosomatic effects of abuse appeared in books for therapists a few years later. A theory of how child sexual abuse affected sexual behavior, creating either sexual inhibition and aversion or sexual compulsivity, also emerged from discussions in self-help groups, co-counselors, writing workshops, and writings by clinicians. The idea that "speaking out" and telling the story of one's experience of child sexual abuse was central to both individual recovery and social change stemmed from these groups, as did the emphasis on peer support. In short, they contributed to emerging lay and professional therapeutic practices and constructed new knowledge about child sexual abuse.

Experiential Knowledge

Central among contemporary strategies of domination is the use of expert knowledge to control behavior and justify inequality (Rose 1990, 1999). Consequently, the survivors' movement, like other movements of the late twentieth century, focused considerable attention on constructing new knowledge specifically aimed at challenging the expert knowledge that maintained the status quo. Major changes occurred in psychotherapeutic and popular understandings of child sexual abuse between the 1970s and the 1990s. Feminist survivors groups like IR and the Pleiades were central in developing the new knowledge that drove these changes. They did not do so alone, but in tandem with professional therapists and social workers.

A widespread understanding of changes in knowledge is that they are driven primarily by the actions and perspective of credentialed professionals, who then pass their knowledge on to laypeople. A detailed examination of knowledge constructed by grassroots activists paints a different picture. Lay people played an active and influential role in developing both theory and practice about child sexual abuse, its causes, and its treatment. They were not just the spark for professionals' work (as Davis [2005] suggests), but worked autonomously and in collaboration with therapists to produce knowledge that was more varied in perspective than professional therapy texts. These variations were often reflected in mass media accounts as well as in state-funded programs, as we will see in subsequent chapters.

In Davis's (2005) view, anti-rape feminists' early work was quickly professionalized, as feminist therapists like Judith Herman expanded on feminist analyses of child sexual abuse as rape. Over time, Davis suggests, feminist professionals developed a trauma model that emphasized the uniquely damaging effects of child sexual abuse on the individual's psychological functioning and that cast the scene in terms of a purely innocent victim and a purely evil offender. The trauma model emphasized the child's dissociative response to abuse; that is, that the child compartmentalized the abusive experience from the rest of her/his life, and often repressed it from memory. The focus on dissociation and trauma, according to Davis, led to an emphasis on recovering repressed memories of abuse.

My data paint a different picture of the construction of knowledge about child sexual abuse. First, some of the changes Davis attributes to professionals actually occurred first among lay activists and only later spread to professionals, or continued to take somewhat different form at the grass roots. Second, feminist self-help groups combined a political approach emphasizing the problems of the patriarchal nuclear family with elements of what Davis calls the trauma model, emphasizing serious psychological effects on individuals. The emphasis on dissociation and repression was, at most, tangential to the new knowledge constructed by these organizations. Third, these groups did not always conceptualize victims' innocence and offenders' evil in black-and-white terms, but rather discussed often-uncomfortable aspects of child sexual abuse that complicated both characterizations. Finally, nonprofessional survivor-activists worked actively to construct and disseminate knowledge about child sexual abuse based on their own experiences. This knowledge influenced how professional therapists understood the issue and often carried more weight at the grass roots than professionally validated information. These mutual influences emerged in a climate where the line between survivor, professional, and activist was blurry and often-crossed, where professional therapists participated in activist groups alongside laypeople, participants in self-help groups sometimes were inspired to pursue professional training, and many therapists were also survivors.

Both IR and the Pleiades focused much of their energy on creating a new model for thinking about incest and child sexual abuse, including theory about its causes, effects, and how individuals could heal from it. Like earlier organizers based in the anti-rape movement, they conceptualized child sexual abuse as a form of violence against women. They added a greater focus on the damaging effects of sexual abuse on individuals and on how these effects could be challenged. This was similar to the "trauma" approach that Davis (2005) outlines, but predates it and casts individual hurt in more overtly political terms. They also began to rethink the idea that women were inevitably innocent victims, and men inevitably perpetrators of abuse, while retaining a critique of the patriarchal nuclear family.

Their theories and information drew on work by professional therapists and academics but also were rooted in their own experience and informal research. For example, both Incest Resources and the Pleiades collected and reported information about the prevalence and nature of child sexual abuse. They drew on the scant published work, but also on their own experiences and the patterns of experience among group members. Incest Resources assembled such information in an educational brochure, the bulk of which consists of information about incest presented in question-and-answer format, addressing basic definitions, discussion of the demographics of perpetrators and victims, frequency of incest, and myths about incest. The brochure analyzes the societal roots of incest in a section asking, "Why does incest happen?" The answer explains first that offenders may have been sexually abused themselves as children (an explanation that is primarily psychological). It then goes on to explain that another factor is "the misinformation which the society as a whole maintains with respect to men, women, and children. Females and children are stereotyped in ways that make them targets for particular kinds of abuse. Furthermore, the perception of children and women as acquired possessions or 'property' persists in our society. Consequently, parents may exert certain rights over children and men may exert certain rights over women." Here we see the hybrid of feminist and therapeutic analyses with information from professional sources and their own experiential data.

Central to both groups' definitions was the view of incest as an act of violence rather than sex, drawn directly from earlier published feminist work and grounded in anti-rape organizing. For example, Maggie outlined the Pleiades' view:

> We...called [incest] not sexuality, but violence, in the same way that Susan Brownmiller had done for rape—we lifted it directly from that.... That it had nothing to do with sexual desire for children, that it was an instance of power, and that fathers needed to have the power taken away from them in order for things to change. We named the nuclear family as the source of the problem.

The critique of family systems theory that emerged in the late 1970s and early 1980s among many feminist therapists (Davis 2005) occurred simultaneously at the grass roots. Maggie reflects this critique of family systems approaches that blame mothers or family dynamics for incest in a 1981 letter, writing, "The causes for incest are much more deeply rooted than an individual family situation, because it is just too widespread."[31] In contrast to the emerging trauma model among professionals, Maggie's statement clearly emphasized the societal roots of incest rather than the individual trauma of victim. IR made similar statements.

Organizers also consistently stressed the problem of blaming mothers for failing to protect their daughters from incestuous fathers. In her address to the American Psychiatric Association, Morrissey advised clinicians, "In cases of father-daughter incest, do not suggest to or agree with the incest survivor that the incest was the fault of her mother." The women of IR and the Pleiades strongly critiqued several other aspects of psychological and psychiatric theory and practice that dominated at the time, including blaming incest survivors for their victimization, suggesting that they are deeply and permanently damaged, or suggesting that they should be able to simply "move on" from the experience. And while they emphasized victims' innocence, they also discussed contradictory feelings of sexual arousal or complicity, or their own sexual feelings as adults toward children.[32]

Both groups discussed the effects of child sexual abuse, drawing on their own experiences and observations in self-help groups as well as the scant literature. A 1981 IR brochure asks "Is incest harmful?" "Very," it answers. "The incest experience is particularly damaging with respect to trust of other human beings. Detachment is common. Self-esteem and sexual functioning are generally affected." The Pleiades also developed a model of how incest affects victims based on their reading of published sources and their practices and experiences within the self-help groups. As Maggie wrote, "I am an incest survivor, and it has affected every single moment of my life, it feels like.... I learned that love meant someone was going to hurt me.... I learned to lie, to conceal who I was.... I learned to feel dirty and unclean."[33] Maggie's understanding of her experiences, drawn from reflection, participating in self-help groups, and reading, is indistinguishable here from the clinical descriptions of effects of child sexual abuse in general that she found in the few published reports available in 1982. Both groups were beginning to emphasize some elements of what Davis (2005) terms the trauma model; namely, the assumptions that incest is harmful despite the fact that the harm may not be immediately apparent. Yet the elements of dissociation and memory repression that are central to Davis's conceptualization of the trauma model were not part of their understanding.

Over time, both groups adopted from outside a more detailed model of the psychological dimensions of child sexual abuse. A large part of the impetus for their shifts came from the growing visibility of female offenders and male victims.[34] Activists learned of these, not from professionals, but from participants in their own self-help groups and from male survivors who began to speak of their experiences. It was hard to reconcile these situations with the patriarchy discourse. Maggie Jochild turned to trauma theory to understand, noting that, "We did not have the piece that people who molest were molested themselves.... We thought it was connected to male domination and the expression of male violence. Now I don't think that's totally wrong. I think men tend to externalize what happens to them in a way that women don't because of male domination. And that those are perceived as lesser than on the power rung are available targets, and again, that's defined by male domination." Along the same lines, Elaine and Kathy explained in an interview that IR had expanded its attention to male survivors and female perpetrators over the years. As we will see later, these expansions came as the movement changed quite dramatically, making the trauma model more central and moving toward a nonfeminist model.

Both groups defined incest based on their own experiences and those of other women. Their emphasis on experience as a basis for knowledge was consistent with the earlier activism that grew from the feminist consciousness-raising model. They emphasized that women were the authorities on their own experiences. They generated theory based on these experiences and believed that it was important to trust and take seriously how women perceived and reported their past. Maggie explained, "One of the stances that the Pleiades took is that whatever someone tells you happened, happened.... We were adamant about that. It's more of a tactical step and it's a psychological approach to say, "Whatever you tell me is the truth..." and to trust that the survivor herself will sort through it." This approach did not suggest that memories of abuse were likely to be repressed, or that the "recovery" of these memories was an important task of the self-help groups. Rather, they simply took members' reports of their experiences as a given.

The focus on experience as the basis for knowledge complicated the image of the pure victim or offender that Davis (2005) found in published literature. For example, Pleiades members talked about the idea of "feeling arousal during molestation." Maggie reported that this piece of knowledge about the effects of child sexual abuse emerged because a member of the self-help group disclosed her own experience:

> She was the one who first ever had the courage to say, "Well, sometimes I got turned on and I feel betrayed by that. And does anybody else know what I'm talking about?" God, you know? And so, then we started putting that out there and I remember getting shit for putting that out. And we were like, "No, if a woman feels that, it's her body."

Here we see again the emphasis on experience as the basis for knowledge. The critics Maggie describes were concerned that women's feelings of sexual arousal during abuse were a product of the patriarchy and therefore not to be acknowledged. The Pleiades, in contrast, justified this controversial material with the feminist frame of, "It's her body." They believed in breaking silence about this issue like others, and placed paramount value on a theory that was consistent with what they thought were women's authentic experiences. Similarly, other respondents reported discussing their anger at nonprotective mothers or their ongoing love for abusive fathers. They did not attempt to construct either victims or offenders as simplistic or absolute categories.

The views presented by the Pleiades and Incest Resources were not unique. They show the influence of the books that the founders report reading, such as *The Best-Kept Secret, Against Our Will, Conspiracy of Silence, Father-Daughter Incest*, along with feminist perspectives on male power over women and children. In this, they are consistent with the earliest feminist activists described in chapter 1. They differ in their emphasis on the effects of incest on individuals and their focus on the need both to provide self-help and support and to change how professional therapists and physicians treat incest survivors. Developed in 1980 and 1981, their new knowledge predated the publication of most of the professional handbooks for feminist therapists (Davis 2005).

Identity Politics

As survivors of incest and child sexual abuse began to speak publicly about their experiences and organize activist and self-help groups, they formulated a new view of their identity as a group, a new definition of what it meant to have experienced child sexual abuse. They became "survivors" rather than simply people who had been sexually abused as children. For them, survivors shared a perspective that was different from all others and that uniquely qualified them to offer interpretations of incest and child sexual abuse and provide support to other survivors. This point of view was grounded in a model of identity politics that was emerging at the time from black feminists, emphasizing the right and necessity of oppressed groups to speak for themselves. Yet even as abuse survivors crafted their own sense of collective identity, they also grappled with issues of internal diversity, particularly around differences of race.

The theory that direct experience lent credibility to social change work was influential in the late 1970s and 1980s. Jewish feminists, young women, old women, international feminists, disabled activists, and others developed specialized organizations, based on the assumption that experience with a particular form of oppression provided the best vantage point from which to understand and challenge that oppression.[35] This view influenced survivors' groups that, in turn, elaborated the approach and helped disseminate it to the women's movement and the larger progressive movement community.

As we saw above, the organizers of Incest Resources and the Pleiades believed that, because they were incest survivors, they had a unique perspective on the issue that gave women attending support groups or workshops a sense of safety. The notion that members of a particular group are uniquely qualified to speak about the experiences of that group was a widespread—although not undisputed—tenet of feminism at the time. The importance of listening to women's own experiences and respecting their accounts of those experiences stemmed both from early feminists' disgust with their marginalization in the male-dominated New Left and from consciousness-raising, with its process of telling individual stories in order to generate collective theory and action. Groups that were marginalized within the women's movement adopted the emphasis on self-definition. Women of color organizing within (and against) the white-dominated women's movement, for example, argued that they alone were the authorities on their own experiences, as the Combahee River Collective, a Boston organization of black feminists, declared eloquently in their classic 1977 statement:

> Above all else, our politics initially sprang from the shared belief that Black women are inherently valuable.... Our politics evolve from a healthy love for ourselves, our sisters and our community which allows us to continue our struggles and work. This focusing upon our own oppression is embodied in the concept of identity politics. We believe that the most profound and potentially most radical politics come directly out of our own identity, as opposed to working to end somebody else's oppression. (274–275)

The Combahee River Collective, in what was probably the first use of the term, called their approach "identity politics."

Being a "survivor" was central to members' individual identities and political work. Constructing and defining what it meant to be a survivor was important, not just as a way of personally coping with the effects of child sexual abuse, but as a route to changing views of child sexual abuse and its victims. For example, in a 1981 letter, Maggie explained, "We use the word survivors instead of victims deliberately.... [T]he memory of what happened to us as children will cease to control our actions unconsciously as adults when we take power over our own lives now and act as survivors."[36]

During the early 1980s, grassroots activist/self-help groups were establishing the collective identity of "survivor" around the country. For example, a Vermont group's flier, with a graphic of a shouting woman and the bold headline "Incest survivors speak out!" advertises:

> We are creating safe space for us to tell our stories, go through our anger and pain, explore how incest has affected our lives, and transform ourselves from **victims** into **survivors**.... Incest continues by our silence. ... Sharing our experiences, we learn and begin to know deeply: **INCEST IS NOT OUR FAULT, WE ARE NOT ALONE.** [emphasis in original][37]

To be a survivor not only meant the psychological change inherent in "transforming ourselves from victims to survivors." It also meant speaking out and, therefore, ending incest, because "incest continues by our silence." This conceptualization of collective identity spread through groups' participation in national conferences and festivals, published work, and traveling speakers and writing workshops.

Racial Identities in a Predominantly White Movement

Virtually all of the work that the Pleiades, IR, and similar groups did during the early 1980s—with the exception of IR's resource list for male survivors—was geared to female survivors. They did not assume that all women experienced child sexual abuse in the same way, however. Alongside their emphasis on a shared identity as survivors, their belief in each woman's authority to define her own experience helped them attend to differences of race and class. The founders of IR tried to address incest for women of color, as Elaine described:

> It was sort of by friendship circles. We each knew other survivors.... We were trying to sort of culturally expand and have some facilitators would could do some outreach in the black and Hispanic communities. Another was an Hispanic clinician who we just sort of knew community-wise and then found out was a survivor as well. So she joined Incest Resources, and basically that was in the hope of providing more expansive services to a broader range of survivors.

These efforts, like those of many predominantly white organizations that attempt "outreach" to people of color, were not terribly successful (Breines 2006). Kathy described the tribulations of attempting to "diversify":

> We would often have difficulty with applying for money, because we didn't have enough diversity in the group. It was tremendously frustrating because it was difficult enough to have survivors self-identify, and then on top of that to sort of be blamed by default that we weren't [racially] diverse. We weren't discriminating against anybody, we were actually trying to find people.

As Elaine elaborated, " I think there was a kind of ignorance of what the multiple issues are for women of color around [child sexual abuse], at the same time... and why survivors [of color] don't become more involved."

Elaine echoes recent activism by women of color who suggest that many women of color have more difficulty confronting incest and child sexual abuse because of notions of loyalty to family and community and a taboo on "airing dirty laundry in public"; that is, giving racists any ammunition to use against their group (Wilson 1994, hooks 1993, 2003). At the same time, the frustration that they describe reflects the approach of many white feminists to issues of race. They hoped (with all good intentions) that they could reach out to women of color within the group's existing structure, without recognizing that a genuinely multiethnic organizing effort would probably take quite a different form (see Lynn 2001; McIntosh 1988). Furthermore, the idea that identities or structural locations shaped perspective and political allegiance indirectly justified separate organizing by survivors of different groups (see Roth 2004).

Survivor activism was not always welcomed by other feminists, who sometimes saw it as overly psychological or infantilizing and who objected to the notion that survivors occupied a privileged political position. Survivor activists, in turn, sometimes felt alienated within feminist or Left organizations. Political struggles between survivor-activists and other feminists over organizational or ideological focus and the place of emotion erupted in Boston and San Francisco, as in other cities. Critics later charged that the emphasis on identity reified distinctions between groups and essentialized their nature, upholding the very inequalities that the group opposed. Some later used the term "identity politics" to critique politics that divided one group from another or fostered squabbles over whose oppression was worse. Initially, however, the emphasis on identity as a basis for knowledge and politics arose in response to exclusivity in a white-dominated women's movement and a male-dominated Left (Roth 2004; Springer 2005). In its initial formulation, identity politics was a way of calling attention to the importance of dispossessed groups' speaking for themselves and prioritizing their own issues, emphasizing the unique intersections of forces that shaped particular groups' experiences. At the same time, the privileging of experience as the most legitimate basis for knowledge proved alienating to many activists and could work to foreclose discussion and dissent (Breines 2006).

By defining themselves as a group that shared a common perspective, activists legitimated the view that their experience gave them a privileged position from which to discuss child sexual abuse. Speaking out meant, not just overcoming one's own sense of shame, but declaring an alignment with other women who had similar experiences. This sense of solidarity was diametrically opposed to the silence and isolation that characterize child sexual abuse, and it was exhilarating for participants. Activists declared themselves *survivors* instead of *victims*, and set about analyzing and combating the traces of victimhood within themselves.

Internalization

As the groups worked against child sexual abuse, they developed a new theory of oppression and domination, along with other feminist and progressive activists. According to this view, oppression not only operates from the outside, controlling and restricting individuals' opportunities and subjecting them to discrimination and prejudice; it also operates from the inside, limiting people's aspirations, views of themselves and others like them, and sense of what is possible and just. Termed *"internalization"* or, later in the 1980s, *"internalized oppression,"* the idea was that societal oppression affects individuals' psyches and emotions. As a result, members of oppressed groups accept stereotypes of themselves or feel powerless or worthless (Stout 1996). Many activists came to believe that internalization helped maintain inequality by justifying the existing order and preventing members of oppressed groups from banding together to challenge their subordination. By the early 1980s, many activists saw internalization as an important problem, particularly when the early gains of the civil rights and women's movements didn't translate into sweeping improvement in the position of women and African-Americans. As activists settled in for the long haul, they sought to address the more subtle and persistent ways that inequality was maintained.

The idea of internalization was not new. Even before the 1960s, some activists discussed how members of oppressed groups could come to believe stereotypes about their group or limit their behavior according to societal dictates of what was appropriate (Weigand 2001). By the late 1960s and early 1970s, with the rise of feminism, African-American organizing, and gay liberation, the idea that oppressed groups needed to throw off negative views of themselves was growing. The Black Power movement sought ways to value the appearance and culture of African-Americans, challenging their constant negative comparison to whites. In consciousness-raising groups, women worked to change their feelings of inadequacy, intellectual inferiority, and sexual dissatisfaction. Groups like the Gay Liberation Front, Radicalesbians, the Furies, and Radical Faeries challenged the devaluing of lesbians and gay men. The Combahee River Collective's 1977 statement directly addressed the pernicious effects of racism, sexism, and homophobia on black women:

> The psychological toll of being a Black woman and the difficulties this presents in reaching political consciousness and doing political work can never be underestimated. There is a very low value placed upon Black women's psyches in this society, which is both racist and sexist. As an early group member once said, "We are all damaged people merely by virtue of being Black women."

By the early 1980s, the concept of internalization was widely discussed in the women's movement. The women who organized Incest Resources and the Pleiades would have been familiar with the concept, and their background in co-counseling inclined them to conceptualize oppression in terms of its effects on individuals' interior lives. Along with other activists against child sexual abuse, they developed an analysis of internalization and how it might be overcome. For survivors of child sexual abuse, they argued, internalization entailed believing that they were at fault for abuse, feeling ashamed and guilty or otherwise stigmatized, and complying with the dictate to remain silent and keep the secret. It could also mean accepting the idea that girls and women are defined by their sexual use, that women ought to be sexually accessible to men, and that they are powerless to challenge the will of others. Activists conceptualized these feelings as more than psychological damage, because they reflected society's approach to children, women, sexuality, and abuse. Because such feelings had systemic roots, rather than just being the product of the actions of a criminal or mentally ill offender, activists believed that they were a political issue, a form of oppression. Survivor activists believed that if adult survivors of incest could resist their internalized oppression, they would not only improve their own lives, but help end the sexual abuse of children more generally.

Co-counseling, similarly, stressed both psychological healing and social transformation, and the effects of oppression and stereotypes on individuals were a central concern. Co-counseling developed an extensive analysis of "internalized oppression," although it used the term only sporadically until the late 1980s. It is not clear where the concept of internalization originated within the co-counseling organization, but it was in wide use in the progressive movements that influenced its members and leaders, from the idea of Black Is Beautiful, to the feminist notion of the personal as political. In turn, co-counseling analysis and practice around internalized oppression influenced progressive movements during the 1980s.

Feminist self-help activists believed that they could change how women felt about their abuse experiences by making the issue visible and encouraging survivors to come out. Recall the Pleiades' plan to have survivors in the audience at the Michigan Womyn's Music Festival stand and embrace each other. They believed that visibility issued a fundamental challenge to stigma and blame and saw this as key to social change. For many activists, child sexual abuse had a key role in maintaining oppression more generally. As Maggie argued in a 1982 letter, "I think the way we learn to accept the fucked condition of the world and to play our role as oppressors/oppressed is from that very early training we get in our families. I think returning their human rights to children might just be the one key to all of it, all the revolutionary work we do."[38] Correspondingly, they believed that it was impossible to end child sexual abuse without ending male dominance, as another activist explained:

> One of the ways the patriarchy operates is that it engenders hopelessness and this sort of sense of, "This is inevitable, and we can treat the wounded but we can't stop it from happening."...To think about

stopping it, you have to think about what keeps it going, what perpetuates it. Silence perpetuates it, secrets perpetuate it, myths about the family perpetuate it.

Like the Combahee River Collective (Springer 2005), the Pleiades and IR experienced internal conflicts that some members saw as rooted in internalized oppression—specifically the patterns of emotion and interaction that group members carried as a result of having been sexually abused as children. Other activists since then have similarly argued that internal conflicts gain heat from members' emotional histories related to the issue the group deals with. The argument is that members' negative beliefs and feelings about themselves and other group members interfere with organizing for social change (Stout 1996). Grassroots therapeutic techniques are, therefore, not just a means of changing psychology, but a route to increased mobilization.

Some participants saw the focus on internalization as potentially changing the women's movement as a whole, challenging inequality at a more fundamental level. As Andrea said, "I thought [the survivors' movement] certainly changed feminism because so much of the emphasis was on [the fact] that it was ideas that kept women in place in a way, and not concrete oppression. That these ideas were being acted out. It really was a revolution...." No one suggested that internalization should be the sole focus of either survivor activists or feminists. To the contrary, the groups also sought to change external institutions. Psychotherapy was foremost among them.

Transforming Psychotherapy

By advocating self-help, the feminist survivors' movement deliberately sought to influence therapeutic knowledge and practice about child sexual abuse and its treatment. They worked both from the outside and through alliances with sympathetic professionals, mostly feminist therapists. As Rochon (1998) argues, the professionals who first adopt a new approach are crucial in changing views among their profession more widely. As professional feminist therapy grew during the 1980s, it influenced the practices and theories of lay counselors, who in turn changed the practice of professional psychotherapy (Davis 2005).[39] Self-help activists engaged in an ongoing exchange of ideas and practices with sympathetic therapists, and directed pressure against those who were less sympathetic.

Changing how the institution of psychiatry and psychotherapy dealt with incest was an explicit part of IR's agenda. As Leslie explained, "for years and years there were no therapists working with survivors, and part of why we had to create self-help things is that they were clueless." IR addressed this "cluelessness" by keeping books in which members could comment about therapists. Women reported therapists who suggested they had provoked incest, who were unwilling to discuss the subject, who told them they were over-reacting, or who were well intentioned but untrained.

The IR analysis of incest and its aftereffects and their model of bringing together support for survivors with public education were influential among professionals. Their influence was heightened by their professional allies, particularly Judith Herman, Ann Burgess, and Emily Schatzow, local feminist professionals working on the issue. Early on, members began to speak to professionals who worked with child sexual abuse survivors, including therapists and physicians. Kathy explained that "many of them got in touch with us, because they actually were open." Through IR members' participation in the Boston Area Sexual Assault Coalition, they became resources for professionals more accustomed to working with adult rape survivors. When Elaine later entered a doctoral program in counseling, she found "there was really nobody in the university system who knew about incest and sexual abuse either.... People there were very receptive, and I ended up doing a lot of teaching within the university system." They also gave guest lectures at colleges and universities. They also experienced hostility and difficulty gaining access to professional and clinical settings. As Elaine explained, "There were a lot of professionals who... were not receptive to learning from a survivor."

Professional allies brought survivor-activists into places they could not have entered alone. For example, Judith Herman invited IR member Kathy Morrissey to speak at the 1982 annual meeting of the American Psychiatric Association on self-help and the treatment of father-daughter incest. While Morrissey felt comfortable with the other panelists, who were all professionals working on the treatment of child sexual abuse, she recalled, "The audience was another story. That was scary.... If you ever want to truly know nausea, you have to tell 200 psychiatrists in 1982 that they've missed several beats, and be talking about incest on top of it." Yet despite her anxiety, the experience contributed to her feeling that she was an authority on the issue of incest.

Morrissey framed her address in terms of her own experience of incest and her participation in self-help groups, beginning by saying, "As a woman who was a victim of both father-daughter and grandfather-granddaughter incest, and one who kept silent for 15 years, I feel triumphant to be here today."[40] She went on to discuss the myths and damaging practices of treatment of incest survivors, and the practice of self-help. In doing so, she disseminated the model of incest and child sexual abuse and the practices of self-help that the group had created.

Morrissey offered specific guidelines for clinicians that drew on basic insights about child sexual abuse grounded in the anti-rape and self-help movements. For example:

> Be sure that you hold out to the incest survivor that the abuse was never, in any way, her fault.... Most incest survivors need to understand why

they could not say no to their abuser. They need to realize how powerless they were in the situation and know that they did not have the adult resources for autonomy that they have now.... Let those you are helping know that sexual abuse is very harmful.

The movement's redefinition of child sexual abuse was so successful that these ideas soon seemed self-evident (Davis 2005). But they were not in 1982, when incest was just beginning to be discussed publicly with any frequency.

Morrissey also admonished therapists to remember the survivor's authority about her own experience: "Therapists should listen, support, and provide helpful comments and information. It is important that the incest survivor make her own connections and conclusions about her experiences. It is also crucial that she know that the therapist believes her story." This approach differs from the portrayal of feminist therapists as leading their clients to develop false memories of abuse by suggesting that generic symptoms are due to abuse or as encouraging "memory recovery" even when the client does not see it as relevant to her (Davis 2005). Although it is clear that some therapists indeed led or even pressured their clients to produce reports of childhood abuse (Davis 2005), this is far from the movement's goal of the survivor (rather than therapist) as authority. It nevertheless signifies the dramatic change—in a very short time—since clinicians' typical response to accounts of incest was minimization or outright disbelief.

Some of the developments that came out of the self-help approach mirrored developments in professional treatment of incest survivors. It is hard to determine whether these developments originated in self-help groups, were introduced to self-helpers by professionals, or simply evolved independently in the two settings. My interviews suggest, however, that these developments often appeared in the self-help groups before publication of professional literature on the same topic; respondents suggest that they were drawn from their experiential "research" and do not report adopting them from professionals. For example, Andrea, a Boston therapist and survivor activist, reported that IR had constructed a checklist of common symptoms of child sexual abuse well before such checklists became widespread (and infamously misleading).

Similarly, the Pleiades used "affirmations," phrases that contradicted myths and internalized negative beliefs about child sexual abuse. These included, "It wasn't your fault. You did not in any way ask for it," and "We are completely lovable. There's not a thing wrong with us." While affirmations later became widespread in the mass culture self-help movement, in 1981 they were unusual. Within a few years, published works included similar affirmations and suggested that survivors repeat them regularly to help themselves shed the effects of abuse. But it is difficult to determine whether these were influenced by the Pleiades. The Pleiades' tactics certainly made diffusion possible. Maggie explained that she and another member "wrote up this statement and these affirmations and we had copies there [at workshops] and we handed them out. I'm relatively certain that if we put any name on at all, we put 'the Pleiades.' But we may not have [included any name]...there was a fairly strong cultural imperative to not claim ideas for yourself, to make them community property instantly" (Freeman 1972/3). Thus, even if the Pleiades' affirmations had influenced other writers or activists, it is unlikely that later incarnations would have been attributed to them.

Certainly, change did not come solely from the grass roots. Networks of feminist therapists treating child sexual abuse survivors were growing in the 1980s (Davis 2005). Some members of these nascent networks had extensive contact with the self-help groups, and a number of professional therapists were themselves active in self-help and feminist organizations. Andrea reported that one professional therapist involved with IR "brought a lot of what Incest Resources and the survivor community was doing into [clinical practice]." Andrea herself, a clinician who had initially become active by attending an IR group, was important in bringing specialized therapy for child sexual abuse to the gay and lesbian community and organized open forums on the topic for therapists. As she described that period in her political and professional life, "I was there as a therapist and I was also out as a survivor." Nevertheless, she differentiated the emerging professional model in which "professionals wanted three stages to dealing with incest" from the activist approach.

In sum, both laypeople and professionals were activists in the development of grassroots counseling and professional therapy for survivors. Activists targeted professional therapy for change at the same time that a movement of feminists within the profession advocated similar changes. Professionals both brought their specialized knowledge into the movement and brought movement insights into psychotherapy. This dual structure—activists training professionals, and professionals developing their own expertise and networks around child sexual abuse—produced significant changes in treatment of survivors during the 1980s. And as we will see in chapter 3, an influx of government funding helped support such activist-professional collaborations.

Conclusion: Self-Help and Social Change

A cursory analysis of new activities IR and the Pleiades engaged in might lead us to conclude that the movement had degenerated into apolitical personal improvement. After all, if their major focus was grassroots counseling and other activities designed to make women feel better about themselves, what is the connection to a larger political agenda? Indeed, influential critics suggest that the women's movement turned away from advocating social change in favor of an essentially apolitical therapeutic focus during the 1980s (e.g., Brown 1995; Kaminer 1992; Rapping 1996; Roiphe 1993). The actual picture is more complicated, however.

Activists believed that changing how they thought and felt about child sexual abuse entailed challenging a social system that indirectly sanctioned incest, failed to attend to children or adults who spoke out about their experiences, and subjected them to stigma and ineffective treatment when they did speak out. The shame that victims felt about having been abused was not simply a psychological artifact, but a product of social forces. Thus, challenging that shame by undertaking emotional work in self-help groups and speaking publicly about one's experiences was not simply psychological change, but social change. For them, the transformation from "victim" to "survivor" was not just about improving one's own functioning, but about coming to see abuse not as an individual problem, but as a collective and political one.

As the state and other institutions attempt to construct particular versions of subjectivity, they do so in part by casting people's difficulties as individual rather than collective. Thus, the mother who feels torn between the demands of her job and caring for her children is encouraged to find ways of "balancing" these demands and to see her failure to do so as her own fault rather than as a result of gender expectations and a workforce structured on the assumption that workers all have wives. Making collective what is constructed as individual is a challenge to such constructions of subjectivity. Through analysis of internalized oppression, activists attempted to make explicit how hierarchies are maintained by gaining the psychological and emotional cooperation of the dominated. They used therapeutic language and practices to do so, working together to cast off feelings of personal inadequacy and blame, recognize their commonalities with other survivors, and attribute blame not only to individual perpetrators but to the social system that created them.

This fairly abstract point relates directly to an aerobics class for incest survivors, mass meetings in which women recited affirmations, or small self-help groups. In each of these cases, activists sought to challenge sexism and the exploitation of children in the locations where they affected individuals' subjectivity. About the aerobics class, for example, organizers argued that both incest and sexism alienate women from their bodies. Physical activity can bring women into touch with their bodies—but it rarely does so in conventional aerobics classes because of objectification of women's bodies and focus on weight loss. At IR*obics, attendees knew that they all were survivors of child sexual abuse, and they were able to exercise and regain control over their bodies while simultaneously being visible as survivors. Certainly this was personally beneficial for participants, but, in the eyes of organizers, it was also a way of overcoming the internalization of societal inequalities based on gender and a societal silencing of incest survivors.

For activists, self-help more generally was profoundly political work. As one put it, "We were actively trying to start a revolution in this area." They were not interested in a revolution that changed policy but left daily life or consciousness untouched, and they had little faith that policymakers could create deeper change. Instead, they sought to change the world by combining strategies aimed at changing how individuals thought, felt, and talked about having been sexually abused with strategies aimed at raising social consciousness on the topic. They worked at the grass roots to build the kind of communities and support systems they envisioned, and they worked at the individual level to create the kinds of consciousness and sense of self that they believed would characterize truly free women.

Expanding on the new feminist paradigm of child sexual abuse that began in the 1970s, they challenged authorities on their own turf. Activists contested who is authorized to speak the truth about child sexual abuse, arguing that they alone were entitled to define their experiences and identities. The politicized forms of self-help they developed directly rejected the subordinate forms of consciousness that both women and survivors of childhood abuse were expected to develop. In doing so, they challenged established practices and assumptions about abuse victims that shaped therapeutic practices and state policies. As they sought to retake control of the self and daily life, they took on the therapeutic ethos using some of its own tools. Resistance to therapeutic coercion, thus, did not entail rejecting a concern with subjectivity and identity, but rather redefining identity and using therapeutic approaches for different ends.

Yet therapeutic and feminist approaches were by no means the only ones contributing to social change around child sexual abuse. Nonprofit organizations, social work, child protective agencies, and federal and state governments became increasingly involved with the issue of child sexual abuse during the 1970s and 1980s. As more funding became available for local work against child sexual abuse, the movement at the grass roots grew and left its feminist roots behind. Yet the work of feminist self-helpers influenced the new organizations that benefited from state funding and support in often-unexpected ways.

3

Social Services, Social Control, and Social Change

The State and Public Policy in the 1970s and 1980s

Feminist survivor activists in the 1970s and early 1980s did not see government as an ally. They lacked access to the political process, but they did not believe they could accomplish much through the government anyway, and they preferred to create radical alternatives. Largely unbeknownst them, however, major changes occurred in federal and state policy about child sexual abuse during this same period. During the 1970s and 1980s, the federal government developed new mandates for reporting child abuse and providing child protective services and made numerous grants to states agencies, organizations, and individuals for social services and research on child sexual abuse. The first policy initiatives focused on physical abuse, but they rapidly expanded their purview to include sexual abuse, as well as neglect (Nelson 1984). This expansion resulted in part from the movement's success in increasing the visibility of child sexual abuse, although the channels of influence were sometimes indirect. Pressure from physicians, growing interest in sexual abuse among child welfare advocates, legislators' desire for visibility on an uncontroversial issue, cultural and political changes wrought by the various movements of the 1960s and 1970s, and the feminist survivors' movement converged to produce substantial new policy on child sexual abuse (Davis 2005; Downs, et al. 1996; Nelson 1984).

In turn, the changing federal and state policy climate affected the directions that the movement took, the kinds of influence it had, and the ways that the issue was conceptualized as it pervaded popular culture. State priorities favored medical and criminal approaches to child sexual abuse, such as treatment programs or improvements in police investigation, prosecution, or child protective services. While activist organizations not infrequently secured such grants, they had to submerge other parts of their agenda to do so. The funding provided an opportunity for activists to influence state approaches to child sexual abuse, making the criminal justice system and medical institutions more receptive to survivors and their concerns. Yet their influence over the state was subject to selection processes that filtered out the most challenging elements of their agenda.

State institutions for dealing with child sexual abuse are numerous. While most scholars argue that the state uses therapeutic techniques for social control (Brown 1995; Nolan 1998; Polsky 1991; Rose 1990), I will show that the institutions of the therapeutic state were a location of both control and resistance, providing activists a point of entry and influence as well as imposing limits on the scope of that influence. Activists challenged therapeutic modes of social control not just by appropriating therapeutic discourses and techniques for their own ends, as we saw in chapter 2, but by entering and reshaping the state itself. In addition, when state funding led to expansion of non-profits focused on child welfare, these organizations provided an additional source of support and resources—and sometimes an institutional home—for movement groups and individual activists.

Without federal and state funding, organizations working against child sexual abuse could never have grown so dramatically in the 1980s and would have taken very different forms. Conversely, without activists' efforts, federal and state policy on child sexual abuse would have moved in different directions. Yet the connections between grassroots activism, the rise of professionalized organizations dealing with child abuse, and federal funding—and the often-arcane minutiae of how that funding was disbursed and what strings were attached—have remained largely invisible. After a review of theories of the therapeutic state, this chapter traces federal policy on child sexual abuse, these policies' effects on the state level, and the role of social work and related professions in the management of child sexual abuse. I follow the money trail in order to show the influence of these developments on activists.

The Therapeutic State, Social Control, and Resistance

No longer achieved primarily through brute force or threat of it, much contemporary social control is maintained by persuading citizens to cooperate. This kind of social control uses therapeutic discourse and techniques to shape citizens' mental states—their beliefs, sense of self, emotions, and sense of moral order—in an attempt to direct their behavior in accordance with collective notions of what is acceptable, desirable, and "normal." Such forms of social control have been termed "therapeutic" or the "therapeutic state" by numerous theorists from diverse perspectives (Giddens 1991;

Habermas 1979; Nolan 1998; Polsky 1991; Rose 1999, 1990; Szasz 1961). Theories of the therapeutic state seek to describe and explain how state power affects all areas of life, such as child-raising techniques, consumption habits, attitudes toward work, self-esteem, bodily practices, and so forth. Practices of the therapeutic state draw on specialized knowledge and psychological techniques to influence individuals' interior lives, and are often implemented by social workers and related professionals employed in government agencies that intervene in people's lives (Polsky 1991).

Nikolas Rose (1999: 90) defines "therapy" as a way of "rendering experience into thought in a way that makes it practicable, amenable to having things done to it." Therapeutic practices are those "in which one problematizes one's existence in terms of an interpretation of its inner psychological and psychodynamic meanings and determinants, acts upon one's dilemmas in terms of psychological interpretations of their implications, and intervenes upon oneself (alone or with the assistance of others) in terms of psychological norms and techniques—through self-inspection, self-problematization, self-monitoring and self-transformation" (ibid., p. 90). Rose and others show how state agencies persuade or coerce their clients to engage in therapeutic or self-reflexive practices in order to change their behavior and worldview. For example, drug courts mandate that those convicted of drug and alcohol use go through addictions therapy and define themselves as addicts (Nolan 1998), and welfare-to-work programs attempt to instill a "work ethic" and middle-class values in poor people (Polsky 1991).

While theorists of the therapeutic state differ, they agree on several crucial elements. First, authorities seek to *regulate and control wide-ranging spheres* and activities. Rose (1990: 4) argues that "Our personalities, subjectivities, and 'relationships' are not private matters, if this implies that they are not the objects of power. On the contrary, they are intensively governed." Second, and perhaps more important for our purposes, the late modern state[1] has developed structures and techniques for *regulating daily life and interiority* that Rose (1990: 2) calls "technologies of subjectivity." Rose argues that the state and other authorities attempt to shape conduct by acting directly upon subjects' thoughts, feelings, and personalities through means such as parenting advice and surveillance, workplace training programs about personality types, or advice about how to balance work and family obligations. Professionals such as psychiatrists, psychologists, and social workers who are "experts in subjectivity" (Rose 1990: 2) provide the knowledge and the personnel for carrying out these attempts to regulate the "internal workings of citizens" (Nolan 1998: 298). Their expert knowledge includes means of examining, describing, and modifying personality, mental state, and emotion (Rose 1990: 7).

Scholars who write about the therapeutic state vary widely in their political allegiances and their analysis of the role and culpability of ordinary people, the larger culture, and movements for social equality in the rise of the therapeutic state. While Polsky and Rose recount the state's imposition of therapeutic modes of control onto a population that sometimes resists, others take a neoconservative approach in which social control is secondary to the deleterious effects of the therapeutic ethos in culture and daily life (Bellah et. al 1985; Lasch 1978; Nolan 1998; Sykes 1992). These include the elevation of the self over community and moral values, an excessive value placed on uncensored expression of emotion, and an emphasis on individual victimization rather than personal responsibility. Claims of "victimization," in Nolan's view, encompass virtually any mention of inequality: "[T]oday many groups claim the status of victim, for any number of reasons. They are victims because of their race, gender, sexual orientation, physical or mental impairment, and so on" (Nolan 1998: 16).

It is hard to avoid noticing that many elements of the maligned therapeutic ethos were also elements or outcomes of the social movements of the 1960s and 1970s. Indeed, conservative critics of the therapeutic state blur the distinction between the state's therapeutic modes of control and "therapeutic" tendencies in the larger culture, particularly what they see as an elevation of victimhood and the individual at the expense of traditional values, such as religious and community-based standards, emotional discretion, and acceptance of the social order.[2] Critics on the left, conversely, see activists' use of therapeutic techniques or emotion, or their discussion of psychological effects of oppression, as playing into the hands of a state that uses these very techniques to control (Brown 1995; Kaminer 1992; Polsky 1991).

There are thus two main thrusts to the literature on the therapeutic state: the focus on social control and the critique of individuals' recourse to claims of victimization. I will take issue with both of these claims. First, while the state uses therapeutic modes of control, these are not absolute, and they can also enable resistance from inside therapeutic discourse and institutions. Second, "victimization" is far from the only way for people to discuss individual difficulties and injustice, even within a therapeutic discourse. Although state initiatives did sometimes cast people as victims, they did not always do so, and many individuals actively resisted this classification or addressed the state from other standpoints.

Public policy and state agencies that deal with issues of child sexual abuse are clearly part of the therapeutic state. They not only use therapeutic techniques (along with other means of coercion), they do so in order to maintain social control (Scourfield and Welsh 2003). At a straightforward level, this social control aims to prevent the sexual abuse of children by identifying and prosecuting offenders, imprisoning or treating them, improving parenting techniques, and surveilling schools and day care centers. In the process, agents of the state promote particular models of parenting and interaction with children as acceptable and attempt to change the worldviews, daily lives, and selves of those they target. The therapeutic techniques used include clinical case-management for families deemed "at risk" for abuse; counseling for offenders, victims, and family members;

training programs for teachers, day care workers, physicians, and others who come in contact with children; and public education programs. These therapeutic interventions exist alongside more directly coercive efforts to deal with child sexual abuse, such as prosecution and incarceration of offenders and removal of children from abusive parents. Therapeutic and other forms of social control overlap, for example, when the child, non-offending parent, or offender receive therapeutic treatment or parenting education along with incarceration for the offender and child welfare supervision of the family. The state's power of coercion is never far behind its therapeutic programs, compelling citizens to engage with therapeutic agencies and to at least appear to adopt the prescribed points of view (Nolan 1998; Polsky 1991; Rose 1991, 1999).

State officials did not address child sexual abuse simply because of an interest in social control, however, but also because of pressure from activists from the survivors' and child protective movements. These activists raised public consciousness about child sexual abuse and influenced the directions that federal and state policy took, how funding was implemented, and the organizations and treatment programs that emerged. Conversely, the kinds and amount of funding available trickled down to affect even grassroots activists. Although state policy and practice dealing with child sexual abuse are an instance of social control and the expansion of the therapeutic state, they are also a location of resistance to that control and to the therapeutic state.

The federal agency charged with administering and funding initiatives against child abuse, the National Center on Child Abuse and Neglect (NCCAN), did not initially fund child sexual abuse, focusing instead on physical abuse and neglect.[3] But as activists and advocates pressed and reports of child sexual abuse poured into agencies, NCCAN expanded its focus. Beginning in 1978, NCCAN began to include sexual abuse in its priority areas during most years. While the amount of funding and the proportion devoted to child sexual abuse fluctuated from year to year, as figure 3.1 shows, it provided a steady source of support to both professionalized and grassroots organizations. The amount of funding, while relatively small, spurred related funding at state and local levels, and research and demonstration projects gained wider influence.

The priorities of federal and local government favored some movement organizations and goals over others, however, showing the operation of selection processes as the movement came into contact with the state. Federal legislation and funding set yearly priority areas. As child sexual abuse entered these priority lists, activists were able to gain access and resources. But the state focus on treatment and prosecution meant that efforts in these areas received a boost while other areas languished. Later, as funding favored collaboration between community organizations, police, and medical facilities, the interests of police or hospitals selected the social movement organizations that entered these collaborations and the kind of

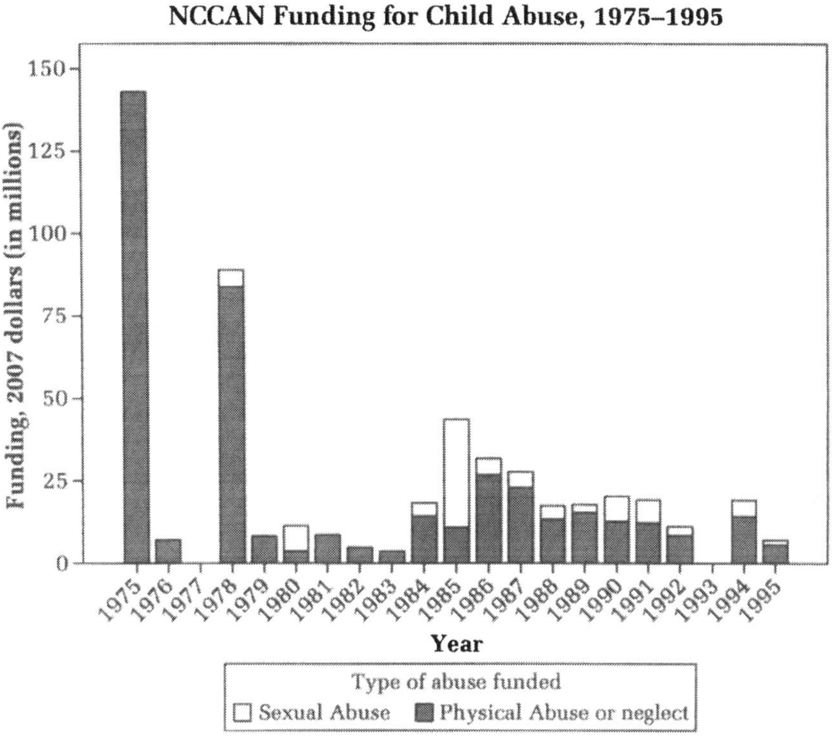

NCCAN Funding for Child Abuse, 1975–1995

Figure 3.1. NCCAN Funding for Child Abuse, 1975–1995
Source: NCCAN Clearinghouse Compendium of Discretionary Grants, Fiscal Years 1975–1995

training they offered. In sum, while the movement and state influenced each other, they did so within the parameters set by the state itself, even as activists worked to shift those parameters.

Federal Legislation about Child Sexual Abuse in the 1960s and 1970s

Prior to the mid-1960s, as discussed in chapter 1, there had been little discussion of child abuse by physicians, by policy makers, or in mass culture since the early part of the century. Beginning in the mid-1960s, physicians began writing about the severe physical abuse of children, terming the medical consequences "battered child syndrome" (Kempe et al. 1962). As the issue became more visible in the medical literature, it came to the attention of policymakers. The federal Children's Bureau, along with the Children's Division of the American Humane Association, drafted a model child abuse-reporting law in 1963 and began to support research on child abuse. This early research began to raise interest in the topic in medical and child welfare circles. Very rapidly, between 1963 and 1967, all 50 states adopted laws mandating the reporting of child abuse (Nelson 1984, chap. 3). Because of the initial focus on physical injury and the role of doctors in raising the issue, policymakers conceptualized child abuse in medical terms. They also viewed it as quite rare and therefore assumed that bringing individual cases of child abuse to the attention of authorities would be sufficient (Nelson 1984).

The first federal legislation on the issue passed Congress and was signed (reluctantly) by President Nixon in 1974. The Child Abuse Prevention and Treatment Act (CAPTA) provided grants to states, government agencies, schools, and other organizations for prevention campaigns and demonstration research, and established the National Center on Child Abuse and Neglect (NCCAN) under the Department of Health, Education, and Welfare (Nelson 1984: 104, 115). CAPTA assumed a medical model of child abuse, and physicians had more influence than child welfare workers over the crafting of the legislation (Nelson 1984: 106–9, 113–115). Consequently, CAPTA provided relatively little attention to services or prevention efforts that treated child abuse as a social problem rather than the result of pathological parents (Nelson 1984).

CAPTA mandated greater and more coordinated child welfare services at the state level, and required states to have procedures "for the prevention, identification, and treatment of child abuse" in order to receive service grants (Nelson 1984: 104, quoting Hoffman 1978: 86). As Nelson describes, the volume of cases reported to state agencies far exceeded both their expectations and the capacity of social service agencies. Reports of sexual abuse in particular were more widespread than expected. As a result, mandatory reporting laws created a need for many more social services, which were required under CAPTA, but not federally funded. The rapid expansion of child protective services during the late 1970s was a direct result.

The expansion of child protective services is precisely the kind of change that theorists see as instantiating the growth of the therapeutic state. Not only did the numbers of offices and clients served increase, the growth coincided with a broadening definition of child abuse. The child welfare advocates who staffed the expanding state offices were more inclined than physicians to a broader definition of child abuse, one that included, not only sexual abuse, but also neglect.

Media attention to child pornography also increased legislative attention to child sexual abuse. Public awareness of child pornography originated largely from the efforts of Judianne Densen-Gerber, who directed the Odyssey drug treatment centers and had previously attempted to bring public attention to physical child abuse, and Frank Osanka, a professor who taught a class on child abuse. Osanka and Densen-Gerber publicized child pornography through press conferences and demonstrations in major cities around the country (Bridge 1978; Dudar 1977).[4] Public and legislative outrage led to congressional hearings on child pornography at which Densen-Gerber and Osanka presented evidence (Dudar 1977) and the Protection of Children Against Sexual Exploitation Act passed in 1977, establishing federal criminal penalties for the production or sale of child pornography and for interstate transport of minors for prostitution (which previously had been illegal for females but not males) (Ascher 1978; Kinnear 1995: 104). By 1978, twenty-two states had passed legislation outlawing the use of minors in pornography, with approval expected in six more states and eleven others expected to begin considering such bills (Bridge 1978).

Little other federal legislation focused on child sexual abuse until around 1980. CAPTA came up for an uncontroversial reauthorization in 1978. With new provisions on child pornography and adoption reform, it was renamed the Child Abuse Prevention and Treatment and Adoption Reform Act (CAPTARA) (Nelson 1984: 117–118). The reauthorization increased the proportion of federal funding that went to state programs, shifting authority to state child welfare services (Nelson 1984: 118) and boosting the trend toward expansion of social services that had been under way for over a decade. Even prior to 1980, funding and policy were shaping both social control and resistance, as we will see by examining the relationship between funding, state agencies, and social movement organizations.

Federal Policy, Funding, and the Rise of Social Services, 1960s and 1970s

CAPTA and the mandatory reporting laws sparked significant changes in the provision of social services and the profession of social work, but many changes were already underway. Changing federal approaches to dealing with poverty during the 1960s led to an increase in social service infrastructure and laid the groundwork for the expansion and direction of child welfare services over the next couple of decades. In particular, the "War on Poverty" initiated an expansion in public social work and social welfare between 1965 and 1966. Previously, direct services had mostly been left to the variable efforts of the states and localities, but during the mid-1960s, federal grants-in-aid to the states began to increase (Leiby 1978: 297, 301). Such grants to the states would become the central funding strategy of CAPTA, supporting the expansion of specialized child welfare services in the 1970s. As social programs shifted toward offering services rather than direct financial support, a broader range of families became eligible for these services. Attempts to ensure "maximum feasible participation" in program design by the people being served allowed activists a point of access. These earlier developments laid the groundwork for activist organizations to receive funding under CAPTA for their work.

Anti-Poverty Programs and Child Welfare during the 1960s

New approaches to dealing with child sexual abuse emerged in the context of programs aimed at reducing poverty and lowering welfare caseloads. In the 1960s, the federal government attributed the problem of child welfare in part to the "multiproblem, hard-to-reach family, [and] the absence or inept fragmentation of constructive help" (Leiby 1978: 303). It dealt with the "multiproblem family" by requiring states to expand child welfare services through the 1962 amendments to the Social Security Act, which increased reimbursement to states for casework services, with the goal of increasing direct intervention with poor families and reducing dependency on Aid to Families with Dependent Children (AFDC) (Polsky 1991; Specht and Courtney 1994). In order to receive the higher rate of reimbursement, states were required to "prepare a 'social study and plan for services' for every child on AFDC; and offer services to people not actually dependent [on AFDC] but in danger of becoming so" (Leiby 1978: 303–304).[5] These amendments expanded the number of families subject to intervention by including families who were only "at risk" of becoming dependent on AFDC. They also established the therapeutic approach within social welfare services more firmly through the emphasis on casework, and increased the need for social workers in order to provide the prescribed services (Polsky 1991).[6]

Michael Harrington's influential 1962 book, *The Other America: Poverty in the United States,* intensified interest in alleviating poverty among policymakers and the general public (Leiby 1978: 312–313). Harrington argued that ending poverty required cultural change to "destroy the pessimism and fatalism that flourish in the other America" (quoted in Leiby 1978: 313). This view supported the kinds of social welfare and community mental health services that were fed by other streams as well and lit a fire under the fledgling War on Poverty (Piven and Cloward 1979; Naples 2002). The growing civil rights movement heightened the urgency (Piven and Cloward 1979; Leiby 1978: 313). These programs led to an expansion, not only of social services, but of social work as a profession. By any calculation, the number of social workers necessary for the newly created social services, child welfare, and community mental health programs far exceeded the supply. Consequently, federal funding for training and research in social work was plentiful during the 1960s. Enrollment in social work programs tripled and the number of social workers doubled during the 1960s and early 1970s (Leiby 1978: 341, 343).

The new approaches went beyond traditional casework and illustrate the growing involvement by the government in managing clients' daily lives and points of view. Increasingly, social service agencies provided direct services such as day care, housing assistance, and parenting training (Polsky 1991: 184; Specht and Courtney 1994), partly because individual casework on such a large scale was impractical, and the new services and programs were a more efficient way to deal with large numbers of clients (Leiby 1978: 331 et seq.). Although the new programs were not "therapy," narrowly defined, they certainly intervened in individuals' lives in an attempt to change beliefs and feelings.

Social workers were not only expected to work sympathetically with clients, but to "carry out the state's social control functions with respect to the protection of children... [and to] represent the interests of the courts and law enforcement agencies" (Specht and Courtney 1994: 66–67). Many found the latter unappealing, if unavoidable. Although social workers are thus drawn into acting as agents of social control (Polsky 1991: 208), they remain potential sources of resistance or allies to activists. As the 1970s progressed, social work drew veterans of the New Left, civil rights, and women's movements, who hoped to put their political goals into practice by working to alleviate poverty and social problems (Leiby 1978: 340; McAdam 1988; Specht and Courtney 1994; Whittier 1995; Whalen and Flacks 1989). The activist history of some social workers enhanced their potential support for social movements.

"Maximum Feasible Participation" and Activist Access to the State

Social movements had an important effect on these new social programs. The civil rights and welfare rights movements, in particular, helped spark a change in how policy was implemented and how social service and welfare agencies were governed. They built on the Economic Opportunity Act of 1964, which mandated the "maximum feasible participation" by affected populations in community and service programs (Polsky 1991: 173). As a result, boards of directors began to include representatives from the populations that agencies served. This proved contentious, as activists attempted to use social service organizations to politicize and mobilize the poor (Leiby 1978). State and local governments opposed what they saw as the federal sponsorship of radical politics, while bureaucracies themselves resisted their own restructuring (Polsky 1991: 173–177). Nevertheless, activists made a few inroads and formed networks with agency workers, and the notion that citizens should shape the social welfare interventions that affect them would prove to be a powerful one.

During this same period, community mental health care emerged, funded by the federal Mental Retardation Facilities and Mental Health Centers Construction Act of 1963, which supported the construction of community mental health centers (Leiby 1978: 308; Polsky 1991: 274). It was driven by the conviction of NIMH experts that treatment for mental illness was most successful when it was rooted in patients' community and family relationships and tied to local social welfare agencies (Leiby 1978: 305–307). Like other social service agencies, community mental health centers (CMHCs) included the mentally ill and representatives of "community groups" (often social movement organizations) on their boards of directors (Polsky 1991: 271). CMHCs proved to be receptive to activists' new ideas about child sexual abuse, and many went on to receive federal funding to host self-help groups for survivors during the 1980s.

The inclusion of affected populations in CMHCs and social service agencies meant that potential opposition to the therapeutic state was part of their structure. Members of affected populations were often marginal to decision making or internalized the perspective of the "experts" in charge, but they also not infrequently challenged that perspective. Later, feminist and survivor activists gained access to professional therapists and agencies partly because of this idea that affected populations deserved a voice in their treatment (Polsky 1991: 177). Conservatives overstated the critique of the welfare state as an arm of radical social movements, but they were correct in pointing to a connection between activists and social service agencies, however fraught and contradictory. "Maximum feasible participation," while limited, contributed both to activists' development of therapeutic modes of resistance and to the later conflicts and coalitions that opposed those activists, as we will see. It was not the primary route for activist access to the state, but it laid groundwork for activists' use of other routes.

Social Service and Grant Funding for Child Sexual Abuse in the 1970s

Funding for services around child abuse during the 1970s occurred through several means. The federal government provided funds to the states, and states also allocated their own funds to child welfare programs. By the time CAPTA passed in 1974, almost all federal funding for social services came in the form of block grants, which allowed states to determine how to distribute the funds, but NCCAN also administered grants to organizations and individuals. Simultaneously with CAPTA in 1974, Title XX of the Social Security Act greatly reduced federal control over how states structured services and paved the way for a dramatic expansion in the populations who were affected by programs around child sexual abuse (Polsky 1991: 184; Specht and Courtney 1994) by allowing states to use social services block grants (SSBGs) for services to people who were not on public assistance, and for a wider range of services.[7]

Despite this leeway, states did not substantially reduce their child welfare programs, largely because CAPTA required them to maintain mandatory reporting laws, investigate reports of abuse, and produce reports on child welfare. In fact, child welfare programs and other social services grew rapidly during the latter half of the 1970s. Social services block grants supported all social services, so precise expenditures for child abuse programs are difficult to obtain. Overall appropriations to SSBGs fell steadily from a high of $6.8 billion in 1977 (in 1996 dollars) to a low of $2.8 billion in 1996. Between 1977 and 1979, funding fell only slightly, to $6.237

billion (in 1996 dollars), but beginning with Reagan's election in 1980, funding levels fell dramatically.[8]

Funding earmarked for child abuse was at the highest level ever (adjusting for inflation) between the 1974 passage of CAPTA and its reauthorization in 1978 (Nelson 1984: 116), as table 3.1 shows. Adjusting for inflation, NCCAN disbursed more grant funding in its first year, 1975, than in any subsequent year, and its second-highest disbursal was in 1978.[9] Decreased levels were authorized again in 1978 for disbursal through 1981, when CAPTARA was reauthorized. Half of the initial funds, and a somewhat lower proportion of the 1978–1981 funds, were earmarked for "demonstration" projects: generally local projects that provided direct treatment, service, or prevention. Social service agencies, law enforcement, hospitals, or community mental health centers organized demonstration projects, but so did social movement organizations and independent advocacy or service organizations. Demonstration project funding was thus an important way that federal funding facilitated grassroots activity. NCCAN, the federal agency charged with awarding grants in the areas of child abuse to organizations and individuals, was the source of most of the demonstration grant funding, as well as funding for research.

Despite its largesse, NCCAN funded no projects that focused on child sexual abuse (or even mentioned it) in its first three years. In 1978, however, it included sexual abuse for the first time, listing "clinical demonstration of specialized treatment of child sexual abuse..." among its priority areas and funding five projects in that area. Two were based in hospitals, and two in state family service organizations, but the fifth recipient was Parents United, Inc., in San Jose, California, a professionally coordinated self-help program for parents of sexually abused children, sponsored by the Giarretto Institute, which ran the Santa Clara County Child Sexual Abuse Treatment Program (Davis 1995: 82).[10] In 1979, NCCAN made the first of several sizeable grants to the Giarretto Institute itself, for a Child Sexual Abuse Treatment Training Institute Pilot Project to train professionals in treatment for child sexual abuse.[11] This and similar programs increased therapists' skills and networking in the field.

Federal and state governments also funded self-help groups led by members of the groups they served. Perhaps in response to the shortage of trained social workers, the Children's Bureau and later NCCAN provided the initial funding for the fast-growing Parents Anonymous, a peer-led twelve-step group aimed at helping parents to stop physically abusing their children (McFarlane 1981). The growing support for treatment and prevention programs could be seen as an instance of the state and professionals extending control over families. However, when state funding trickled down to nongovernmental organizations, organizations sometimes constructed their own definitions of self, family, and community and reclaimed the therapeutic territory from state control, and movement activists sometimes found a source of support in these organizations. Nowhere was this more evident than in the intersections between the state and activists around child sexual abuse during the 1980s.

Federal Policy, Phase Two: Expanding Concern and Constricting Funding during the Reagan Years

Ronald Reagan's election to the Presidency in 1980 changed everything and nothing. The conservative groups that were Reagan's core constituency opposed any government intervention in "family life," including domestic violence or child abuse. The Christian fundamentalist organization Moral Majority, for example, opposed child abuse laws on the grounds that parents had the authority to discipline their children as they saw fit. But although the ideological climate shifted rightward and legislation around child abuse faced opposition, funding levels and concern about child sexual abuse continued to rise. Policy toward child abuse and social services proceeded under three contradictory dictates: a general move toward cutting funding for social programs; a shifting from federal to state oversight and administration; and the political unpalatability of appearing to be "soft" on child abuse.

In 1981, the Reagan administration eliminated all federal funding to states for specific social programs, subsuming it under the Social Services Block Grant, which provided greatly reduced funding with no federal requirements about how the funds should be allocated (Specht and Courtney 1994: 103). SSBG funding levels dropped by 38 percent in Reagan's first two years,[12] with net losses for most states in federal funding between 1980 and 1985, even as the number of child abuse cases increased (Select Committee on Children, Youth, and Families 1987: 43–49). CAPTA funding increased during this same period, but the increase was far too small to make up for the loss of funding through other programs (Select Committee on Children, Youth, and Families 1987: 48).

Nevertheless, in the first half of the 1980s, states reported that they targeted sexual abuse with major initiatives or programs more often than any other form of child abuse. The majority of these initiatives were prevention programs aimed at children or parents, but there were also treatment programs and training for service providers (Select Committee on Children, Youth, and Families 1987: 106–107). In general, federal funding for anticrime programs was more readily available than for social services, and this helped increase prosecution and the role of law enforcement and strengthened discourse that viewed child sexual abuse as a criminal rather than medical matter. The growth in social services—and the therapeutic model of social control—had acquired their own momentum, however, and continued to be influential despite reduced funding (Polsky 1991).

Child abuse legislation faced heavy opposition federally, but ultimately with little effect. Under the Republican administration in 1981, CAPTARA was almost allowed to expire (Nelson 1984: 119). The administration opposed both its federal coordination and the notion of federal intervention into family affairs (Nelson 1984: 120). One critic wrote that the legislation would "open a Pandora's box of federal intrusion into the family and assist the government in its attempt to revolutionize the traditional American family" (Gasper 1980: 36). The bill survived, but with decreased funding (Nelson 1984: 121). When CAPTARA came up for renewal again in 1983, it passed more easily, partly because of rising rates of reported child abuse (Nelson 1984: 121).

Even as Congress opposed child abuse legislation, the federal government's own agencies released studies showing far higher rates of abuse than previously suspected; much of the evidence of high rates of child abuse came from studies produced or funded by NCCAN. In 1979, Diana Russell, a feminist sociologist who had been one of the organizers of the International Tribunal on Crimes against Women, conducted a random sample study of the childhood sexual experiences of women in the San Francisco area, finding that 38 percent had been sexually abused (using a broad definition of abuse) (Russell 1986).[13] NCCAN released its own major study of the incidence of child abuse and neglect in 1981, which found that 44,700 cases of abuse and neglect (a rate of seven per 10,000 children) were reported to professionals between April 1979 and May 1980 (Kinnear 1995: 104). An earlier study funded by HEW and published in the "Child Protection Report" had estimated ten million children a year were physically or sexually abused or severely neglected (Crawford 1981).

This research, combined with activists' dogged attempts to make child sexual abuse visible, consolidated a broader definition of child abuse that included sexual abuse and was endorsed by medical experts, social workers, and activists. The 1980 third edition of Kempe's classic *The Battered Child*, for example, moved beyond earlier editions' focus on physical abuse to "include the vast array of manifestations of abuse and neglect of children" (Helfer, Kempe, and Krugman 1997: xvii). Professionals in the field of child abuse noted the rising interest in child sexual abuse. For example, Douglas Besharov (then director of NCCAN), reported about the 1981 Third International Congress on Child Abuse and Neglect, "If any one topic dominated the Congress, it was child sexual abuse" (Besharov 1981: 12). This interest stemmed from the sharp increase in reporting of child sexual abuse. David Finkelhor (whose influential research was funded by NCCAN for several years, beginning in 1981)[14] found that sexual abuse was the "fastest growing form of abuse among those being reported to public agencies," with the "percentage of reports involving sexual abuse doubling" between 1977 and 1978 (quoted in Besharov 1981: 13).

Finkelhor attributed increased reporting to "parallel efforts by the child protection movement and the women's movement" (Besharov 1981: 13). Davis (2005) concurs that the alliance between the child protection and feminist movements helped to bring attention to child sexual abuse. But although the two movements worked along parallel paths, they did not join forces on a large scale until later. Consider the degree of separation between the feminist activists in Incest Resources and the Pleiades and the social workers working in child protective agencies. Although they were dimly aware of each other, they had little contact, and didn't really influence each others' views until later in the 1980s, as we will see in chapter 4. The spate of feminist analyses of child sexual abuse published in 1980 and 1981 were one of the routes of mutual influence, and Finkelhor, like a few other academics, was one of the first to bridge the two movements. An intellectual history, such as Davis's (2005), is more likely to emphasize such connections early on since they existed primarily among theorists and authors, while my focus on activism and policy highlights the lag between academic connections and their influence on social movements.

Increasing concern ensured that NCCAN funded numerous influential projects on child sexual abuse throughout the 1980s, despite the cutbacks. NCCAN funded many demonstration projects, which, by definition, are funded only temporarily, with the assumption that state agencies or nonprofits will assume ongoing funding. In practice, ongoing funding was hard to come by. But even when short-lived, demonstration projects served as models for best practices and built connections among different agencies dealing with the issue—social services, child protective services, law enforcement, community mental health, and dedicated child abuse agencies—and between agencies and activists. Thus, although NCCAN funding was paltry compared to the funding that went to other issues and compared to what was needed, it catalyzed organizational networks and increased publicity about child sexual abuse.

NCCAN's yearly "priority areas" reflected current questions in the field, but also helped to shape the direction of both practice and research. In the first half of the decade, NCCAN priority areas related to child sexual abuse focused on treatment and prevention. By the latter half of the 1980s, the focus on prevention was joined by an increased emphasis on law enforcement. By establishing the areas for which organizations could receive funding, and by encouraging institutional connections between mental health, law enforcement, social services, and survivors' organizations, NCCAN funding reshaped the social movement and the large nonprofit sector in the area that grew in the 1980s.

NCCAN Funding in the Early 1980s

NCCAN funding on child sexual abuse began in earnest in 1980, when it disbursed a relatively small amount of money ($5,535,555 in 2007 dollars), but all but one grant were in the area of child sexual abuse. These grants supported four additional regional treatment and resource centers focused on developing and disseminating treatment techniques (Kinnear 1995: 105).[15] These served as a focal point for nonfeminist organizing around child sexual abuse that flourished in the 1980s (see chap. 4), and also were a resource for feminist therapists. For example, respondents who were therapists in two different cities reported connections with their local centers and noted that the centers provided resources for the local movement.

In addition to the regional centers, NCCAN funded six projects in 1980 focused on educating elementary school children about child sexual abuse, two of which went to independent nonprofits.[16] Prevention programs in the schools were very influential throughout the 1980s and were central to the popularization of the movement's agenda. They provided a hook for many magazine articles aimed at parents, introduced parents and children to the issue, and, perhaps most important, developed the curricula that were later adopted by countless school districts. Programs such as the ones funded by NCCAN built on the work of the feminist Child Assault Program, but downplayed explicitly political and feminist stances.

NCCAN also funded fourteen projects in 1980 aimed at developing specialized services for dealing with child sexual abuse or coordinating among existing specialized services. The Oregon chapter of Parents United was the recipient of one of these grants, indicating the interpenetration of that hybrid professional/self-help organization with the state; most of the remaining grants went to hospitals, children's services agencies, and police departments.[17] These grants, while small in the context of total funding, were significant because they pulled together law enforcement, child protective services, mental health centers, and hospitals under the ideal of a "multidisciplinary" approach to addressing child sexual abuse. The grants increased networking and exposed law enforcement workers to the therapeutic approach to the issue.

The next few years were much leaner, as the expanding definition of child abuse collided with the shrinking federal budget. At the federal level, proclamations of "National Child Abuse Prevention" months or weeks (e.g., in 1982 and 1983) took precedence over significant appropriations.[18] Virtually no grants went to child sexual abuse projects in 1981, 1982, or 1983. However, funding priorities in 1982 and 1983 emphasized demonstration projects in the prevention of child abuse based on collaboration between state agencies and the general public. One such grant, for example, went to Parents Anonymous in New York State to "develop strategies for an effective working relationship between Parents Anonymous and child protective service agencies," while another went to the National Office of Samoan Affairs in San Francisco "to create and validate a child abuse and neglect training, service improvement, and prevention model implemented by urban Native American Samoan community volunteers."[19] This kind of effort no doubt gained steam from agencies' desperate need for staff due to cut-backs; but it also allowed volunteers some measure of influence.

Overall, during the early 1980s, NCCAN funding in the area of child sexual abuse focused much more heavily on psychological treatment than on prevention or law enforcement. Compared to NCCAN funding overall, a much larger proportion of grants in the area of child sexual abuse focused on treatment. This began to change in the mid-1980s.

Crime and Prosecution, Mid- to Late 1980s

By the mid- to late 1980s, as policymakers increasingly framed child sexual abuse as a crime rather than as a psychological problem, law enforcement took a growing role alongside social services. There was a steady stream of federal legislation during the mid- and late 1980s, mostly focused on criminal penalties or procedures for investigating charges of child abuse, aside from routine reauthorization and minor amendments to CAPTARA in 1984 and 1988. The expanding focus on child pornography, treatment of child witnesses in abuse cases, and highly publicized criminal cases of mass abuse in day care centers increased visibility for the issue of child sexual abuse. But questions of treatment took a back seat. Social service agencies continued their efforts, but with ever-decreasing funding, and under fire for ineffectiveness.

Child pornography remained a major locus of federal efforts during the mid-1980s, with congressional hearings and the passage of the 1984 Child Protection Act, which amended the 1977 Protection of Children against Sexual Exploitation Act to increase penalties.[20] The focus on child pornography gained heat from the broader anti-pornography climate of the Republican administration (Nelson 1984: 118). The legislation and, indeed, almost all of the discussion of child pornography, focused on criminal penalties rather than prevention or treatment of those involved, reflecting the overall punitive approach.

Procedures for investigating and prosecuting child sexual abuse also received considerable attention. Much research and legislation centered around the testimony and treatment of child witnesses. A 1984 report from the Attorney General's Task Force on Family Violence found that child victims were subjected to excessive interviewing (up to 12 interviews) in the course of prosecution. The Task Force recommended changes including allowing "hearsay evidence at preliminary hearings" and videotapes, the use of anatomically correct dolls and victim advocates for children, and "presuming that children are competent witnesses" (Kinnear 1995: 107). Congress took up the issue in 1986 with the Children's Justice Act, which required states to set up multidisciplinary task forces that included law enforcement, medical and psychological professionals, and child advocates to investigate and prosecute child sexual abuse, and funded training of police in order to "improve the chances of prosecution while reducing the trauma to victims" (Kinnear 1995: 107). The 1990 Victims of Child Abuse Act codified most of the remaining recommendations of the Attorney General's report (Kinnear 1995: 108).

Numerous articles in publications aimed at judges and lawyers addressed these issues, from many perspectives. For example, a 1988 article in *The Judges' Journal,* titled "Child Sexual Abuse: Whom Should the Judge Believe?" guided judges through the investigation, decision-making process, and disposition of these cases while recognizing various positions on the issues. The article addressed the various kinds of allegations of child sexual abuse that emerge in custody and visitation cases and showed that such allegations were fairly rare, only about one-third were believed to be untrue, and fathers as well as mothers made allegations (Thoennes 1988: 17–18).[21] While child sexual abuse allegations were relatively infrequent in domestic relations courts (where custody and divorce are handled), they were more common in criminal court. Not surprisingly, federal grant funding continued to emphasize law enforcement.

NCCAN Grant Funding, Mid and Late 1980s

NCCAN grant funding followed the focus on crime and prosecution and the emphasis on multidisciplinary investigations. In fact, 1984 and 1985 were banner years for NCCAN-funded projects on child sexual abuse. Funding for projects on child sexual abuse increased, to $11,008,457 and $27,156,624, respectively (in 2007 dollars), and the issue returned to the priority agenda. Most of the funded projects focused on law enforcement, collaboration between law enforcement and other agencies, and direct intervention by child protective services, but a sizeable number also focused on child sexual abuse prevention. The prevention projects were a major point of entry for movement organizations.

Major priority areas in both years focused on projects that supported child protective services' (CPS) connections with school systems, police, and the justice system. Although not all grants in these areas went to projects focused on sexual abuse, many did, and the resulting institutional connections carried over in any case. Most of the projects seeking to increase coordination between CPS and school systems produced educational materials or set up support groups for parents deemed at risk (teen parents, for example). Most recipients were state offices of social services, with some educational institutions and a smattering of independent nonprofits.[22]

NCCAN also prioritized "judicial and social service management of sexual abuse and exploitation cases" in 1984, described as addressing "practices that compound trauma to the child, lack of legal representation for the child in criminal cases ... and little attention to protection for the child victims."[23] These grants went to programs as varied as evaluations of sexually abused preschoolers; training for lawyers, investigators, prosecutors, and volunteer guardians *ad litem*; and improving law enforcement in child prostitution.[24] Atypically, most went to independent nonprofits, despite the stated focus on law enforcement. Independent nonprofits also received grants in 1985 and 1986 to develop programs to train and coordinate volunteer guardians *ad litem* or Court-Appointed Special Advocates for children. Although these programs did not focus specifically on child sexual abuse, they represent another way that citizens were brought into the state's justice system.[25] Recipients tended to be legal or psychological practitioners or community groups concerned with child abuse who aimed to bring about change in law enforcement, improving prosecution and conviction rates as well as the treatment of child witnesses. They were, in effect, receiving state funding to change the state. Although one might argue that techniques for interviewing child witnesses or training investigators, prosecutors, and guardians *ad litem* reflect a "therapeutic ethos" (Nolan 1998), they were a challenge to state power over children who enter the legal system and to the process by which child sexual abuse cases are prosecuted.

Emphasizing NCCAN's focus on sexual abuse in the mid-1980s, the National Children's Advocacy Center received $804,853 in 1985 for a national resource center on child sexual abuse. The NCAC was formed in 1985 in Huntsville, Alabama, and focused on promoting the use of child advocacy centers, which pull together multidisciplinary teams to deal with child abuse allegations. The grant, and their status as a national resource center, encouraged the development of local child advocacy centers, which became widespread by the 1990s.[26]

Numerous other grants in 1985 also focused on building institutional connections between law enforcement, educators, treatment professionals, and child protective services.[27] These went to police and law enforcement, children and family services, independent nonprofits such as the Children's Institute International and the C. Henry Kempe National Center, and state departments of education.[28] They worked to foster multidisciplinary investigations, bringing together treatment, law enforcement, and child protective services.[29] The emphasis on a multidisciplinary approach fostered organizational networks within the field and drew therapeutic modes of thinking into law enforcement, and vice versa; and it brought professionals in contact with the activists who staffed some nonprofit organizations. This was important as the focus on child sexual abuse as a crime increased, because it meant that even those within law enforcement were exposed to a therapeutic orientation, while those in other fields could frame their efforts so as to be eligible for funding despite the focus on law enforcement.

In addition to law enforcement, NCCAN's other major focus during the mid-1980s was child sexual abuse prevention, primarily through educational programs aimed at children. While funding for prevention did not aim to increase prosecution, it shared the assumption that sexual abuse was a common, lurking danger for children, a view made possible by feminist activists' work to make the issue visible and to document the large numbers of survivors.

Funding of prevention programs increased dramatically during the mid-1980s. NCCAN funded such programs beginning in 1984 and increasing heavily in 1985, when it made 29 grants related to education about child sexual abuse for children from preschoolers to adolescents and for public awareness. The programs included programs aimed at all ages of students, training teachers or other volunteers to conduct prevention programs, and adapting prevention curricula for special populations such as Native American, Alaskan village, Spanish-speaking, Southeast Asian, Haitian, migrant, or hearing-impaired students. Grants supported multimedia education campaigns, street theater presentations, and community exhibits of children's art. Recipients included schools of education, parent-teacher organizations, state departments of education, hospitals and health departments, community mental health centers, and independent nonprofits such as rape crisis centers, Parents Anonymous, and Girls' Clubs of America, as well as nonprofits focusing specifically on prevention.[30] States also funded prevention programs, as did local school districts. California, for example, funded prevention programs in the schools in 1984 to the tune of $11.25 million (Bowen 1984: 91). Resources for prevention programs, including curricula, publications, and videos, were produced in rapidly growing numbers in the mid-1980s. Paramount Home Video, for example, produced a video starring Henry Winkler, Mariette Hartley, John Ritter, the Flintstones, and the Smurfs, titled "Strong Kids, Safe Kids" (Bowen 1984: 92) and bearing many striking resemblances to the Child Abuse Prevention Project's programs.[31] The prevention curricula were possible in a climate of rapidly increasing visibility and awareness about child sexual abuse, and they carried over into mass culture, as we will see in chapter 5.

Many groups conducted workshops in the schools. One teacher described the common themes of these programs: "Each person's body is his or her own. They have a right not to be touched if they don't want to be" (Bowen 1984: 91). With the slogan "Safe, strong, and free," Columbus, Ohio's Child Abuse Prevention Project (CAP) sought to empower children and give them a sense of control over their own bodies. Illusion Theater in Minneapolis took a similarly direct approach, and like CAP, addressed incest. For example, in a program for high school students, Illusion Theater presented "a chilling family meeting in which a daughter admits, 'I've been having sex with my dad since I was a little girl'" (Bowen 1984: 91). The emphases on assault by family members and children's empowerment were controversial; ultimately, most school-based programs downplayed abuse by family members in favor of teaching "stranger danger." For a while in the 1980s, however, CAP and similar programs held contracts with many schools. According to a 1984 article in *Time*, "more than 50,000 children in Ohio and 80,000 in California" had participated in CAP workshops, and numerous school systems in other states employed either CAP or similar programs (Bowen 1984: 91).

Despite the boom in prevention sparked by NCCAN funding, the following years saw relatively little funding activity from NCCAN on child sexual abuse. Between 1986 and 1989, very few priority areas focused on sexual abuse; few grants were issued under these, and only a handful for dealing with child sexual abuse under other priority areas.[32] Two priority areas related to sexual abuse in 1986, significantly, focused on constituencies that were just emerging within the survivors' movement: "child sexual abuse by women" and "male victims of sexual abuse."[33] The years 1987, 1988, and 1989 were even leaner than 1986, with almost no grants related to child sexual abuse.[34] NCCAN did fund a parents' self-help group in Puerto Rico in 1989, noting that "from its inception, NCCAN has supported efforts of national networks of parent groups that utilize techniques of self-help for the treatment of parents who abuse and neglect their children and also serve as a resource to other troubled parents who believe that without this help they might harm their children.[35] While minimal, such funding helped self-help for survivors, the offspring of feminism, twelve-step programs, and psychotherapy, to become widespread by the late 1980s.

Overall, NCCAN funding in the late 1980s continued in the same areas as the earlier 1980s, but at a much more minimal level. By the mid-1980s, more grants were going to prevention than to treatment, but the number of grants related to law enforcement and child protective services was the largest of all. The emphasis under the Reagan administration in both legislation and funding was on criminal investigation and punishment. NCCAN grants reflected this emphasis in their funding of cooperative ventures between law enforcement and children's services and of studies of child victims, their testimony, and the prosecution of child sexual abuse cases. Simultaneously, though, extensive funding of prevention education programs for children kept the activist wing of the movement alive, as we will see below. Meanwhile, highly publicized cases of apparent abuse in day care centers fueled the rise of a view of abuse as primarily a crime and led to unexpected coalitions.

Ritual Abuse, Day Care, and Changing Political Alignments

Governmental framing of child sexual abuse as a crime to be prevented or prosecuted, rather than a psychological or political problem, helped to ensure that the cases of child sexual abuse that most captured public attention were criminal prosecutions. Public outrage and fear ran high over allegations of abuse at day care centers and stories of children raped and murdered by offenders who had recently been released from prison after serving time for similar crimes. These cases were related to the tightening of sentencing guidelines, publicity about how to prevent child sexual abuse, and the law-and-order conservatism of the era. In addition, outrage over abuse and neglect cases in families that were under the oversight of Child Protective Services merged with conservatives' criticism of CPS to bolster massive cuts to social services. Together, these forces led to political realignments by the end of the 1980s.

Beginning around 1983, a series of allegations about child sexual abuse cases with multiple offenders and multiple victims emerged around the country. While the specifics varied, most followed a general pattern. One or two children reported having been touched inappropriately by a caretaker, usually telling their parents, who then either reported it to authorities or began calling other parents. In either case, eventually large numbers of children were questioned, often using techniques since discredited as leading. Generally several adults were accused, including both men and women. While accusations often began with "garden variety" sexual assault, they also included allegations of organized child pornography and prostitution, torture, Satanism, elaborate rituals, animal sacrifice, and sometimes murder. About one-quarter of these cases initially ended either without indictments or in acquittals, while the remainder resulted in convictions of at least some defendants. The majority of convictions had been overturned by the early 2000s.[36]

Public assessment of these cases has changed over the years. Initially, professionals involved in questioning the children and prosecuting the cases were certain that ritual abuse, including murder, had occurred, and believed that their questioning techniques could not produce false allegations of the kind and detail that the children recounted. Established figures in the field were very alarmed by the cases. Kee MacFarlane, at the time with Children's Institute International and previously with NCCAN, told a congressional hearing in September of 1984 that, "I believe we're dealing with a conspiracy—an organized operation of child predators designed to prevent detection" (quoted in Chaze 1984). Over time, some of these same professionals and their critics came to believe that children are more suggestible than initially realized, and standards for forensic interviewing of children changed. By the late 1990s, it became quite rare for a multiple-offender case to be brought to trial, primarily because acquittals and overturned convictions on the earlier cases, combined with the skeptical public discourse about them, made district attorneys doubtful about the allegations, rendering conviction unlikely.

Many now argue that those accused in the day care cases were innocent and that repeated and aggressive questioning created false allegations (Nathan and Snedeker 1995; Ofshe and Watters 1994). Others argue that, at least in some cases, genuine ritualized sexual abuse did occur. Some of these believe that the alleged perpetrators were actual Satanists who conducted real animal sacrifices and child murders, while others believe that they simply created the illusion of extremely violent acts to intimidate the children (Scott 2001). Still others believe that at least some of the children were actually sexually abused—in some cases by one or more of the alleged perpetrators, and in some cases by family members who were spared from suspicion because of the focus on child care workers—but that false allegations of ritual abuse were created in the course of questioning (Goodman and Quas 1997; Cheit 2007).

Regardless of what actually happened in these cases, they changed the political and social climate surrounding child sexual abuse, contributing to changes in child care practices and the treatment of child witnesses, and ultimately to the rise of the successful countermovement. Some observers argued that the day care cases reinforced—or even resulted from—cultural anxiety about women's employment outside the home. The allegations resonated with the assumption that young children were better off at home than in day care, and parents' fears about entrusting their children to others. Indeed, advice to parents about protecting their children overwhelmingly focused on risks from strangers in public places or in unsafe day care centers.

Nevertheless, the majority of such articles published in popular magazines did not caution mothers to quit their jobs and stay home, but rather publicized guidelines about how to select a safe day care center.[37] Along the same lines, the U.S. Department of Health and Human Services issued a Model Child Care Standards Act in 1985, to provide states with a standardized approach to preventing child abuse in day care. The report declared that "speedy and sure implementation of the following proposals can do much to prevent child abuse in day care."[38] These guidelines were widely publicized and quickly adopted: parents ought to be able to visit the center without notice at any time, staff should have criminal background checks, and no staff member should be left alone with a child. Their rapid dissemination meant that the public quickly came to see day care centers as relatively safe.

Perhaps more significant, charges of Satanism and the demonization of working mothers dovetailed with the rising influence of Christian fundamentalism in both cultural and political institutions during the 1980s (Victor 1993, 1994). This was a decade when a majority of Cabinet members were born-again Christians, when the Moral Majority rose to prominence, and when the president advocated the return of school prayer and the teaching of religiously based "moral standards" (Irvine 2002). Indeed, although many conservatives abandoned support for these cases, as I will discuss below, fundamentalist Christians remained among the embattled believers in the existence of satanic ritual abuse into the early 2000s, and Christian counselors were a main source of psychotherapy in the area.

Political alignments around these cases have changed dramatically over the years. Civil libertarians opposed the cases fairly consistently all along, although more so after questions were raised about defendants' guilt. But many conservatives, liberals, and feminists changed their positions over time. Initially, conservatives championed the prosecutions as part of a crackdown on heinous crimes. Even opponents of child protection laws, such as the Moral Majority, did not object since the prosecutions did not intervene in family affairs, but in the already-suspect realm of child care. Fundamentalist Christians were already inclined to believe in Satanism, so the day care cases allowed them to reaffirm their religious mission and promote the idea (embraced by then-President Ronald Reagan) that Armageddon was near (Victor 1994). Over time, however, many conservatives came to view the cases as an example of the liberal state run amok and accusing innocent victims of committing crimes. This change was facilitated by the fact that most of those charged were white, many were women, and most could be portrayed as respectable, upstanding members of society. Similarly, many feminists and liberals initially supported the prosecutions, but over time also came to see them as examples of sloppy interviewing, prejudice against working women, or capricious law enforcement; increasingly, their position merged with the civil libertarian and conservative arguments, which became accepted as fact.

In other words, some feminists, civil libertarians, fundamentalist Christians, and other conservatives all ended up on the same side. These groups came together particularly strongly because of the nature of the day care cases, more strongly than they could have around child sexual abuse more generally. Because the allegations were so sensational, hard to believe, and were based on evidence that was widely challenged, the critical position gained large-scale public and media support. Although the countermovement did not emerge until nearly a decade after the first multiple-offender cases, it had its roots in the unexpected political alignments that developed following those cases, and it was those alignments that made its success possible.

Because conservatives held political power, the addition of liberal allies tended to strengthen conservative positions: that state funding for social services should be cut because it encourages intrusions into family autonomy; that the changes in treatment of child witnesses gave too much credence to children, who are essentially unreliable; that the prosecution of child sexual abuse cases is often misguided; and, ultimately, that the feminist approach to child sexual abuse was overblown. Skepticism about satanic ritual abuse transferred easily to disbelief in, and opposition to prosecution for, child sexual abuse in general. The discrediting of child witnesses who claimed ritual abuse extended to the discrediting of child witnesses in sexual abuse cases in general, and then to the discrediting of adults who recalled their own childhood sexual abuse, as we will see in chapter 6.

In sum, by the end of the 1980s, social services were under attack from both the right and the left (Nelson 1984: 90–91). As Polsky (1991: 209) writes, the critique of the therapeutic approach to social services "while avowedly liberal, resonates nicely with the conservative diatribe against big government." Because of the movement of feminists into social service agencies and the funding of feminist agencies themselves, the critique (from both left and right) often expanded into a critique of feminism (Brown 1995).

Conclusion

The rise of governmental concern with child sexual abuse was fueled in part by the social movement, which contributed to the broadening of state definitions of abuse. The state's use of therapeutic interventions into child sexual abuse provided both a point of entry and a target for activists and their allies. At the concrete level, the targets and entry points were NCCAN and its funding, CAPTA, and child welfare agencies at the state and local level (which, in turn, were supported and shaped by funding priorities and legislative mandates). Activists' own therapeutic discourses and practices differed markedly from those of the state, but overlapping goals and shared terminology sometimes allowed access to funding and collaborative relationships with state agencies. As a result, the state response to child sexual abuse took a somewhat different form than it would have without the social movement.

Although some movement organizations benefited from state funding or alliances with other organizations that received state funding, they did not all benefit equally. As federal and state governments invested in child sexual abuse programming, they favored medical and criminal approaches over feminist ones and credentialed experts over activist laypeople. Funding priority areas further selected organizations whose approaches to treatment, collaboration with law enforcement, or prevention focused on individual rather than social ills. These selection processes provided greater resources, credibility, and visibility to the parts of the movement that could take positions consistent with those of the state. They contributed to a mainstreaming of the survivors' movement in which the politics and practices of feminist activists lost ground as a new version of self-help grew.

Public awareness and mass media coverage of child sexual abuse grew to an unprecedented level in the 1980s, spawning nonfeminist organizations devoted to the issue, and, ultimately, widespread opposition. Although federal funding for child sexual abuse was relatively paltry, it both contributed to and fed off of larger cultural trends. When NCCAN funded five regional child sexual abuse and treatment centers in 1980, it charged these centers not only with conducting research on child sexual abuse treatment and prevention, but also with disseminating the results. Such initiatives, along with the continuing efforts of the feminist movement and the proliferation of prevention programs, produced an incredible increase in mass media coverage and cultural awareness of child sexual abuse in the 1980s. They paved the way for a new version of survivor activism and self-help to enter mass culture in the early 1980s. Many new groups sprang up. These new groups were not grounded in a feminist—or other larger political—analysis, but were focused on recovery from and prevention of child sexual abuse. These activists and the mainstream attention to child sexual abuse transformed the earlier movement. At the same time, the feminist strands persisted, making their way into the new nonfeminist organizations and into the state and treatment bureaucracies that dealt with child sexual abuse.

4

Going Mainstream

Self-Help Activism During the 1980s

> At the end of the '80s survivors didn't feel apologetic for it... There wasn't as much silence, shame, or isolation... Survivors were angry and they weren't feeling apologetic, and in some ways there was safety in numbers. Women were out there and were speaking, they wanted to have voices. In the early '80s [a survivor appearing on television]... actually had her face blacked out on the TV show. By the end of the decade women weren't needing to black out their face.
> —Elaine

Changes in federal and state policy and increased funding came together to increase the visibility and networks of services around child sexual abuse steadily throughout the 1980s. But despite the vibrancy of the feminist survivors' movement, it entered public consciousness and policy only indirectly, through its influence on prevention and other grant-funded programs, the entry of feminists into social work and therapy, and books written by feminist activists. Although feminists remained active on the issue throughout the 1980s, their visibility and influence shrank in proportion to the growth of a new, nonfeminist survivors' movement. Feminist analyses of societal silence and internalized oppression laid the conceptual and institutional groundwork for nonfeminist groups to take up the issue, but the new groups approached it in their own way.

New grassroots activity against child sexual abuse grew rapidly outside the women's movement during the 1980s. Most new groups were self-help—oriented and focused primarily on the healing and recovery needs of survivors. The rise of twelve-step recovery groups for addiction and "co–dependency" as well as incest and child sexual abuse fed into and from these survivor groups, with many members participating in both. These new survivor activists did not overlook societal factors, however; they advocated public policy changes and worked with social service agencies to promote treatment and prevention. They emphasized survivors' visibility and public education, both as part of their own process of healing and as a means of reducing the stigma and silence surrounding child sexual abuse.

In this, they were influenced by the feminist approach. But they were single-issue groups, focused on child sexual abuse in its own right, rather than as a symptom or linchpin of women's and children's oppression.

Nonprofits devoted to working against child abuse also proliferated during the 1980s. The child protective movement, which had been active for a century or more, was the basis for these new organizations. Most were highly professionalized, with paid leaders and little or no grassroots membership. They blossomed in response to increased federal and state funding and brought together therapists, social workers, child protective services, and researchers with concerned citizens and policymakers (Davis 2005). Although many focused on child abuse in general, they formed an important part of the context in which the new grassroots groups operated. For the first time, there was a large and well-established collection of organizations that worked to combat child abuse.

Earlier feminist organizing had operated in a vacuum in which the state, mass media, and nonprofit world had not yet weighed in on the issue. The new survivor organizations operated in a different world, and their approaches to the issue both accommodated and challenged the other organizations and institutions that were weighing in on the issue. Activists in the nonfeminist organizations understood child sexual abuse in a new way, deemphasizing patriarchy as the problem and integrating a focus on male survivors and abuse by women, and focusing on concrete services, policy changes, and reducing social stigma, rather than broad social transformation to end women's subordination. More socially, politically, and religiously diverse than their predecessors, the single-issue survivors continued to develop experiential knowledge. As their membership and their collective identity expanded to include men and women with varied social and political outlooks, they addressed different questions about child sexual abuse and its effects. Their politics and knowledge incorporated concerns like how child sexual abuse affected religious faith, marriage and parenting, or mainstream employment. Their approach was not apolitical, but it embodied a different kind of politics, one not closely tied to feminism or other progressive movements. Instead, they focused on the single issue of child abuse and formed alliances with both the left and the right around specific issues. This chapter tells their story and shows how they shifted the politics of child sexual abuse.

The Emergence of Grassroots Self-Help

Two influential organizations, Incest Survivors Resource Network International (ISRNI) and VOICES in Action, epitomized the new wave of survivor activism. Both began as small self-help networks and quickly expanded into national organizations that provided education and referral to local resources, facilitated self-help groups, and mounted conferences. The organizations overlapped with each other during their founding year, but parted amicably shortly afterward and developed somewhat different niches. Both pioneered a distinctive form of self-help activism that combined peer therapy, twelve-step recovery, and a focus on public education and visibility. They were not feminist in orientation, but saw child sexual abuse as rooted in children's powerlessness and social policies that failed to provide either prosecution or treatment in abuse cases. They identified stigma and lack of treatment for adult child sexual abuse survivors as an injustice. They promoted peer and professional treatment, advocacy, and public education, and engaged with the state on policy issues. Nevertheless, they saw their work as "nonpolitical" because it was not linked to political parties, ideological frameworks, or other social movements.

In 1980, Diana Carson, a layperson in Colorado who had been sexually abused as a child, started an organization to promote self-help, which she originally called VOICE (Victims of Incest Can Emerge) and then renamed "VOICES," loosely interpreted to stand for "Voices of Incest Survivors."[1] The group held its first national meeting in 1983 in Colorado and "was meant to be in the beginning an alliance of all the survivors working together."[2] Meanwhile, in New York City, Mary was also beginning to think about how to organize adult survivors. Mary also had been sexually abused as a child, and had learned more about the issue through her work as a probation officer and by serving on the New York City Advisory Task Force on Sexual Assault. She commented, "Working with adult survivors was an idea whose time had come. A lot of [people] individually, without even knowing about each other, were starting to think of what to do." As Carson, Mary, and others began to "think of what to do," they helped create a survivors' movement that was larger, more visible, and more palatable to the mainstream.

Incest Survivors Resource Network International

Mary's motivation for organizing sexual abuse survivors stemmed from her contacts with survivors through her job and Task Force service, and her desire to further her own healing from sexual abuse and give something back to the larger community. She explained, using the language of twelve-step programs, "I think all of us, as part of our recovery, find that we have to do something to help change other things out there in the world in one way or another." Mary was unsure about how to proceed, in part because she did not want to organize a group that would be perceived as too political or controversial. She tried sending around memos about the issue in her workplace, hoping to start an organization dealing with child sexual abuse in the courts, but nothing came of that. Mary explicitly did not want to be associated with the active and visible women's movement in New York, not because she opposed feminism, but because she wanted to be perceived as moderate, mainstream, and uncontroversial.

In fact, however, feminist networks were central in getting Mary's activism off the ground. She knew authors Louise Armstrong and Florence Rush, and another woman she met at a New York Women Against Rape workshop, Kate Brady, provided the initial contact with Diana Carson and the fledgling VOICE. Mary decided to form a New York City chapter of VOICE. She explained that this resolved her dilemma about being perceived as too controversial, laughingly reminiscing, "I thought, if I can say that a group of housewives [started this], maybe that would be acceptable."

Mary recruited members by posting notices at various organizations, including the Manhattan Inter-Hospital Sub-committee on Child Sexual Abuse, with which she had been involved. People called her, and they began planning a first meeting. The group gathered for the first time on February 16, 1983, at the Quaker meeting house where Mary was a member. She reported that she "didn't know who would be showing up. And lo and behold, some of my colleagues were showing up... We had about forty people." The fact that some of Mary's colleagues attended the meeting, although she had not previously realized that they had been sexually assaulted as children, is testimony to the invisibility and silence surrounding incest and child sexual abuse at the time. As she recalled, laughing, "I had never knowingly met a survivor before, but then I found out that I knew loads of them."

Right away, they had to decide who could be a legitimate member of the group. Mary reported that some attendees were part of "the lesbian community [and]... called themselves separatists... They didn't want anything to do with men, couldn't even have a man in the room." This presented an issue, because one man had attended, Arthur, who was later to become Mary's husband and co-coordinator of ISRNI. Mary reported that, "there was a quite a bit of discussion about [Arthur's presence], but then when he started talking about being a survivor [of sexual abuse] from both his mother and father that quickly broke down." One woman who had been raped as an adult but not sexually abused as a child also attended that first meeting, but she and the group decided that her attendance was not appropriate, and she left. Overall, Mary reported, "there was group consensus that it should be open only to survivors... and that it was okay for men who were survivors, but it was not okay for people who were not."

These were not just pragmatic matters, but questions of collective identity and political orientation. The group typified the new style of organizing in which an identity as "survivor" trumped any divisions of gender and political ideology. Although indebted to feminist identity politics, this was an identity politics based not on structural inequality (such as gender, race, or sexuality), but on experience (such as child sexual abuse). This proved a major distinction between earlier feminist survivor activism and the new wave.

Seven members of the New York group traveled to the first national conference sponsored by VOICES on Memorial Day weekend in 1983, and they found it both inspiring and disturbing. Mary reported, "It was a very exciting conference, but of course there were a lot of things to be ironed out, because it was sort of meant to be sort of an umbrella group for all survivor things going on, which was good but there wasn't total agreement among some of the other groups." Mary and other New York VOICES members made important and lasting contacts with other activists and with professionals working in the field. On their return from the conference, however, they decided they would rather be autonomous from VOICES. Mary explained that their decision stemmed partly from specifically their reluctance to become involved with legislative campaigns:

> They were at that time thinking of going into a lot of legislative things and so forth which we didn't know whether [they] would be suitable for us in New York... We decided that... maybe we should go a little slower and not get into so much legislation because we didn't know whether that would have the approval of the Quaker meeting...

Approval from the Quaker meeting was important, not just because it provided meeting space, but because Mary had requested "oversight" from the meeting, which meant that she met regularly with a small committee to receive advice and support. (The group later affiliated more formally with the Friends.) In addition to their substantive differences, Mary and others also had a more general discomfort with being "controlled" by a non-local organization. They decided to rename themselves and establish an independent organization.

Selecting a name for the group was shaped by their desire to promote the visibility of incest survivors, just as it had been for Incest Resources. As Mary explained, "the idea sort of came up that we should really get a phone [listing] in the phone book and have it start with the word 'incest.'" They decided to call themselves "Incest Survivors Resource Network International" (ISRNI), adding "international" because Arthur and Mary planned to travel to Sweden that summer and anticipated that international calls would follow.

By virtue of their location in New York City, ISRNI quickly received considerable publicity and became a source for media contacts and information. Mary described how, early on, "We got a lot of media calls because we were in New York City and we were willing to be visible as survivors... We had about seven, eight, nine, ten people from that original group that were quite willing to do TV things, radio things. So the media in New York sort of knew that they could [call on us]." For example, ISRNI provided speakers to the media after the airing of "Something About Amelia," a 1984 TV movie about incest. They also publicized the group by having a table at the 1983 conference of the National Organization on Child Abuse and Neglect (funded by NCCAN).

Around this time the group established a more formal structure, initially experimenting with an open membership structure, but ultimately settling on a smaller, board-controlled structure. Mary and Arthur became early board members along with one other person; they married in 1984 and continued to run the organization together until their deaths nearly twenty years later. In 1984, Mary quit her job and devoted herself full-time to ISRNI. ISRNI continued to hold monthly meetings until 1987. It was a busy time, Mary laughed, with "one thing after another. I think some weeks, we were coming in [for meetings] four evenings a week."

ISRNI never received any grant funding. Mary explained that they avoided such funding deliberately in order to maintain autonomy. She explained, "The first year it's fine and then the second year, new rulings may come down [from the] federal [government as] to what they want or don't want, and then all of a sudden, the purpose of what you want to do may get changed. We decided that we'd rather not get involved in any of that." When ISRNI incorporated, it did so as a private foundation, supported by "Arthur's money" (which was not vast). According to Mary, the organization never received more than a few hundred dollars in donations during its entire lifespan.

In addition to facilitating monthly meetings for incest survivors, ISRNI (mainly Mary and Arthur) quickly became a clearinghouse for referrals and information about incest. They ran a 24-hour "help line" for ten years, which they continued at more limited hours after that, and also provided online contact. They offered callers support and referred them to resources in their own communities. Arthur often talked with the men who called, so that they could connect with another male survivor. Mary reported that they "worked very closely with the self-help clearinghouses all over the world," explaining that "I try to get them hooked up with some of the main national organizations and let them know about what's going on in their own [area], because a lot of people call and they don't know what's happening two blocks from them." She sent out packets of information including materials from VOICES, Survivors of Incest Anonymous (SIA; a twelve-step group), and any local groups; therapists also received information about the International Society for Traumatic Stress Study (ISTSS) and the American Professional Society on the Abuse of Children (APSAC). Their international contacts came in handy, as they were often able to refer international callers to groups in their own countries.

In keeping with their decision not to be a membership organization, ISRNI did not attempt to persuade callers to join the group, preferring to make referrals to other organizations or encourage callers to start their own groups, as Mary explained:

> We've always sort of considered ourselves a catalyst to encourage other people to form their own organizations and to do things. We've had a lot of people that wanted, like, to become chapters of us and stuff and we didn't want to go that route. [We've] always encouraged people to be, you know, joining VOICES.

Not surprisingly, ISRNI maintained ties with many other organizations. As Mary said, "One of our big things is the network, introducing people to other people." From the beginning, ISRNI representatives went to conferences of organizations focused on child sexual abuse and to twelve-step organizations, particularly Survivors of Incest Anonymous. Arthur's job involved traveling, and both he and Mary used these trips to extend their networks. Mary reminisced, "I would visit the rape crisis centers or anything else that had to do [with sexual abuse]. We started to go to the Parents United chapter down in Virginia Beach, and got to talk to quite a few people there." Mary and Arthur became involved with Parents United and attempted unsuccessfully to get a chapter of the group going in the New York area. Arthur made a presentation at a Parents United conference in 1985 in Santa Clara, California, and met many activists with whom they stayed in touch for years. Both Mary and Arthur also helped to found Survivors of Incest Anonymous chapters and volunteered for the organization; later in the 1990s, Mary served as SIA coordinator in their new home of southern New Mexico, as well as serving on the board of directors of VOICES in Action beginning in 1994. Mary also served on the membership committee of APSAC, and coordinated a group in the International Society for Traumatic Stress Studies on building bridges between self-help groups and the professionals.

ISRNI leaders and members also participated in public workshops, primarily in New York. Mary explained, "We were doing quite a few workshops and stuff with the professionals where they would present the material from their professional hat and then Arthur and/or I or some of the others would then sort of illustrate what they were talking about from some of our own life experience...that went very well, it was very well received by the professional community in New York." This kind of event, although effective, set up the professional as the expert on the issue and cast the ISRNI speaker in the position of "client," or example. Through such events, ISRNI became well known and somewhat influential in professional circles. Yet they supported rather than challenged expert knowledge.

In other ways, experiential knowledge was central to ISRNI's approach. The group's web site reported that "ISRNI was a pioneer in discussing: the aftereffects of incest; female offenders; the vital need for effective treatment programs for juvenile offenders; the role of the mother in father-daughter incest; the concept of emotional incest."[3] Indeed, it was one of the first organizations to raise such issues and to frame them in terms of members' own experiences, echoing the epistemology of the feminist organizations, which saw survivors' experiences as a primary source of data and theory about incest. The group's emphasis on respect for individual differences allowed them to discuss female offenders without prejudgment based on the prevailing opinion that mothers did not commit incest. It allowed them to discuss "the role of the mother in father-daughter incest" without worrying about reinforcing sexist tendencies toward blaming the mother, since survivors, after all, were simply acknowledging their own experiences.

The group's approach in this regard owed a debt to members' involvement with twelve-step programs such as Alcoholics Anonymous, with their value on personal testimony and accountability.

ISRNI was also concerned with matters of policy, which they understood in light of survivors' experiences. Members strongly advocated effective treatment and an improved child welfare system. Mary explained that they saw the issue of child welfare policy as complex, however:

> We've been very active in encouraging communities to start decent treatment programs where every member of the family can be helped ... A lot of us, when we were kids, did not want to have a teacher finding us out unless we knew that the community had the treatment, because if you find us out... then what is the community going to do? I said [to child welfare advocates], "Get some decent treatment out there, and then the kids will be coming to you because kids know."

While ISRNI was not alone in raising these issues in the mid-1980s, many other survivors' organizations were not as engaged with questions of policy and social service. Certainly the feminist organizations discussed in chapter 2 were not. And there was a general skepticism about treatment—or any sympathy—for offenders. Yet, along with Parents United, ISRNI saw intervention with offenders, particularly adolescent offenders, as crucial. Although some nonprofits received NCCAN or other state funding for treatment for offenders or for families as a whole, this approach did not really catch hold within the larger survivors' movement until the late 1990s.

Mary and Arthur continued their work until their health failed in the late 1990s. Although ISRNI officially dissolved its incorporation in 1998[4], the organization remained remarkably consistent over its decades of existence. Over time, it amassed more contacts, but its basic form did not change substantially. Even after Arthur had moved into a nursing home and Mary, at home, battled breast cancer, she continued to send out information, admitting that, "I'm trying not to send out more than like 3, 4, 5 packages a day. I was sending out quite a few more before. It's just that my energy level has gotten [low] and it's pretty much [just] me doing it now... I'm just trying to still be of service."

Mary and Arthur saw their work with ISRNI as a form of service, which was important to them from both Quaker and twelve-step traditions. Building on twelve-step programs, in which the final step is to "carry this message to alcoholics, and to practice these principles in all our affairs" (Alcoholics Anonymous 2002), Mary explained that she and Arthur saw service as important for their own recovery:

> That's why even now that the organization has stopped as an organization, I still want to keep doing. And it's helpful to me now, too, because when I'm on the phone with somebody calling or something, I forget about my aches and pains and it's a great help to me that it gives me some purpose.

Their combined religious, recovery, and service motivations served them well, keeping both Mary and Arthur committed to ISRNI as their lives' work. Yet because the organization never developed a large or durable membership base—by design—Mary and Arthur carried the majority of the burden of maintaining the group and its activities. When they both became ill in the mid-1990s, a third board member endeavored to pick up some of the slack, but his other responsibilities made this difficult. Although the organization was unable to survive their deaths, it survived for more than fifteen years, no small feat in the competitive and stressful world of social movement organizations.

Throughout its history, ISRNI remained relatively low profile. Mary and Arthur were well known within the treatment and prevention worlds as effective public speakers, and they had connections with most survivors' organizations worldwide.[5] Yet their contact with people seeking resources was brief—sending them information and referring them to other organizations. If these people went on to become involved with the survivors' movement, they did so through other organizations, not through ISRNI.

VOICES

VOICES, meanwhile, was developing along very different lines, seeking to establish itself as a mass membership organization for survivors. Radically grassroots in its early years, VOICES held national and regional conferences, published a newsletter, and connected members with similar experiences or interests through a pen pal network called "Special Interest Groups."[6] Like ISRNI, and in some ways like the feminist groups of the early 1980s, VOICES focused on members' helping each other to recover from the effects of child sexual abuse. Like the feminist groups of the early 1980s, these activists believed that visibility and connections with other survivors were powerful antidotes to the silence and isolation that frequently characterized survivors' experiences. Laura, who joined the organization in 1986, explained that they were "trying to make an organization work so it reaches out to survivors everywhere, so that it's a voice that people can hear...and know that we're here and [they can] come to us."

The organization's structure in its early years included a volunteer president, vice president, secretary, treasurer, and board of directors; volunteers also performed all the clerical and organizational work, which was considerable, given the newsletter and the coordination required for the Special Interest Groups. Like ISRNI, VOICES was constrained from political lobbying by its tax-exempt status, but the group's self-help orientation was primarily a function of its membership and mission.

The group was open to anyone who wanted to join and tended to attract people who were just beginning to come to terms with their experiences of abuse. It was a haven for those with psychological symptoms that might have made them less welcome (and less able to participate) in groups more oriented toward political action. Its focus on self-help and healing was useful to people who were not ready or able to take other kinds of action on the issue. As Laura noted, "I think a lot of people who are wanting some shelter from the storm, in the self-help kind of way, are very largely apolitical."

The group initially emphasized the commonalities among different kinds of abuse by including them all under the rubric of "incest" to emphasize the common betrayal of trust, its aftermath, and the abuse of power. In addition, the group did not interrogate members' recollections of abuse for accuracy. Laura continued, "All comers were welcome. We didn't feel any particular need to say, 'Uhh, we're not so sure that your memories are accurate. Get out of here.'" The group's willingness to welcome anyone who identified as an incest survivor, combined with their broad definition of the term, made it a target later when critics charged that many memories of child sexual abuse were false. Yet what Laura described as the "incredible amount of acceptance for people" was a powerful antidote to the shame, skepticism, and shock that members had encountered outside the group, and as such was an important component of the self-help approach.

VOICES members developed a collective identity that was quite similar to that of ISRNI. They prioritized common experience as "survivors" over other distinctions and emphasized the similarities between different kinds of child sexual abuse, subsuming them under the term "*incest.*" Members included both women and men, those with political allegiances from left to right alongside those with little interest in politics, lesbians as well as heterosexuals,[7] professional therapists and laypeople. The group was also more diverse in economic class, educational level, and race than many other survivor organizations.[8] Although there were conflicts within the organization, my observation and reports by respondents suggest that they did not tend to occur along these lines. The overwhelming focus on a common "survivor" identity and the emphasis on members' providing support for each subsumed other fault lines.

The group did not limit itself to self-help. It did public education and sent spokespeople to the media with the aim of fostering awareness and thus improving adult survivors' experiences. Members also provided information to mental health professionals through workshops and, beginning in the early 1990s, a continuing education track at the annual conferences. Some members, along with other activists around the country, sought legal remedies for adult survivors through efforts to extend statutes of limitations on child sexual abuse to enable criminal prosecution, and they advised victims about civil suits against offenders. Laura saw these activities as "political," in contrast to self-help, explaining that, "The whole cause of trying to encourage people to use lawsuits to say, 'Hey, this is a crime!' was an activist thing to do." While Laura saw the group's self-help activities as distinct from work on legal remedies, the dichotomy between political and therapeutic is not so clear-cut. VOICES, like its feminist predecessors, was a hybrid organization, addressing both emotional and societal change.

While VOICES and ISRNI were developing broad-based survivors' organizations, other groups were developing more specialized approaches. A Christian survivors' movement grew during the 1980s, and twelve-step programs for survivors proliferated. VOICES and ISRNI took a more explicit advocacy stance than the other groups. All of them, however, were part of the popularization and explosive growth of lay therapeutic approaches that politicized the personal. As such, all of them are offspring of both the feminist survivors' movement and the state-supported child protective movement.

A Christian Survivors' Movement

It is perhaps misleading to speak of a distinct Christian survivors' movement. In fact, the major self-help organizations included many people who found comfort and guidance in their predominantly Christian faiths. VOICES members discussed the effects of sexual abuse on religious faith, how to reconcile their faith in a loving God with the fact that that God had not prevented their abuse, and the strength that God, Jesus, or religious communities provided in their recovery. ISRNI was based on the Quaker practice of Mary and Arthur. Certainly survivors of other faiths also brought their religious beliefs into their recovery and activism, but Christian spirituality was by far the most evident, even in organizations that were not specifically religious.

In addition, explicitly Christian organizations grew throughout the 1980s and 1990s. A 1985 article in *Christianity Today* described the efforts of Alice Huskey, who founded an organization to educate the public about child sexual abuse after being sexually abused by her father (Frame 1985). Through this organization, Counter Abuse, Inc., Huskey gave workshops at local churches and schools. Oriented toward Christian women, Huskey's work was as much about her religious faith as about her experience as an abuse survivor. Saying that "offering 'hope and help' to both the abused and the abusers presents Christians with a major opportunity for evangelism," Huskey also acknowledged that "talking to abuse victims about God is no easy task." The *Christianity Today* article cites difficulties with trust, including trust in God, as an effect of incest, and notes that "to some women, the word 'father' invokes fear, not comfort" (Frame 1985: 34). Yet healing in a religious context was important to some survivors and entailed not only a psychological transformation, but a spiritual one.

Christian activists also argued that the specific effects of child sexual abuse were shaped by their religion's attitudes toward sexuality and abuse. As one woman recounted, "I thought I was the one who had sinned and was going to hell because I'd been sexually active early" (Mahany 1990: 37). Another, calling for a stronger response from the Catholic Church to "heal and support victims," complained of the "totally inadequate" response of her confessor when she finally disclosed that she had been abused as a young adult (Mann 1989: 38). For her, talking more openly about abuse, training for priests from whom victims might seek help, and fostering healthier sexuality were necessary. Of course, these same critiques returned, redoubled, as the scope of clergy abuse became evident in the 2000s.

Countless abuse victims sought help from ministers and pastoral counselors. While many reported that pastoral counselors disbelieved or dismissed them, others found specialized counseling. Some organizations, such as the conservative evangelical Focus on the Family, developed a focus on child abuse, answering mail from incest victims (Frame 1985: 33). Later, in the mid-1990s, Focus on the Family became involved with policy around incest in order to advocate the preservation of traditional families, under the rationale that stepfathers or boyfriends were more likely than biological fathers to abuse children in their family. The group was also inevitably drawn into debates over the effects of incest because it opposed abortion even in cases of rape and incest. Its publications contain many articles about the failure of abortion to resolve trauma following rape or incest, and the ability of women to love and mother their children conceived through rape or incest (Mathewes-Green 2000).

The concern with child sexual abuse dovetailed with other parts of the evangelical Christian agenda on the rise throughout the 1980s. Beyond their concern with Satanism, both fundamentalist and mainline Christian denominations incorporated self-help and personal growth techniques into the idea of "spiritual growth." Pastoral counseling flourished, and sermons and church publications included themes of healing from painful experiences, forgiving those who had caused harm, and reconciling faith in God or Jesus with the existence of abuse or evil. The parishioners who heard such messages and sought pastoral counseling were predominantly dealing with abuse by family members or others, not ritual abuse.

Not all religious discourse about child sexual abuse was consistent with the survivors' movement. The Catholic Church's efforts to maintain confidentiality and its opposition to extending mandatory reporting laws to clergy were significant issues in the mid-1980s. For example, in 1986, *The Christian Century* argued that mandatory reporting laws could damage relationships, invite "backlash from the betrayed party" (the suspected abuser), and "violate the sanctity of the confessional" (Scott 1986: 174). This stance drew intensely critical reader response in the following issue. One abuse victim wrote that because of the "sanctity of the confessional," "it took me several years to escape the abuse," and another complained that the article "notices the violation of a 'sacred and moral' trust in reporting the offender, but never reflects upon the sacred and moral trust between the victim and the pastor" ("Readers' Response" 1986). These latter views came to be widely reflected in Catholic and other Christian *discourse* about child sexual abuse. However, the defense of confidentiality, opposition to mandatory reporting laws, and the practice of dealing with child sexual abuse internally rather than reporting it to external authorities remained dominant in institutional *practice*, as we see in the information that later became public about the Catholic Church's response to abusive priests (Castelli 1993; Investigative Staff 2002).

As publicity about sexual abuse by clergy, especially in the Catholic Church, grew during the later 1980s, religious organizations developed an expanded official response that drew on therapeutic and legalistic approaches. Throughout the 1980s, the Catholic Church paid numerous settlements to people who had been sexually abused by priests. Churches that housed child-care centers developed training programs for staff (Lindner 1985). An interdenominational Christian group formed in 1989, under the sponsorship of the Minnesota Council of Churches, to conduct seminars (titled "Healing the Wounds") on how congregations could recover from the effects of an abusing pastor, and to develop recommendations for such congregations (Hopkins and Laaser 1995: viii–xi).

Most visible Christian activity against child sexual abuse was very similar to mainstream self-help approaches because of the dominance of religious ideologies in everyday life. For example, in 1987, a six-year-old singer, Sharon Batts, recorded a "prayer for abused children," entitled "Dear Mr. Jesus." The song became a phenomenon. Radio stations received huge numbers of requests for it—the director of the American Society for the Prevention of Cruelty to Children called it one of the most-requested songs in history (Day of the Child 2000)—and the album sold more than 100,000 copies. The song told the story of a child physically abused by her mother, praying to Jesus, "Please don't let them hurt your children." It increased visibility of child abuse among Christians, and made a Christian approach to healing and redemption visible to the mainstream. As with most mass media programming on child sexual abuse, when radio stations played the song they sometimes provided a hotline number, connecting listeners to resources provided by groups like VOICES and ISRNI ("Dear Mr. Jesus," 1987).

Twelve-Step Recovery Groups

Twelve-step organizations were influential in virtually all survivors' organizations and were an important element of the new wave of survivor self-help in themselves. Alcoholics Anonymous was perhaps the first self-help group. Founded in 1935, AA has core texts and practices based on spiritual principles, but little to no central coordination; it organizes primarily through local meetings in which members tell their stories of drunkenness and recovery and offer support to each other (Rapping 1996). Twelve-step groups focused on other issues spun off from AA. In 1980, child sexual abuse survivors in Long Beach, California, who had been involved with twelve-step groups founded Incest Survivors Anonymous. Two years later, another twelve-step group for incest survivors, Survivors of Incest Anonymous, formed. Modeled closely on AA, ISA and SIA adapted the twelve steps into a recovery programs for people who had been sexually abused as children and operated through local self-help groups, emphasizing "anonymous fellowship," mutual support, and spirituality as a source of recovery. While there were reports of rivalry between the two groups, at the grass roots they were more similar than different.[9]

Twelve-step discourse affected how survivors thought about incest and recovery. Even some other self-helpers criticized the twelve steps for their emphasis on the "powerlessness" of the individual and making amends to people one has harmed. In the context of incest, this plausibly implies that the victim is ultimately responsible for any effects of the abuse (Armstrong 1994). But the grassroots practices of ISA and SIA meetings point us to a more complex view of the political ramifications of the rise of twelve-step groups. On the one hand, the meetings took up time that activists might otherwise have used for organizing. On the other hand, many people involved in twelve-step groups retained their political analyses and involvement outside the groups. For example, Boston activist Leslie reported that members of her local ISA meeting were able to organize in support of increasing the statute of limitations for child sexual abuse primarily because of their feminist activist background. Further, ISA and SIA—like VOICES—also attracted many members who would not otherwise have been politically active at all. In this sense, they helped create a constituency of survivors, a group with some sense of a collective identity.

Conclusion

Twelve-step groups, Christian recovery groups, ISRNI, and VOICES were all part of a new wave of self-help organizing. They shared a similar model of injury and recovery that emphasized speaking about one's experiences and finding support from other survivors, and they were committed to building a community of survivors. They emphasized commonalities across gender, class, and race, and among survivors of different forms of child sexual abuse, creating a broad collective identity. They focused on issues of child sexual abuse rather than other political issues or ideologies, and were oriented culturally and politically to the mainstream (despite some individual members' connections to other movements). Alongside their focus on individual healing, they also incorporated work toward social change, whether through advocating legislation, publicity and outreach, attempting to change religious organizations, or simply attempting to help other survivors of child sexual abuse.

Activists in the new wave saw child sexual abuse in a very different way from the feminists who first began working on the issue. Instead of seeing it as a result of patriarchal power, they viewed it as largely gender-neutral. In their view, child sexual abuse resulted from the dysfunctions of individual families and offenders and from society's willingness to turn a blind eye. The solutions these activists advocated addressed what they saw as the roots of the problem. In self-help groups, survivors could recover from the effects of abuse. Treatment programs for offenders and families addressed the problem for others, and prevention and training programs for families tackled the pathologies that could lead to child abuse. Educational programs helped children avoid or speak up about abuse. Activists spoke publicly about their experiences with child sexual abuse in order to reduce the invisibility of the issue, and organized outreach and referral so that other survivors could find support and healing. They advocated legal changes that would allow more effective prosecution and extend statutes of limitations, the reform of religious organizations that failed to intervene in sexual abuse, and improved treatment and social services.

Overall, these activists moved from an understanding of child sexual abuse as part of a larger problem—patriarchy and children's subordination—to a view of it as a single issue. This shift was not a simple rejection of feminism, but a response to the limitations of a narrow patriarchy frame for conceptualizing abuse of boys, or women as offenders. These issues became pressing as the movement diversified and addressed the range of experiences members brought, ironically the process and basis for theory that the feminist self-helpers had honed.

Meanwhile, feminist activism around child sexual abuse continued, but it was influenced by the growing nonfeminist self-help and twelve-step movements, leading to conflicts within the women's movement. Numerous cities report splits between "twelve-step" and "political" feminists in the mid-to-late 1980s, including Boston (according to respondent Andrea), and Columbus, Ohio, where activists bemoaned that all the political lesbians were joining twelve-step groups (Whittier 1995; Blessing 1992). These conflicts were real, and some activists did turn more toward personal transformation.

However, the fabled substitution of therapeutic practice for political action has been greatly overplayed. For one thing, the same individuals who were involved in self-help continued to undertake policy work and confrontation with authorities. For another, the mid-to-late–1980s were an extraordinarily difficult time for social movements across the progressive spectrum, including feminism, quite apart from the rise of self-help (Whittier 1995; C. Smith 1996). The broader feminist movement declined more as a result of this hostile climate than as a result of activists' own choices to move in a therapeutic direction (Whittier 1995). As we have seen, the notion that a focus on individual subjectivity is inherently apolitical is theoretically problematic as well.

Social movements in a given time period tend to interpret issues in similar ways, drawing on the "master frames" developed by particularly influential movements (Snow and Benford 1992). For progressive movements in the 1970s and for some time afterward, the master frame was that of civil rights. Feminists, gays and lesbians, ethnic minorities, disabled people, and many other constituencies declared their status as minorities who were entitled to rights (Skrentny 2002). The self-help survivors' movement of the 1980s, however, did not adopt a rights frame. Instead, it emphasized *individual empowerment* through *collective therapeutic practice* and called on the state to protect its citizens and alleviate their suffering. This change is what scholars, contrasting it to the heyday of Left activism of the 1960s, decry as individualistic, therapeutic, and problematic in its relationship to the state (Brown 1995). To the contrary, I believe that the change suggests a new model of politics, one that challenges therapeutic means of control by the state and medical professionals and attempts to return that control to citizens. This approach does not stop at individual "therapy," but makes demands on the state that are analogous to demands for freedom from nontherapeutic modes of coercion. As we will see, like all social movements, this one was neither entirely successful nor entirely co-opted.

The single-issue self-help groups affected vast numbers of people and, for a while, characterized mainstream discourse about child sexual abuse. They adopted the emphasis on self-help and healing that the earlier feminist movement promoted, but without its analysis of internalized oppression or larger structural causes. Self-help discourse provided a conduit through which the therapeutic elements of feminists' approach to child sexual abuse made inroads into mainstream culture and policy, but without the controversial baggage of institutional critique. The mainstreaming of self-help and survivor visibility represented a sea change in how people talked about and understood child sexual abuse. These changes were not what the initial feminist activists sought, but nevertheless resulted in part from their efforts. Similarly, mainstream discourse about child sexual abuse changed during the 1980s, incorporating some aspects of both feminist and non-feminist activists' perspectives and omitting others.

5

Diffusion and Dilution

Mass Culture Discovers Child Sexual Abuse

During the 1980s, discussion of child sexual abuse exploded into the mainstream, in magazine and newspaper articles, self-help books, talk shows, and television specials. This was both a blessing and a curse for activists. They sought increased attention for child sexual abuse in hopes of decreasing the stigma that survivors felt and galvanizing wider support. If child sexual abuse flourished in silence and secrecy, they believed, greater visibility could reduce it. As the issue received more attention, potential recruits contacted self-help groups, and policymakers became more receptive (Koopmans 2004). Yet activists had little control over the media coverage, which underplayed incest, instead emphasizing abuse by strangers, and often focused on survivors' psychological damage rather than the recovery and resilience that the movements emphasized. Nevertheless, mass media coverage was far from uniform. It was shaped by the interplay of media constraints and practices with activists, credentialed experts, and professional treatment, child protective, and criminal justice organizations (Beckett 1996).

In this chapter, I use the mass media as a lens through which to examine the spread and transmutation of activists' approaches to child sexual abuse. As Rochon (1998) writes, cultural change is evident in mass media adoption of "altered language to express a newly developed discourse." The mass media are particularly relevant to the question of cultural change in this case because one of the goals of the movement was to make the issue of child sexual abuse visible, thus breaking the associated stigma and encouraging both adults and children who had been sexually abused to come forward.

The more successful a movement is in changing the culture (short of revolution), the less it can maintain control of the content of the message. As Williams (2004) puts it, social movement "expressions, to the extent that they do become authentically part of the public cultural repertoire, do not stay the sole symbolic property of the groups who first used them." Yet activists who hope to change attitudes or discourses cannot simply abstain from engagement with mainstream culture. Instead, they attempt to navigate the strait between promoting ideas that are too challenging to mainstream beliefs to get media coverage and promoting ideas that challenge mainstream beliefs so little that they no longer constitute meaningful change (W. Gamson 2004; Maney et al. 2005).

Whether issues get media coverage and how they are portrayed result not just from what activists do or say, but from *selection processes*. These include activists' credibility and access to the media, publishers' demands for stories that will sell, conventions about how stories are framed, and the degree to which movement formulations of issues are seen as relevant or comprehensible within prevailing understandings of the world (W. Gamson 2004; Ryan 1991; Beckett 1996; Williams 2004). When an issue is portrayed in a way that taps into an established worldview, it is likely to gain more coverage in the mass media (Gamson 2004; Williams 2004; Williams and Kubal 1999). When a movement contains multiple messages about an issue, those that are most consistent with existing understandings are the ones most likely to be represented.

The movement against child sexual abuse contained a wide range of positions and frames, some similar to established understandings, and others diverging dramatically. The feminist view of the issue challenged established understandings of gender, family, sexuality, and childhood, while the single-issue wing emphasized recovery for adult survivors. Treatment and child protective organizations emphasized professional therapy, connections to child welfare, and access to the criminal justice system. In general, the perspectives of professionals and the single-issue movement received much more media play than those of feminists.

Some elements of the movements' positions resonated easily with existing belief systems and media conventions: breaking silence about abuse, extra-familial abuse, how parents could protect their children, prevention efforts, the symptoms and professional treatment of survivors, and the importance of criminal prosecution. The feminist frame that linked child sexual abuse with patriarchy was not palatable; the gender-neutral approach advocated by the self-help movement was more so. Although mass media were most likely to portray female victims and male offenders, the gender breakdown was almost always implicit. Therapeutic elements of activists' approach reached the mainstream along with elements of their institutional critique. But in both cases, the more challenging aspects, such as the analysis of internalized oppression and the importance of mutual assistance among survivors (on the therapeutic side) or the critique of the nuclear family or children's structural powerlessness (on the institutional side) remained unheard.

The selection process does not depend solely on the content of the message, but also on the characteristics of the messenger. Access to the media depends on a credentialing process through which individuals or organizations establish themselves as legitimate commentators on the issue (Beckett 1996; Gamson 2004; Rochon 1998; Ryan 1991). Credentialed experts are likely sources for media stories because journalists view them as more authoritative than the activists who, ironically, are responsible for arousing media interest in the first place. Research and organizations funded by federal initiatives were a frequent source of experts and "hooks" for articles, although feminist authors achieved some access to the media because of their public status. Furthermore, journalists' desire to provide first-person narratives of abuse meant that they often sought out participants in activist or self-help groups, such as ISRNI and IR. Nevertheless, when these authorities or activists were cited in articles, their comments on child sexual abuse were edited so that the most acceptable were the most audible.

There is no question that the amount of media coverage skyrocketed in the 1980s and 1990s. The number of articles on child sexual abuse indexed in the *Reader's Guide to Periodical Literature* increased steadily, and the proportion of articles on child abuse that focused on sexual abuse grew as well (see figure 5.1). The number of articles on child sexual abuse increased

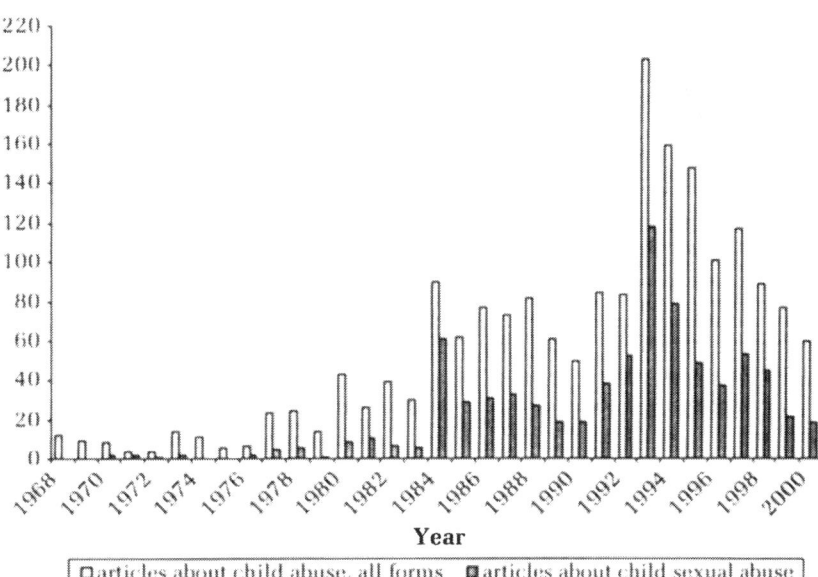

Figure 5.1. Number of Articles about All Forms of Child Abuse and about Child Sexual Abuse Indexed in the *Readers' Guide to Periodical Literature*, 1968–2000

throughout the 1980s, with a mean of 23 articles per year between 1980 and 1983, which grew to a mean of 44 between 1984 and 1989. The numbers continued to increase in the early 1990s, peaking in 1993 and declining to the previous decade's level by 1999.

Articles' central themes changed over time, showing both the influence and dilution of activists' approaches to the issue. Personal narratives of abuse became common during the 1980s, after being virtually nonexistent previously, reflecting activists' commitment to visibility and speaking out. Drawing on activists' work on abuse prevention, parents received enormous amounts of advice on how to protect their children from sexual abuse. But by the late 1980s, medical and criminal frames for understanding abuse dominated, and the movement's emphasis on peer support virtually disappeared in favor of professional therapy. Medical and criminal experts dominated in the 1990s, as skeptical coverage of abuse and false memories grew.

Beginnings: The 1970s

Mass media coverage of child sexual abuse during the 1970s was notable for several reasons. Most obviously, there was very little of it. The minimal coverage was oriented toward providing basic information and debating whether it was acceptable for adults to have sex with children. In the absence of competing frames, feminist interpretations of child sexual abuse and the balance of power in the family appeared fairly regularly, although they were far from dominant.

Much of the material framed incest as "the last taboo" remaining after the sexual revolution. For example, a 1976 article in *Redbook* by William Masters and Virginia Johnson provided an overview of sibling, father-daughter, and mother-son incest, arguing that mother-son incest was "the most traumatic of incestuous relationships." For victims of father-daughter incest, in contrast, "the greatest difficulty young girls encounter is the father's jealousy as they grow older and show interest in boys their own age." While the article's account of the long-term effects of parent-child incest reflected sexological belief at the time, it differed strikingly from those that appeared in the 1980s.

Several articles discussed "sex with children" as a topic of controversy, quoting people who advocated intergenerational sex as healthy for child and adult alongside those who opposed it, often feminists. Uniformly critical of advocates of incest, these articles nonetheless gave them a hearing (which would soon end). For example, a 1979 article in the left-leaning *New Times* presented "sex with children" as a new American "obsession," citing films such as *"Pretty Baby," "Taxi Driver,"* and *"Night Moves,"* as well as hardcore child pornography. Whereas "[l]ibertines," the article states, take the position that "If it feels good, do it," the author ultimately took the feminist stance on child sexual abuse and rape: "The central issue is power, which cannot be separated from sex... In male-dominated America, sex is in the hands of men" (Coburn 1979: 71). A similar article in *The Progressive* in 1981, "Breaking the Incest Taboo," made its feminist frame apparent from the subtitle, "Those who crusade for family 'love' forget the balance of family power" (Yudkin 1981). It quoted Florence Rush, indicating the influence of the landmark books published by the initial feminist knowledge-producers (Rochon 1998), but also quoted the NCCAN-funded 1979–1980 National Incidence Study and included information on child prostitution and pornography that reflected legislative concerns. The government studies provided information about the frequency of child sexual abuse, but they did not provide a framework for understanding why it occurred. Feminist analyses filled this gap, emphasizing power imbalances within the family.

In contrast, coverage of child pornography, which peaked in 1977 and 1978 in conjunction with congressional hearings on the issue, did not take a feminist perspective either implicitly or explicitly (with the exception of two articles in the feminist *Ms.*). Articles in *Time*, *U.S. News and World Report*, and *People* recounted stories of "kiddie porn" and profiled law enforcement efforts. An article in *Parents Magazine* advised parents to maintain good communication with their children in order to prevent them from running away and becoming the "raw material for kiddie porn" (Bridge 1978). An article in *Redbook* written by Judianne Densen-Gerber (1977), the principal activist against child pornography at the time, was a more direct call to arms, urging readers to support pending legislation and exhorting that "you and I can make a difference."

With the exception of child pornography, coverage during the 1970s did not generally discuss the legislative and policy changes going on at the time. Two exceptions were articles critical of increased intervention by state agencies following the recent passage of mandatory reporting laws. One such piece, in *The Progressive*, argued that "some of the proposed preventive steps [against child abuse] are creating new abuses against privacy and civil liberties" (Zeldin 1978: 11). In a response published in the letters section, the supervisor of a child and family services unit contrasted Zeldin's focus on civil liberties and privacy with children's rights, asking, "how about the freedoms and rights of young children? Who speaks for them?" (Reed 1978). Framing the debate in terms of children's rights v. civil liberties was common during the 1970s, but virtually vanished during the 1980s, only to reappear with the rise of the countermovement in the 1990s. In contrast to later years, only one article published during the 1970s focused on the author's personal experience of abuse (Angel 1978).[1]

The federal programs described in chapter 3 influenced media coverage by providing information, but also were newsworthy themselves. Early prevention programs for children garnered publicity in journals aimed at teachers and school administrators. One such article, originally published in the U.S. Children's Bureau journal *Children Today*, reported on one of the first federally funded children's prevention programs (Broadhurst 1975); the author of another, Alice Low (1979), was a "technical information specialist" with NCCAN, and another author, Barton Schmitt (1976), was associated with the NCCAN-funded University of Colorado National Center for the Prevention and Treatment of Child Abuse and Neglect, indicating the very direct effect of federal action on mass culture's coverage of child abuse. The scant coverage aimed at parents drew on the same sources. *Parents Magazine* published a 1977 piece entitled "The Terror of Child Molestation" emphasizing safety measures that children should take and discussing how parents should respond to children who report molestation (Schultz 1977). Most of the experts cited were law enforcement or medical professionals, their credentials providing them access and authority. The only reference to incest came from feminist author Susan Brownmiller (Schultz 1977: 70).

During the 1970s, activists, policymakers, and the mainstream media were in the process of defining child sexual abuse. Government studies and programs had begun to view it as widespread, as did feminist activists. Feminists had defined silence and invisibility as major barriers to addressing abuse. Yet aside from a handful of articles, child sexual abuse remained virtually invisible in the mass media. This invisibility was a double-edged sword. Activists wanted to break silence around child sexual abuse and call public attention to the problem. At the same time, lack of interest from mainstream media and culture allowed them maintain ownership of how the issue was framed. Already, experts involved in treatment or policymaking were given considerable weight in articles, but many articles also invoked feminist experts and frameworks. Once popular culture weighed in, activists' framing gave way to frames that did not challenge gender, familial, or age inequalities.

Publicity and Concern: The 1980s

By the early 1980s, the tone and content of media coverage had changed considerably. More stories appeared each year, and they were more varied. Personal stories of child sexual abuse were the major new theme during the early 1980s (Beckett 1996). They carried the message that "coming out" about abuse was important for both individual healing and preventing abuse more broadly. Many articles advised parents on how to protect their children, and a large number of articles discussed allegations of abuse at day care centers and the growing concern with satanic ritual abuse. These themes continued in the later 1980s, but the tide began to turn, with more stories about false accusations of abuse, particularly in multiple-victim cases. Coverage of child sexual abuse in other media also grew, including self-help books for survivors, television talk shows, and made-for-TV movies.

None of this would have happened without the activism by feminists and self-helpers, but their voices were increasingly drowned out by those of experts, and their frames for understanding abuse were distorted, even as important elements of their analyses remained. Federal funding and the organizations it supported played a background role in the cultural shift, providing a venue for personal disclosures, research reports that constituted "events" for reporters to focus on, and experts who provided explanatory quotes.

"Coming Out" and the Flowering of Mass Media Coverage, 1980–1985

Personal narratives of experiences with child sexual abuse were the most striking new direction in media coverage during the first half of the 1980s. Whereas in the 1970s only one such narrative appeared, they appeared in many major outlets every year during the 1980s, and nearly all of these stories emphasized the powerful effects of "breaking silence." The effects were also powerful for readers, who encountered detailed stories of incest and molestation and their effects. Gaining the most publicity, a steady stream of celebrities disclosed that they had been abused as children. The poet Rod McKuen revealed in a 1982 speech to the National Committee for the Prevention of Child Abuse (funded by the federal government) that he had been sexually abused, and proceeded to go on tour speaking for the committee (McKuen 1982). Senator Paula Hawkins disclosed that she had been sexually abused at the age of five by a neighbor, in a highly publicized speech to the 1984 National Conference on Sexual Victimization of Children (which was also funded by NCCAN). In the context of high-profile child sexual abuse cases at the McMartin day care center and Minneapolis Children's Theater Company,[2] Hawkins' evocation of "the horror of the trial... how tiny I felt..." helped lend urgency to efforts to ease the trauma of children's testimony and to view child witnesses as credible ("A Senator Recalls a Wrong" 1984: 27).

Noncelebrities also "came out" in print about child sexual abuse. Such stories often focused on incest and brought unprecedented mainstream attention to sexual abuse within the family. Virtually every article about incest, and most articles about other forms of child sexual abuse, began with the personal story of a victim. A typical 1984 article in *Mademoiselle*, titled "Incest: The Crime That's All in the Family," began, "Twelve-year-old Lisa had the kind of father her friends labeled neat and told her she was lucky to have... What they didn't know was that he was sexually abusing his daughter," and proceeded to recount the father's sexual assaults in graphic detail (Mithers 1984: 125). Personal stories were almost invariably accompanied by professional resources: For example, a sidebar to a similar story in *Glamour* (O'Neill 1984) quoted psychologists about the effects of incest, advised that victims get "professional help," and gave contact information for Parents United, the San Jose, California-based organization (partially funded by NCCAN) that ran self-help groups for family members.

Even articles that did not center on survivors' personal narratives used "coming out" as a device. For example, an article in *People Weekly* interviewed Florence Rush about the controversy over child pornography laws. Most of the article was a substantive discussion of child pornography, freedom of the press, and the protection of children. Embedded, however, was the question, "Were you molested as a child?" to which Rush replied by recounting her molestation by a dentist at seven and how, "when I was 11, men sitting next to me at the movies would try to reach up my skirt." Rush discussed these incidents in *The Best-Kept Secret*, but presented them as part of the near-universal experience of girls with male sexual imposition. The magazine article, in contrast, framed these experiences as "molestation," a more individualized "crime," and Rush as an individual victim rather than a girl experiencing the consequences of sexism. Even as this moved away from Rush's feminist point, it reflected the value the movement (if not Rush herself) placed on experiential knowledge, suggesting that her own experience made Rush better qualified to write about abuse.

In the early 1980s, numerous articles that focused specifically on incest drew on new resources such as counseling centers and research projects to emphasize the psychological damage and treatment of incest survivors. A typical a 1981 *Redbook* column entitled "Incest: Why Is It Our Last Taboo?" by prominent sexologists Lorna and Philip Sarrel, outlined types of incest (father-daughter, mother-son, and sibling) and their aftereffects. The authors' expertise as a social worker and psychiatrist, respectively, were the source of authority for the article, which was framed in psychological terms, with professional therapy as the only recommended treatment. Although the authors decried victims' feelings of secrecy and shame, they did not engage with activists' frames about breaking silence, let alone those that emphasized links between incest and patriarchy.

Articles that focused on child sexual abuse more generally, rather than incest specifically, tended to frame the issue in terms of the risk of abuse in public places by strangers or by trusted adults such as teachers or priests. Their focus was on what parents could do to protect their children. A typical article in *McCall's* titled "How to Keep Your Child Safe from Sexual Abuse" stressed talking regularly with children about sexual abuse from a young age and encouraging them to yell and say no. The article quoted a number of experts, including Sally Cooper of the Child Assault Prevention Project, whose prevention programs for children it profiled (Kleinmann 1984). A similar lengthy article in *Ladies Home Journal,* called "Molesters Beware: What Kids Must Know," profiled a New York group that taught self-defense to women and children, and discussed several other prevention programs, including CAP. The article encouraged parents to replicate the programs' classes at home (Benedict 1984: 52–53). Even Spiderman got into the act, with a 1984 special issue, sponsored by NCCAN, that showed Spiderman rescuing a boy from a babysitter who was molesting him, and "reveals that even he, Spider-Man, as a youngster had been abused by an older friend"

(Bowen 1984: 92; "Spider-Man and Power Pack" 1984). (Spiderman's focus on male victims was unusual for the time.)

In general, these articles drew heavily on feminist-inspired prevention programs for their advice to parents. Recall that NCCAN funded numerous prevention and education programs in the mid-1980s, many of which were profiled in popular magazines. In addition to their direct effects on the children they served, the programs provided the "hook" that journalists needed for their stories. Federal funding and feminist prevention programs thus came together neatly to increase public awareness.

In addition to their focus on prevention, articles on "molestation" by non-family members emphasized the frequency of such incidents, often calling them an "epidemic." These articles stressed the need to take incidents seriously, recognize the negative consequences for the victim, and report the offenders to authorities. Again, several articles quoted Florence Rush on the significance of sexual assaults even when they do not involve intercourse (e.g., Jacoby 1981). The "epidemic of child abuse" frame, while designed to raise readers' concerns (and thus magazine sales), also emphasized the widespread yet invisible nature of child sexual abuse. It was consistent with activists' emphasis on the scope and serious nature of the problem, but it also relied on a medical model of abuse, consistent with the approach of physicians and many nonprofit advocacy groups. For example, a 1981 article began in hugely oversized type, "If as many children were stricken by a disease as are victimized by child abuse, a national emergency would be declared" (Crawford 1981).

There was steady coverage of child sexual abuse in the African-American press, especially *Jet* and *Ebony*, throughout the 1980s. Much of this was virtually indistinguishable from the coverage in white women's magazines, with the exception that their illustrations used black models. For example, a lengthy article on child abuse that appeared in *Ebony* in 1985 gave general information about physical and sexual child abuse and neglect, and quoted and included photos of two African-American professionals in the field, both housed in agencies that received federal grant funding ("What to Do About Child Abuse" 1985).[3] Other articles focused on cases or issues of particular interest to African-American readers. For example, *Essence* published the story of a mother whose daughter was sexually assaulted when she was on vacation with the Fresh Air Fund, an organization that matches low-income children from New York City with host families in more rural areas (Hechler 1985).[4] *Jet* published many articles on cases where black children were sexually abused, including a series of articles on sexual abuse by a white offender. Later, *Jet* followed cases where famous African-Americans were accused of sexual abuse, such as the Michael Jackson case. Predominantly white mainstream news journals and magazines paid little attention to race or to the experiences of African-Americans. Even in cases involving people of color, both black and white media took a "race-neutral" approach.

Calls for action took on more urgency as several cases of alleged sexual abuse in day care centers emerged. Media attention turned to advising parents how to choose safe day care centers. Articles appeared about the Jordan, Minnesota, McMartin, and other smaller scale day care cases in large numbers in 1983 and 1984. A typical 1984 *Newsweek* article about charges at the Puerto Rican Association for Community Affairs (PRACA) day care center in the Bronx[5] managed, in one page, to discuss the McMartin case, the Country Walk day care case in Florida, and another case in Chicago. The article charged that there was an "epidemic" of child sexual abuse cases, but it only discussed cases with multiple offenders or multiple victims (Beck and Namuth 1984).

This period has been written up in later accounts as a time when hysteria about Satanism, ritual abuse, and predatory day care teachers was rampant, and attention to "garden variety" child sexual abuse and incest got short shrift (Armstrong 1994; Jenkins 1988; Victor 1993). In fact, the bulk of media attention during this period continued to focus on sexual abuse of children by individual strangers or family members. Such articles were less dramatic than those focusing on ritual abuse, but they were also very numerous and represented far more attention than the issue had received previously. Frequently, articles used the day care cases as the initial hook, and then went on to discuss other forms of child abuse. For example, "The Scandal That Shocked the Nation" headlined a lengthy feature on child sexual abuse in *Working Woman* that began with the McMartin preschool case, but proceeded to discuss abuse by strangers, acquaintances, and relatives; prevention programs, treatment, resources for parents of abused children; and necessary legislative changes (Olson 1984).

Jenkins (1988) argues that the moral panic over child sexual abuse built on *faux* ritual abuse to equate all child sexual abuse with satanic ritual abuse, thus viewing sadistic abuse as very common, all sex offenders as psychopaths, and all abuse as inevitably leading toward sex murders. In contrast to Jenkins' argument, the actual media coverage suggests otherwise. Rather than equating all sexual abuse with ritual abuse, the stories discussed other forms of child sexual abuse as distinct from ritual abuse. To be sure, the fear and publicity surrounding ritual abuse cases served to bring more attention to other forms of child sexual abuse. As coverage of satanic ritual abuse increased, so, too, did coverage of incest, which averaged 6.2 stories per year between 1984 and 1988 (the years of highest coverage of ritual abuse) in the periodicals indexed by the *Readers' Guide*, compared with 3.75 stories per year between 1980 and 1983. But the coverage of incest decidedly did not emphasize its extreme frequency or its propensity to cause sex murders. Instead, it focused on family dynamics, the shame and symptoms victims experienced, and the treatment of victims and offenders.

Television

Child sexual abuse saturated all the media, including television. The format of the TV movie was perfectly suited to dealing with incest, and the 1984 movie *Something About Amelia* gained a great deal of attention. The story of a girl who is sexually abused by her father, *Something About Amelia* starred Ted Danson as an incestuous father driven by "moody sexual maladjustment" ("Sick Fathers" 1984) who initially denies but ultimately admits his actions. The movie ends with the family in therapy, modeled on the Giarretto Institute approach, and the hope that they may be reunited. Following the same formula as most magazine articles, the film depicted Amelia's tormented reaction and reluctance to disclose the abuse, along with her mother's initial skepticism. As all the magazine articles reminded their readers, the incestuous father appeared, from the outside, to be a nice, normal man (Ted Danson, even!). The movie was framed solidly in the psychological and medical perspective, from its focus on therapy as the solution to its reliance on a "medical consultant" to ensure that it got the psychological details correct (Estrin 1984).

The movie galvanized incest survivors nationwide. The network broadcast hotline numbers after the movie, and ABC reported 5,000 calls (Stark 1984). My interviewees reported that they helped to set up hotlines in New York, Boston, and Chicago, and that hotline staff made referrals to Incest Resources, ISRNI, and VOICES. The executive director of the Chicago-based National Committee for the Prevention of Child Abuse, Anne Cohn, reported receiving letters from more than 3,000 people who had seen the movie, saying "that they had been sexually abused as children" (Stark 1984). Clearly, the movie was a result of cultural change around incest, but it was also a catalyst for such change.

Several other films and television specials during the 1980s dealt with child sexual abuse, including Oprah's *"Scared Silent."* These films were not calls to arms, but they were highly visible depictions of father-daughter incest and other forms of child sexual abuse. They presented a view in which the victims were not to blame and encouraged victims to speak out. This was a remarkable success for activists. Yet the films did not critique the underlying structures that feminists believed led to abuse and its invisibility, nor did they show survivors' ties to each other as central, as single-issue activists believed. Once again, the parts of the movement's message that were the least threatening to the status quo drowned out the larger societal critique.

Selection Effects, Experts, and Feminist Voices: The Impact of Activists on Media Coverage, 1980–1985

If the articles on nonfamilial abuse generally showed the influence of activists through their profiles of prevention programs, the picture was more mixed for those on incest. Media attention challenged the idea that incest was extremely rare and should be kept secret, yet much of it presented incest as shocking and titillating. Most of these articles featured eye-catching headlines with the word "INCEST" or a phrase like, "MY FATHER ABUSED ME SEXUALLY" printed in oversized text. Most recycled the same stock phrases, such as, "incest, the last taboo," or "the ultimate taboo," and contained explicit details of the assault. Some dredged up the notion that mothers were responsible for incest, such as a *Glamour* piece that quoted a child psychiatrist as saying, "Classically, the mother is a co-perpetrator... Consciously or not, she knows the incest is going on and encourages it" (Keslow 1981).

Most articles used the word "victim," with very few adopting the movement's preferred term of "survivor," even though many of the women who were profiled probably participated in self-help groups of some kind. There were few other sources for journalists who wanted to talk to survivors; the major New York media outlets contacted groups like ISRNI when they needed spokespeople, and members of Incest Resources and the Pleiades also reported media contacts. Yet the articles never mentioned subjects' involvement in such groups or, indeed, any kind of connection with other survivors. Instead, the articles presented them as victimized by their abuse, seeking recovery through professional therapy and supportive relationships with husbands or boyfriends. When articles gave resources for victims, they did so in a box at the end of the article and usually referred to Parents United, which, although a self-help group, was professionally sponsored and viewed self-help as an adjunct to professional treatment (e.g., Baye and Nelson-Ricks 1984; O'Neill 1984; Tunley 1981).

Furthermore, most of the experts quoted in these articles held professional credentials: they were medical or psychological experts, child protective workers, and, very often, people associated with the Child Abuse Centers funded by NCCAN. Although feminist authors and academics were sometimes quoted, feminist analyses of incest as political or as a result of the patriarchal family were almost entirely absent. For example, activist sociologist Diana Russell was described as "a sociologist at Mills College," and Judith Herman, also a noted activist, scholar, and clinician, was described as an "assistant clinical professor of psychiatry at Harvard Medical School and director of the Women's Mental Health Collective in Somerville, Massachusetts" (Stark 1984). NCCAN grant recipients and others affiliated with NCCAN-funded centers appearing often in the articles. Thus we see the direct impact of federal funding on mass media coverage and the associated cultural change.

Media reliance on personal narratives provided activists some access, but they could not control how journalists framed their stories. Unsurprisingly, horrific childhood experiences and ongoing symptoms received more play than activists' collective work to reduce child sexual abuse and empower laypeople to help each other recover. The selection process ensured that the most palatable, or resonant, elements of movement frames reached the furthest into the mainstream (Rochon 1998). Nevertheless, some activist frames did enter the media coverage, albeit unevenly. Virtually all articles stated that the victim was never to blame, and showed incest's negative effects, an important change from the idea that it had positive or neutral effects. Many articles contended that incest was far more common than suspected and occurred in "nice," respectable families. Many emphasized the need for victims to speak up, using Florence Rush's phrase to decry that incest remained "the best-kept secret."

Some articles, even in mainstream outlets, framed incest in feminist terms. Some mentioned male dominance as one root of fathers' sexual abuse of their daughters and made the point that mothers were not to blame (e.g., Stark 1984). For example, describing Lisa's rape by her father in *Mademoiselle*, the author used a patriarchy frame, quoting Susan Brownmiller's assertion that incest is permitted because of the dictate that "There shall be no outside interference in the absolute dictatorship of the father," and Judith Herman's description of "a family atmosphere in which male rule is unquestioned'" (Mithers 1984: 126). This article and another in *Ms.* (Clearly 1984) outlined how survivors could bring civil charges against their fathers, giving publicity to this important tactic of activists in both wings. Overall, however, nonfeminist self-help frames outnumbered feminist frames, individual struggles outnumbered collective ones, and medical and therapeutic frames were at least as visible as movement ones. Experts, many from NCCAN-funded organizations, were a mix of feminists and others, but almost always appeared politically neutral in the media. Media outlets and authors selected among the available frames and interview subjects according to what was comprehensible and marketable within existing understandings of abuse, family, and gender.

Shifting the Balance: Critique and Medicalization in the Late 1980s

By the later 1980s, the balance of stories had begun to shift. The overall number of stories increased steadily, and they continued to recount the experience of adults who had been sexually abused, report on prevention and treatment, and advise parents about how to protect their children. Simultaneously, stories dealing with false accusations appeared in increasing numbers. The Left and feminist press joined conservatives in decrying excesses and "hysteria" surrounding child sexual abuse and supporting defendants seen as innocent. Articles raising questions about the veracity of children's testimony or the existence of ritual abuse ranged from 3 percent to 20 percent of the total stories on child sexual abuse each year between 1984 and 1989. Despite being a small fraction of the total, they had a disproportionate impact and lent credence to a brewing countermovement.

Many covered the acquittals of defendants in high-profile ritual abuse cases such as the McMartin Preschool case.[6] A 1985 article in *Newsweek* focused on skepticism about children's testimony, asking "Is there a 'witch hunt' mentality in sex-abuse cases?" as it discussed acquittals and dropped charges numerous cases (Press 1985: 75). Another piece in *U.S. News and World Report* focused on "the other victims of child abuse"adults falsely accused—and decried "child abuse hysteria." (Gest 1985). As the decade went on, such stories increased in number, until the media consensus was that cases in which ritual abuse was alleged were generally false.

Marking the beginning of a trend toward criticism of child sexual abuse prosecutions and child protective services in the Left press, *the Progressive* ran two articles in 1985 under the heading "Invasion of the Child Savers." One argued that the "hype and hysteria" surrounding missing and abused children was a "media fad" that led to state intervention against poor and single-mother households, and false accusations against ex-husbands and day-care workers (Elshtain 1985). A companion article argued that "child savers" in social services exaggerated the frequency of abuse, disregarded due process, and penalized poor parents for "neglect" (Wexler 1985). These authors' opposition to state intervention targeting marginalized citizens is consistent with larger Left concerns. Yet the language of "hysteria," "media fad[s]," and "child savers" and their opposition to child protective services echoed conservative opponents of intervention into child abuse, men's rights activists, and conservatives who opposed social service funding more generally. They presaged an odd alliance with these conservatives in opposition to child abuse interventions.

A similar article in *Ms.* dealt with children's removal from families because of false reports to Child Protective Services (Zegart 1989). Presenting several cases in which children were placed in foster care following unambiguously false accusations, the article profiled an accused mother who founded the southern Colorado chapter of VOCAL (Victims of Child Abuse Laws). VOCAL, as we will see in the next chapter, worked with both men and women accused of child abuse. However, it took many explicitly anti-feminist positions and almost always advocated for fathers in custody cases where abuse was alleged. The article also quoted Douglas Besharov, who had been the first director of NCCAN, but, by the time of the article, was a fellow at the conservative American Enterprise Institute. It is hard to imagine an article on another topic that would lead *Ms.* to quote such conservative sources favorably. Yet child sexual abuse created many such strange alliances, which only increased in the 1990s.

Despite the increasing skepticism about reports of abuse, the majority of articles published in the popular press through the end of the 1980s took the position that children's allegations were usually believable and that child sexual abuse was widespread. This was essentially the same line put forward by the feminist and single-issue survivors' movements. For example, a typical 1989 article in *U.S. News and World Report* quoted a family therapist that "1 in 4 girls and 12 to 15 percent of all children may be sexually abused," and "children rarely make up abuse stories" (Moore 1989). First-person accounts of abuse remained common in women's and news magazines, and continued to be framed in terms of "coming out," "speaking out," or "breaking silence." Both feminist and nonfeminist self-helpers promoted this frame, which implied that challenging secrecy would help decrease child sexual abuse and foster recovery.

But, in the media accounts, professional therapy was necessary once the issue was out in the open. For example, a long piece in *Parents* recounted a mother's discovery that her husband was molesting their daughter (Marks 1987). Accompanied by a column by the treating therapist, the article explained the abuse as a result of the wife's depression and the husband's own experience of childhood sexual abuse by his father. Family reunification came as a result of lengthy treatment and family members' participation in support groups, an approach typical of the Child Sexual Abuse Treatment Centers funded by NCCAN. Other articles advised parents of abused children to find a "good therapist" through their pediatrician, department of social services, police department, or the National Organization for Victim's Assistance (a federal agency) (Thompson 1987), never mentioning peer support or therapist referrals available through grassroots groups.

Beginning in the mid-1980s, a series of articles covered allegations against clergy, particularly Catholic priests. When attention to child sexual abuse within the Catholic Church peaked in the early 2000s, it appeared that the issue had been brought to light only recently. But in fact, there was sporadic media coverage throughout the 1980s and 1990s, including an extensive 1985 investigative piece in the *National Catholic Reporter.* By the early 1980s, families of abuse victims were receiving civil settlements and complaints abounded about inadequate response from bishops ("Painful Secrets" 1985). Over the course of the 1980s and early 1990s, the Catholic Church reportedly paid $400 to $500 million to litigate and settle cases of child sexual abuse by priests, and at least 400 priests were charged with child sexual abuse or treated for pedophilia at the Church's treatment centers (Castelli 1993: 8; Horn 1993: 54). While some cases received publicity, many more were settled quietly. It was not until the 1990s that evidence about the number of cases in previous decades really emerged and the scandal erupted (John Jay College of Criminal Justice 2004).

Contrary to the "moral panic" model, the media and the experts who issued their opinion did not speak with a unified voice. For example, several articles focused on the wide range of acts that fell into the category of molestation. In "Was I Molested? The Gray Area of Sexual Abuse," Carol Kirschenbaum (1987) addressed the question of whether exhibitionism or a "teacher who fondled and French-kissed [a] 12-year-old" are molestation. Kirschenbaum quoted Florence Rush and Henry Giarretto of Parents United on the negative effects of even "minor" forms of molestation, but also quoted a psychiatrist who opined that effects vary and depend on the overall context of the child's life. The focus on the "gray area" and the presence of the psychiatrist's dissenting opinion exemplify the variety of views present in media accounts, even at the height of publicity and concern.

The Paradox of Therapy: Effects of the Movement on Late 1980s Coverage

The emphasis on molesters' mental illness and victims' psychological symptoms grew during the later 1980s, as illustrated by the articles discussed above. The focus on victims' symptoms tended to cast them as damaged and to emphasize their limits rather than their strengths. The focus on therapy framed child sexual abuse as an essentially medical problem that was the result of offenders' psychological disorders, produced psychological symptoms, and required professional treatment.

Increasingly, first-person narratives described professional therapy and articles included resources to locate therapists. Although the resource lists also usually included Parents United as a source of self-help groups, Parents United also was a conduit to intensive professional therapy with victims and families through its affiliation with treatment facilities. Even *Ms.*, which referred survivors to VOICES, along with the National Center for Missing and Exploited Children, the hotline sponsored by Childhelp, and Parents' United, made no mention of feminist self-help groups (Goldsmith 1987). Without state funding or a service orientation, feminist survivors' groups remained too small and locally focused to serve as resources in national publications. The selection processes that shaped access to funding in turn limited access to publicity and the recruits that followed.

Both feminists and self-helpers pushed for publicity about abuse, and they achieved it. They pushed for acknowledgment that abuse carried heavy emotional costs for victims, and they received it. They pushed for more effective help for victims, and for training for therapists. This demand, combined with government funding and feminist therapists' efforts, fed the huge increase in therapists and treatment programs for child sexual abuse. These individuals and organizations then served as expert resources for journalists, who unsurprisingly focused on the psychotherapeutic dimensions of child sexual abuse. The undeniable absence of other elements of movement analyses from mainstream media does not mean that the movement had no impact. Instead, it underscores the pattern of selecting from the elements of activists' approaches those that were most consistent with preexisting frames and discourses.

Self-Help Books

In addition to the coverage in magazines and television, a burgeoning number of books aimed at survivors of child sexual abuse were published during the 1980s, most focusing on recognizing and recovering from its effects.

Books were more likely than other media to discuss child sexual abuse in the context of gender, often alongside self-help suggestions. Book publishing (at that time) was less centralized than other media and included feminist presses that published books on child sexual abuse. Furthermore, the greater length of books allowed authors to present themes that resonated with the mainstream alongside feminist themes. An emphasis on empowerment through self-knowledge, with minimal overt political content, proved immensely popular and profitable (Rapping 1996, Simonds 1992).

Perhaps the best indicator of the increase in the number of books aimed at survivors is the "resources" sections at the back of major self-help books. *The Courage to Heal* (Bass and Davis 1988, 1994), arguably the most widely read self-help book on child sexual abuse, listed 13 books in its 1988 edition under the categories "Survivors Speak Out" (first-person accounts of abuse) and "On Healing." By the 1994 edition, it listed 42 books in these same categories, many published between 1987 and 1991, plus 27 books related to healing listed in other categories.[7]

Before the late 1980s, most of the books available were either feminist analyses such as Florence Rush's *The Best-Kept Secret* and Sandra Butler's *Conspiracy of Silence*, first-person narratives edited by feminists, such as the anthologies *Kiss Daddy Goodnight* (Armstrong 1978) and *I Never Told Anyone* (Bass and Thornton 1983), or studies by feminist scholars, such as David Finkelhor's *Sexually Victimized Children*, Judith Herman's *Father-Daughter Incest*, and Diana Russell's *The Secret Trauma*. While survivors read these books in an effort to understand and cope with their own experiences, the books did not prescribe self-help or therapeutic practices.

In contrast, later books focused directly on what people could do to recover from abuse. This kind of self-help book became ubiquitous in the late 1980s. General self-help books were published in large numbers in the 1980s, dealing with subjects such as codependency, "women who love too much," intimacy, anger, adult children of alcoholics, sexuality, and specialized topics such as postpartum depression (Rapping 1996; Simonds 1992; Taylor 1996). Some respondents reported using these as early resources, and *The Courage to Heal* listed several of the leading books on codependence, alcoholism, and intimacy in its 1988 resources section.

It was not until the late 1980s that self-help books oriented specifically toward survivors of child sexual abuse were published. *The Courage to Heal* itself was the best-selling of these. The book combined personal narratives, explanations of the effects of abuse, and suggested healing exercises. It later became controversial because it treated recovered memories of abuse as valid and stated that people could accurately conclude that they had been abused, even in the absence of clear memories, based on symptoms and a gut sense. The 1994 edition toned these statements down, but retained strong support for the validity of recovered memories.

For our purposes, what is important about *The Courage to Heal* is not its stance on repressed memory but how it influenced activism, self-help practice, and the broader culture. The book exemplifies the combination of feminism and self-help. It analyzed abuse in feminist terms, discussing male power in the family and how societal constructs of women's sexuality affect those who are sexually abused. Emphasizing the need for women survivors to speak up and to define their own lives, the book echoed the feminist survivors' movement in which it was born. Co-editor Ellen Bass had led the writing workshops during the late 1970s that led to the publication of *I Never Told Anyone*. Several of the feminist activists I interviewed had worked with Bass or attended her writing workshops, and they saw *The Courage to Heal* as "their" book, reflecting their perspective. At the same time, its influence went far beyond the feminist survivors' movement. Virtually every participant in survivors' self-help groups of any political stripe read the book, and many other survivors did, too. It thus served as a link between the feminist survivors' wing, the larger self-help movement, and mainstream culture.

Many other self-help books aimed at child sexual abuse survivors came out at around the same time. The 1988 edition of *The Courage to Heal* listed only four items under its "On Healing" heading, none of which were focused specifically on child sexual abuse. The 1994 edition listed 23 books in this category (mostly published in 1989 and 1990) and 18 additional books on self-help and healing in other categories.[8] In addition, it listed three "meditation books" aimed at facilitating healing; three books on choosing therapists; three books on starting self-help groups; and 37 magazines, newsletters, organizations, or clearinghouses for survivors.[9]

What these varied books shared, marking a departure from both feminist and single-issue self-help movements, was a set of suggested (or even prescribed) exercises and approaches to healing. Rather than finding their own way with the help of others in self-help groups, survivors could read about a likely sequence of feelings and responses and ways to cope with them. Certainly self-help groups also affected how individuals viewed their own experiences as they developed norms for expressing emotions, accounts of typical paths through healing, and so forth. Self-help books codified and homogenized the findings of lay psychotherapy and combined them with professionals' theories and insights. Thus the lay knowledge constructed on the ground became an expert knowledge validated by authors' professional credentials and the solidity of print.

Yet self-help books are credible, not just because of the professional credentials of the author, but because of how the narrative resonates with readers' own experiences. Readers do not simply accept whatever a book tells them, but tend to reject books that conflict with their worldviews, are "facile," or "intrusively instructive" (Simonds 1992: 28–29). Readers use self-help books as "tools" to help them work on specific issues or problems in their lives (Simonds 1992: 32). In my observation, attendees at survivors' conferences talked with each other about which self-help books were particularly helpful and why; they recommended *The Courage to Heal* nearly universally, and commented about the strengths and weaknesses of other books.

These books could not have been written the way they were without the influence of feminism, and specifically feminist survivors' movements. Many of the earliest authors' interest, evidence, and expertise came, not from professional work, but from their activism. As Rapping (1996: 153) writes, "That Norwood's book [*Women Who Love Too Much*], like virtually every other of the hundred or so [self-help] books I read, drew its analysis of female experience and behavior from feminism seems to me so obvious as to make it rather amazing that none of the authors credit this intellectual source." Yet at the same time, most books watered down feminism's analysis of systemic inequality in favor of a view that problems could be solved through individual psychotherapeutic practices (Simonds 1992: 48). The books that were published later did so much more than the early ones, as professionals took a larger role in publishing on the issue, with the institutionalization and mainstreaming of the issue.

How did self-help books change the movement and survivors' own perceptions and experiences? They created a stronger norm about what those experiences should be like and laid out a path that survivors might expect to follow. They also made the approach of the movement, thus modified, much more widely available. When people could buy *The Courage to Heal* in their local chain bookstore, the self-help approach became available to people who would never have come in contact with either a feminist survivors' organization or a single-issue self-help group. Despite the toned-down political analysis and the prescriptive elements of many self-help books, their proliferation advanced some movement goals—visibility, decreased stigma, support for survivors—even as they sidestepped questions of larger social change.

Conclusion: Moral Panics and Cultural Change

It has become widely accepted that media coverage during this period fueled a "moral panic" over child sexual abuse centered around allegations of satanic ritual abuse, abduction, and murder (Jenkins 1998; Victor 1993, 1998). This accepted narrative argues that, during a moral panic, the extreme case (satanic ritual abuse and child sex murders) comes to stand in for the routine case (incest and child sexual abuse), and both are viewed with exaggerated alarm as extremely common and dangerous, with no room for dissenting views. My examination of the full scope of media coverage does not support this account. While there were indeed many articles about satanic ritual abuse, disproportionate to the number of alleged victims, they never dominated the overall coverage, which remained focused on assault by offenders known to their victims. Press coverage did not generally conflate incest and nonritualized child sexual abuse with satanic ritual abuse or child abduction.

Furthermore, media contained a range of views about the symptoms resulting from child sexual abuse, including experts who saw the effects as catastrophic along with those who saw effects as variable. A similar range existed in coverage of offenders, with some articles suggesting they were irredeemable and others profiling treatment and family reunification programs. Favorable coverage of Parents United was widespread, for example, although the group worked with offenders and nonoffending parents, as well as abuse victims—far from the demonization of offenders that the moral panic model assumes. The multiplicity of viewpoints, from nonprofit advocates, researchers, feminist authors, and the occasional activist, belies the moral panic account (McRobbie and Thornton 1995). Perhaps most important, the scope of coverage was not out of proportion to the actual problem of incest and child molestation. In fact, Cheit (2003) shows that the majority of criminal cases of child molestation are not mentioned at all in news coverage.

In addition to its poor fit with the evidence, the moral panic account is problematic on theoretical grounds. Panics—in which individuals are mindlessly swept up in the group—are not very good explanations for human behavior. Critiques of panic theory have become routine in studies of collective behavior and social movements (Clarke 2002, Quarantelli 2001). The panic model is no more apt for explaining periods of rising concern with social problems. The notion that a populace speaks with one irrational voice as it is swept up in a panic that transcends previous beliefs and established norms is no more logical and no more supported by the evidence in the case of concern over child sexual abuse, than it is in the case of people's behavior as they participate in a demonstration. Concern with social problems is different from other forms of collective behavior because of the central role of the mass media, which seek to raise concern in order to increase readership. But the media published various views of abuse and were influenced by multiple constituencies. Their reliance on experts mitigated against the equation of all forms of child sexual abuse with satanic ritual abuse or sex-murder, because the research and treatment centers that provided most experts dealt with more mundane issues.

Instead of analyzing cultural change as a moral panic, we can understand how views of child sexual abuse changed by examining interactions between activists and other players. The idea of selection processes, in which elements of movement understandings enter mass media according to their resonance with preexisting views of the issue, allows us to recognize the multiple views that are generally present outside the media at any given time, as well as to think systematically about why some views are more widely disseminated than others.

Culture changes partly through the efforts of activists, to be sure, but those efforts alone rarely produce widespread change in the mainstream.

Diffusion and Dilution   131

As Rochon (1998) argues, expert allies can legitimate new approaches. In the case of child sexual abuse, the movement itself produced or influenced many of these allies. As child sexual abuse entered mass awareness in the 1980s, experts produced by the movement of the 1970s and early 1980s helped legitimate the issue. These experts produced knowledge about child sexual abuse that mirrored the knowledge lay activists produced, but with a greater focus on "treatment," contributing to the definition of child sexual abuse in medical terms.

The media's general acceptance of abuse allegations as true and of abuse as widespread, the rise of personal accounts by survivors, and the publicity about treatment programs all brought a selected part of the movement's ideology into the mainstream. Yet only selected parts of movement analyses of child sexual abuse gained the public eye. Whereas the feminist survivor movement cast child sexual abuse as the result of systemic inequality, particularly patriarchal power and the power of adults over children, media discussions of fathers' presumed access to their children were rare. The activist idea that children were not to blame for having been sexually assaulted became widespread, as did the view that child sexual abuse was far more common than previously assumed. If children were not at fault, though, the media laid the blame at the feet of criminally deviant pedophiles who, like victims, needed professional treatment. The emphasis on individual treatment and recovery was more consistent with the single-issue wing of the movement, but activists' emphasis on survivors' self-definition and mutual assistance shrank under the media emphasis on experts and professional therapy. While few activists in either the feminist or single-issue survivors' movements saw child sexual abuse as purely a criminal or a medical issue, the elements of their views and activities that did take criminal or medical approaches fit neatly into the state, treatment institutions, and mainstream media, where they flourished, as we will see in chapter 8. Alternative points of view survived among activists, but did not benefit from the issue's mainstreaming; if anything, they became more marginalized within a movement that turned to therapy on one hand, and criminal prosecution on the other.

At the same time that the movement against child sexual abuse influenced popular culture, it was influenced by the dominant discourse. The question of cultural *resonance*, usually used to understand why certain activist approaches are well received by the mainstream, also helps us understand why certain institutional approaches are well received by activists. The links that the movement itself drew between healing and politics, and the necessities brought about by activists' engagement with state and therapeutic institutions, meant that the professionalized therapeutic approach resonated with many activists. But their adoption of a therapeutic approach did not mean simply giving over control to professionals. On the contrary, as the self-help wing of the movement flourished, it democratized and deprofessionalized the practices of listening to others' stories, interpreting one's own and others' experiences and emotions, and suggesting alternate ways of thinking and feeling about one's experiences (see Polletta 2002).

Without an overtly feminist analysis, self-help practices could spread far more widely. The media explosion brought recruits into self-help groups whose understanding of child sexual abuse was shaped by the submerged politics of mass culture. When a countermovement mobilized in the early 1990s, previously apolitical self-helpers found themselves pulled into a pitched battle. The countermovement resisted both the media acceptance of child sexual abuse as a widespread and legitimate social problem, and the policy and legal practices that permitted the accused to be found guilty. With a dual focus on the unreliability of adults' memories of abusive childhoods (whether the memories were "recovered" or continuous) and the unreliability of children's testimony about sexual abuse, the countermovement effectively reversed many of the cultural and policy changes that occurred during the 1980s.

6

Turning Tides

Countermovement Organizing, "False Memory Syndrome," and the Struggle over Scientific Knowledge

A surprising thing happened in 1992. A small group of parents, accused by their adult daughters of childhood sexual abuse, formed an advocacy organization. Within a short time, this organization attracted large numbers of parents whose children had accused them of sexual abuse, inspired academic research into the nature of childhood memories, recruited numerous experts to serve on its advisory board, garnered extensive media coverage, and gained widespread respectability. At first blush, parents accused of child sexual abuse would seem a very difficult constituency to mobilize. The accusation carries heavy stigma, and one would expect that parents claiming to be falsely accused would find it difficult to convince the media of their innocence or the importance of their cause, particularly in light of increasing sympathy for people who had been sexually abused as children. In the face of these obstacles, the False Memory Syndrome Foundation (FMSF), mounted a successful campaign.[1]

In this chapter, I examine the emergence and trajectory of the FMSF and other countermovement groups and their interactions with the survivors' movement. I show how the FMSF used scientific discourse and expert knowledge to promote its view of memory and abuse. Its success stemmed both from its promotion of a scientific frame and from its successful coalitions across the political spectrum.

The FMSF and related groups emerged in response to the movement against child sexual abuse and are best understood as a *countermovement*. Countermovements organize in response to the claims and gains of another social movement (Meyer and Staggenborg 1996).[2] Although the small amount of scholarly literature on the FMSF discusses its opposition to "recovered memory therapy" (Davis 2005), its goals extended beyond therapeutic techniques to a broader range of issues about child sexual abuse. It directly challenged legislation and policy about child sexual abuse, the issue's representation in the media, the ideologies and collective identities of survivor activists, and specific activists and organizations in the movement against child sexual abuse. Most members were drawn to the FMSF because they had been accused of child sexual abuse, but the organization was more than a support system for accused parents; it organized systematically and effectively to oppose many of the premises and gains of the movement against child sexual abuse. In this way, it, too, was a hybrid organization, combining service to members with advocacy for social change.

As the survivors' movement grew, more and more adults (mostly women) spoke publicly about their childhood experiences. As a result, more parents were accused. As therapeutic practices to address child sexual abuse grew, more clients recounted their experiences and received encouragement to take those experiences seriously, confront their parents, and protect their own children by keeping them from their grandparents. A small but significant minority of these adult survivors pursued legal remedies, most often by bringing civil suits against their parents (because statutes of limitations for criminal charges had run out). As a result, parents accused of sexually abusing their children faced a greatly increased likelihood of public exposure and legal or financial penalties.

Of great concern to the FMSF, many adults without previous memories of child sexual abuse recalled childhood sexual abuse. Some of these recollections occurred in the course of therapy, while others occurred in daily life, often after hearing or reading about child sexual abuse. It is impossible to determine how many parents were accused of child sexual abuse as a result of previously forgotten memories, or "recovered memories" as both movement and countermovement termed them, but it was certainly a significant number. These parents and their spouses formed the core of the FMSF, and they vehemently declared both their own innocence and the unreliability of recovered memories and memory in general.

Although the FMSF framed its focus as questioning the validity of recovered memories, its activities, publications, legislative initiatives, and informal coalitions with other organizations and networks show its opposition to the broader gains of the movement against child sexual abuse. This is not to say that it favored child sexual abuse, but rather that it opposed the major elements of the movement's *approach* to the issue. Namely, it opposed the claims that child sexual abuse is widespread, that it leads to predictable negative effects in individuals, that children's reports are reliable, that publicity about child sexual abuse is a social good (instead, it saw publicity as inciting false memories of abuse), that child welfare intervention in its present form is appropriate or effective, and that legislation on the issue (such as CAPTA) is warranted. Yet, ironically, because it framed its claims primarily in terms of a critique of recovered memory, its influence on policy and attitudes toward child sexual abuse more generally was limited, although still significant.

The battles over recovered memories were battles over the construction of knowledge and authority. The public battle between the FMSF and the movement against child sexual abuse centered around the question of whether adults' memories of child sexual abuse were reliable. The weapons activists used in this battle were primarily discursive (Katzenstein 1998). Each side conducted research on the nature of memory, attempted to align its approach with science, and sought media publicity and academic legitimacy. By aligning itself with scientific research, the FMSF sought to counter survivors' epistemological claim that their own perspectives on their experiences held the ultimate validity, and thus to construct a different consensus about the nature of child sexual abuse and recollections of it.

As both the FMSF and its opponents have pointed out, without external corroboration we have no means of distinguishing between true and false claims. Accordingly, I attempt to make no judgment about individual cases or about the balance between false and true accusations of abuse, and use language that is as neutral as possible. This does not mean that truth is not important; on the contrary, it matters very much to both adult children and parents whether particular instances of abuse actually occurred.[3] Instead, I focus on the sociological explanations for the FMSF's emergence, direction, and success, and ultimately on what it can tell us about how social movements influence knowledge.

Competing claims about the nature of memory are important, not just for their scientific accuracy, but for understanding how knowledge about child sexual abuse is socially constructed and why particular constructions gained credence at particular times. Dominant understandings of memory, like any other scientific topic, are not a simple product of accuracy or truth. We do not believe what we do simply because it is correct; paradigms or beliefs become dominant because they make sense within social arrangements and other cultural and scientific beliefs, and because of effective advocacy by their proponents (Kuhn 1996; Swidler and Arditi 1994).

The Contested Construction of Knowledge

The survivors' and FMSF movements constructed competing bodies of knowledge about child sexual abuse and memory, and the contest between them played out according to the different political and cultural opportunities available to each group and to the version of "truth" that it promoted. The basic premise of the sociology of knowledge is that knowledge is not a simple matter of accurate information, but is shaped by the social context in which it is produced and the social location of its producers. Beliefs about what is true change over time. These changes are not just a matter of progress, in which scientists gather more accurate information and learn more about how the world works. They are also a reflection of cultural worldviews, patterns of authority, and structures of knowledge production (for example, inside or outside the academy) and knowledge dissemination (for example, technological advances such as the printing press or the Internet, and consolidation or independence of media outlets) (Swidler and Arditi 1994). Knowledge gains credence in part because of the authority of those who promote it, and scientific data and analyses are produced within specific institutional settings with agreed-upon procedures for arbitrating among competing versions of the truth (Swidler and Arditi 1994: Wuthnow 1985). Patronage from government or private sources can promote particular forms of knowledge over others (Swidler and Arditi 1994).

Recognizing that knowledge is socially constructed does not relegate us to an uncritical relativism. Some "truths" are more consistent with existing bodies of evidence than others, and some accounts of "reality" bear little resemblance to observable phenomena. Nevertheless, plausible scientific findings can be ignored or submerged in academic journals where they never reach the popular eye, and areas of research can be hotbeds of activity or languish in the intellectual hinterlands. Questions can be formulated and researched in many different ways depending on grant support, institutional context, and the larger cultural context. All of these factors and more affected the rise and popularization of memory research and the idea of false memory syndrome in the 1990s.

Social movements shape knowledge. Activism against child sexual abuse by feminists and self-helpers contributed to new definitions of child sexual abuse, its frequency, causes, aftereffects, and treatments. As these new definitions gained credence, the countermovement began to advocate alternate approaches through its own activist efforts, academic research, and media coverage. In political systems like the United States', social movements have many venues in which they can try to achieve victories: the courts, state and federal legislatures, state and federal executives, as well as nongovernmental institutions and popular or academic opinion. When a movement faces difficulty within one arena, it can move to a different arena; unsurprisingly, when one movement does so, its opponent is likely to follow (Meyer and Staggenborg 1995). When activism against child sexual abuse gained public acceptance, the emerging countermovement challenged its view of child sexual abuse in a venue that the movement had not penetrated: scientific research on the nature of memory. Once the countermovement did so, the movement against child sexual abuse also began to conduct research on memory and seek academic support.

The relative success of movements and countermovements depends on their political and cultural opportunities (Meyer and Staggenborg 1995). Although the FMSF faced serious cultural obstacles in mounting a defense of people accused of sexual abuse during a period when the credibility of such accusations had increased, it was able to make use of other cultural resources. By aligning itself with science and promoting academic research on the unreliability of memory as more legitimate than survivors' accounts, the FSMF was able to borrow the credibility granted to science in this culture. When the survivors' movement attempted to don the mantle of science itself, it relied more heavily on clinicians than on Ph.D. researchers, thus decreasing its credibility, particularly in professional and academic realms. Some research was conducted to show the possibility of accurate recall of previously forgotten memories of child sexual abuse. While persuasive (for example, Professor Ross Cheit assembled a large database of corroborated cases of accurate repressed memories of child sexual abuse), the reliance on case studies rather than the experimental method distanced it from the authority of science.[4] Furthermore, the survivors' movement had a strong tenet that individuals were the ultimate authority on their own experience, making it unlikely to embrace a scientific approach and opening a gulf between survivors and experts.

Ties among social movements also affect their ability to achieve their goals. The countermovement was able to establish coalitions across the political spectrum by highlighting shared beliefs and downplaying differences. It emphasized civil rights and the right to a free trial, the presumption of innocence, and opposition to intrusion by social workers into families' private lives. These charges resonated with the beliefs of many progressives and civil libertarians, and the FMSF and the cases it championed received favorable coverage in the progressive press. By focusing on multiple-offender/multiple-victim cases where investigation techniques were extremely problematic, rather than the accusations of familial abuse that were more common among FMSF members,[5] the FMSF was able to extend support from civil libertarians to familial abuse cases. Less widely publicized were the anti-feminist and sometimes anti-gay elements of countermovement ideology, which could have decreased its support from liberal quarters. Meanwhile, the survivors' movements' ties to religious organizations, social services, and state institutions tended to increase progressives' skepticism toward its claims.

In fact, the FMSF was not the first group to organize in response to accusations of child sexual abuse. In the early 1980s, Victims of Child Abuse Laws (VOCAL) formed in Jordan, Minnesota, in response to accusations of abuse in a day care center. The organization, which survives today, established chapters in many states, often run by a handful of families. It served as a resource for people accused of child sexual abuse, connecting them with defense attorneys and advising them on their rights (Fine 1995; Hechler 1988).[6] Various other groups addressing fathers' custody rights also sometimes dealt with accusations of child abuse. VOCAL and related groups remained small and relatively ineffective because they relied on claiming innocence in particular cases of child abuse. Even when the cases were persuasive, activists had to mount a separate defense for each case. This not only was inefficient, it did not challenge the overall claims and gains of the movement against child sexual abuse. While VOCAL attempted a broad critique of child protective services and the foster care system, it tended to couch this argument in conspiratorial terms and often included virulent misogyny; it was, therefore, limited in appeal. The FMSF made a broader argument that went beyond individual cases. Its focus on the nature of childhood memory and traumatic events enabled a much broader challenge to the changes wrought by the survivors' movement during the preceding two decades *and* a more effective defense of individual cases.

The Emergence and Consolidation of the Countermovement

The founding story of the False Memory Syndrome Foundation has been widely told (Champagne 1996; Davis 2005). It goes like this: In 1992, a small group of parents who had been accused of sexual abuse by their grown daughters began talking with each other about their experiences. The founders, Pamela and Peter Freyd, sought to counter their daughter Jennifer's accusations of incest against Peter. A prominent cognitive psychologist, Jennifer had recalled child sexual abuse shortly after entering therapy. (Before founding the FMSF, her parents attempted to proclaim their innocence in other ways, including contacting Jennifer's professional colleagues (J. Freyd 1993, 1996).) Placing advertisements in newspapers, they contacted scores of other parents in similar situations. As they shared their experiences, these parents realized that their daughters (and a few sons or other family members) had all participated in similar forms of therapy aimed at recovering repressed memories of child sexual abuse. Misled by unscrupulous or uninformed therapists, the daughters confronted their parents and, when the parents denied the abuse, severed contact. As researchers and professionals heard about the issue, they shared their expertise on the unreliable nature of memory, joined the Foundation's advisory board, and conducted research on memory inspired by the parents' plight. The organization caught the eye of journalists, who publicized it, bringing more members to the group and helping to shift public views of recovered memories and psychotherapy for child sexual abuse.

Like the founding stories of most social movement organizations, this account is both accurate and incomplete. The organization's explosive growth and influence stemmed from a "perfect storm" of political and cultural opportunities and its founders' fortuitous location within academic and media networks.

From its inception, the FMSF had two constituencies: parents who had been accused of abuse by their children, and researchers who focused on the malleability of memory and opposed therapeutic techniques aimed at recovering memories of abuse. The Foundation served as a support system for accused families, providing them resources and information, and connecting them with its network of state organizations and contacts.[7] Many researchers supported the group, joining its "scientific and professional advisory board." Initial support came from the Institute of Psychological Therapies, the private practice of Hollida Wakefield, an M.A.-level psychologist, and Ralph Underwager, a psychologist and Lutheran minister, which focused on child sexual abuse. Wakefield and Underwager had published work on false accusations, and they often provided advice and expert testimony for the defense in child abuse cases.[8] Their interest in false accusations brought them together with the founders of the FMSF, and they supported the initial toll-free hotline for the FMSF and "help[ed] develop material to send to callers."[9]

Although the FMSF claimed the mantle of science, Wakefield and Underwager were clinicians and advocates (usually for the defense) in child sexual abuse cases, not research scientists with expertise in memory.[10] The organization, then, did not spring from an alliance with professionals in memory research, but rather one with professionals with a particular perspective on child sexual abuse allegations. This is not surprising, given the scant research on memory when the FMSF originated. Indeed, researchers in memory also joined the advisory board in droves within the group's first few years.

The FMSF leased an office and incorporated as a nonprofit charitable organization in June of 1992.[11] It quickly established a solid financial footing and relied on a small corps of dedicated volunteers and two part-time paid office workers.[12] A network of volunteers throughout the country shared the burden of responding to messages left on the toll-free phone line, using a protocol and resources developed by the organization.[13] The Foundation's initial activities included the hotline, the newsletter, a survey of the families who contacted the group, press releases about child sexual abuse and memory, and the collection of legal resources.[14]

Publicity through notices in newspapers and the hotline garnered immediate attention from the media and accused parents. After the *New York Times* and the Sally Jesse Raphael talk show covered the group in July, 1992, they reported receiving "over 600 phone messages in three days."[15] The following month, Pamela Freyd recounted that "the number of families who have called to tell us the same story has almost doubled (1,132 as of August 28)."[16] Like many movement organizations, the FMSF's self-reported numbers are likely to be inflated, and not all calls were from families facing accusations (Champagne 1996). Nevertheless, it is clear that the organization grew rapidly in its first years. In 1992, Freyd reported state liaisons in 44 states;[17] by 1993, there were 50 state liaisons, as well as many local and national committees and meetings.[18] That year, the national organization moved to a new and larger office.[19] By 1994, the national office was publishing a second newsletter, "The Retractor," which told the stories of people who had accused their parents of child abuse and later retracted those accusations.[20]

Financial support came from individual donations (some quite sizeable), bequests, stock gifts, employer matching donations, and membership dues, which were set at $100 annually in 1992 and remained at that level through 2006.[21] Fund-raising presented challenges because of the stigma associated with being accused of child abuse, as Freyd wrote in a fund-raising appeal: "We have a committee willing to help with fund raising, but we will not give them names to call because we understand the need for anonymity in so many cases."[22] By 1994, the FMSF appointed a volunteer with financial experience to chair a successful fund-raising drive.[23] The organization reported raising $150,000 between December 1, 1994, and February 28, 1995, in response to a $100,000 matching grant from a member. By then, the annual operating budget was $1 million and, reportedly, only one-third of these monies came from membership dues.[24] Survivors' organizations never reached these financial heights.

The bulk of expenditures, around 75 percent in most years, went for research and education or member services: mainly publishing the newsletter, disseminating information about memory and false accusations, surveying member families, and gathering information about civil suits alleging parental abuse or, a few years later, suits by parents against their children's therapists alleging negligence.[25] These activities were the cornerstone of the FMSF's approach, which focused on changing the state of knowledge about memory, therapeutic practice, and public opinion.

The FMSF made a dramatic impact very quickly. It brought large numbers of families together, reported on and facilitated retractions of abuse accusations or family reconciliations without retraction, produced a tidal wave of publicity, and coined the term "false memory syndrome." The notion of false memory syndrome spread rapidly. By 2001, the newsletter hailed the inclusion of the term in several dictionaries,[26] and in 2003 Freyd celebrated the use of the phrase "false memories" in a Supreme Court decision.[27]

In addition to fewer new accusations based on recovered memories, the FMSF soon reported increasing numbers of retractions of accusations. In 1997, Freyd claimed that seven percent of member families surveyed had a child who had retracted and over 25 percent had a child who had resumed contact without retracting their accusation.[28] By 2000, Freyd described a "flow of letters from parents describing the return of their children,"[29] and a year later, a reader wrote to report that among the "dozen" attendees at her local FMSF meeting "almost everyone present had some current contact with the accuser."[30]

Calls to the national office decreased after 1995, and dropped dramatically by 1998.[31] By 1999, the FMSF was scaling down. As Freyd wrote, "Because families need less personal support, in the future we can put more effort into 'watch dog' activities. Because families are no longer in crisis and there are now many sources for information about FMS, we can reduce the number of newsletters this year."[32] In its later years, the FMSF increased its focus on questions of children's suggestibility and the unreliability of children's accusations of contemporaneous abuse, again emphasizing a scientific approach.

Reinterpreting Recovered Memories of Child Sexual Abuse

The FMSF's main strategy was the production and dissemination of new knowledge about memory, aimed at convincing the public, therapists, and their accusing children that recovered memories of child sexual abuse were most likely false. Using members' own experiences and scholarly research, the FMSF and its allies developed a sweeping critique of therapeutic practice around child sexual abuse, arguing that therapists fostered clients' false memories of sexual abuse in order to promote their own preconceptions, to increase their earnings, or out of irresponsible ignorance. Science, they argued, proved the inherent unreliability of any memories of long-past events, particularly those produced through techniques aimed at retrieving or enhancing memory, which gave therapists unprecedented levels of control over suggestible clients. Many therapists, they argued, were motivated by radical feminism, despising the nuclear family and seeing all men as likely abusers. In any case, a therapeutic focus on childhood trauma was ineffective and not supported by research, which favored short-term cognitive-behavioral treatment aimed at improving present functioning, rather than coming to terms with past events. Caught up in a cult-like world of victimhood, people with recovered memories of abuse needlessly cut themselves and their children off from their loving families. Their claims served only to divert attention and funds from the relatively rare problem of genuine child abuse.

The FMSF, in other words, employed a panoply of frames for understanding the experiences of its members and persuading others to support them. Common to all of these was an emphasis on science as the only legitimate source of knowledge, and the claim to be the voice of scientific reason in the debates over memory and abuse. In its first year or two, the FMSF used many different frames, often in combination, as organizers tried to figure out both how best to understand their own experiences and how to communicate their perspective persuasively to outsiders and to their own children. In the first few years, two frames rose to the surface most often: recovered-memory therapy as a cult, and memory science. Fairly quickly, as legal strategies using scientific evidence were increasingly successful, the "memory science" frame virtually eclipsed other frames.

Cults, Alien Abduction, and Other Frame Extensions

> How cult-like this "therapy" is.... There is the blind faith—the hypnotic acceptance of the teachings of the gurus—the unquestioning and uncritical incorporation of the far-out tenets into the personal lives of the adherents—no matter how outlandish the teachings—no matter who gets hurt, or how much. There is the missionary zeal and closed-minded, narrowly focused, head-in-the-sand determination to

vindicate a social agenda (a product of fuzzy emotional, convoluted thinking) at any cost.

—A Dad[33]

The cult frame was very common in the early years, and cropped up occasionally later. Framing recovered-memory therapy as a cult allowed parents to view their children's separation from them as the result of indoctrination, rather than as the child's own rejection of the parent. It was also a comprehensible way of explaining the child's disappearance from family life, given publicity about cults and brainwashing. One letter-writer explained that she told curious neighbors or friends that their children had joined "a sort of therapy-cult that is obsessed with sexual abuse," noting that, "People seem to understand cults."[34] When sons or daughters cut off contact with their families of origin following accusations of sexual abuse, accused parents saw this as similar to how cults required isolation from family and friends.[35]

The cult explanation waned by the mid-1990s, but the newsletter raised it periodically in conjunction with relevant events. The suicides of members of the Heaven's Gate cult in 1997 provided a hook that Freyd used to remind readers that "the similarities of [FMS families'] situations to those whose children have entered formal cults are striking. Perhaps the most notable is the aspect of cutting off contact with the family or anyone else who does not subscribe to the new belief system."[36] In 1999, the Waco tragedy made the cult frame resonant again, with a member writing that people with false memories "are, in effect, no different than the followers of Jim Jones or David Koresh and would drink poisoned Kool-Aid or burn themselves to death had their therapists requested them to do so."[37]

The FMSF also compared recovered memories of child sexual abuse to recovered memories of implausible events, such as abduction by aliens. In an early issue of the newsletter, a typical analogy stated:

> Just because a person recovers vivid memories of abuse by space aliens does not mean that space aliens have invaded our planet. Just because someone recovers vivid memories of past lives does not establish the reality of such lives. Just because someone recovers memories of abuse during some sort of therapy does not mean that it really happened.[38]

In the FMSF view, the key similarity between memories of alien abduction, past lives, or child sexual abuse was the "mechanism of recovered memories," by which experiences could be forgotten and later remembered accurately.[39] But the organization used the improbability of alien abduction to cast doubts on the validity of recovered memories of abuse. For example, a 1993 statement implied that if readers doubted the existence of alien abduction or Satanic cults, they must also doubt accusations of more common events (such as incest) against families who claimed to be falsely accused:

> This is a scientific issue. Either there is "massive repression" or there is not. Either people have been abducted by space aliens or they have not.

Either there is an intergenerational conspiracy of satanic abuse cults or there is not. Either the families who claim they have been falsely accused are criminals or they are not.⁴⁰

By the turn of the century, the newsletter no longer made the comparison with past lives or alien abduction, which had become less visible in the larger culture by then. As other related issues gained public attention, however, the newsletter continued to attempt to link them to child sexual abuse. For example, claims of post-traumatic stress disorder (PTSD) among soldiers received media attention in the mid-2000s. As PTSD became more widely accepted, it threatened to validate claims of PTSD due to child sexual abuse. Not surprisingly, the newsletter focused on suspicions about soldiers' claims of PTSD and the scientific findings that arose from research on these claims, writing in 2003, for example:

> There is disturbing evidence that many veterans appear to have deliberately exaggerated symptoms in order to obtain a PTSD diagnosis.... Additionally, there is the problem of "phony combat vets."... If this is the case, it means that much of the research in the field is not reliable.⁴¹

In making these comparisons, the FMSF was engaging in what theorists call "frame extension," an attempt to connect recovered memories of child sexual abuse with other already widely accepted issues and thus to persuade potential supporters of the validity of their cause (Snow et al. 1986). Most social movements, including the survivors' movement, engage in such efforts. Despite the links it drew between false memories of child sexual abuse and other issues, however, most of the FMSF's focus was on memory and child sexual abuse in particular, emphasizing how "memory science" supported the organization's claims.

Memory Science

The FMSF's central argument was that it had science on its side. It sought to disentangle the question of child sexual abuse, which it routinely noted was a reprehensible reality, from "memory science," which it argued showed that memories could not be repressed and later recalled, and that false memories could be created by researchers (and thus by therapists). A typical 1993 comment summed up this perspective:

> REPRESSION OF MEMORY IS A HIGHLY CONTROVERSIAL THEORY.
> ... In order to fully evaluate the authenticity of a memory report, it must be examined in light of current knowledge about how memory works. Certainly it is the case that people remember things that they haven't thought of or remembered for quite some time. But when someone claims sudden memory for a series of horrible events spanning years and years, a serious question about whether any current theories of memory can

accommodate this arises.... We need to see the scientific evidence that this can be possible and how probable.[42]

Instead, they contended:

> Researchers agree that memory does not work like a video tape recorder. Researchers agree that memories are reconstructed and reinterpreted and that there is no scientific evidence for any other type of process for memory of events. Researchers agree that some memories are true, some memories are confabulated and some memories are false. Researchers agree that misremembering is the norm.[43]

The organization mustered considerable scientific evidence for their view of memory, and many researchers in the field served on the group's scientific and professional advisory board. Experimental research by Elizabeth Loftus (e.g., 1994) and others showed that research subjects could be convinced that they had experienced events that had never occurred, essentially creating a false memory—such as having been lost in a shopping mall as a child—in the laboratory. These researchers argued that such studies proved that false memories of child sexual abuse could be similarly induced in therapy.

Early on, the newsletter added a column entitled "Focus on Science," featuring summaries of research showing the unreliability of memory and critiques of research suggesting that memories of trauma could be repressed and later recalled.[44] In general, it attempted to show that research supporting its position was more scientifically valid than its opponents', and it often used methodological critiques to dismiss findings that contradicted its position. For example, a critique of one study about corroboration of memories of child sexual abuse raised many legitimate methodological issues, and concluded that the study "cannot be considered definitive, or for that matter even relevant in any way to the question of the validity of long-repressed memories of child sexual abuse."[45]

In addition to casting doubt on the legitimacy of recovered memories, the FMSF questioned the symptoms assumed to result from childhood abuse, in an attempt to rebut the idea that clients who entered therapy with no memory of abuse might have unremembered sexual abuse as the underlying cause of their problems. The newsletter regularly synopsized articles showing that problems such as eating disorders, dissociative disorders, or sexual dysfunction were not the result of child sexual abuse. One such column critiqued a study showing that people who had been sexually abused as children had physical differences in their brains compared to those who had not and proposed a methodologically complex—indeed, impossible—alternative. The author conceded that, "If this sounds like a difficult and expensive study, it is...Pending studies with such scrupulous methodology, we must remain very skeptical of any statements we hear about the long-term effects of sexual abuse."[46] The author essentially set an unachievable methodological bar for studies opposing FMSF positions.

Studies supporting FMSF positions were not subject to similar review. For example, a 1997 "Focus on Science" column by Advisory Board member Harrison Pope addressed PET scan studies showing differences in brain activity between people in traumatic and nontraumatic situations. Pope argues that these studies cannot be seen as evidence for repression of memories of trauma because one cannot "take a series of scientific findings, link them together, and *safely extrapolate to conclusions about some other phenomenon which one has not studied directly*" (emphasis added).[47] This extrapolation, however, is precisely the approach of experiments showing that false memories can be created through suggestion, such as Elizabeth Loftus's (1994) famous studies in which adults came to believe, falsely, that they had been lost in a shopping mall as children.

As time went on, the newsletter critiqued studies showing corroboration for recovered memories on different grounds. Instead, Freyd wrote, "the position of the FMS Foundation has always been that whether they are continuous or recovered—some memories are true, some a mixture of fact and fantasy and some false. Of course some recalled events will be true, but that does not change the fact that the only way to determine the historical accuracy of a memory is through external corroboration." She went on to suggest that the theory of "repression" as a specific mechanism by which traumatic events were forgotten was the problem; people might simply forget and later remember traumas, without necessarily *repressing* their memories. When the accuracy of previously forgotten memories of abuse was corroborated, the claim was attacked because it did not demonstrate repression, although the mechanism of forgetting and remembering need not have any bearing on the accuracy of recollections (Freyd 1998).[48] Studies that documented forgetting and remembering actual events thus could not refute the FMSF stance that repression itself did not exist.[49]

The organization portrayed therapists who accepted the credibility of repressed memory or encouraged clients to attempt to remember forgotten events as opposed to science. Therapists' ties to activism or their reliance on experiential knowledge were presented as damning evidence. For example, an article in the 1992 newsletter wrote, "We also know that the therapists who have alienated children from their families ignore research evidence. Most of them urge their clients to read *The Courage to Heal* which states in its preface that it is based on no psychological theory."[50] The problems with therapy went beyond recovered memories to the underlying assumptions of clinical work. As Freyd wrote in 1999, "Evidence abounds for problematic beliefs within the mental health community: blaming problems on others ... and believing that current problems stem from childhood trauma."[51] Blaming therapists for their children's memories of sexual abuse helped parents view their accusing children as blameless (Davis 2005). As "Mom of a Retractor" wrote, "Don't blame your daughter for all the grief that has been wrought. Blame Recovered Memory Therapy!"[52]

Persistently, the newsletter drew a sharp distinction between researchers and clinicians, portraying the former as concerned with science, and the latter as unable to evaluate empirical evidence. Instead of science, the FMSF suggested, therapists were motivated partly by financial gain. As Freyd asked, in 2002, "Why the gap between research and practice in the trauma field? Could it be related to the fact that there is less work for therapists if people get better from traumas by themselves?"[53]

In contrast to unscientific and greedy clinicians, the FMSF portrayed itself as interested in pure science. Over and over, statements like, "Perhaps the most disturbing aspect of the current phenomenon, is the misuse of science to promote a political end. It is the scientific issues that are the focus of the False Memory Syndrome Foundation"[54] appeared in the newsletter. In contrast, it portrayed its opponents as ignorant about science and motivated by politics. As a 1996 Focus on Science column put it, "The 'science' of the 'memory' is established. We are dealing with a sociopolitical movement."[55] Of course, the FMSF itself was a political entity, but portraying itself as purely scientific was advantageous in the courtroom, legislatures, and public opinion.

Memory science was clearly the most persuasive frame the FMSF used, and perhaps the most useful to member families in understanding their children's accusations because it blamed therapists and exonerated their children. In the larger culture, the use of scientific discourse increased credibility and insulated the FMSF from claims that it was motivated by members' desire to deny guilt. The memory science frame was often accompanied by claims about the organization's concern for the well-being of their grown children, family reconciliation, and children who were genuinely abused.

Larger Concerns: Family Reconciliation and Genuine Abuse

The FMSF stated repeatedly that its concern was not with child sexual abuse, but with the science of memory. This contention and the organization's statements of support for accusers and genuine victims of abuse allowed it to avoid much political challenge. From its beginning, the FMSF sought to promote family reconciliation, either what they called "returning," in which accusers reestablished contact with their families without withdrawing their accusations of abuse, or "retracting," in which accusers explicitly withdrew the accusation. The group encouraged parents to provide their children with information about false memory syndrome, allow contact without recrimination, and avoid discussing the accusations until their children brought them up. Most families embraced this strategy and, as the years went on, the newsletter published increasing numbers of letters from parents rejoicing at their renewed contact with their children and grandchildren. Most such letters agreed that the parents' lack of expression of anger toward their children was crucial in allowing reconciliation.

In the foundation's later years, increasing numbers of families reported reconciling with their children. In 1997, 7 percent of FMSF members reported that the accusation had been retracted, and another 24.6 percent reported that the accuser had resumed family relations without retracting. By 2001, still only 7 percent reported retractions, but 36 percent had resumed contact with their families.[56] In 2004, a survey by the Illinois chapter found that 11 percent had children who had retracted the charges, 37 percent had resumed contact without retracting, and another 19 percent had "minimal contact" with families.[57] Many conferences included panels of retractors and their parents and siblings advising other families about how to promote reconciliation.[58]

Throughout, the organization and parents writing to the newsletter emphasized their overriding love and concern for their accusing children. These children, they believed, were victims of therapeutic mistreatment that was making their symptoms worse, not better. Freyd wrote of members' "profound anxiety about the safety of the children who have acquired memories and redefined their histories," because, "They may be grown ups, but they are in trouble."[59] Letter-writers expressed similar views, writing that "Our primary concern is for her to get competent care,"[60] and, "my own feeling of relief that she no longer sees me as a perpetrator is minor compared to my joy that she is emerging from a black hole and will have a chance now for a fuller family life instead of a bitter future based on false memories."[61]

Not all parents were so sanguine about the accusations. For example, a 1999 letter described rewriting wills to exclude accusing children and their children.[62] By 2004, such language was more common, as "not-so-grieving father" wrote:

> Instead of viewing the accusing daughter as the "victim," let's see her for what she is: a willing co-conspirator who, along with a smug therapist, has intentionally made her father or mother the scapegoat for her personal problems. That being the case, it's sensible to say to her: "You made your decision so... good riddance!"[63]

Despite occasional anger, most of the group's members focused on changing therapeutic practices in order to bring about their children's return. They also regularly professed their concern for genuine cases of child sexual abuse.

The FMSF made two kinds of statements about child sexual abuse. First, the newsletter often noted that child sexual abuse was less common than widely assumed, and did not have predictable negative effects on victims. A typical statement noted, "We suspect that much fuel for the belief in the memories comes from the conflicting and possibly inflated statistics about the actual incidence of child sexual abuse."[64] The newsletter regularly printed summaries of findings from government incidence studies on child abuse, focusing on the relatively small percentage of cases of sexual abuse as opposed to physical abuse and neglect.[65] A commentary following one such report noted that even these figures might be inflated by false accusations by children under leading questioning by caseworkers:

The techniques for implanting memories in children are similar, if not identical, to those employed by "recovered memory therapists." Another parallel is the belief that certain behaviors and "symptoms" are definitive indicators of sexual abuse, despite the fact that such beliefs have been consistently debunked in the reliable research literature. Consequently, the testimony of caseworkers is typically replete with myths and "junk science."[66]

Nevertheless, the newsletter frequently included statements about the horrific nature of genuine child sexual abuse and the Foundation's concern for actual victims. Spokespeople took pains to say that they did not oppose action in cases of genuine child sexual abuse, as Freyd wrote in 1995, "For three years, critics have tried to portray the FMSF as an organization of perpetrators, as a group against therapy, and as a backlash against child abuse. None is correct. The Foundation is very much concerned that those found guilty of abuse are appropriately punished and that every effort be made to stem child abuse."[67] The FMSF, they argued, was dealing with an issue that was completely separate and distinct from child sexual abuse: false memories and false accusations. Underlining the distinction, Freyd wrote, "the 10,000 reports that we have received don't really seem to be about child abuse."[68] While this protected the organization from stigma, it ultimately limited its ability to influence public policy around child sexual abuse.

Science and Social Change: Countermovement Tactics

The FMSF and its allies pursued their goals using several major approaches. The most influential was simply the creation and dissemination of knowledge—the frames outlined above—that could make sense of accusations of child sexual abuse as something other than literal truth. Claiming science on their side, supporting networking among researchers, and circulating research findings on memory were the central mechanisms by which the FMSF changed public opinion. In addition, the FMSF compiled and publicized its members' experiences, both through formal surveys and, informally, through "speaking out" (ironically borrowing the tactic of personal testimony used by feminists and survivors). FMSF members tried countless other approaches to get public attention, from a National Day of Prayer for parents accused of abuse,[69] to accusing books about child sexual abuse of being pornographic,[70] and they occasionally used confrontational tactics such as picketing. They relied most heavily on legal strategies and attempts to regulate and restructure therapeutic practice. Regardless of the means and the venue, the countermovement's emphasis was on its scientific accuracy as opposed to its opponents' irrationality and incompetence. This approach was quite effective, especially in the legal arena.

Experiential Knowledge: Family Surveys and Speaking Out

The FMSF collected data about the families who contacted it, surveying members and gathering copies of letters written by accusers to family members.[71] The FMSF argued that by collecting data about families' experiences—what kind of abuse they were accused of, by whom, what kind of therapy the accuser had been in, and the demographics of the family—it could gain insight into the larger phenomena of recovered memories and therapeutic practice.[72] Just as the survivors' movement relied on experiential knowledge to redefine child sexual abuse, the FMSF relied on experiential knowledge to redefine recovered memories and false allegations. Rather than gathering information informally through support groups, as the survivors' movement did, the FMSF gathered information through surveys and tallied it systematically. This gave it a more comprehensive picture of the experiences of large numbers of families. Nevertheless, the basis for this knowledge was direct personal experience, and the claim for its validity rested on the consistency in families' reports. If so many families were reporting the same experience—accusations based on long-forgotten memories, recovered in therapy, of events for which there was little or no external corroboration—then this experience must reflect a genuine social pattern or truth. This rationale is identical to that of the survivors' organizations—if so many survivors reported similar aftereffects as adults and denial or silencing by family members and the larger culture, then these must reflect a genuine social pattern or truth.

By conducting and tallying its survey, the FMSF cloaked experiential knowledge in the mantle of science, presenting results in quantitative tables and reporting statistically significant differences between groups.[73] The FMSF surveys are, of course, distinct from academic research on memory. However, the FMSF and its surveys are the major source of published information about the nature of false memories of child sexual abuse (as opposed to false memories of other events created in experimental research) and are, therefore, foundational to many statements about these topics in academic and journalistic publications.

The FMSF also encouraged members to speak out about their own experiences and provided them with the contacts and resources to do so.[74] By telling their own stories, they believed, they could put a sympathetic face on the false memory phenomenon and help change minds, including those of their accusing children. The newsletter regularly exhorted members to help with "publicity" by writing letters to "papers, to television shows, to lawyers, to government officials, [and] to medical people...."[75] Members often wrote in to describe their own experiences with speaking out, like this woman:

> I teach CPR classes three-four times a month. As I finish my lecture, I will stand there and hold and cuddle the infant mannequin and tell

how my husband and I were not allowed to see our new granddaughter for almost a year—all because we were accused of crimes that never happened. I then take a few minutes and talk about FMS.[76]

Other members wrote letters to the editor, or spoke at colleges or senior centers.[77] Members placed books about the FMSF in libraries and asked bookstores to stock and display them, and their affiliated publisher (SIRS Publishers) offered free library displays.[78] Members were urged to contact their favorite authors and encourage them to write on the topic,[79] and to write reviews of books about false memory or survivors' therapy on Amazon.com.[80]

Like the survivors' movement, the FMSF sympathized with the shame and stigma that accused families felt, but encouraged them to transcend those feelings and speak out. The FMSF even talked about "coming out" in order to bring about social change. For example, in 1995, the newsletter introduced the "Make a Difference" column with, "Like us many FMSers have come out of the closet in the last few years and would play an active role in combating the repressed memory craze—if they knew how to go about it."[81] Like survivor activists, FMSF members hoped that by sharing their personal experiences, they could change minds.

Picketing and Confrontational Tactics

The use of confrontational tactics was less common, but several countermovement activists organized picketing at conferences and lectures and therapists' offices and homes. Chuck Noah, an accused parent associated with the FMSF, picketed throughout the early 1990s at events and at a therapist's office and home in Washington State.[82] The FMSF newsletter and therapists' publications included other reports of pickets at therapists' offices.[83] FMSF members also picketed survivors' conferences and appearances by authors Ellen Bass, Laura Davis, and Judith Herman.[84] Psychologist Anna Salter and psychotherapists Laura Brown and David Calof (also the editor of *Treating Abuse Today*, which had published articles critical of the FMSF) reported pickets of their homes and offices. Calof (1998) reported that the demonstrations, organized by Noah, had occurred more than 100 times, "sometimes stretching over three city blocks," and that Noah also picketed Calof's attorney's home, where he was arrested after refusing a police order to leave. Noah was found guilty of assault and violating subsequent anti-harassment and no-contact court orders.[85] The FMSF vociferously denied that it encouraged such pickets, writing in an editor's note following a laudatory description of a picket, "The FMS Foundation does not encourage picketing. If individuals, for whatever reason, decide this is something they should do, we report on such events as part of the ongoing documentation of the FMS phenomenon."[86] Denying association with picketers who used insulting and harassing tactics was important to maintaining the FMSF's public face of scientific neutrality.

Legal Tactics

The FMSF engaged with the legal system in many ways: assisting parents accused of abuse, facilitating parents' and retractors' lawsuits against therapists who assisted with memory recovery, and sharing strategies with attorneys defending child abuse cases that were not based on recovered memories. In all of these cases, science-based assertions of the suggestibility of memory were central.

While abuse charges themselves were profoundly troubling to FMSF families, civil suits from their accusers were a more immediate threat for those who faced them. In 1992, the newsletter claimed that 17 percent of families in contact with the FMSF had been threatened with or involved in such suits. The organization gathered lists of lawyers, and kept track of statutes of limitations and rulings about delayed discovery and the admissibility of evidence based on recovered memories.[87] By 1994, the "Legal Corner" appeared in every newsletter, reporting in detail on relevant cases.[88] The FMSF filed amicus briefs in numerous cases, alleging the lack of scientific support for memory repression, and regularly advertised copies of documents from relevant cases.[89] FMSF conferences and continuing education programs provided information to attorneys and others, including advice about serving as expert witnesses.[90]

Although lawsuits were a burden for families, they provided an opportunity to establish favorable case law and, ultimately, to force the end of particular therapeutic practices or the closure of treatment facilities. Fairly quickly, court rulings favorable to FMSF members began to emerge. Most significant was the 1994 *Daubert* ruling (not specific to recovered memory) which required a hearing to establish scientific validity before evidence could be admitted. When lawyers in cases involving recovered memories raised questions about the validity of those memories, a *Daubert* hearing was required to determine the scientific validity of the phenomenon of memory repression and recovery. The hearing often led to the exclusion of testimony based on recovered memories, which meant that many suits by adult children against their parents could not proceed.[91]

Expert witnesses on both sides lined up to testify about the accuracy of recovered memories and the scientific acceptance of techniques used to assist recall. The experts associated with the FMSF position usually prevailed, in large part because they used what attorney and psychologist Christopher Barden, a frequent expert witness and consultant to defense attorneys, termed "science-intensive litigation." As he described the process:

> [W]e presented peer-reviewed scientific literature to judges and juries proving that "dissociation," "repression," "recovered memories" and similar concepts have no empirical support—"it's a bunch of crazy nonsense" as one juror reported.

The approach emphasized differences in education and credentials between expert witnesses for the prosecution and those for the defense, and sought to discredit defense witnesses by using what Barden called "detailed social science cross examination (e.g., explain the terms 'reliability and validity,' tell us the methodological errors in your research, define the term 'Kappa coefficient')."[92] Parents accused of child sexual abuse used the "science-intensive" approach not just to defend themselves, but also to bring malpractice suits against their children's therapists. It was very effective, leading to many large verdicts against therapists. As Barden explained, the first large verdicts drew other attorneys to the field by convincing them that such lawsuits "were winnable and economically viable."[93]

Statutes of limitations were another battleground. Some states had extended or repealed statutes of limitations for child sexual abuse during the 1980s and early 1990s, based on the idea that victims might be unable to appreciate the damage they incurred until years later, or that they might not recall the incidents. Several states' legislation specifically addressed delayed recall, typically specifying that the statute of limitations would begin at the time that memories were recollected. By 1991, 14 states had passed such laws (Darnton 1991: 72). As skepticism grew about recovered memories, however, the extensions came under fire. For example, Illinois considered reinstating its statute of limitations for child sexual abuse, after repealing it in 1994, reportedly because of doubts about the legitimacy of recovered memory, heightened by the accusation against Cardinal Bernardin by a man who later recanted his recovered memory.[94]

In general, the FMSF newsletter reported favorably on attempts to limit the statute of limitations for child sexual abuse[95] and viewed extensions as a means of allowing cases based on recovered memories to go forward.[96] In 2003, Freyd complained that "at least three states are considering extending the statutes of limitations to allow those who "repressed" their memories of child sexual abuse to bring lawsuits." However, in none of these cases was the statute of limitations extended specifically for those with repressed memories. Freyd wrote, "Extending the limitations is one issue, and it can be debated. Having a provision that would allow unreliable evidence is another matter."[97] Of course, extending the statue of limitations does not in itself allow unreliable evidence. Interestingly, the FMSF supported case law tolling (suspending) the statute of limitations based on mental illness in a case where the plaintiff was a retractor suing her therapist.[98]

The FMSF and its members acquired a reputation for litigiousness, with rumors and actual threats of lawsuits for defamation running rampant. Freyd wrote, in 1995, "The FMS Foundation has not been involved in any lawsuit either as defendant or plaintiff. None of its directors, advisors or staff members are involved in any lawsuit stemming from their association with FMS." Immediately following this denial, she went on to threaten suit against the authors of an article opposing the FMSF because the authors claimed Freyd made "untruthful and malicious efforts to damage their daughter's career and reputation."[99] While the FMSF apparently never sued these authors, they unsuccessfully sued another author in 1997.[100] Advisory board members Wakefield and Underwager unsuccessfully sued psychologist Anna Salter when she disputed their findings and their representation of the literature about false accusations by children (Salter 1998). Further, FMSF members filed many suits against therapists using the encouragement and information they got from the organization and its members. Freyd's statement was, therefore, disingenuous and served mainly to maintain the FMSF's public stance of scientific neutrality.

Throughout its coverage of legal efforts, the FMSF insisted that it had "never been involved in any lawsuit."[101] It did, however, provide information, referrals, and networking for those who were involved in lawsuits, in addition to highly laudatory coverage in the newsletter, and the legal victories went a long way toward achieving the group's goals. In all the legal cases, the countermovement's main argument was the essential scientific accuracy of their view. Although political and judicial policy is rarely a simple outgrowth of scientific knowledge, the memory science frame was enormously effective.[102]

Targeting Therapists and Therapeutic Practices

Like the survivors' movement, the FMSF and its members targeted the structure and practice of psychotherapy for change. They did so by filing legal or licensing complaints against specific therapists and advocating legislation and training to change the practice of therapy as a whole. Here again, the countermovement's focus was on clinicians' unscientific activities in contrast to its own model of scientifically valid psychotherapy.

On the individual level, many FMSF members explored filing complaints with licensing boards against their children's treating therapists, and some actually did so, with assistance from the national and state offices of the FMSF. The newsletter instructed families in how to learn the identity of the therapist from the client's family or friends or by hiring a private investigator[103] and asked parents to send information about complaints they had filed with licensing boards.[104] Early on there were few successes; families reported that their complaints were rejected because as third parties they had no standing.[105] But the number of complaints grew, and licensing boards began to respond. In 1994, for example, the Colorado Mental Health Grievance Board reported 90 complaints in the preceding two years, mostly from third parties.[106] Members also filed complaints with accreditation agencies over hospitals' inpatient programs for treating child sexual abuse or multiple personality disorder/dissociative disorder.[107]

FMSF members also sued their children's therapists for defamation and damages. The first such case to receive a verdict in favor of the third party was filed by Gary Ramona against his daughter's therapist after the daughter accused him of child sexual abuse. The FMSF newsletter lauded the case, writing that, "Many lawyers around the country now feel that the door is open to seek truth and redress in our court system for the unscientific and negligent conduct of some therapists."[108] The FMSF submitted amicus briefs in similar cases,[109] and local chapters sponsored programs on third-party litigation.[110] Such suits grew from a trickle to a steady stream, but it is unclear how many resulted in awards for the parents.[111]

Former patients who came to believe that their memories were false also pursued lawsuits against their therapists. By and large, the successful ones were those in which plaintiffs had been diagnosed with dissociative identity disorder and had come to believe that they had been victimized by Satanic cults. The legal strategies were "science-intensive," and the charges were that the psychotherapy was negligent, failed to include informed consent, and failed to notify plaintiffs that "the diagnosis and treatment of Multiple Personality Disorder [dissociative identity disorder] is highly controversial," and the therapeutic techniques used were "not based on current science regarding memory."[112] After initial difficulty, such clients won numerous large settlements against their treating therapists.[113] The cases wound down by 2006, as most had already been litigated and practitioners had changed their approach to avoid liability.

The FMSF emphasized "quality control" and "informed consent," criticizing the use of "unvalidated" therapies and lack of randomized trials in treatment of child sexual abuse.[114] Much was made of the need for "safe and effective" psychotherapy.[115] The FMSF itself offered accredited continuing education programs for mental health workers.[116] Arguing that because professional associations had failed to police their members, the courts and legislatures must step in,[117] the FMSF supported informed consent legislation aimed at regulating mental health treatment. These included various state bills that focused on child sexual abuse treatment and recovered memories in particular, such as a New Hampshire bill that "require[d] patients undergoing experimental methods such as Recovered Memory Therapy be informed of the risks and limitations of the treatment if government or insurance monies are involved,"[118] and a Colorado bill requiring "mental-health workers to document that they advised their patients of the nature and possible consequences of repressed memory therapy."[119] Indiana passed an informed consent bill in 1996,[120] but despite the campaigns, no other state did.

Despite the newsletter's advocacy of informed consent legislation and the active involvement of FMSF members and allied professionals in that advocacy, FMSF board member Alan Feld denied that the FMSF itself sought to pass such legislation, writing that a critic "fails to distinguish between the Foundation and the actions taken by some of its members and other professionals who are actively seeking to get informed consent legislation passed."[121] Such statements, like Freyd's denial that the FMSF promoted lawsuits, worked to maintain a nonpolitical, scientific image.

The FMSF's critique of therapy dovetailed with larger shifts in healthcare, particularly the rise of managed care and associated attempts to curtail the cost of mental health care that led to changes in psychotherapy in line with FMSF goals. As one respondent, a psychotherapist, noted, "In some ways the managed care companies welcomed the backlash [i.e. the countermovement] because it becomes part of the justification for not dealing with those issues [multiple or complex symptomology of child sexual abuse survivors]." Another noted that instead of workshops about abuse, therapists were "doing workshops about managed care." In other words, the external context favored the FMSF critique of therapy. The FMSF picked up on this as it crafted its message, emphasizing that most therapeutic techniques were not proven effective and that scrutiny of childhood experiences was not only potentially harmful but expensive. It is impossible to determine whether the FMSF influenced a managed care approach to therapy, but some of its prominent board members were outspoken in favor of short-term cognitive-behavioral therapy, the favored form under managed care.

Knowledge Battles

Regardless of the tactics the FMSF used, the underlying issues were ones of knowledge and truth—about particular accusations, but more generally about the nature of memory and child sexual abuse. The FMSF shifted the terms of the debate over knowledge by emphasizing scientific epistemology. Clinicians working with survivors responded by creating and disseminating their own expert knowledge couched in the language of science. But in doing so, they distanced themselves from the survivors' movement, which relied on experiential knowledge. Many grassroots activists were skeptical of experts and resentful that they didn't defend the movement more fully. This wedge weakened the political power of the experts and lessened the movement's ability to respond to the FMSF in the media and courts. At the same time, the experts couldn't make use of many of the movement's most persuasive pieces of "knowledge," because they were not couched in scientific language and method. The FMSF attacked attempts to legitimate this knowledge in a scientific framework—for example, by studying survivors or documenting recovered memories of genuine events—on methodological grounds (while sparing research supporting its own position from similar attack).

In its confrontations with the survivors' movement, the countermovement generally maintained its veneer of scientific objectivity, stating that its goal was to give accusers accurate information about recovered memory so that they could return to their loving families. The survivors' movement and its allies responded in two ways. Grassroots activists responded politically, viewing the countermovement as an attempt to silence survivors and, hence, legitimize abuse. Professionals and researchers responded by developing a counter-science, attempting to document corroborated cases of recovered memories and specify mechanisms of forgetting and

156   The Politics of Child Sexual Abuse

remembering. This bifurcation ultimately rendered both lay and professional activists less effective.

Confrontations with Survivor Activist Organizations

The FMSF was the subject of discussion and criticism within survivors' organizations from its inception, and it responded in kind. FMSF newsletters dismissed survivors' advocacy and recovered memories as a "sociopolitical movement," while survivors' organizations termed the FMSF a "backlash organization" that defended "perpetrators."

The FMSF newsletter regularly refuted what it called "Our Critics." For example, in response to a therapist quoted as saying she "believes FMS is nothing more than 'a massive denial and justification' movement started by perpetrators of child sexual abuse," Freyd reported that "We have given this information to our lawyers because people have suggested that this is libelous," and, if the legal threat were not enough, speculated that the therapist "knows so little about psychology that she failed to recognize the names of the distinguished researchers who comprise the FMS Foundation Advisory Board."[122]

The newsletter also featured Freyd's pleas for survivors' organizations to cover the issue of false memory. In 1993, for example, Freyd wrote, "Survivor newsletters have a very important role to play in the dissemination of information about memory and a very difficult task ahead of them if they are to help their constituency (our children).... We hope that they will print our message: WE LOVE OUR CHILDREN. WE WISH THAT THEY WOULD TALK WITH US."[123] Even negative coverage of the FMSF in survivors' newsletters was seen as potentially spreading the message to those who needed it most—people who falsely believed themselves to be "survivors" due to recovered memories.[124] Many survivors' newsletters did cover the FMSF in its early years. As the publisher of one explained in an interview, "We needed to address it in a way that would empower survivors, give them arguments they could bring up if they wanted to get in a discussion with someone about the whole issue of false memory."

The FMSF generally wrote as if all participants in survivors' organizations had false memories, with phrases like "their constituency (our children)" and "publications aimed at our accusing children." This neutralized criticism from survivors' organizations because it presumed that their grievances were not due to genuine child sexual abuse. Similarly, survivors' organizations' assumption that the FMSF was made up of actual "perpetrators" allowed them to neutralize FMSF criticism because it presumed that parents' grievances were equally illegitimate.

Countermovement activity had a dramatic effect on survivors' organizations and individual activists. Most interviewees reported that membership in survivors' organizations declined in the 1990s, and they blamed the countermovement. Professional therapists were increasingly hesitant to be visible as activists or speakers, because they were afraid of being sued. Organizations focused on ritual abuse experienced particularly severe repercussions, including other survivor groups' increasing reluctance to associate with them.

The cultural climate also changed dramatically between 1990 and 1995, because of the FMSF's success in garnering positive media coverage. Many respondents reported that they felt renewed stigma if they "came out" as survivors. One noted that "it's become a liability to be an out survivor." Another contrasted her earlier activism with the late 1990s, saying, "I used to feel a lot of sort of pride.... That shifted as the political climate shifted. I started feeling much more stigmatized." Another commented, similarly, "I've had people tell me that it's almost an embarrassment to identify as a survivor." Many, even those with continuous recall of abuse, described personal experiences of having friends, colleagues, or classmates question whether they had actually experienced child sexual abuse. As one explained, "the backlash isn't about childhood sexual abuse, it's about repressed memories...[but] I think that their attacks have tarred all adult survivors, not just those with repressed memories." Some respondents, mostly therapists, acknowledged that the FMSF had changed some of their own views. For example, one therapist noted that, "Obviously, it's an oppressive backlash, but there's a gift in that backlash and the gift is that, as therapists, we get clear about when it can be disempowering to a survivor to lead her remembering process."[125]

Most of the countermovement's "gifts" to the survivors' movement were not as well received. Survivor activists and sympathetic professionals reported being "harassed" by picketing, "nasty" letters, attempts to persuade professional colleagues to oppose them, "bogus complaints" to professional licensing boards, and "hang-up phone calls." Professional therapists reported a disproportionate number of such actions, but virtually all publicly visible activists I interviewed reported at least one or two incidents.

Survivor organizations attempted to mobilize in response. There were isolated protests against FMSF authors or activists. For example, a reading by FMSF supporter Mark Pendergrast, author of *Victims of Memory* at a Santa Cruz, California, bookstore drew a picket line, and a few members of the survivor activist group Run Riot entered the reading to "confront" the author and tell their own stories. Student activists at Evergreen State College in Washington demonstrated in opposition to countermovement activist Chuck Noah, who picketed on the campus. When countermovement members filed a lawsuit against Laura Davis and Ellen Bass (authors of *The Courage to Heal*, which was reviled by the countermovement and widely adored in the survivors' movement), a defense organization formed and successfully raised funds for their defense.[126]

Mostly, though, respondents bemoaned the lack of response. One longed for a collective response, "wanting to see people, women, standing shoulder to shoulder on this issue." But time and again, countermovement victories drew little response. For example, the verdict in the *Ramona* case, in which Gary Ramona successfully sued his daughter's therapist, was a cause for great celebration in FMSF quarters, and demoralized and outraged many survivor activists. Yet, one activist described her inability to muster a collective response:

> It was like there was no response here.... A friend of mine who is an activist [said] "Let's do something.... Let's write up a pamphlet right now and go and start something." That is totally what, in the past, I would've done [but].... I just couldn't.

Because of the success of the countermovement, she worried about opposition. She explained: "I felt like there was this shift in the climate enough that we might not be well-received.... I just could not bear the idea that we might go there, it being just the two of us, and that we might not get a good response."

In addition to the relative lack of protest or other activity to oppose the countermovement, survivor activists engaged in relatively little meaning-work to reframe the debate. Activists did attempt to counter the FMSF's arguments. They suggested that parents involved in the FMSF were trying to deny their own guilt and avoid financial ruin through civil suits. They suggested that the general public did not want to believe that child sexual abuse was widespread. The FMSF's appeal, in this account, was that it allowed people to deny the reality of child sexual abuse. For example, one activist commented, "People don't want to believe that there might be an offender in their midst and they can't recognize him, or that they might be married to one, or that their kid might be being abused." Another interviewee thought that this denial stemmed in part from conservative elevation of the traditional nuclear family, commenting, "To me the false memory syndrome is a way that the system tries to ignore how prevalent incest is in this country.... Because what we're saying is, "No,... [the] family is not safe."

Surprisingly few nonprofessionals addressed the issue of recovered memory directly, although Frank Fitzpatrick, founder of Survivor Connections, did trademark the name "The True Memory Foundation," explaining, "I just thought, because I had [corroborated] recovered memories, The True Memory Foundation would be a good secondary name for Survivor Connections.... It contradict[s] the notion that survivors who had recovered memories are liars, or that we've been forced to falsely accuse people by therapists." By and large, activist attempts at counter-framing received little play in the mass media. The most direct response to critiques of recovered memory came from researchers and therapists.

Professionals Respond

The FMSF gained ground by referring to scientific knowledge and marshalling experts to support its position. These experts targeted therapists working with survivors, who attempted to respond and were also the first sources that the media turned to for comment. (Many had also been sources for favorable media coverage during the 1980s.) They tried to muster scientific evidence to support their claims, but were hampered by the necessity of distancing themselves from the experiential knowledge of the movement (now discredited by the FMSF's emphasis on science). Yet that experiential knowledge was central to many movement claims about the frequency, nature, and effects of child sexual abuse, as well as to therapeutic techniques that emerged from feminist and self-help groups. Without it, experts had trouble making their case; but with it, they were seen as unscientific.

Activists noticed professionals' attempts to distance themselves from experiential knowledge. A respondent who was a Ph.D. therapist saw the distinction as useful, explaining, "As Dr. X I can do things in the public eye and say very radical feminist things that will be listened to." But to lay activists, the attack on experiential knowledge seemed like an assertion of the notion that "women cannot be experts on their own lives. We have to defer to people that have the appropriate degrees, went to the appropriate schools, and know our psychology better than we do." For professionals trying to craft a credible response to the FMSF's experts, a reliance on science was crucial, and being overly close to clients or activists could impugn their credibility.

Researchers from clinical and academic psychology conducted a variety of studies of the veracity, frequency, and explanations for forgetting and remembering of child sexual abuse. These included studies of long-term memory for documented cases of child sexual abuse and experimental examinations of forgetting and remembering in the laboratory. The most methodologically sound of these studies began to appear after 1995, and they increased in number after 2000.[127] By then, however, the publicity over recovered memory was dying down and the academic research supporting its veracity received little play in mainstream media, leaving the FMSF's scientific credibility unchallenged.

Style and content made the majority of professional writings advocating the legitimacy of recovered memories unintelligible to nonprofessionals, as many interviewees commented. Several respondents lauded a prominent book by Jennifer Freyd (1996) (the cognitive psychologist and daughter of FMSF founders Peter and Pamela Freyd), *Betrayal Trauma*, which outlined a causal explanation for memory repression of incest. It is unclear how many actually read the book, but they saw the author as "one of us" because of her high-profile conflict with her parents and her status as a credible professional advocate on their behalf. Judith Herman had a similar stature as a credentialed professional whose writings were claimed by movement activists. But the wealth of other books and articles supporting recovered memory that appeared after the FMSF's ascent remained obscure to most participants.

The distance between therapists and survivors also reflected the success of the FMSF's strategy of encouraging parents to sue their children's therapists. As one interviewee noted, therapists became more cautious about allying themselves with self-help organizations that might advocate positions about recovered memories that were less scientifically defensible. In addition, both the FMSF and professionals themselves focused on the importance of therapists in memory recovery, thus obscuring the role of grassroots and feminist self-help and lay therapy. One respondent explained, "The falsies [false memory advocates]...say therapists created this thing, when in fact therapists just kind of jumped on the bandwagon after a lot of stuff had already happened.... It's like, 'No, wait a minute. Therapists did not plant these ideas. We had these ideas a long time before there were any therapists willing to work with us about it.'"

In fact, some activists were angry about the expanding role of professional therapists in dealing with child sexual abuse, as well as their failure to mobilize politically in response to the FMSF. Respondents complained about what one called the "lily liveredness" of therapists in responding to the FMSF, proclaiming, "It makes me want to just throw up, considering how much money they've made off us." But professional therapists were not just throwing in the towel for no reason. Lawsuits by third parties and retractors, complaints and queries to professional licensing boards, and the threat of "mental health consumer" legislation were highly effective in stifling advocacy by therapists. Treating clients who had been sexually abused became riskier for all therapists, not just those who used suspect techniques.

These conflicts and differences, combined with very different approaches to knowledge construction, made it unlikely that professionals and grassroots activists would ally to challenge the FMSF's view of memory. The FMSF did not have this problem, because there was no sizeable preexisting movement of the falsely accused. Furthermore, the FMSF developed alliances across the political spectrum, while the survivors' movement was increasingly isolated politically.

Alliances and Opponents: Feminism, Anti-Feminism, and Coalitions

The FMSF formed coalitions with progressive groups, as well as with father's rights groups over child custody disputes where child abuse was alleged. It also formed an alliance with people accused of abusing children who were currently minors and the attorneys who defended them. In contrast, the survivors' movement formed few effective coalitions. While diverse constituencies coexisted amicably within survivor organizations, their respective movements did not ally so easily. Feminist politics reduced support from conservatives, while religious elements (including twelve-step discourse) and support for child protective intervention threatened support from feminism and the Left. The FMSF's emphasis on science and the rights of the accused, and its de-emphasis on gender, facilitated the coalitions across the political spectrum that helped it win the knowledge battles.

Accusations by Children

Parents accused of abusing their minor children by ex-spouses or child welfare agencies were the first two major constituencies outside their immediate purview to face the FMSF. Initial professional advisors Ralph Underwager and Hollida Wakefield worked with such parents, so the issue was not foreign to the organization. However, it staked out a narrower turf, as Freyd wrote in the newsletter during the first year: "[W]e have nothing to say about children or believing children. FMS Foundation is concerned about adults and the techniques some therapists are using to 'help' adults find memories."[128] Part of the concern was maintaining the organization's focus, but just as important was protecting its reputation, as Freyd wrote the next year:

> There have been hundreds and hundreds of callers who have told us stories of their children being taken from them by human services organizations. These are not repressed memory issues. There have been letters from people in prisons and there have been people who have told us that indeed they were guilty of abuse but not of the things for which they are currently accused. These are not considered "clear" cases.... In addition to the moral considerations, FMSF has too much to lose to "harbor perpetrators."[129]

Despite these distancing measures, the FMSF newsletter consistently reported on cases where the accusers were minors and the issue was suggestibility rather than memory recovery. The newsletter reviewed articles and books related to the day care cases and accusations in the course of divorce and custody disputes.[130] The FMSF even produced its own resource booklet in 1995 entitled "Resources for Families Accused by Minor Children."[131]

The FMSF argued that memory science raised the same questions about leading questioning by child protective workers and by therapists. For example, a contributor argued that "accounts voiced by adult psychotherapy patients about events in the distant past and those voiced by children about events in the recent past are both accounts regarded as memories. (Ultimately, both are mistaken beliefs cognitively processed as memories.)"[132] He termed false accusations by children a "related civil liberties issue."[133] As convictions in day care cases were overturned, Freyd accurately claimed some credit, writing, "This shift follows in the wake of better public understanding of issues of memory and suggestibility. The Foundation has played a pivotal role in the change."[134]

The newsletter reported from 1999 through 2004 that the "vast majority"[135] of new callers faced accusations from "young children, almost always in the context of divorce and custody proceedings."[136] And by 2004, the

FMSF made a strong connection between children's accusations and false memory, labeling children's reports "recovered memories": "[C]laims about recovery of memories have moved to younger and younger children. For example, it is not unusual for us to get phone calls about eight-year-olds remembering abuse from age four years."[137] Thus, Freyd linked children's "recovered memories" of abuse earlier in their childhood to the recovered memories of adults that had been the primary concern of FMSF members. Expanding to a new, related issue is not uncommon as social movement organizations achieve a measure of success on their initial goals (Meyer 2006).

By 2000, the FMSF was publicizing conferences organized by the National Child Abuse Defense and Resource Council, an organization for attorneys who defend people accused of child abuse. The group's 2001 conference, entitled "Child Abuse Allegations in the Courts: Science and Reason v. Myth and Emotion," focused "on children, child suggestibility and special laws applying to children," in contrast to the FMSF's focus on accusations by adults. The Council was certainly part of the countermovement coalition, since it was publicized in the FMSF newsletter, used the "science versus pseudoscience" frame, and featured speakers such as FMSF advisory board member Richard Ofshe.[138]

Unsurprisingly, groups defending adults from children's accusations saw themselves as allies of the FMSF. From the beginning, many of the major players in the FMSF, VOCAL, and smaller efforts were part of an Internet listserv, "Witchhunt."[139] Established in the mid-1990s, Witchhunt served to connect participants in different organizations and locales. On the listserv, they shared frames and ideas, and connected issues of recovered memory, criticism of child protective services, and what they saw as wrongful prosecutions for child sexual abuse. They also vilified feminism, and many posters used intensely misogynist language.

Over the years, VOCAL (initially "Victims of Child Abuse Laws") had evolved into a collection of small state affiliates, loosely linked by a national association and by shared language and documents. Its rhetoric focused on the evils of child protective services, emphasized "family rights" in the face of state intrusion, and drew heavily on conservative language. For example, the group's "About VOCAL" statement proclaimed: "VOCAL believes the family is the foundation of society, and any activity which weakens families is a threat to our entire society. Strengthening family unity makes for a stronger America."[140] VOCAL provided accused parents with referrals to attorneys and information to about how to document and defend their cases. Like the FMSF, VOCAL defined its clientele as the falsely accused; however, its provision of information to any accused parent was controversial. Doubtless some of the parents who contacted VOCAL were falsely accused, but equally certainly, some were not, and many fell into a gray area, in which they had punished their children physically but believed they were entitled to do so. Advocates in VOCAL assumed that CPS workers were bent on destroying the American family and fathers' role in it, and that the majority of cases investigated were bogus. They also shared with the FMSF a critical relationship to feminism.

Feminism and Anti-Feminism

While VOCAL was overtly anti-feminist, the FMSF had a more contradictory relationship with feminism. It criticized feminist denigration of the family and the assumption that men were naturally prone to violence and incest, and claimed to be more truly feminist because it defended falsely accused women, challenged the relegation of women to victim status, and took a scientific rather than emotional approach to child sexual abuse.[141] FMSF members argued that that feminists, especially therapists, had fueled the false memory problem because of their hatred of men. Feminists, in this view, were predisposed to see all men as sexual abusers. For example, Laura Bass and Ellen Davis, authors of *The Courage to Heal*, the newsletter accused, "know that every woman with or without memories really was abused by some evil male, probably her father. They seem to know that any male suspected of being a perpetrator is a perpetrator."[142]

Feminists came in for special scorn for their critique of the traditional patriarchal family. One writer in the newsletter referred, for example, to "the wave of child-abuse hysteria that has fueled the most virulent anti-family policies in our nation's history,"[143] while the newsletter argued that "therapists and lawyers who encourage" clients to sue their parents do so either out of greed or because they "have belief systems that hold that the family as we have known it throughout history is bad and should be destroyed."[144] The critique of a feminist agenda to destroy the family solidified a bond between the diverse interests represented in the countermovement, but had to be downplayed in communications with the larger public.

The Countermovement and the Left

In addition to alliances with conservatives and anti-feminists, the countermovement formed alliances with the Left, while survivors found themselves increasingly marginalized. While feminists remained divided on the politics of recovered memories, the rest of the progressive Left swung more toward the FMSF position. Major progressive magazines, such as *Mother Jones* and *The Nation*, took the position that recovered memories were likely to be inaccurate and accusations of satanic ritual abuse were factually impossible, and supported the defendants in high-profile child sexual abuse cases. Some respondents reported opposition from progressive organizations. As one public figure active in Left politics said, "There is a sector of political people... who sort of feel that I'm weird." Despite the countermovement's anti-feminism, such coalitions were not unexpected. The emphasis on civil liberties was compelling to many progressives, as was the opposition to psychotherapy, which dovetailed with the Left's critique of the supposed turn away from political engagement (Brown 1995). The FMSF received much more support from progressives than did their allies in VOCAL, however, many of whom were more virulently anti-feminist.

The survivors' movement's allies, on the other hand, made many progressives (including some in the movement itself) uncomfortable. Many survivors' organizations had an overtly religious tone, for example. Those that advocated increased prosecution and criminal penalties for offenders sometimes aligned with conservative "law-and-order" groups, while those that worked to improve child welfare drew criticism for encouraging the expansion of state authority. As one activist described, these "funny alliances" produced "tensions" because, "There are people who are active in [the survivors' movement] who come from the Christian Coalition perspective and, if you come from a feminist perspective... there are real difficulties with homophobia, with parental rights questions, with theocracy as a desirable goal."

Internal splits among survivor activists and the overall weakening of the women's movement rendered it unable to shift the debate. The FMSF's emphasis on accusations of satanic ritual abuse rather than familial sexual abuse weakened the link to feminist anti-violence work. And because of the greater visibility and influence of single-issue self-helpers and advocates in mass media and public policy, the movement's link to feminism was shaky in any case. All this facilitated the FMSF's simultaneous coalitions with progressive groups and anti-feminist, "pro-family" organizations.

Conclusion

The development of knowledge about child sexual abuse and memory was inseparable from its political context. The countermovement and survivors' movement battled over beliefs about child sexual abuse, including people's memories of abuse, its effects, means of treatment, and children's credibility. Both sides constructed knowledge using research by credentialed experts alongside grassroots experiential knowledge. While each side criticized the other for flawed methodology, in fact, both sides tended to misrepresent the research by the other side (Freyd 1998), overemphasizing weaknesses while failing to acknowledge strengths, and subjecting it to critiques that also applied to research on their own side.

The FMSF drew on scientific discourse to frame the issue as the accuracy of memory, or "memory science." It focused on establishing its objectivity compared to opponents' emotionality and irrationality. Even when it discussed issues such as accusations from minors or the effects of abuse, it relied on scientific language and the contention that its approach alone was scientifically correct. Its varied tactics entailed publicizing the "scientific" view of memory, criticizing the nonscientific approach to therapy by advocates of memory recovery, and excluding evidence based on recovered memory from court by demonstrating that it was counter to research on memory.

Knowledge construction and dissemination are subject to political opportunities. It takes resources, expertise, and access to conduct and disseminate research. The survivors' movement was dominated by grassroots activists committed to experiential knowledge and clinicians, rather than by academic researchers. The FMSF, in contrast, attracted academic researchers who employed experimental methods, and their reliance on scientific techniques and discourse enhanced the Foundation's credibility. The FMSF's use of credentialed "experts," who are the likely sources for reporters, facilitated their media connections (Rochon 1998). If its members had been less educated, with fewer ties to academia, their attempts at knowledge construction would probably have remained small-scale and unknown.

The countermovement also benefited from other political opportunities. The legal climate allowing trial lawyers to earn huge commissions from suits against therapists, and the early success of such suits, attracted many lawyers willing to represent clients. The favorable *Daubert* ruling allowed them to present their scientific evidence about memory repression, and their use of the scientific frame and credentialed experts gave that evidence credibility. The shift to managed care dovetailed with the FMSF attack on long-term therapy.

Cultural opportunities were also important. The memory science frame resonated with existing beliefs about evidence and modes of gaining authority. FMSF emphasis on family reconciliation and its stated concern for the well-being of accusing children lent credibility and sympathy, as did its statements in opposition to genuine child sexual abuse. It kept its opposition to feminism fairly quiet, although that, too, saw more cultural receptivity than it would have a few years earlier.

The memory science that the FMSF promoted was quite convincing, particularly when read apart from the studies supporting the accuracy of some recovered memories or when FMSF summaries of the literature served as a primary source. But memory science did not receive such wide support, including on the Left, simply because it was convincing. Rather, it confirmed the political stances of its supporters, who embraced evidence that state agents were violating civil liberties and that the apparent emotional distress and hidden sexual violence that fueled the therapeutic turn were actually the creation of therapists who stood to gain professionally. In contrast, science on the biological differences between women and men, or the genetic roots of homosexuality, was subject to vigorous debate on the Left about both accuracy and political ramifications. The difference is that such research challenged the political outlook of the Left, while "memory science" did not.

Overall, however, the FMSF's focus on memory and its stated exclusion of issues of child sexual abuse more generally limited its effects. It made considerable inroads in the practice of therapy and in views about recovered memories. But by excluding child sexual abuse more generally, its effects on public policy—legislation, funding, victims' compensation funds—were relatively limited. Nevertheless, survivor activists responded vigorously, renewing their efforts to promote visibility and self-definition.

7

The Politics of Visibility
Coming Out, Activist Art, and Emotional Change

The countermovement politicized self-help activists even as membership in self-help organizations shrank. What resulted was not an explicitly feminist movement, but one that sought to provide emotional support to survivors even as it worked to end child sexual abuse by bearing witness to the pain it caused, claiming a politics of visibility that emphasized personal identity disclosure, or "coming out." Activists aimed to transform the meanings and emotions attached to child sexual abuse both by survivors and by others, and to retain their identities and voices in the face of the countermovement's challenge. They constructed a stronger network of national and local groups and sought to form a culture of opposition to the growing skepticism of survivors' claims in mainstream culture. Their focus on emotional transformation through visibility politics characterized the grassroots movement of the mid-1990s and beyond. By relying on coming out and expressions of identity outside of mainstream culture, the movement retained influence despite the successful countermovement and the homogenizing selection processes in the mass media. Activists maintained cultural visibility and promoted emotional and cognitive approaches to child sexual abuse that emphasized the survivors' right to define their own experience. This view of child sexual abuse and the visibility that accompanies it are major long-term effects of the movement against child sexual abuse.

"Coming out" was a key component of visibility politics. As a self-conscious strategy for social change, it began in the late 1960s with gay men and lesbians who publicly disclosed their sexual identities in order to celebrate their identity; display their rejection of conventional sexual and political strictures; and create social change by challenging invisibility, stigma, and assumptions about homosexuality. In the following decades, coming out became a common way for many groups to conceptualize identity disclosures as a strategy for social change. People "came out" as feminists, conservatives, people of color who could otherwise pass as white, Christians, Jews, and survivors of childhood sexual abuse. Activists saw speaking about identity and experience as promoting social change because of its effects on individuals' emotions (reducing shame, promoting pride) and because it strengthened individuals' alignment with a collectivity. By disclosing individual experiences and identities, participants declared their allegiance to a social movement and challenged dominant notions of that group's nature and position. Even people who did not participate directly in movement groups could adopt the identity strategy of coming out to attempt to change attitudes in their own circle and declare allegiance to a movement.

Like many other groups, survivors of child sexual abuse conceptualized their identity disclosures as "coming out" and understood coming out on multiple levels. At the individual level, it referred first to acknowledging and understanding one's own experiences and coming to identify as a "survivor," and second to disclosing one's identity in daily life and in the course of participating in movement activities. At the movement level, "coming out" referred to public events at which individuals displayed their identity as a group, such as demonstrations or speak-outs. Participants saw coming out strategically, as a route to social change, but also saw it as transformative for individuals, changing the emotions associated with child sexual abuse. Because individuals' feelings about their own experiences were a target for social change, activists saw transformations of individual feelings and identity as significant beyond individual well-being. They also directly confronted countermovement organizations and public cultural projects, creating in the process a strong oppositional collective identity as survivors that drew together otherwise ideologically diverse individuals and groups.

Because of the countermovement's influence, survivors understood their attempts at healing and speaking publicly about abuse as political in a new way. They were struggling simultaneously with how to live well and unashamed and how to change the larger culture. They did so in a context where other social movements were relatively quiescent nationally. The feminist movement remained small, and many survivor activists saw it as disconnected from their own interests and concerns. They sought an ideologically flexible, racially diverse movement, and, rightly or wrongly, many saw the women's movement as wedded to a white perspective and to male dominance as the explanation for all ills (Reger 2005). Queer Nation and ACT UP, so active a few years earlier, had largely died down by the mid-1990s, but they provided a model of "in your face" coming out that was very appealing to some survivors' groups. They wanted a proactive approach that focused on preventing child sexual abuse, and they sought it in emotional and cultural change.

Emotional transformation was inseparable, for them, from broader social change. Many believed that activists needed to reckon with the emotions that survivors and others brought to the issue in order to move forward with prevention. Despite the success of the countermovement, activists working in this model made inroads into cultural and policy change. They illustrated the connections between emotions and mobilization and the role of visibility tactics in social change. Visibility politics worked effectively to change emotions and beliefs among those who came in contact with them, but were limited in range. Activists also found allies in larger and more mainstream movement organizations.

In this chapter, I examine how visibility politics played out in a re-politicized self-help movement and in public collective action. Activists sought to change individual emotions through therapeutic activities in self-help groups and workshops. They sought to change others' emotions through public, visible displays of identity: coming out individually and collectively and creating and displaying political art.

Self-Help Re-Politicized

> For me, really, the point of excitement is to politicize psychology and to psychologize the political.... Can we create a politics that is capable of spanning our lives from the most intimate details... to the biggest macro organizational kind of global issues? Because I don't see anything else being effective enough.
>
> —Diana

Self-help practices and organizations dealing with child sexual abuse persisted despite the challenges to belief in recovered memory and to therapeutic practices around child sexual abuse. Self-help books continued to sell in large quantities, and self-help and 12-step groups remained well populated. Voices in Action, ISRNI, and Incest Resources, as well as countless smaller local groups, continued organizing conferences and support groups, sending out information packets, publishing newsletters, and referring survivors to resources for therapy. A sizeable number of (primarily) women continued to practice self-help and to define themselves as survivors of incest and child sexual abuse.[1] Despite the overwhelming success of the countermovement in changing beliefs about memory recovery, self-help organizations retained credibility among many adults who had been sexually abused as children, and their significant others. But whereas earlier self-helpers had relied on lay-led support groups, by later 1990s therapeutic efforts were dominated by professionals, even within survivors' organizations, which assumed that participants also received private therapy. Most self-help groups were interpenetrated with treatment facilities, professionals, the state, or religious institutions.

Whereas the earlier movement's social change efforts were either overtly feminist or focused on issues of basic visibility and education, by the mid-1990s, the movement was engaged in a pitched battle with the countermovement. The countermovement made it clear to self-helpers that they were engaged in a political endeavor. They saw themselves as battling the forces of denial and backlash, countering the shame and invisibility promulgated by perpetrators of child sexual abuse. Instead of defining the struggle in gender terms, they viewed it as a struggle between abusers and their supporters and survivors and "pro-survivors." Being part of a self-help group or undergoing therapy for child sexual abuse transformed people's sense of themselves and the world. They not only reassessed their own experiences, but often came to see child sexual abuse as a widespread social problem that could be reduced by making their own experiences visible. The countermovement thus challenged survivors' new cognitive and emotional perspectives and their individual and collective identities. The struggle was as much about the nature of child sexual abuse itself as it was about "recovered memories, as we saw in chapter 6." Participants in the self-help movement understood it as such, linking their own emotional path to questions of larger social change.

Countless self-help groups existed around the country. Some were large and nationally oriented, like Voices in Action, the largest nonfeminist survivor organization. It recruited a relatively stable board that included mental health professionals, mounted annual conferences that profited from a continuing-education track for mental health professionals, published a regular newsletter, and received some state funding. Voices in Action members attended annual conferences and participated in pen pal "Special Interest Groups" pegged to shared identities (such as male survivors, or people abused by clergy, or survivors who were artists). Other organizations were smaller in scope, ranging from formally structured centers that housed peer and professionally led groups, to church groups, to informal gatherings of friends. Resources were plentiful for people who wanted to start their own self-help groups, which participants saw as contributing to social change. For example, at a Voices in Action annual conference, the National Black Women's Health Project sponsored a workshop on how to start and run a self-help group. Explaining the goals of self-help, the presenter noted that it "doesn't stop with the self" but "expands to help the world."[2] Similarly, the Healing Woman Foundation aimed to "teach women that: They are not alone; Healing is possible; [and] When they are ready, they can make a difference by taking their healing into the world. Our goal is to create a strong, organized, vocal community of women survivors of childhood sexual abuse and their supporters, who can speak out about violence against women and children."[3]

Diverse constituencies came together in the large self-help organizations. In Voices in Action, for example, conservatives and feminists coexisted, drawn together by a shared identity as survivors. A visible Christian presence at the Voices in Action conference staffed literature tables, and participants talked about the effects of abuse on their religious faith and offered to pray for each other. This coexisted with "New Age" spirituality, including workshops on flower essences, chakras, and spiritual healing. A visible lesbian presence included a musical performer who sang about her relationships with women and analogized coming out as a lesbian to coming out as a survivor. After her performance, I observed participants who had spoken earlier from an explicitly Christian and heterosexual perspective telling this performer how much the song had moved them.[4] Participants and publications talked about survivors as a unified group and emphasized commonalities over differences of status or of type of abuse. The confrontations with the countermovement described in chapter 6 heightened the sense of being part of what one presenter called the "survivors' rights movement."[5]

Conferences typically included a mixture of workshops on individual emotional change ("healing") and collective issues. For example, at the 1998 Voices in Action conference, plenary talks were given by State of Illinois Attorney General Jim Ryan and *Courage to Heal* author Ellen Bass, representing the group's dual foci on state policy and individual transformation. Both speakers emphasized the importance of providing help and healing to individuals and both also raised social issues—Ryan by talking about legislation creating Child Advocacy Centers and educational programs for mandated reporters, and Bass by talking about social silencing of survivors and the importance of visibility for change. Another presentation exhorted survivors not only to "take control" of their own lives (a message consistent with a focus on individual emotions) but also to take control of their communities by becoming involved in advocacy organizations.[6] Publications framed around "healing" also regularly published updates and calls to action regarding policy. *The Healing Woman*, for example, contained a regular column entitled "Fighting Back," which asked readers to write to elected officials to support legislation and publicized speak-outs and other public events.[7]

Most Voices in Action conference presentations focused on "healing" topics such as "Boundary Issues: Knowing and Caring for Ourselves," or "Retrieving the Masculine Spirit: New Perspectives for Male Survivors." Others, however, ranged wider, such as, "A Critical Review of False Memory Syndrome," and "Socialization, Violence Against Women and Action I Can Take Now!"[8] Similarly, a 1999 conference in New York City, sponsored by the Incest Awareness Foundation, had a dual focus on healing and strategies for improving the mandated reporting system, with addresses on how to educate mandated reporters and strengthen the child protective system, and keynote addresses by Ellen Bass and former Surgeon General Joycelyn

Elders. Workshops were a mix of individual healing topics (such as "Sexual Healing") and policy-oriented topics (such as "Supporting Authenticity in Children's Allegations of Sexual Abuse in the Court System"). In a classic hybrid format, one morning's workshops consisted of individual survivors recounting their experiences of abuse and recovery with the goal of helping mandated reporters better understand child sexual abuse.[9] Informal conversations at conferences ranged from experiences of personal healing, to debates about how to intervene in suspected child sexual abuse, to questions about how the government could improve prevention efforts.[10]

The dominance of professional therapists in survivors' organizations was a major change from the previous era. The seeds were sowed in the overlap between therapists and self-help organizations in the 1970s, and germinated in the 1980s as professional therapy for child sexual abuse grew more common. As movement organizations offered continuing education for professionals at conferences and solicited professional board members in order to improve finances and credibility, the trend increased. It led to a professionalization of many groups in which many workshops and decisions were led by credentialed therapists. For example, a professional therapist founded the Incest Awareness Foundation, and its workshops were dominated by professionals, who listed their degrees and therapy practices in the program to legitimate their offerings. In many sessions, attendees became, in effect, clients, who received wisdom from the therapists presenting.

But despite the formal dominance by therapists, attendees continued to offer their own interpretations, raising questions of race, gender, educational disadvantage, and the adequacy of social responses. For example, during a Voices in Action conference workshop entitled "Moving Beyond Survival: Is It Okay to Be Successful Now?" participants talked about having been raised to take traditional female roles and how sexual abuse in their families had been an outgrowth of traditional notions of gender. Unlike the speaker, they framed their attempts to be "successful" as changing the gender system. Similarly, when a Latina participant commented on how American culture's discouragement of emotional expression affected her experience, another Latina agreed and talked about how cultural differences and discrimination affected survivors; and a disabled woman brought up the stigmatization of disability.[11] This dynamic, in which nonprofessional participants challenged and extended the points made by professional presenters, was common.

While many participants in the self-help groups during this period saw them as part of a social movement that challenged the FMSF and advocated for children, many longtime activists saw the groups as largely apolitical. Some longtime activists were unhappy with what they saw as a shift to an apolitical, therapeutic approach that abandoned feminist tenets. One, for example, deplored "the eagerness to go to therapy...and the inability to reinforce women's self-confidence and self-esteem by supporting them to be independent and strong." Others argued that although individual emotional health was a precondition to activism, it did not constitute activism in itself. For example, one longtime activist wished for more overtly political activity, yet felt strongly that, "I don't think people can be effective activists if they're in excruciating pain all the time [laughs]...but I also can't see any possibility of success of building the kinds of emotional support that women need without being out there willing to fight for it." Ironically, though, as participants in self-help groups began to feel better, they were likely to leave those groups. As several organizers described to me, "They move on, to where it's no longer such an important issue."

Some activists wished, conversely, that participants would spend more time on their individual psychological health, and commented that organizing a movement of people who had been traumatized carried special challenges. Andrea, for example, described her travails organizing a demonstration:

> Part of what's hard about doing survivor activism [is that]...most of the people that helped us didn't help us. They demanded enormous emotional support to do very little work, or no work. The day of the [protest] I gave people jobs like, go find a roll of masking tape on the other side of town, because they were a lot more help if they weren't there. It's a movement where people have shifting levels of ability and disability at any given moment.

Most activists saw healing as political in itself, not just a precondition to effective movement participation. For some, encouraging others' recovery from sexual abuse was their own political contribution, one that they saw as inseparable from other kinds of social change. For example, an African-American woman who facilitated self-help groups for women through a multiracial, mixed-class church, explained how her political view of incest had emerged:

> The first part was helping women to see that they were not alone and that they no longer needed to be isolated or ashamed....But then as I worked for the issue more and more I said, "Wait a minute. As we change, we need to help change the world."...So then I began to look at what supports our environment that incest can live in. It was like: the patriarchy. Uh-huh. It began to hook up with my feminism. So then, it was like, "Ok, this is an oppression." I began to name it as oppression and injustice. And so at that moment, then I looked around and said, "Oh, the same kind of changes that are necessary for me to be free as a Black woman are the same kind of changes it takes [to end] incest."

Another African-American woman who performs theater and musical pieces about child sexual abuse defined social change similarly:

> Part of what the movement has to be about, in terms of social change, is giving people the idea that those who are silent, who are not able to

come out, who are suffering in silence...or who feel isolated and alone, or who feel crazy because of all the crazy stuff that's happened to them, or somehow feel different, unworthy to be respected or loved...give them a space where they can see that it's okay.... Their soul can be resurrected, the essence of who they are, which is sometimes buried underneath all this bullshit, can be resurrected. They can be whole.

A white woman in her thirties similarly described the connections between her own healing and politics:

Oftentimes I was able to have the power and the passion about healing myself that I did because I knew I was part of a bigger chain. Like a link in the chain that was trying to create freedom for people. And by me telling the truth about my life and by me healing, I was taking political action. Like, when I couldn't heal for me, I could heal for, you know, for justice.

For participants who had not been activists previously, the heavy professional component in the organizations enabled them to see the groups as simply an outgrowth of private therapy, rather than a collective response to a social problem. Those activists who understood their healing work as political tended to be those who had prior involvement with social movements. They attempted to draw in less-political survivors by reframing the issue. For example, one leader attempted to reframe child sexual abuse in terms that seemed more clearly political, explaining that, "For example, when I talk publicly or when I do groups for survivors, I talk about what I do as 'atrocity work.'...It is a wound, to be sure, but it is a political wound as well as a psychological wound."

The FMSF attack on recovered memory, survivor groups, and therapy made pursuing those things political in a new way. While participants with other activist experience understood survivors' issues as connected to broader social change, other participants saw their search for emotional support as resistance to the influential countermovement. Its political meanings thus differed from those of the self-help movements that preceded the countermovement, even when its activities were similar. Similarly, being visible as survivors of child sexual abuse acquired a different significance in the wake of the FMSF.

The Politics of Visibility

As long as we're silent and kind of in the corner just doing our therapy by ourselves and not saying that we exist, then people can say, "Oh, it's one or two women." No, it's not... excuse me, we're out there!
—Amali

The Politics of Visibility   175

The survivors' movement used strategies that emphasized identity disclosure in several ways. At the individual level, in daily life, activists "came out" about their experiences of child sexual abuse. At the collective level, they organized "speak-outs" and conferences under the theme "To Tell the Truth." Finally, they made art—written word, performance, and visual art. Through visibility strategies, they sought to transform the beliefs and emotions of observers, as well as themselves. Activists displayed a politicized, reclaimed version of what it meant to have experienced child sexual abuse in order to foster personal transformation, overturn the invisibility of child sexual abuse, and change cultural discourses and institutions. Activists "came out" in a variety of ways, from the obvious (talking about their experiences with people in their daily lives) to the less obvious (creating activist art). Amali, who sought to be open everywhere she went, explained, "I don't make any bones about it. I don't apologize to any community for being who I am. I talk about it to anybody and everybody. I go, 'Yeah, this is who I am.'" Respondents also came out to larger audiences, as did Amali, whose church support group "did a Mother's Day performance...about being survivors.... There we were, and we were not anonymous."

In addition to transforming the emotions of individuals, the politics of visibility sought to change attitudes and feelings of others through speak-outs and public art projects and performances. The feminist movements for legalization of abortion and against rape first developed the "speak-out" in which women recounted stigmatized experiences in order to show that ordinary women had them and to challenge their invisibility. Take Back the Night marches against violence against women often included speak-outs, in which some of my respondents reported participating. For example, Arthur first spoke publicly about his childhood abuse by a priest at a speak-out organized by a rape crisis center, naming the perpetrator and performing original music.

Speak-outs specifically against child sexual abuse first became nationally visible in 1992, when an activist in Santa Fe, New Mexico, organized a local speak-out, attended by 500 people, under the name "To Tell the Truth" (Miller 1992). The concept spread rapidly, and a coordinated national effort has organized yearly To Tell the Truth events, including speak-outs, marches, public speeches, and conferences, in many localities since then. Twenty-five states had such events in 1993,[12] while in subsequent years the numbers were lower.[13] Local groups also organized speak-outs. Speak-outs were personally transformative for participants, who reported feeling less shame and stigma after speaking openly about their experiences. Their collective nature enhanced the effect; as the organizer of the first event said, "The more people speak out, the faster we heal" (Miller 1992).

The experience of being open about having been sexually abused as a child changed people's sense of themselves. Leslie, like many, saw change in individuals as significant in itself, commenting, "Even if we don't stop child sexual abuse, I think that there are numbers of people having that experience of... 'I'm public and I'm doing it.' I think that's just, in and of itself, a really profound thing. I mean, it *is* social change." Many activists assumed that they would face negative reactions if they spoke about their experiences. Discovering that this was not the case could be immensely liberating. Amali put this common experience into words, describing the first time she came out as a survivor in a public setting:

> I was reading a poem...and for some reason I ended up saying I'm a survivor of incest [in my introduction].... There was that moment when I realized that I had said that, when the audience realized that they had heard that, and at that moment I felt so alone standing there.... So I took a deep breath and I was looking at women in the audience...and there were women whose eyes welled up tears. I understood that I was standing in front of a lot of women who were survivors, and that I was speaking for them. I was able to say what they hid away, and that they loved me for it. From that moment on it became very easy to speak and say, "Yes, I'm a survivor."

Most respondents talked about how claiming an identity as a survivor of child sexual abuse—rather than remaining silent and ashamed—increased their sense of belief in themselves. These experiences did not come in the context of psychotherapy or self-help groups, but through collective action or collective coming out.

Coming out was an inevitable feature of any public demonstration, since participants felt that they were revealing their own identities as survivors. One regular demonstration was a contingent in the San Francisco Gay Pride Parade organized by Run Riot, a local survivors' activist group. Participants carried signs reading "Speak Up" and "End Abuse," and chanted: "Hey, hey, ho, ho, sex abuse has got to go," "Sex is good, sex is great, it's molesters that we hate," and "Tell, tell, tell." They wore stickers proclaiming "Proud Survivor," "The abuse stops here," and "Sex Positive Incest Survivor" and handed out fliers about child sexual abuse to observers. They found that disclosing that they had been sexually abused as children was exhilarating and transformative. Staci Haines, co-founder of RunRiot and Generation Five, described her feelings as "deeply empowering. We were elated afterwards...the level of joy in the group was so high.... There's...this sense of, 'I can do it!' this sense of, 'I can tell!' this sense of, 'We can have an impact, we're not alone!'" For Staci, as for others, "telling," "having an impact," and "not being alone" were connected.

Activists connected their identity-disclosure strategies to those of other social movements. In a typical comment, Ella analogized, "The civil rights movement is a great model for speaking your truth. The courage to identify an injustice, and to have the courage of your convictions....I find a lot of inspiration in the children who are speaking out on anti-child labor movement in India. Children are speaking out about their experiences, saying, 'This is happening. This is what it's like, world. Come here and have a look.' And I think that's what survivors are doing too." For some, speaking out about child sexual abuse was linked to a specifically feminist tradition—the idea that, because women have been silenced institutionally and culturally, speaking out is a form of resistance. African-American women understood this institutional silencing in both race and gender terms. For others, it had to do with child sexual abuse in particular. They felt that speaking out gave them a sense of self and an ownership of their own experiences that had been barred to them by silence around child sexual abuse. Because their power had been taken away as a result of the issue they were trying to change, they saw reclaiming it as a political act.

Other activists saw their coming out as giving voice to others who could not. For many interviewees, this was profoundly moving. For example, one activist felt that "what the visibility with the movement can do... for survivors who are not strong enough to be out there [is] to say,'You are not alone, and I will stand here for you when you are unable to stand for yourself. And when you're ready, come out, come out, wherever you are.' " She linked this to black feminist traditions, describing talking with other survivors as "a laying on of hands.... Many black women writers have sometimes written about the laying on of hands, and it is that connection that saves their lives. So when I give, I lay on hands." Another activist explained that when he is open about his experiences being sexually abused by a priest, his visibility affects others. For example, he said:

> If I'm on a plane, I'll start talking to people [who ask], "Where are you going?" [I'll say] "I'm going to this sexual assault conference... I'm going to this speak-out. I was sexually abused by a priest...." And the lady next to me said, "Yeah, it happened to me too." And she showed me a picture in her wallet of her uncle that she still had thirty years later.

In these ways, coming out effects a personal transformation—a change in subjectivity—not only for the individuals who come out themselves, but for others.

Most of the activists I interviewed also felt a strong sense of responsibility to children in abusive situations and believed that speaking out could help them. One articulated this sense of responsibility, saying that, "When I was five, maybe I needed to be silent as a female, and seven and eight and twelve, for my own survival. But now I can speak, and I do have a voice.... [I'm] feeling responsible for all those other little black girls that arecoming now." For another, being visible as a male survivor was important because there are so few men who speak out about having been sexually abused:

> The message I've told men is... it's your duty as a survivor to give a voice to these issues and the reason it's your duty is because [you should] think of yourself as that child. What you needed then was to hear men come forward and speak openly with courage and without shame about sexual victimization, the same message that women get:

it's not about you. It's about what happened to you. You're not responsible. You couldn't prevent it.

Activists also hoped that speaking about their experiences would raise awareness more generally. As one woman put it, "I think most people are shielded from it. So I try to unshield. I think people have to get unshielded if we're ever going to really stop it."

In addition to speaking out, art activism was a major component of the survivors' movement after the mid-1990s and reflected another kind of visibility politics. Protest art is a common means by which movements communicate their new meanings publicly and can gain a hearing where a speech or educational program about an issue cannot (Krouse 1993). Respondents who were artists hoped that their art would produce social change. For example, one performer argued that, "theater is a real interesting tool to use in terms of social change, particularly when you talk about issues that people don't want to deal with, like sexual violence, like child abuse." She described her theatrical performance as depicting both unrelenting violence and irrepressible strength and intended to evoke an emotional response in her audience. In a piece about "a fifteen-year-old African-American girl child who was raped and murdered in a schoolyard in Oakland, California," she sought to "bring people in and ... knock them over the head, you know ... [*laughing*]." In another piece, she said, "I get to belt, I get to be fierce in my indignation about this shit, you know? ... By that time people are on their feet—you know—chanting, and screaming, and yelling, and whistling, and that's a more empowering sort of thing."

The emotional response she desired was not simply a moral shock (Jasper 1997), but the emotional changes associated with resistance, such as a sense of empowerment to speak out about child sexual abuse (Whittier 2001). Similarly, another organization, People of Fire, brought a traveling exhibit of three statues representing the stages of response to and healing from child sexual abuse to conferences and workshops. The organization's founder contended that the project promoted emotional change, writing, "The POF art bypasses ... resistance because it's about 'speaking up,' breaking silence, in a way that can be 'heard' first at a level of image, emotion, and experience."[14]

Activist art appeared in many venues, including poetry and drawings in newsletters, performances and art shows at conferences, independent theater performances, and collective public art projects like the Clothesline Project, which holds T-shirts painted by visitors to the exhibit depicting experiences of abuse and violence. Conferences often included a talent night where attendees read poetry or sang original compositions. Such artistic productions depicted the experience of abuse, the emotions felt by children and adult survivors, the brutality of offenders, the indifference or cruelty of other adults, and the triumph of emotional transformation. Individuals working in theater produced numerous shows about child sexual abuse, and theater workshops in settings from prisons to colleges often included participants' experiences of abuse. Artistic quality varied considerably, but was not the central point. At its core, the art aimed to break the artist's own silence and transform how audience members think and feel about child sexual abuse. For example, an announcement of an art exhibit sponsored by a survivors' organization explained that such art was a route to social change because it bore witness to atrocity:

> It is our belief that we contribute to the healing of child sexual abuse by our willingness to bear witness to its reality, in spite of our discomfort in doing so.... The Art of Healing is a forum for healing and empowerment, an opportunity for adult survivors to share with a strong, clear voice, to tell the truth, and to reclaim their power.[15]

Without mass visibility, many respondents argued, it was impossible to mobilize survivors. At the most basic level, any form of collective action entails coming out. As Ella put it, "The invisibility of the survivor...plays against us." Kimberly expanded on this dilemma, making the analogy to the lesbian and gay and civil rights movements, saying, "What really catapulted those other movements was when a massive group of people came together and were visible." By countering the invisibility of child sexual abuse, Kimberly believed, mass collective action by survivors could change how people conceptualize the issue:

> We have to march on Washington by the millions. We have to come out of the closet, if you will.... There's nothing that identifies us as survivors in society if we don't say that we are.... One of the points that we have to make in coming out is that we are everywhere. You know, we are from every class, we are from every neighborhood, every family, every community, every race. And when we come together in that mass and we are visible, I think it could say to this society—it *will* say to this society—that this is a real problem.... Once we are visible, it exposes the insidious perpetration of violence that has persisted and continues to persist unchecked.

The fact that collective action entailed coming out was both its central problematic—how to mobilize a constituency to proclaim a stigmatized and personally painful experience publicly—and the source of its power.

Conclusion

The survivors' movement is one among many that employ the politics of visibility. Identity disclosure, activist art, and demonstrations that "bear witness" to violence are common to women's, lesbian/gay, transgender, and anti-racism movements, and bearing witness to collective violence has been a major tactic of antiwar groups such as the Women in Black, who hold silent vigils worldwide (Benski 2005). These strategies aim to change the individuals who participate and those who observe, bringing attention to issues that might otherwise go unspoken and dramatizing the problem in ways that bypass observers' preconceptions and evoke an emotional response. They provide the movement an avenue through which to shape cultural images of child sexual abuse.

Coming out as a strategy has significant limitations, some of which are at the heart of the critique of "identity politics." For one, identity strategies limit the role of people who do not share the identity—in this case, people who have not experienced child sexual abuse. The survivors' movement, like others, created identity categories for nonsurvivors, terming them "allies" or "pro-survivors," but these categories carry different assumptions about the perspective and experiences of those within them. In addition, identity-based movements can oversimplify the experiences and commonalities of their members or treat the meaning of experiences as straightforward, rather than as a matter of interpretation, constructed in specific cultural contexts.[16] A final risk is of simply being discredited. Institutions are dominated by a discourse that casts victims of child sexual abuse as seriously and permanently wounded and subject to interpretation and treatment by experts rather than themselves. In addition, credentials and authority in both the state and the mass media rest on standards of objectivity. Consequently, the credibility of activists who speak based on their own experience is suspect (Coy and Woehrle 1996; Nepstad 2001).

The grassroots activists of the 1990s and early 2000s operated in a world where media and scholarly debates over memory defined child sexual abuse, and where their own identities as survivors were questioned more than any time since the beginning of the movement. Whereas earlier activists fought the invisibility of child sexual abuse when they came out, activists now fought a skepticism toward their claims to have been abused and the idea that they were duped by unscrupulous therapists rather than defining their own identities. Participants saw self-help and therapy as political in part because of the countermovement's opposition to them, not just because of their connection to broader social change. Theater, art, and coming-out strategies made up a strong politics of visibility in which individuals—not professionals, the media, or opponents—defined their identities and worked to influence how others saw and felt about abuse. In contrast to the earlier emphasis on commonalities among survivors, the new visibility politics emphasized self-expression and individuality, focusing on expressing multiple perspectives as a means of healing and of bearing witness.

Visibility politics illustrate how collective action can transform emotions of participants and others and, conversely, how transformations of emotion and identity are also preconditions to collective action. Particularly around child sexual abuse, activists believed, individuals' thoughts, feelings, and behaviors were as important for social change as were cultural representations, policy, and legislation. They wanted people—survivors, offenders, and bystanders—to recognize abuse when it was occurring, to feel both outrage and empowerment, and to intervene. Activists wanted visibility to occur on their own terms, controlled by survivors themselves. They achieved this imperfectly. The growing role of professionals in the self-help movement was possible because of the movement's success in changing psychotherapy, but it also decreased lay control.

But visibility alone can affect only some kinds of social processes and structures. To the extent that a movement relies on it to the exclusion of other tactics, or assumes that coming out will work in all situations, it can limit movement effectiveness. As individuals came out to friends and strangers, and as outsiders viewed activist art, activists were able to affect how others understood and felt about child sexual abuse. Their reach was limited, however, by their lack of access to mass media and their political marginality. Their connections to policy reform existed mainly through their participation in larger movement organizations. As the grassroots activists worked to define the issue outside of mainstream culture, these major movement organizations moved into ever closer alliance with the state and powerful institutions.

8

The Paradoxical Consequences of Success

In 1998, a national survivors' organization received funds from a state crime victims' compensation fund, which it used to provide scholarships to its conferences for members of underrepresented groups, primarily people of color. These well-attended national conferences included continuing education workshops for therapists alongside workshops for survivors. The income produced by therapists' attendance at the conferences, along with the state funding, supported a paid executive director, who brought organizational and fund-raising skills despite his lack of experience with the issue of child sexual abuse. In short, it was an institutionalized and professionalized organization, although it relied on a volunteer board of directors and volunteer labor for many tasks, such as mailing out newsletters, organizing conferences, and planning and executing educational campaigns. Simultaneously, it had a strong presence of lay survivors, who set the tone for the organization's self-help activities. This organization was Voices in Action, the same group that had been radically grassroots and nonprofessional a decade earlier.

Despite the countermovement, growing numbers of survivors' organizations and individuals became engaged with the state throughout the 1990s and 2000s. Voices in Action, like other organizations, began to professionalize in the late 1980s with available of grant money and the rise of a therapeutic specialization in treating child sexual abuse and became increasingly professionalized in the 1990s. Ironically, greater acceptance and access to state resources weakened some earlier movement gains. As survivors' organizations professionalized and allied with state agencies, their boards of directors and staff were increasingly occupied by credentialed experts, and networks of nonprofessional survivors declined. Adopting medical or criminal discourses in order to gain access to the state and mass media, the most "successful" organizations minimized other aspects of their political agenda, despite the broader interests and commitments of individual members.

These were the paradoxical consequences of the movement's success. Although the movement made progress in policy change by challenging the state on its own territory, it simultaneously became subject to greater control by state agencies and more vulnerable to adopting state discourses about child sexual abuse. Earlier activists had demanded that the state treat child sexual abuse more seriously: that police no longer dismiss accusations, that judges no longer let offenders off with a slap on the wrist or a promise of therapy, and that social service agencies do their utmost to prevent and end children's victimization. By doing so, the movement put child sexual abuse on the "political agenda of the state," demanding, as Proffitt (2000: 23) says of the battered women's movement, "that the federal government and society as a whole share responsibility for eliminating" child sexual abuse. But as with mass media representation, the movement's closer relationship to the state was not a simple success. Instead, it brought a mixture of gains and compromises. Those who seemed to gain power often gave it up in the long run; those who avoided alliance with the state often lost autonomy anyway; and those who gained government resources often ended up losing status rather than improving it.

Movement organizations were not equal in their access to institutional and state support. The movement against child sexual abuse contained activists who defined being a survivor and the problem of child sexual abuse in different ways and called for drastically different solutions. As we have seen, medical and criminal approaches dominated state and mass media approaches to child sexual abuse. Unsurprisingly, organizations that advocated goals consistent with the state's preexisting priorities and discourses were the most likely to influence policy and gain access to state resources. Organizations with a therapeutic or individual focus were no more likely than those that made an institutional critique to gain access to the state. Elements of both approaches influenced state responses to child sexual abuse, but in both cases, selection processes ensured that the more challenging elements remained outside. While a therapeutic or institutional focus did not determine organizations' access to the state, the use of medical or criminal discourses did. Overall, organizations that gained access to the state used medical or criminal frames for child sexual abuse, whether they focused on changing individuals or changing institutions.

In this chapter, I examine how selection processes shaped activists' access and influence and show the gains and compromises that came with various forms of state involvement. As we will see, movement organizations entered the state apparatus in numerous ways and locations, including social services, criminal justice, and public health. Few organizations became fully institutionalized or absorbed into the political process, although many individual activists entered the state directly. More often, organizations developed relationships with the state as clients or service providers. They preserved the most autonomy working with public health agencies, where they retained a critique of criminal approaches to child sexual abuse even as they built on medical metaphors. In their range of relationships to the state, they typify the multiple paths to movement institutionalization and how it varies in both kind and degree (Meyer 2006). Table 8.1 provides an overview of organizations' use of medical and criminal discourses, their emphasis on individual or institutional change, and their relationship to the state.

I identified five main types of relationships between the movement and the state. First, some activists were able to enter the state directly,

Table 8.1. Types of Movement Organizations and Their Institutional Allies

Level of Change: Individual vs. Institutional	Discursive Focus	
	Medical	Criminal
Individual Change	Quasi-Governmental Organizations: professionalized movement organizations, therapeutic services, professionally-guided self-help, training programs for state agencies and professionals	Clients of the State: Victim Services: crime victims' compensation, civil litigation, support and therapeutic services to crime victims
State and Institutional Allies and Funding Sources	NCCAN; VOCA; VAWA; Psychotherapeutic professional associations	VOCA; VAWA; local law enforcement agencies
Institutional Change	Public Health: Movement advocacy organizations, publicity campaigns, capacity-building	Law Enforcement: Movement groups focusing on enforcement and legislation
State and Institutional Allies and Funding Sources	Centers for Disease Control; Surgeon General's office; U.S. Justice Department; professional associations for treatment of offenders; medical professional associations	VAWA, local law enforcement, some Bar Associations

assuming positions within governmental agencies. These *"femocrats"* (Eisenstein 1991) made substantial compromises, but their influences on relevant government agencies are real gains of the movement. They worked in many of the state and institutional allies listed in table 8.1.

Second, some movement organizations remained officially outside of government, but worked in close alliance with state agencies as consultants or trainers, performing tasks that were integral to governmental needs in a privatized setting. Serving as *quasi-governmental organizations or subcontractors*, they received financial support and had the opportunity to influence policy and practice, but had to attend to state goals as well as their own. Even when movement organizations formed peer relationships with state agencies, their status often hinged on the distinction between professionals and the lay survivors who were their clients. They adopted a medicalized view of abuse and focused on individual change, with a therapeutic orientation.

Third, some movement groups did not form peer relationships with state agencies, but rather appealed to the government for funding and special accommodations, primarily through crime victims compensation funds or on grounds of trauma-related disability. Like the quasi-governmental organizations, their focus was on change at the individual level. While the financial support they received allowed these groups to do things they could not have done otherwise, their role as *clients* of the state also pushed them toward formulating the issue as one of crime and survivors as victims in need of services. Even activists who saw themselves as outsiders to the state sometimes attempted to use its enforcement power by filing civil suits or criminal charges against offenders. Despite their intentions, doing so could easily place them in a subordinate position and reinforce the very views of abuse that they sought to challenge.

Fourth, other activists pushed for increased penalties and better enforcement of child sexual abuse cases. These *enforcers* both challenged the state in their efforts to increase criminal justice responses to abuse and strengthened the state in their efforts to bolster its enforcement arm, while they rarely departed from criminal and medical discourses. Drawing on a view of child sexual abuse as a crime, the organizations working in this area focused on change at the collective level, emphasizing policy change and law enforcement.

Fifth, a growing number of organizations sought to work within both the state and mass media, innovating a *public health* approach to child sexual abuse prevention. These organizations applied visibility politics to the issue of child sexual abuse as a whole and worked successfully with advertising agencies, governmental agencies, and medical associations. In part because of the intense racial inequality in the criminal justice system, they eschewed an emphasis on law enforcement. They, too, included many professional staff, but continued to emphasize the visibility and self-determination of survivors. Their access to government agencies, however, owed much to their use of medical discourse, and, despite their critique, they were unable to weaken the dominant criminal approach.

Although some individuals and groups remained firmly outside the state, they were marginalized in an era when other groups gained legitimacy through their ties to the powers that be. More commonly, organizations that did have established relationships with institutions included individual members with divergent views. Many of these individuals employed the visibility politics discussed in chapter 7. They found a home and institutional support within movement organizations for which visibility politics was a secondary focus that remained largely *in*visible in grant proposals and public discourse.

Many authors argue that the therapeutic dimensions of the state simply serve to extend state power (McGee 2005; Nolan 1998; Polsky 1991; Rose 1990, 1999; Sommers and Satel 2005). Yet some of the programs that are part of the therapeutic state represent concessions to activist demands that state institutions—including police departments, the justice system, and child protective services—do more to address and reduce child sexual abuse. To complicate matters further, what one movement organization considers a success, such as the passage of laws that require registration of sex offenders, another organization considers a failure. The mixture of gains, compromises, and losses that comprise the outcomes of the movement result from the interaction between movement strategies and the selection processes that privilege some organizations, frames, and goals over others.

Joining the Government: Femocrats and State Agencies

To hear some conservatives tell it, the U.S. government is run by "feminazis," radical feminists who wield extraordinary power to demonize men, separate fathers from their children, and funnel resources and privileges to women, people of color, and homosexuals. To hear some critics on the Left tell it, entering the state constitutes co-optation almost by definition. The truth, as usual, is more complex. At certain times, feminists and other activists have been able to move into state agencies and affect policy. They are more likely to move into state and local government than federal, and into low-level rather than high-level positions (Boles 1989, Eisenstein 1991). They may not be able to design public policy, but they can affect how policies are implemented, which can be as important (Burstein et al. 1995). In this section, I will discuss both the entry of individuals into the state and the role of state agencies in working against child sexual abuse.

While some countermovement critics charge that social service agencies are dominated by feminists and activists against child sexual abuse, my data do not suggest this.[1] Instead, the most common agencies that employed activists in my sample were those that served crime victims and witnesses.

For example, Judy, a driving force behind the National Assault Prevention Center, took a position in her state attorney general's office as Chief of Crime Victim Services in the early 1990s. She saw this position as a way to continue working on "larger victim issues" and on the protection of children. Kathy, who worked as a child advocate in the child abuse prosecution unit of a district attorney's office beginning in 1985, started a victim witness program in the early 1990s at the criminal bureau of the attorney general's office in her state. She thought that "any situation where someone's in a position to raise someone else's awareness can only help." Some states, at some times, reached a critical mass of activists in governmental positions. These networks made a real difference, because, as Kathy said, "people are planted places and rely on each other through coalitions or informal networks ... and people will have some awareness about what you're dealing with."

While "femocrats" influenced policy and its implementation, they faced substantial limitations. Their positions often hinged on the shaky candidacies of progressive elected officials. They rarely retained their positions for long or were able to set up programs that endured when new administrations entered, and they were constrained by the regulations on their agencies. In her position as victim-witness advocate, Kathy, for example, was unable to directly advise survivors about the process of filing a civil suit to recover damages from offenders, although she had considerable experience and expertise in that area.

The establishment of state agencies is one form of a movement's institutionalization. The movement against rape and domestic violence made inroads into the federal government under the Clinton administration through the Violence Against Women Act (VAWA), passed in 1994 and renewed in 1999 and 2005 under President George W. Bush. Activists made headway by linking to the issue as it became institutionalized, but child sexual abuse took a back seat. VAWA focused on adult women, mostly addressing child abuse when it occurred along with domestic violence, and defining both domestic violence and rape as crimes that primarily targeted adult women. It contained some provisions dealing indirectly with child abuse, including a national hotline for victims of domestic violence or rape, grants for local shelters, education programs, and reforms of police procedures (Laney and Siskin 2003). More directly, it funded child abuse law enforcement, court-appointed advocates for victims, training for judicial personnel, and programming to reduce sexual abuse of runaway and homeless youth. The 2005 reauthorization of the Act added programs related to dating violence, making unmarried teens eligible for domestic violence programs. Yet despite the office's own statistics on the prevalence of rape of minors,[2] it makes little mention of youth as victims outside of dating violence and homeless or runaway youth (Meyer-Emrick 2001; Matthews 1999; Clinton 1995; Shalala 1994). Funding for programs focused on children was a small fraction of its budget: In 1996, VAWA's spending for programs focused on children was $12.36 million, representing 5.4 percent of overall spending on violence against women programming.³ Consequently, VAWA had relatively little direct impact on child sexual abuse.

VAWA was an institutionalized arm of the movement against rape and domestic violence, although in collaboration with "tough on crime" forces in the federal government. By the 1990s, child sexual abuse as an issue had largely separated from the movements against rape of adults and domestic violence, and few activists or organizations fully addressed violence against both adults and children. Thus, VAWA provided few opportunities for activists against child sexual abuse, who had to lobby VAWA to consider child abuse and help protective parents.⁴ VAWA gave a sympathetic hearing to such efforts, but it was not a route through which child abuse activists could readily enter the state.

NCCAN, the other federal agency addressing child abuse, continued to exist during the 1990s and 2000s, but ceased to be an independent agency after the 1996 CAPTA renewal, when the Children's Bureau absorbed its functions.⁵ While NCCAN still issued grants, its demotion signaled a decreased priority for child abuse prevention, and its funding levels decreased over the 1990s. Further, the vast majority of NCCAN grants issued during the 1990s went to research projects, rather than demonstration projects. As we saw in chapter 3, it was funding for demonstration projects that generally supported movement organizations. Overall social service spending, through federal block grants and the requirements they placed on states for matching funds, also declined in the 1990s. The Child and Family Services Block Grant bill of 1996 no longer required states to continue to spend their own funds for child protective services, as previous block grant bills had. In other words, states could receive federal funds for CPS without appropriating their own funds. In practice, states maintained some expenditures, but not necessarily at previous levels. At the same time, the 1996 block grant bill decreased authorized federal funding by 14 percent, and in general even lower levels were actually appropriated. All this increased advocates' sense that federal commitment to child sexual abuse prevention and services was dropping.⁶

The decreased federal funding was due to the actions of the Republican Congress, but also to efforts by countermovement activists. FMSF advisory board member Herman Ohme explained his work against CAPTA reauthorization in 1994 as follows: "When the Republican Party took control of the U.S. House of Representatives in 1994...I saw the opportunity to change the CAPTA laws...which had been the root cause of the child sex abuse hysteria and false accusations. I had been an active member of the RNC (Republican National Committee) for years and had some voice with the new party in control. I enlisted the help of nationally known CAPTA experts, Richard Gardner, M.D., [and] Carol Hopkins, San Diego Grand Jury Foreman, to testify before the U.S. House and Senate Committees....Our team was successful in correcting some of the worst features of the old CAPTA law but were blocked from deleting the "mandatory reporting" feature."⁷ "Child abuse," as defined in the reauthorized CAPTA, had to be a "*recent* act or failure to act on the part of a parent or caretaker" [emphasis added]. Despite these changes, federal and state funds continued to support some movement organizations, including many that were outside the official state.

Circling the State: Quasi-governmental Organizations in the Social Services

No government operates solely through its official institutions (Rose 1999; Nolan 1998; Mitchell 1991; Polsky 1991). Many of the tasks of government, particularly those that provide services or regulate the daily lives of citizens, are performed by sub-contractors of a sort, nominally autonomous civilian agencies that work closely with official branches of the state. When government agencies mandated programs to deal with child sexual abuse, they often subcontracted these programs out to existing agencies. The centers that NCCAN funded in 1980 were a model for such programs. Receiving heavy federal funding, the centers developed treatment and prevention programs that sought in part to meet state requirements for response to the rising numbers of mandated reports of child sexual abuse. Similarly, while some states' departments of social services administer preventative services for parents considered at high risk of abusing their children, in other states, services are subcontracted out to groups such as Parents Anonymous or community mental health centers. The boundaries between the official state and autonomous agencies are thus indistinct.

In the mid- and late 1990s and early 2000s, Parents Anonymous benefited from numerous NCCAN grants to "develop a national network of mutual support/self-help organizations."[8] Local agencies received grants to incorporate Parents Anonymous into their work. By 2006, Parents Anonymous was a registered trademark, available only to "accredited organizations and local affiliates." It still relied on mutual support between parents in free meetings, and parents remained involved in leadership, but professionals had become key leaders. Parents and professionals co-led the meetings, and the organization was far from a grassroots self-help network, or even the more highly organized but peer-led other "Anonymous" programs. Parents Anonymous groups for parents and children operate in homeless shelters (among other locations), where parents who are already in contact with state or state-contracted agencies can participate.[9] In other words, Parents Anonymous became a quasi-governmental organization, providing social services as mandated and supported by the state, diminishing the role of non-professionals, and potentially playing a stronger social control role.

When activists or organizations formed alliances with government, they became part of the web of support services on which official state agencies rely. For example, some autonomous organizations received federal or state grants to provide services such as telephone crisis lines and referral to law enforcement or counseling. Countless such agencies provide services to rape survivors, and a significant number of those also have resources and referrals specific to child sexual abuse, such as RAINN, the Rape, Abuse, and Incest National Network. Founded in 1994, RAINN operates a national sexual assault hotline that links callers to local hotlines and resources.[10] Since 1996, VAWA has also supported a national domestic violence hotline that refers callers to shelters and other resources, most of which are not official state agencies.[11] Voices in Action, too, provided services directly to people who might otherwise have made use of community mental health centers or other state resources, although it received relatively little state funding to do so. By facilitating support groups, providing public education about the prevention and treatment of child sexual abuse, and referring survivors to state resources, Voices in Action filled a role that the state might otherwise have had to assume. The degree of association between the state and organizations with state contracts or funding varies; some organizations are closely associated with the state, others receive funding for more narrowly-bounded projects.

State funding rarely comes without strings attached. Anti-violence movements that received extensive state funding, such as the anti-rape and battered women's movements, changed substantially as a result. Shelters or rape crisis centers had to report data on the women they served, requiring them to ask detailed demographic questions that could deter crisis callers (Matthews 1994; Gornick and Meyer 1998). They had to provide job-training programs and group therapy to women staying in shelters, or encourage women to press charges, which could particularly discourage women of color skeptical of a racist criminal justice system (Crenshaw 1991; Proffitt 2000: 24–5; Fraser 1989). Over time they moved from a self-help model, in which women who had survived violence were central in running the group, to one in which those women were clients, receiving professional services. Instead of analyzing violence against women in feminist terms, they increasingly focused on family pathology and the need to increase women's self-esteem (Fraser 1989; Matthews 1994; Martin 2005; Proffitt 2000; Walker 1990).

The movement against child sexual abuse shared some of these problems, but to a lesser extent, partly because it wasn't a candidate for the same level of funding as the battered women's or anti-rape movements. Most activist organizations that sought funding, such as Voices in Action, did not deliver direct services, but rather facilitated self-help. With funding they operated more efficiently with professional staff, but lay involvement balanced professional influence. And because parts of the existing movement weren't candidates for extensive funding, they survived to put forward a different view of child sexual abuse.

Activists also tried to influence the content of official state programs through workshops and training programs. Much of the training and education given to police officers, case workers, and other bureaucrats is designed and administered by outside agencies. The vast number of state agencies dealing with child sexual abuse and thus needing such training provided an opportunity for activists seeking to influence them. Education and training programs provided a point of access for activists to influence protocols for dealing with child sexual abuse and domestic violence. Larry, for example, who focused on male survivors of child sexual abuse, described a typical regimen of training activities that included working with hospital emergency room staff, police departments, and sex crime units, and speaking in high school classes. Voices in Action, through its professional track at conferences, provided training to therapists. Even smaller conferences often included some continuing education component for professionals.[12] Another activist taught classes through her state university, the Department of Health and Human Services, and to social work supervisors and lawyers, and gave in-service trainings at the state attorney's office and at group homes.

While a medical or criminal framing was necessary to secure state funding, the content of training programs or continuing education sponsored by activist organizations is not directly regulated by the state or professional associations, once the organization is accredited. In fact, movement organizations may present views of child sexual abuse that are at odds with state interests in these workshops, such as critiques of the foster care or criminal justice systems. Recall, as well, that the FMSF was an accredited continuing-education provider, providing content that was drastically different from the content provided by Voices in Action. Thus, relatively unmonitored continuing-education credits for therapists, along with training programs for other state entities, provide an opportunity for activist influence on both sides, even as they fulfill a state-sanctioned role.

At the same time, many movement functions were assumed by government agencies or other powerful institutions. Prevention programs in schools, for example, were generally run by independent organizations until the early 1990s or so. Under increasing budgetary and political pressure, such programs were largely abandoned in favor of in-house classes taught by school personnel. Over time most such programs succumbed to shrinking funds, leaving little more than an hour or two of cautioning against "stranger danger." Not only did the sponsoring organizations lose the contracts that were their lifeblood, the school-based programs abandoned controversial elements that dealt with assault by family members or that focused on empowering children.

As movement organizations professionalized, psychotherapeutic professionals gained control at the expense of lay survivors. Thus, the earlier movements' critique of professional psychotherapy and drive for survivors' self-determination fell prey to the dominance of expert knowledge. These professionals did not seek out power at the expense of laypeople. As we saw in chapter 7, laypeople continued to assert their experiential knowledge within self-help and visibility politics, and many professionals continued to support them. Nevertheless, selection processes favored organizations with credentialed experts on the board of directors, and these professionals had considerable credibility both with the state and with organizations' members. While diverse perspectives remained inside of organizations, it was medical and professional perspectives that were externally visible and that drove the funded programs.

Entry into the state or the circle of quasi-governmental organizations and sub-contractors that it supported was a double-edged sword for the movement. Activists gained influence, but only to a point. The processes by which contracts or grants were awarded favored organizations that framed their actions in terms familiar to the state. State agencies selected organizations that provided services in line with the medical view of child sexual abuse and that appeared credible, usually because of participation by credentialed experts (Coy and Woehrle 1996; Nepstad 2001). These selection processes meant that the more radical elements of the movement, such as its critique of the patriarchal family or of children's powerlessness, never made it into official policy or procedure (Currie 1990). At times, activists aided the state in its social control function, in effect "policing" people referred to Parents Anonymous by courts or placed in court-mandated counseling. While many activists saw this policing as a good thing, it nevertheless meant that the state's interest in social order trumped activists' interest in social change. When activists entered the other side of the equation, as the state's clients rather than its proxies, the ramifications were even more complex.

Clients of the State: Crime Victims and Disability

While some funding remained available to movement organizations, most self-help and activist groups could not compete for large grants. Crime victims' compensation funds were a primary alternative source of funding for some groups, including national organizations like Voices in Action and many state and local groups. While these funds allowed organizations to mount programming, they required framing child sexual abuse as a crime and survivors as victims of crime. As such, they placed survivors in a subjugated position even as they supported programs that survivors desired and that might work against that subjugated position.

All states have crime victims' compensation funds, mostly established in the early 1970s in response to the Federal Uniform Crime Victims Reparations Act of 1973.[13] While it initially primarily compensated individual crime victims for expenses related to their injuries, in 1984 the federal Victims of Crime Act (VOCA) expanded funds to organizations that provide services to crime victims. Currently, about half of the funds go to compensate individual victims, and half to organizations that provide assistance to crime victims.[14] Victim assistance funds support an estimated 5,600 organizations nationwide such as "domestic violence shelters, rape crisis centers, child abuse programs, and victim services in law enforcement agencies, prosecutors' offices, hospitals, and social service agencies."[15]

The federal contribution to such funds is rather modest; most monies come from the states. Nevertheless, federal requirements shape the programs, which are similar from state to state.[16] Federal VOCA provisions ensure funding for child sexual abuse victims, both for child victims and adult survivors. Federal statute requires that 10 percent of all grants go to each of four priority categories, including child abuse (including both sexual and physical abuse) and adult sexual assault (including "adults molested as children").[17] Funding to victims of sexual assault, both children and adults, often went beyond this required minimum. For example, in Massachusetts, 9.5 percent of 2001 VOCA grants to individuals went to child sexual abuse victims and another 3.8 percent to adults molested as children.[18] One such grant provided services to the parents of a young rape victim, therapy for their daughter, assistance with pressing charges, and police protection "when the abuser's wife began harassing the family."[19]

Child sexual abuse self-help and advocacy groups became eligible for VOCA monies by framing their activities in terms of *providing direct services to crime victims*. Paradoxically, although groups gained access to these funds by defining abuse in criminal and medical terms, they often used the funds to support self-help activities that took a broader view. In order to be eligible for VOCA funds, organizations were required to be nonprofit, use volunteers, and "promote coordinated public and private efforts to aid crime victims within the local community."[20] These requirements were tailor-made for many organizations that originated in activist efforts and had expanded into facilitating self-help, providing resources and referrals to survivors, and doing public education. For example, in Colorado the Wings Foundation, Inc., received a $35,050 grant in 2000 to support its work in "provid[ing] facilitated peer support groups, orientation for prospective new members, a speakers bureau, advocacy and other forms of support to adult survivors of childhood sexual abuse."[21] Crime victims' compensation and assistance funds allowed Voices in Action to hire an executive director and provided scholarships to conferences for underrepresented minorities. Many government agencies also received support from VOCA, including interdisciplinary child advocacy centers that both investigated child abuse charges and provided support and treatment to victims, and projects within sheriffs' or district attorneys' offices or other criminal justice agencies to provide referrals or victim advocacy.[22]

Advocates inside state agencies worked to ensure that crime victims' compensation funds were accessible to adult survivors of child sexual abuse. For example, Kathy reported that colleagues in her state's Office for Victim Assistance and the Victim Compensation and Assistance Division[23] drafted legislation, which was enacted in 1994. The central issue was how best to deal with crimes that had been committed in the past, often without any police investigation. Kathy saw access to the funds as a matter of justice because "somebody did commit a crime against them." Framing abuse in criminal terms was unavoidable, since VOCA required the filing of a police report.

Closely related to victim compensation issues were accommodations for disability produced by trauma. The Americans With Disabilities Act (ADA), passed in 1990, bans discrimination against people with disabilities and requires employers to make adjustments for employees with disabilities. Activists for adult survivors of child sexual abuse argued that those suffering from post-traumatic stress disorder (PTSD), dissociative disorders, and even chronic depression resulting from abuse should be protected under the ADA. Several respondents advocated for the rights of survivors with disabilities for accommodation in the workplace, including medical leave. In some cases these respondents conceptualized their own experiences, at least at certain points in their lives, as a form of disability. One, for example, described herself as having a "dissociative disability," while others reported taking short-term disability leave in the past. Most respondents, however, did not see themselves as disabled, even when they were coping with considerable psychological trauma. Defining oneself as disabled challenges the identity of the survivor as someone who is stronger than the abuse and who is not permanently injured by it.[24]

VOCA funding consolidated organizations' stability and enabled them to expand their activities, but in other ways it weakened the position of individual survivors and their movement. By basing their claim to funds on survivors' status as crime victims, organizations positioned survivors themselves less as peers or challengers to the state and more as its clients. The legislation required that activists use the dominant discourse that defined child sexual abuse, not as an issue of politics or power, but as the problem of criminal, deviant perpetrators of violence. In order to get compensation, victims had to demonstrate their pain and suffering (for which they could be compensated) and make claims for funding for treatment, usually psychotherapy. This meant using the expert medical discourse to show oneself as psychologically damaged and in need of treatment. Gaining access to disability protections required a demonstration of even more extreme injury and inability to function. In effect, the requirements of such funding make impossible the demonstration of some aspects of the oppositional collective identity, particularly the notion of "survivor" with its stress on strength, empowerment, and action to end abuse publicly. Yet they simultaneously assume the elements of survivor identity that hold "victims" blameless and permit the speaking of what was formerly unspeakable (Davis 2005; Minow 1997). Nevertheless, it is different to define oneself as a crime victim or a person with a medical condition instead of a survivor of patriarchal violence, someone healing from trauma, or an activist fighting to make the world safe for children.

An additional arena in which the criminal discourse and individually-focused activism came together was around civil litigation. Most adult survivors were unable to bring criminal cases against their alleged abusers because of statutes of limitations, but some activists advocated filing civil suits against offenders. These suits draw directly on the model of child sexual abuse as a crime and illustrate both its power and its costs. Civil suits can bring financial settlements that pay for treatment or compensate for pain and suffering. They also serve a symbolic function, as an advocate wrote: "For those women who have reached adulthood without any legal response to the sexual abuse by their fathers, tort remedies provide them with the opportunity to have their day in court, to place the blame for the incest on their father, and to let the world know, through a public court proceeding, that the women themselves were not to blame" (Moore 1986: 12). They have been widely used by people abused by clergy or other authority figures, and less widely used by incest survivors; as we saw in Chapter 6, they became less common as a result of the countermovement, which led to skepticism about most claims of child sexual abuse.

The conventions of civil litigation can work at cross purposes to survivors' goals of breaking silence and exposing a perpetrator. In direct opposition to activists' desire for visibility, when civil suits are settled out of court, the parties are often bound by confidentiality agreements that forbid them to speak publicly about the case. When the defendant is alleged to have other victims, as in the clergy abuse cases, confidentiality agreements can hinder other victims' cases. It was only when large numbers of alleged victims filed mass suits against clergy and refused confidentiality agreements that the scope of sexual abuse within the Catholic Church was exposed, empowering the activist groups that sought structural change in the Church (Investigative Staff 2002).

Civil litigation requires survivors to assume the role of "victim." Damages are awarded to those who are *damaged*. In order to receive damages, plaintiffs not only had to show that the defendant had abused them, but that they had experienced pain and suffering as a result. This often necessitated testimony from therapists about symptoms. One 1985 article about civil litigation, for example, listed a litany of debilitating symptoms under the heading "The Damaged Survivors of Incest." These included: "a pattern of revictimization in their adult lives...severely impaired relationship skills...sexual dysfunction....They are a damaged people" (DeRose 1985: 192–194). Activists emphasized that "taking your perpetrator to court" could be an empowering way of breaking silence and transcending shame and secrecy. Yet, in doing so, they risked losing control over their own image and identity. The model of survivor identity that the movement advocated was someone who speaks the truth about having been abused without shame, and controls her own life rather than being controlled by her past. Such a survivor would be unlikely to win a civil award. Instead, she would need to show that she required extensive therapy and had significant lasting effects from the abuse. It is for these that she would receive compensation, not for the fact of the abuse itself. In other words, the requirements of civil litigation make it almost impossible to maintain an oppositional collective identity as survivor, but rather require participants to display a pathologized identity.

Like civil litigation, increased funding, prosecution, and treatment all rely on bringing the power of the state to bear on behalf of child and adult survivors of child sexual abuse. Financial compensation, free and accessible treatment, and contexts in which to speak openly of one's experience without stigma and to come to see it as less shameful were movement goals. If these goals did not take shape exactly as activists had envisioned, if they were more closely linked to the state's apparatus of social control and to the medical and criminal discourses it promoted, this is less a result of misguided movement strategy than it is evidence of the strength of the state and dominant culture to pick and choose among the goals and discourses of a movement, selecting those that are most consistent with the status quo. As we have seen, policy outcomes are shaped as much by internal government priorities—prosecution and crime reduction over social services, for example—as by actual needs or the demands of activists. Activists' efforts to increase criminal prosecution starkly illustrate this process.

Crime and Punishment: Activists, Sex Offender Policies, and Law Enforcement

Child sexual abuse is illegal and therefore subject to investigation, prosecution, and penalty. Prosecution of child sexual abuse cases was rare prior to the 1980s, and convictions even rarer. By the late 1980s, prosecutions were up and considerable attention was focused on how to investigate child sexual abuse allegations, as we saw in chapter 3. Penalties and conviction rates probably increased, if erratically, but incarceration rates remained noticeably lower than rates of guilty pleas or convictions, and by the early 1990s some evidence suggests that they were declining (Cheit and Goldschmidt 1997; Cross et al. 2003; Cullen et al. 2000).[25] Compared to other felonies, complaints of child abuse in general were "more likely to have charges filed...to be carried forward without dismissal, and had lower incarceration rates" (Cross et al. 2003: 324). Imprisonment rates nevertheless were higher for sexual offenders against children than for other types of offenders against children (Finkelhor and Ormrod 2001) and were highest with female victims and male offenders (Sedlak et al. 2005).[26] Yet, cases where the alleged offender was a parent or stepparent remained much less likely to be prosecuted (Stroud et al. 2000: 6).

These changes did not result merely from law enforcement, but from the changing political and social climate surrounding the law. Activists varied in their approach to the criminal justice system and the view that child sexual abuse was primarily a criminal matter. While some claimed an identity as crime victim in order to gain access to state funding, others took the focus on crime further, advocating increased prosecution, stiffer sentencing, registration and community notification for convicted offenders, civil suits against offenders, and a frame that understood child sexual abuse primarily as a violent crime. Policies in these areas changed substantially during the 1990s and 2000s, as a result of both activists' efforts and other forces.

At the most basic level, activists had been arguing since the 1970s that adults who sexually assaulted children should be punished. Earlier feminist activists framed child sexual abuse as a result of patriarchal control and violence. Because they defined the state as a primary agent of patriarchal control, the idea that they would turn to the state for protection was anathema (Currie 1990). However, they wanted abuse to be taken seriously even though they mistrusted the state. Some early writers preferred the phrase "father-daughter rape" or "sexual assault" to "incest," precisely to emphasize its violent and criminal nature. In a climate where most cases were never reported to authorities, DAs were reluctant to pursue cases, and incest cases were almost never prosecuted (Cheit and Goldsmith 1997), it was inevitable that activists would push for increased prosecution and for defining incest as a crime like any other sexual assault. Activists argued that prosecution is an indicator of how seriously the act is taken by the larger society, and potentially a part of how victims come to terms with their experience. It also serves to deter further assaults. If child sexual abuse can proceed essentially unpunished because of the low rate of conviction, there is little to stop offenders from sexually abusing children (Armstrong 1994; Cheit and Goldsmith 1997). Activists also contended that prosecution could serve a direct prevention role in cases of offenders with multiple victims, preventing offenders from abusing additional children.

While the notion of prosecution as prevention relies on law enforcement, it also assumes a medical frame, resting on the idea that pedophiles have a medical condition that predisposes them to continue abusing children until forced to stop. Yet even activists who did not subscribe to a medicalized explanation for abuse supported prosecution as a way of showing that society took child sexual abuse seriously. As a result, activists, pundits, and policymakers alike called for increased prosecution, and the medical and criminal frames reigned.

It is easier to call for prosecution than to deliver it. Numerous legal and political limits confront those who report being sexually abused as children. Statutes of limitations limit the amount of time that can pass between a crime and its prosecution. They are particular barriers for victims of child sexual abuse, many of whom cannot report the crime when it occurs and are ashamed to report it as adults. Most states extend the statute of limitations for offenses against children, either by allowing for more years from the date of the offense, or by providing that the statute of limitations doesn't start to run until the victim is 18, or until the date that the offense is reported to law enforcement or Child Protective Services. Efforts to extend statutes of limitations for child sexual abuse were perennial throughout the 1990s and 2000s, widely supported by the activists I interviewed, and widely opposed by the countermovement.

Despite publicity about criminal charges filed on the basis of testimony from now-adult victims, the overwhelming majority of child sexual abuse cases go to court when the victim is *still* a child. Some of the changes in treatment of child witnesses funded by NCCAN in the 1980s survived and became institutionalized, and some of the practices that activists encouraged police to adopt also made a difference in how victims and witnesses are treated and in how child sexual abuse cases are investigated. Child victims are less likely to be subjected to repeated duplicate interviews as part of prosecution, and they are perhaps more likely to be viewed as potentially reliable witnesses. The National Network of Child Advocacy Centers promotes the use of multidisciplinary teams to coordinate the investigation and treatment of abused children and their families (Kinnear 1995: 108).

Some movement organizations mobilized specifically to support victims in court and to press for stricter legislative and penal responses to child sexual abuse. They operated in uneasy coalition with other survivors' organizations, took a hard line on offenders, and attempted to work with the federal Violence Against Women office. The first such groups emerged in direct response to the countermovement. The closely associated One Voice and the American Coalition for Abuse Awareness[27] attempted to dispel countermovement claims about the unreliability of memory through media campaigns and lobbying around relevant legislation. After a few years, they developed a focus on children's allegations, particularly in custody disputes where an allegedly abusive parent stood to gain custody, helping people negotiate VAWA and local resources. Their focus on child victims addressed the countermovement's growing emphasis on children's allegations and allowed them to build coalitions with domestic violence groups. In 2000, they merged with Justice for Children, an organization that provided casework and volunteer attorneys to protective parents.[28]

Sex offender registries and community notification laws were another area in which some activists tried to increase state intervention. A wave of legislation and organizing aimed at incarcerating sex offenders even after their sentences ended, tracking their whereabouts after release through registries, and notifying communities of their locations, increased the powers and penetration of the criminal justice system in the late 1990s and 2000s. The federal government established a national database of convicted sex offenders in 1993; "Megan's Law," federal legislation establishing registries and community notification for sex offenders, passed in 1996 (modifying a similar statute of 1994); and federal mandatory sentencing guidelines went through in 1998.[29]

The registries created hardships for offenders and thus can be considered a form of punishment (Tewksbury and Lees 2006). Yet the rationale for registries and civil commitment was not primarily one of punishment; in fact, the minimum sentences for sex crimes remained relatively low (Cheit and Goldsmith 1997). Instead, advocates of civil commitment and community notification laws argued that sex offenders suffered from the intractable disease of pedophilia. Citing high recidivism rates and medical explanations of pedophilia, they argued that sex offenders could not be treated effectively and, if released, were ticking time-bombs waiting to molest and murder more children. Notifying communities of their proximity was the only way to help parents defend their children. This approach was based more on allegiance to a medicalized view of child sexual abuse than on research on treatment of sex offenders, which is relatively scarce and contradictory.[30] While most parties agree that habitual violent sex offenders who repeatedly abduct, rape, and sometimes murder are resistant to treatment and should not be released, there is controversy about the remaining population of offenders.

Even the debate over whether offenders can be successfully treated assumes a medical approach to child sexual abuse, defining it as a matter of pedophilia, rather than as a result of children's objectified and powerless position in society, male domination, a twisted societal attitude towards sex, or any other structural or cultural explanation. This is testimony to the powerful selection process exerted in mainstream culture and the state. The activist movement against child sexual abuse succeeded in bringing greater visibility and state response, but the response itself rested on a medical and criminal, rather than political, understanding of the issue, and reinforced state interests in incarceration and regulation, rather than social change. Furthermore, given the racial inequities in prosecution and sentencing, many African-American and Latina activists were highly suspicious of the criminal justice response. Moving in a new direction, a final set of organizations attempted to change the debate about treatment and prevention through a public health approach.

Public Health: Using Medical Discourse to Change Institutions

Public health initiatives attempt to improve the health of groups of people through education campaigns or public policy initiatives, rather than improving the health of individuals one at a time through medical intervention. They focus on prevention and "harm reduction"—that is, reducing the incidence and impact of a problematic behavior—rather than law enforcement or intervention by social service agencies. The idea is that when people are educated about the problems associated with a behavior and given resources to change it, and when cultural acceptance of the behavior declines, the behavior itself will be less common. Public health campaigns focus on educating people about health habits in order to persuade them to make particular choices. Despite the language of "choice," public health campaigns are undeniably a form of social control, in which the state attempts to bring citizens' behavior in line with its goals, not by imposing external controls, but by changing how people think, feel, and behave. They work upon people's interior lives and are thus a hallmark of the therapeutic state.

Public health campaigns aimed at preventing child sexual abuse employed medical discourses about child sexual abuse alongside visibility politics. Activists viewed widespread publicity about how to prevent child sexual abuse as a way of encouraging people to talk openly about the issue and thus destroying the secrecy and stigma in which child sexual abuse flourishes. The public health approach to child sexual abuse followed a host of successful public health approaches to other issues such as smoking, drunk driving, gun use, domestic violence, and eating habits. Government funding and agencies, especially the Centers for Disease Control, were enthusiastic about a similar approach to reducing child sexual abuse, and the public health organizations received foundation and government funding. They worked with the CDC, the Surgeon General's office, the American Medical Association, and other professional associations; each of these institutional players, in turn, embarked on its own public health campaign against child sexual abuse.

Activists against child sexual abuse found the public health approach appealing for several reasons. First, many longtime activists were frustrated by the movement's lack of impact on the incidence of child sexual abuse. While resources and responses to abuse after the fact had improved, prevention efforts had not. Second, the success of the countermovement had rendered many of the movement's earlier strategies ineffective by impugning the credibility of adult survivors. A focus on prevention sidestepped the countermovement's critique of memory, by focusing on child sexual abuse itself. Third, the movement's own prior successes changed the political landscape and thus led to a need for new strategies. Basic information was widely available, the stigma on speaking out had somewhat decreased, and psychotherapeutic practice had changed, making therapy for survivors was widely available. In contrast, prevention campaigns focused on instructing children in self-defense techniques had not been particularly effective.

Several groups in different areas independently came to the conclusion that they needed to employ sophisticated marketing and community organizing techniques to attempt to reshape the public view of abuse. They were inspired by the ideas of visibility and coming out (from their own experience in the survivors' movement), by the success of other public health campaigns, and often by their own professional experience in marketing or business. Many organizations worked within the public health approach, such as Stop the Silence, which sponsored a walk/run, and Mothers Against Sexual Abuse, which, drawing directly on Mothers Against Drunk Driving in its name, distributed educational materials, referred victims and families to professionals for treatment, and worked on relevant legislation.[31] Three influential organizations represent the range of approaches: Massachusetts-based Stop It Now, Darkness to Light in South Carolina, and Generation Five in the San Francisco Bay Area.

The founder of Stop It Now was a longtime feminist activist and abuse survivor who had extensive corporate and management experience. Focused on the insight that it was adults, not children, who needed to be at the center of prevention efforts, Stop It Now coordinated several statewide campaigns, including advertising about child sexual abuse and toll-free helplines for offenders seeking help and others seeking advice about how to deal with abuse situations. It produced publications on topics such as adolescent sex offenders and how to intervene with an adult who shows sexually inappropriate behavior with a child, it commissioned surveys, and it networked with other groups and government agencies to develop a wider public health campaign. Similarly, but on a smaller scale, Darkness to Light designed and distributed advertising campaigns against child sexual abuse. Generation Five similarly focused on disseminating information and involving adults in prevention. Instead of media campaigns, however, Generation Five emphasized community organizing and capacity building, running training programs for community leaders who could weave prevention efforts into their other work (such as youth or domestic violence organizing), and it focused on working within diverse communities.

The discourse of these organizations built on the themes of visibility and survivor self-determination, but differed in important ways, seeking to establish child sexual abuse as a health issue similar to smoking or drunk driving. For example, Stop it Now framed child sexual abuse as a "public health epidemic," writing, "One in five girls and one in seven boys have been sexually abused before the age of eighteen."[32] They stressed that abusers can change with effective treatment, and that some abusers will "respond to our call to STOP" and call the helpline.[33] In their view, the public health approach addresses the "root causes" of child sexual abuse by:

> Develop[ing] awareness in potential abusers and encourag[ing] them to seek help; Challeng[ing] abusers to stop the abuse immediately and seek treatment through a helpline or on the internet; Work[ing] with families, peers, and friends on how to confront abusers; [and] Join[ing] with others to build a social climate that says "We will no longer tolerate the sexual abuse of children."[34]

These are the key components of a public health approach, aiming to change how both potential abusers and others think about child sexual abuse, changing behaviors by giving people the skills for confronting suspected abusers, and changing the larger cultural view of child sexual abuse.

This is a gender-neutral approach, more similar to the nonfeminist self-help groups than the feminist organizations in which the founder got her start. Yet it maintains an emphasis on familial abuse, writing, "Who Are These Abusers?, ... They are the fathers, mothers, siblings, close relatives, friends, or other caretakers of children. They are rarely the monsters we imagine lurking in the corners of our playgrounds and parks." The advertising campaigns target nonabusive family members who may have suspicions about the behavior of relatives and parents of adolescents with sexual behavior problems.

These groups disseminated their view of child sexual abuse through polished advertising and community outreach campaigns. These campaigns were the offspring of both mass media advertising and the visibility strategies of social movements such as ACT UP, with its attention-getting poster campaigns. Advertisements focused on basic information, such as "Sex with Children Is Wrong," and encouraging people to speak up if they had suspicions. Stop It Now conducted focus groups with offenders, survivors, and family members of offenders and of adolescents with sexual behavior problems, in order to determine the messages that would hit home with the demographics they sought to reach.[35] For example, they adopted the phrase "sex with children" instead of "sexual abuse" because offenders told them that they had not understood their actions as "abuse."

Similarly From Darkness to Light (D2L) sought to increase the visibility of the issue and affect public opinion. Its public service announcements, which appeared on several cable networks and publications, were polished and compelling and referred viewers to a national helpline that connected callers to local helplines.[36] They focused on the high rate of child abuse (one in six boys, one in four girls), using images such as six boys in baseball uniforms or four girls jumping to the popular song "Girls Just Wanna Have Fun," complete with a voice-over by the artist, Cyndi Lauper. One spot showed a girl swinging, the image changing to show her pregnant; a related billboard showed the same image of the pregnant girl with the text, "Stop Adults from Having Sex with Underage Children." The longer television spot emphasized the costs to society, stating, "50 percent of teen pregnancies, which cost the country over $7 billion a year, are the result of adult men having sex with underage girls."[37]

D2L approached the problem of reducing child sexual abuse as if it were a matter, in part, of finding the right image, and they benefited from plentiful funding and connections to the advertising world. They reported "co-branding" with Little League Baseball on an ad about boys, and received advertising development from a prominent Madison Avenue agency, Young and Rubicam. In 2003 D2L consulted "Landor Associates, one of the leading brand consulting firms worldwide, to help reposition the organization as a symbol of hope and strength in the fight against child sexual abuse." Landor and D2L developed a new central theme, "Confronting child sexual abuse with courage," which "meant to encourage adults to face the harsh reality of child sexual abuse head on," as well as a redesigned logo.[38] It sought to craft a message that would resonate with mainstream culture and thus gain access, while also proving effective in reducing abuse.

The groups sought to enter the mass culture in their own terms rather than accepting existing representations of child sexual abuse. Yet in order to make their own campaigns comprehensible, they could not avoid drawing on existing representations. D2L, for example, referred to abuse survivors as "walking wounded," and liberally sprinkled ads with images of cute, innocent, and vulnerable looking children. Similarly, Stop It Now used images of children playing to suggest both their innocence and their vulnerability. The D2L advertisement about the costs to society of teen pregnancy was an innovative way to reach viewers who might not care about other aspects of abuse, yet was framed within the existing discourse about teen pregnancy as a cost to society. That existing discourse generally cast teen pregnancy as the domain of African-Americans, however, while the D2L ad used a conventionally pretty white girl as its subject, and relied on the rapid visual transformation of her child's body to a hugely pregnant one to shock viewers into attention. These efforts to catch attention and remain readable undeniably made the ads more effective, but they also limited their ability to address the more structural and political elements of the groups' analysis, such as the overwhelming prevalence of familial abuse or the ways that institutions collude in concealing abuse.

Generation Five also drew on a public health approach, but added what it called a "family violence" approach and a more explicitly political feminist and anti-racist orientation. It built alliances with domestic violence opponents to emphasize how "communities can help families to prevent violence and seek effective support by creating public discussions that counter the assumption that 'family business' should remain 'family business.'"[39] Because it had less engagement with mainstream media, it made fewer compromises in its message, but the reach of that message was reduced (Johnston and Taylor 2008).

All three organizations presented other elements of their approach in face-to-face campaigns. D2L reached large numbers of adults through a prevention training program called "Stewards of Children."[40] Stop It Now focused on speaking engagements and public dialogues between abuse survivors and offenders, in an attempt to diminish community denial about the existence and nature of child sexual abuse and to raise hope that effective treatment for offenders was available. Only with such hope, the organization believed, would offenders attempt to stop committing abuse and bystanders dare to confront them. Pairing a survivor and a "recovering offender" who had been convicted and served his sentence, the dialogues included each participant's narrative and their questions and comments for each other. The dialogues neatly sidestepped skepticism about claims of abuse by including a convicted sex offender who admitted his own actions and the strategies he had used to lure a victim and conceal the abuse, alongside a survivor who could describe the similar strategies used by the (different) person who had abused her. The offender's testimony about his own treatment and recovery process also offered support for the group's advocacy of effective treatment. But although Stop It Now used experiential knowledge to challenge the assumption that sex offenders could not be treated, they also emphasized the effectiveness of cognitive-behavioral therapy and worked closely with professionals treating sex offenders, many of whom served on their board.

Generation Five, in contrast, relied primarily on face-to-face interactions through a leadership training program that trained people to work against child sexual abuse within their own organizations and communities. Participants developed "Community Action Projects" such as "public prevention and awareness education, advocacy work, art and media campaigns, projects aimed at integrating an ability to respond to child sexual abuse into existing agencies, and offender accountability systems and policies" that aimed to give them hands-on experience. For example, one group "presented to a number of family support and anti-domestic violence programs in local Asian Pacific Islander, Latino and other communities on the relevance of CSA [child sexual abuse] to their current work and community experience, and had child sexual abuse prevention and information materials translated into Cantonese."[41] Partly in response to fear of unjust law enforcement in communities of color, Generation Five emphasized the importance of developing approaches that made sense within a community's own culture and experience.

This approach reflected the emphasis within public health on capacity building, in which community leaders were trained in the skills necessary for them to combat a health problem within their own community rather than relying on outside experts. Generation Five sought to build the skills of community leaders so that they could educate others and develop effective and community-specific means of reducing child sexual abuse. Even more than Stop It Now! and D2L, Generation Five was able to present a political view of child sexual abuse in the project and to present the issue and its solutions as complex and varying across ethnic, age, gender, and sexual communities. Their grassroots approach allowed them more autonomy, but also restricted how broad their influence and visibility could be.

All three organizations had connections to other advocacy groups dealing with child sexual abuse, treatment organizations, survivors' organizations, and other social movements such as the women's, restorative justice, and harm-reduction movements. All three participated in a 2002 retreat sponsored by the *Ms.* Foundation for Women aimed at developing a stronger national movement against child sexual abuse and identifying groups for seed grants.[42] These coalitions were important for providing support to the groups and shaping their work, but with the exception of Generation Five, were rarely publicly apparent. The groups also received institutional support from professional associations that dealt with the treatment of sex offenders and of trauma survivors. While many professional associations dealing with sexual abuse had been effectively discredited by the countermovement, the Association for the Treatment of Sexual Abusers had remained mostly immune, again because it was harder to deny the actuality of sexual abuse when the offender admitted to it and sought treatment. These associations were powerful institutional allies for the public health organizations, lending them legitimacy and sharing networks. In turn, they benefited from activists' attempts to promote the idea that sex offenders could be treated. Whether the public health approach can reduce child sexual abuse remains unknown, but the public health activists did succeed in reframing the issue after the gains of the countermovement. Stop It Now's data about the surprising number of sex offenders who called the hotline and turned themselves in to authorities served as a compelling hook for audiences.

The approach was also compelling to government officials, particularly in the Centers for Disease Control. Stop It Now presented its work several times to the Centers for Disease Control and the U.S. Justice Department as well as the American Medical Association, and Generation Five also participated in meetings sponsored by the CDC. Their access to these agencies was unprecedented for child sexual abuse groups led by nonclinicians, but activist groups dealing with other public health issues, such as drunk driving, breast cancer, and AIDS, had paved the way (S. Epstein 1996). At the same time, political obstacles for the public health approach arose from the dominance of criminal justice frames and policies for child sexual abuse, similar to the obstacles that faced the harm reduction movement around drug use (Weed 1995). Generation Five's advocacy of "restorative justice" and Stop It Now's advocacy of sex offender treatment ran counter to the criminal justice approach, which by 2000 offered little to no rehabilitation. The rise of sex offender registries and indefinite post-sentence incarceration of sex offenders assumed that they were intractable and at high risk to reoffend. As Generation Five and Stop It Now argued, harsh sentences and lifelong stigma prevented offenders from seeking help and made their friends and family members less likely to speak up about their suspicions. In other words, the groups' effectiveness was limited without massive restructuring of the criminal justice system, and that restructuring was extremely unlikely. Thus the organizations had an opportunity to influence individuals' behavior and community responses to child sexual abuse through publicity and capacity building, but they were unlikely to effect the corresponding structural changes.

Public health groups drew on the politics of visibility, but shifted the focus from individual visibility to visibility of the issue, and from relatively unpolished (if formulaic) narratives to highly polished and professional advertisements. Like the self-helpers, they relied on personal experience of sexual abuse to help establish credibility and determine the organizations' direction.[43] Like activists who emphasized coming out as a route to change, they saw visibility as crucial because it reduced shame and would encourage people to report and seek help for child sexual abuse. When the founder of

Stop It Now! said in a speech to a conference on child maltreatment, "Why do we expect disclosure from children when we don't disclose our own personal experiences to each other?" and asked those in the room who has been abused as children to stand, her contention was that adults' shame and fear must change in order to allow them to hear children's disclosures and construct effective prevention.[44] They thus emphasized emotional transformation and used the epistemology of identity politics, despite the homogenized public face of the advertisements.

The public health organizations aimed to enter the mass media on their own terms through advertising, educational campaigns, and capacity building. While these efforts were largely professionalized, rather than being dominated by therapists, they were the domain of managers, advertising professionals, and, in the case of Generation Five, community organizers. Responding to the countermovement, they focused more on prevention rather than adult survivors, although adult survivors founded and animated most of the groups. In their work, as with the work of the other types of organizations, the message of hope and action to end abuse wrestled with attempts to show the seriousness of the issue by documenting the scars of survivors.

Here, too, selection processes allowed some organizations greater access to the state than others. Stop It Now's more conventional public health approach received greater play at the CDC than Generation Five's, for example, and Stop It Now's emphasis on making information available to bystanders and encouraging physicians to address abuse made more headway than their call to increase sex offender treatment and rethink community notification laws.[45] Selection processes were also evident in the media, with D2L's more polished and culturally resonant advertising campaign getting wider play than Stop It Now's more challenging message about offender treatment. In general, however, because the public health approach addressed how communities perpetuated and could reduce child sexual abuse, it tended to shy away from strictly individual and psychological solutions and therefore allowed organizations to maintain a broader social change agenda.

As with other wings of the movement, these organizations walked a fine line between reinforcing and challenging the therapeutic state. The state is not a monolithic entity, however, and its public health arm often warred with its criminal justice wing about how best to approach child sexual abuse. Public health groups put forth an approach that challenged medical and criminal definitions of abuse; they made some headway with medical professionals, but their impact was limited by an inability to change the criminal justice apparatus. The public health movement was thus, in a sense, allied with the state against the state, as well as allied with the state against the common foe of child sexual abuse. The question of whether the movement had become coopted, or served as an agent of state control is thus too simplistic for this case, in which the reduction of child sexual abuse is both a social control goal of the state and a social change goal of the movement.

Conclusion

The countermovement had some effect on policy and funding but was unable to sever the connections between movement organizations and participants and the state. Activists who made inroads into the state framed their work as an attempt to address a crime, to provide treatment to its victims, or to reduce the incidence of child sexual abuse through public education. Although the countermovement had some success in revising CAPTA, it could hardly claim to be in favor of a crime or to oppose humane assistance to crime victims. It avoided this quicksand by framing its claims in terms of memory, rather than abuse, but by doing so, it limited its policy leverage.

Ironically, activists lost power as much from their own success as from countermovement opposition. In this, they shed light on the multiple paths and consequences of institutionalization. Activists moved into a client relationship with the state as crime victims compensation programs grew; organizations that did not become state clients circled around the state, receiving funding to provide services that the state deemed valuable. While state goals were not the whole of their work, more challenging or lay-led aspects often took a back seat, ineligible for state funding or promotion. Self-help groups that did receive state funding, such as Parents' Anonymous, were promulgated as a low-cost way to provide prevention and support to families going through professional treatment or the court system. Public health organizations retained more autonomy and closer links to the earlier movement, but were largely professionalized, without a grassroots constituency. While visibility activists sometimes found a home within other movement organizations, they only indirectly affected those organizations' engagements with the state.

The movement both gained and lost ground, in other words. It did so, not just because of activists' own strategic choices and missteps, but because of state initiatives and selection processes. The selection processes were quite concrete. Agencies such as VAWA and the growth and dominance of a "tough on crime" stance within government provided an institutional location for anti-violence work, but favored organizations that adopted a medical-criminal approach. The process of applying for grants or crime victim compensation sorted out organizations accordingly. Some longtime organizations like Voices in Action adapted by capitalizing on their hybrid structure, developing programs that accessed state resources while retaining autonomous self-help functions. Public health organizations forged new directions and worked effectively within the public health domain of the state. While they maintained activist control, their public health focus risked containment by state agendas as well, as selection processes rewarded research and expert knowledge over experiential knowledge and visibility. After more than thirty years, the movement against child sexual abuse had simultaneously succeeded and failed. In this, it is typical of most influential long-lived movements, and its course provides valuable lessons for analysts and activists alike.

Conclusion

The movement against child sexual abuse is just one of many social movements, from diverse political perspectives, that seek emotional change, construct new knowledge, and bear witness to injustice as often as they confront authorities directly. To understand the nature and impact of these movements, we need to think systematically about therapeutic politics. The state and dominant culture supply social movements with targets, tactics, and discourses for making claims (Tarrow 1994). Therapeutic modes of social control provide such a target, discourse, and tactic. This is particularly salient with regard to child sexual abuse, which was initially conceptualized as a psychological issue and targeted for intervention by social services, with survivors viewed in pathological terms and subject to internal emotional shame and stigma. Not surprisingly, activists saw this approach and its consequences as key to their battle: they both used and challenged the tools of psychotherapy, social services, and criminal justice, and they created their own knowledge to challenge the expert knowledge so central to therapeutic domination. It is ironic, therefore, that they have been roundly dismissed as handmaidens of the therapeutic state, reinforcing state intrusion through social services and cooperating in the substitution of personal well-being for political change. Activists did, indeed, augment state power and professional therapeutic knowledge at some points, but they transformed them at other points (Bell 1993). Their impact on institutions and mainstream culture was limited more as a result of selection processes and opposition than activists' own choices or missteps.

The wave of disclosures and court cases regarding clergy abuse illustrates the vast scope and unexpected directions of the impact of the movement against child sexual abuse. By 2006, hundreds of men and women had disclosed childhood sexual abuse by Catholic priests, often with one priest having molested dozens of people. They initiated successful civil suits that have forced many dioceses into financial crisis, and criminal charges have led to conviction in some cases. Survivors—mostly men—have been very visible in the media, telling their stories of abuse, recounting how they were affected, and denouncing the abusers and the Church for cover-up. Existing groups working against child sexual abuse by clergy became revitalized, and new ones sprang up, notably Voice of the Faithful, which lobbied for greater openness and lay accountability within the Catholic Church.

In 1970, and even 1980, public disclosure on this scale was unheard of, and almost everyone believed that abuse of men was extremely rare. Male survivor activists found the silence and stigma to be almost impermeable. Yet by the turn of the century, men were coming out in large numbers about sexual abuse by men. Their memories of abuse, often forgotten for many years prior, were usually corroborated by the offenders' own admissions or by contemporaneous Church records of accusations against the offender. Court verdicts and public opinion were favorable. Although the False Memory Syndrome Foundation and other countermovement groups criticized some of the cases and used one famous retracted accusation (against Chicago Cardinal Bernardin) as evidence for the unreliability of recovered memories, most of the accusers seemed immune from wider criticism, perhaps because of the solid corroboration for their accusations (Investigative Staff 2003).

In short, these survivors benefited from the activism in the decades preceding them. Changes in cultural views, treatment, research about prevalence, and available tactics and rhetoric for disclosure of abuse all influenced the clergy cases, as did the male survivors' movement that spun off in the late 1980s. They also benefited from professional treatment, expert opinions from therapists about the effects and prevalence of abuse, advocacy from nonprofit organizations, and, in a few cases, extensions of the statutes of limitations. But without the activists who began the whole thing, survivors of abuse by priests would not have been able to stand without shame and pursue justice. If an early activist had been told in 1980 that twenty-five years later, the fruits of her movement would entail male survivors standing up to the Catholic Church, she would probably have been baffled and a bit unhappy. What about girls who are abused by their fathers, she might have asked? What about the problem of male dominance? Why isn't anyone talking about the patriarchal nature of the Catholic Church (Farragher, et al. 2003)? Why aren't girls abused by clergy getting media attention? And, again, what about incest, which remains the most common form of child sexual abuse? Yet the ideas of speaking out, building on experiential knowledge, confronting offenders, and confronting institutions' complicity in abuse rather than seeing it as the action of aberrant perverts, came from feminist and single-issue survivor activists. They dovetailed neatly with the public health advocacy and visibility politics of their descendants in the 2000s.

The men who were sexually abused by priests reaped the benefits of a movement that never dreamed they existed, and that sought to remedy abuse that they believed was overwhelmingly experienced by girls in families. Their critique of the institutional cover-up within the Church, and of the cultural forces of homophobia and male pride that increased their shame and made them hesitate to speak up, was consistent with the earlier movements' frames, building on the male survivors' movement and the institutional critiques of the feminist survivors' movement. But the clergy survivors also reaped the benefits of gender inequality, receiving a degree of credibility that female accusers rarely received, and homophobia, which made the condemnation of abusive priests more palatable since it built on the age-old notion of the homosexual as child molester. Was this a movement success, a case of cooptation, or a failure? And for whom: the feminist survivors' movement, the single-issue movement, the countermovement, nonprofits and advocacy groups, treatment organizations, criminal justice, legislative efforts, or public health and education? The answer is far from straightforward since different parties had different goals, priorities, and political outlooks. Some elements of feminist and single-issue survivors' agendas and discourses shaped the priest cases and societal approaches to child sexual abuse more broadly, but others did not survive to do so. Their influence occurred only in conjunction with that of major institutions, the state, and mass media, which attenuated and redirected activists' goals and discourses. In succeeding, activists lost control of their own agenda.

The feminist movement against child sexual abuse arose in response to institutional and cultural silence about child sexual abuse and the woeful inadequacy of resources for children and adult survivors alike. It broke the silence and brought incest and child sexual abuse to the attention of the public, putting it on the agenda of government and nonprofit organizations that had focused more on physical child abuse. The first activists redefined child sexual abuse, using what they had learned from anti-rape work to understand it in systemic terms as a form of domination of children and women, rather than as the fault of the victim. Their written works were widely read and set the parameters for much of the later discussion. The feminist self-help groups that emerged shortly afterwards melded the emerging political analysis of internalized oppression with existing lay counseling techniques and their own analysis of child sexual abuse to produce and disseminate grassroots therapeutic techniques for survivors. Studying their own experiences for generalizable features of abuse, they discussed unwilling feelings of sexual arousal during abuse, abuse by women, and the persistent sense of self-hatred, shame, and fear that remained long after the abuse ended. In concert with feminist therapists who explored similar territory, they sparked a much wider, single-issue survivors' movement that was an engine for mainstreaming of the issue.

The single-issue survivors' movement drew a broader constituency, including women who were not feminists, men, and people from a range of political backgrounds and religious affiliations. The movement continued to value the experiences of survivors, like the feminist movements, but those experiences were more varied because the constituency was more varied. As a result, the single-issue movement took up issues like the abuse of boys, female offenders, and the effects of abuse on religious faith, parenting, and heterosexual relationships. In doing so, it widened both its appeal and its distance from feminism and other progressive movements, which increasingly sided with the countermovement and its critique of state intervention and infringements on civil liberties.

Like the movements against rape, domestic violence, postpartum depression, medicalized childbirth, and many others, the initial feminist movement against child sexual abuse moved far into institutions, with many of its goals and activities taken up by hospitals, mental health centers, nonprofit organizations, police departments, social service agencies, and government agencies (Davis 2005; Martin 2005; Matthews 1994; Taylor 1996). Like these other movements, it saw many of its ideas enter mainstream media and change the way people understood victims, offenders, and social responses. Unlike the other movements, however, it spawned a powerful countermovement and possessed considerable internal diversity. This internal diversity, combined with the existence of a large industry dedicated to professional treatment and intervention, facilitated the entrance of some elements of movement critique into the mainstream and the exclusion of others.

It was selection processes within the state and mass media that sorted these out. Unsurprisingly, the medical elements of both feminist and single-issue movements, those that focused on treatment and symptoms, received play in both policy and media. The corresponding emphases on reclaiming the self from internalized oppression and the importance of solidarity and mutual support among survivors did not. Similarly, activists' calls for prosecution of offenders and humane treatment of witnesses were more appealing to a criminal justice state than their critiques of the family, major institutions, and the state itself for facilitating or condoning abuse. These selection processes were quite concrete: federal grant funding focused on specific priority areas; police, judicial, and child protective agencies sought training on particular issues; school systems contracted for prevention programming that would not elicit major objections from parents. Mass media chose stories that would grab readers' attention, framed them in terms that resonated with existing beliefs, and sought quotations from credentialed experts (Koopmans 2004; Rochon 1998; Ryan 1991).

The countermovement was subject to the same selection processes. Its critique of memory recovery resonated within the mass media, where parents' narratives of losing their children, therapeutic malpractice, and experimental research demonstrating the implantation of false memories were readily comprehensible and attention-grabbing. Within the state and policy, however, it had less success. Few funding initiatives or government agencies dealt with memory or its recovery, and the issue was salient primarily within the court system, where decisions were made to exclude testimony based on recovered memories. Although countermovement activists sought to influence legislation and child welfare services, they were usually unsuccessful, partly because the countermovement framed itself as not being concerned with child sexual abuse itself.

As the issue of child sexual abuse became mainstreamed, many activists dropped out of the movement or focused on other issues, a common pattern following institutionalization (Meyer 2006). Many others worked with the state in a variety of relationships, but their access continued to be shaped by selection processes favoring experts over laypeople and medical or criminal approaches over more overtly political ones. As some organizations formed closer relationships as quasi-governmental organizations, sub-contractors, or clients of the state, they gained influence and resources, but lost autonomy. They were joined by a re-politicized self-help movement that felt the need to respond to the countermovement's attacks. In the wake of all this, activists who sought new ways to combat abuse crafted a public health approach that built on the visibility politics of the self-helpers, the institutional analysis of the feminists, and the political savvy of those who worked with the state. They deliberately attempted to frame their approach through advertising campaigns that resonated with mainstream themes and in community organizing campaigns that resonated within specific cultures.

The central role of knowledge creation and contestation in all wings of the movement and its opponents suggests an important but neglected engine of social change. While Rochon (1998) insightfully recognizes the role of authoritative knowledge in cultural change, lay activists also play an important role in producing, disputing, and publicizing knowledge that aims to change culture, policy, and institutional practices. Other social movements also engage in knowledge contests, such as those over race and intelligence, causes of poverty, gender and scientific aptitude, effective treatment for AIDS or breast cancer, childbirth practices, and so forth. The contemporary state and major institutions rely on specialized knowledge, especially psychological and medical knowledge, to design and implement programs including child welfare, therapy or treatment, and criminal justice. As a result, challenges to knowledge and the construction of new knowledge have emerged as an important form of resistance.

All of the waves of this movement were hybrid in organizational form, combining therapeutic politics, knowledge creation, and attempts to restructure institutions. Hybrid organizations are common in social movements (Matthews 1994; Minkoff 2002; Taylor 1996). They are internally diverse, combining different elements, primarily advocacy and self-help or service provision; they may also combine ideologies or frames, as activists against child sexual abuse did. Beyond organizations themselves, the overall movement against child sexual abuse was internally diverse. While this hybrid nature undeniably helped activists against child sexual abuse to sustain organizations, by allowing them access to funding for services or training (Minkoff 2002), it did not determine the degree to which their goals were transformed as they entered the mainstream. Instead, selection processes worked on therapeutic and institutional elements alike, giving individualized and less challenging elements of both approaches preferential access to the mainstream. (See table 1.2 in the Introduction and table 8.1 in chapter 8.)

Because hybridity is a common form for movement organizations, its consequences for activists against child sexual abuse have wider implications. Hybridity is a route to resource stability (Minkoff 2002), but not a determinant of substantive outcomes. Instead, selection processes depend on the intersection of movements' particular goals, structures, and frames with political and cultural opportunities. Some therapeutic "services" offered by activists—self-help and 12-step groups, victim advocates in the court system—became widespread and received funding, while others—emphasizing overcoming internalized oppression or fostering solidarity among survivors through peer support—did not. Some institutional changes that they advocated—more sensitive treatment of witnesses in the court system, increased prosecution of offenders, more options for professional treatment—became widespread and received funding, while others—dismantling male dominance within the family, the church, and the state—did not. The same is probably true for other hybrid movements. None of this should blind us to the significance of the changes at both "therapeutic" and "institutional" levels.

Activists against child sexual abuse sought to transform their feelings by challenging the institutions and cultural narratives that produced them, particularly those that produced feelings of shame, invisibility, and worthlessness. They constructed a therapeutic politics that many long-time activists—and social movement theorists—did not recognize as political. But the forms that activism against child sexual abuse took typify the multiple forms that other social movements take in the contemporary period. These forms are more varied and diverse than most definitions of politics—whether academic or political—would suggest.

I hope that this book contributes to a rethinking of the tired distinction between the therapeutic and the political. For activists against child sexual abuse, as for those in the women's, civil rights, environmental, peace, and gay and lesbian movements, social change was about making a different world. This required rethinking what was possible, forming new kinds of relationships and institutions, and ridding themselves of the influences of oppression in their own minds and communities. Few theorists or activists believe that deep and broad social change can be achieved without fundamental change in how people feel, what they believe, and how they negotiate their relationships with each other. Few theorists or activists believe that deep and broad social change can be achieved without changing public policy or the law, or without changing cultural representations.

Our identities and sense of self, our inner worlds, are connected to the larger culture and to the state and public policy. When the state undertakes projects of social control, their effects extend to our identities. Conversely, when social movements try to transform individual thoughts and feelings, these changes echo in culture and policy and ultimately have the potential to diminish state domination. Resistance to therapeutic coercion need not take the form of abandoning concern with subjectivity or collective identity, but can entail reconstructing subjectivity, emotion, and identity in ways that work against coercion. Such resistance is not always successful, and most often, like other forms of resistance, its outcomes are mixed and unpredictable. However, dismissing therapeutic modes of resistance misses a major engine of social change.

These questions are central to how we understand contemporary politics. They tell us about how our lives are shaped and controlled by our contexts, how our very sense of self can be a social product, and how ordinary citizens can change their lot. They cannot do so simply by lobbying for policy change, or simply by meeting in support groups, but must do both, in order to target the intersections between state actions, how people understand the world, and how people think and feel about themselves.

Notes

Introduction

1. It is impossible to obtain accurate information about the prevalence of child sexual abuse. Estimates of frequency vary greatly, depending on the methodology used and definition of child sexual abuse. Studies that rely on incidents reported to the government show lower rates of child sexual abuse, because many cases are not reported to authorities. More reliable statistics come from random surveys of the population, but these vary considerably in quality and findings. In general, studies that ask about specific experiences without labeling those experiences as "abuse" find higher rates of abuse (Bolen 2001, chap. 5; Hopper 2007). Studies that define abuse solely in terms of rape find lower rates than those that define it to include other forms of unwanted sexual contact, while those that include noncontact experiences (such as indecent exposure, sexually threatening or explicit talk, exposure to pornography, etc.) find the highest rates (Bolen 2001, chap. 5; Hopper 2007; Russell and Bolen 2000). National random sample studies find rates of sexual abuse ranging from 8 percent to 30 percent for girls, with a mean prevalence of 25 percent when the results of all valid studies are combined (Bolen 2001: 74). For boys, estimates range from 6 percent (Collins 1995) to 16 percent (Finkelhor 1990). Bolen estimated the mean prevalence of sexual abuse of boys found in national random surveys at 9 percent. For an estimate based on a meta-analysis of existing studies, combined with adjustment for varying methodologies, see Bolen and Scannapieco 1999; they estimate lifetime prevalence of child sexual abuse for girls at 30–40 percent and for boys at at least 13 percent.

There are fewer methodologically sound studies of the frequency of incest. Russell (2000: 211–12) argues, based on her own 1978 research, that 16 percent of females experience incestuous abuse. Other evidence about the prevalence of incest comes from research on sexually transmitted diseases, specifically gonorrhea, in children. Stewart (1992, cited in Sacco 2002: 82) reports that, when the parents and siblings of a girl with gonorrhea agree to be tested themselves, half test positive. Yet, Sacco shows, this seemingly indisputable evidence historically has been vigorously contested. In the late 1890s, improvements in technique allowed doctors to test for gonorrhea on a widespread basis, and they found that the infection was common in girls across ethnic and class groups, particularly those between the ages of five and nine, and they found that many of these girls' fathers also tested positive for gonorrhea (Sacco 2002: 81). Rather than conclude that the girls had been sexually assaulted by their fathers, doctors and scientists developed improbable theories about the casual transmission of gonorrhea and focused on "sanitation" as a solution.

There are also debates over whether the rate of child sexual abuse is increasing or decreasing. After growing dramatically in the 1980s, reports to authorities of child sexual abuse declined by 40 percent during the 1990s, and sexual victimization reports by adolescents who were included in the National Crime Victimization Survey also decreased, by 56 percent (Finkelhor and Jones 2004, 1–2). Finkelhor and Jones suggest that this decrease reflects to an actual decrease in child sexual abuse, due to prevention and deterrence and the increase in the number of offenders who are incarcerated.

2. Exact figures on the gender of victims are difficult to come by. A comprehensive survey of incidents reported to Catholic dioceses found that 19.1% of the victims were female (John Jay College of Criminal Justice 2004). The Survivors' Network of those Abused by Priests (SNAP) reports that "roughly half of our 3,600 members are women" ("The Snap Viewpoint." Available at http://www.snapnetwork.org/clohessys_tough_ questions/clohessy_questions_Page2.htm (accessed 1/20/06)). There is abundant evidence of female victims, despite very sparse press coverage. See Farragher and Carroll (2003) and SNAP, "Female Victims of Clergy Abuse." Available at http://www.snapnetwork.org/female_victims/female_ victims_index.htm (accessed 1/20/06).

3. New social movements theorists made related, although not identical, arguments. See Buechler 1995, Cohen 1985, Melucci 1989. Several other scholars examine the changes in social movements in late modernity. Taylor (1996, 101–102), drawing on Giddens as well as new social movements theorists Melucci and Touraine, suggests that self-help movements emerge in response to grievances such as the decline of community and male domination within the institutions, and that medical, legal, and psychological discourses provide bases for identity. I am less concerned with the novel nature of contemporary challenges than with the interactions between therapeutic movements and the state, which change over time but are not uniquely contemporary.

4. Scholars writing about how social movements change culture use a variety of concepts: *frames, discourses, values, narratives, ideology,* and *meanings*, each tapping a somewhat different dimension of culture (Benford 1997; Benford and Snow 2000; Polletta 2002; Rochon 1998; Skrentney 2002; Snow 2004; Snow et al.1986; Steinberg 1999, 2002; Whittier 2002). Others focus on it attempts to redefine collective identities, or the definitions of who is included in a group and what that group is like (Polletta and Jasper 2000; Taylor and Whittier 1992). The constraints of the existing culture have been termed "discursive opportunity structures" (Ferree et al. 2002; W. Gamson 2004; Koopmans and Statham 1999), "cultural resources" (Williams 1995, Williams and Kubal 1999), "cultural resonance" (Rochon 1998), "discursive fields" (Steinberg 1999), and "emotional opportunities" (Whittier 2001). In discussing how movement groups interpret child sexual abuse—how they explain its causes, effects, and proposed solutions—I use both *discourse* and *frame*. Discourses are broad systems of meaning, whereas frames are more discrete and specific interpretations of particular issues or events. For example, the state or a movement organization might draw on medical discourse (a system of making sense of actions in terms of pathology or illness) to frame sexual offenders as pedophiles. In discussing how movement groups understand themselves, as individuals and as a group, I use *collective identity*. Unlike some scholars, I do not draw a sharp distinction between politics and culture; instead, I focus on specific elements of both, such as public policies, institutional practices, mass-media coverage, and how people discuss child sexual abuse in daily life.

5. I do not intend an allegiance to evolutionary or sociobiological theory (see Koopmans 2004). Quite the contrary.

6. Another extensive literature deals with child sexual abuse itself, rather than social responses to it.

7. For example, Jenkins (1998: 7) writes that, during moral panics, "professionals, the media, and assorted interest groups...argue that the problem is quantitatively and qualitatively far more severe than anyone could reasonably suppose." Davis (2005) is largely an exception to the moral panic approach.

8. Victor (1998: 560) argues that moral panics are based on "cognition and communication behavior," and are thus different from mass hysteria or emotional contagion, which focus on "psychological characteristics of individuals." However, in the collective behavior tradition, the precise point of mass hysteria theories is that individuals adopt behaviors in groups that they would not adopt on their own; that under the influence of groups, they *become* irrational, quite apart from their individual psychological characteristics. The focus in most writing on moral panics is on the irrational nature of people's fears and beliefs.

9. While the moral panic approach recognizes the influence of social movements in passing, it focuses on professionals and others who support the cause from "outside," rather than grass-roots groups who are agitating on their own behalf. Collective actors are seen as emerging as a result of the moral panic, rather than as influencing changing views of the issue. For example, Victor (1998: 2) writes, "A moral panic often gives rise to social

movements aimed at eliminating the threatening deviants and may generate moral crusades and political struggles over the use of the law...."

10. I located these through interviewees, at conferences, on the Internet, and by signing up to receive organizational mailings.

11. The subject headings varied over time, and included "child abuse," "child welfare," "child molesters," "child molestation," and "incest."

Chapter 1

1. "An Introduction to the New York Radical Feminists, p. 4." N.d., probably early 1970s. SSC, WL, Box 27, Folder 259, "Revolution."

2. Terry Hardy, "N.Y. Women Discuss Rape," *The Militant,* May 7, 1971. SSC, Women's Liberation Collection, Box 24, Folder 231. "U.S. Subjects B."

3. But see Gordon (1988) on early 1900s activism on the issue, of which second-wave feminists were unaware.

4. Rush began this analysis in her NYRF talk, and published a full version in the feminist journal *Chrysalis* in 1977.

5. I heard these stories from several interviewees; published reports are also widespread.

6. Erin VanBronkhorst 1973. "Rape Stories Spark Discussion," pp. 1 and 5. *Pandora: The Seattle Women's Newspaper*, October 30, Vol. IV, No. 2:1 et. seq. Herstory Microfilm Collection, Herstory 1, Continuing Update, Reel 6.

7. Sharon Haywood. 1974. "Can Sex Offenders Be Cured?" *Pandora,* May, p. 1 et seq. Herstory Microfilm Collection, Herstory 1: Continuing Update, Reel 6. The article drew only one distinction between men who have assaulted adults and those who have assaulted children: "The problems with child molesters differ somewhat in that these men avoid adult women altogether. The child molester rarely employs violence but rather uses seduction" (p. 10).

8. "Karate Union to Begin Spring Classes." *Pandora* (n.d.; probably 1974). Herstory Microfilm Collection, Herstory 1: Continuing Update, Reel 6.

9. *On Our Way,* Dec./Jan. 1974–1975, p. 4. SSC, WL, Box 7, Folder 67, "Women's Liberation—Connecticut."

10. *D.C. Area Feminist Alliance News,* 1978. Vol. 2, No. 5, Nov/Dec. p. 3. SSC, WL, Box 8, Folder 68, "Washington, D.C."

11. No date, probably mid-1970s. "Southern Female Rights Union Program for Female Liberation." SSC, WL, Box 8, Folder 79, "Louisiana: New Orleans—Southern Female Rights Union."

12. *New Haven Women's Liberation Newsletter,* Vol. II, No. 2. (N.d.— probably 1972.) SSC, Women's Liberation Collection, Box 7, Folder 64, "Women's Liberation—Connecticut."

13. Women's Action Alliance, 1973. Women's Action Alliance Directory, p. 10. SSC, Women's Liberation Collection, Box 6, Folder 41, "U.S./Directories."

14. For examples, see: "Women Against Violence in Pornography and Media," newsletter, Sept. 1978, 2(8), SSC, WL, Box 27, Folder 253; "Men-R; Pornography," Alan Berger, 1979. "Pornography: Is Censorship the

Answer?" *Boston Real Paper*, Sept. 14: 1, SSC, WL, Box 27, Folder 253, "Men-R; Pornography"; Women Against Pornography flier, n.d., SSC, WL, Box 27, Folder 253, "Men-R; Pornography."

15. The subsequent conferences were: Copenhagen 1980, Nairobi 1985, Beijing 1995. United Nations web page, available at www.un.org (accessed July 20, 2007).

16. Alabama Department of Archives and History. Available at www.archives.state.al.us/women/sources.html (accessed July 20, 2007).

17. Newsletter, Lucy Parsons Women's Coalition, August 1977. SSC, WL, Box 27, Folder 252, "Political Action." The group was based in the Boston area.

18. The NIMH grant was for a WAR program entitled "Community Action Strategies to Stop Rape" (CASSR). The other community organization to receive an NIMH grant was the Los Angeles Commission on Assaults Against Women (Matthews 1994: 44).

19. This program, later renamed the Giaretto Institute, is known for its treatment of entire families.

20. The only indexed references to "children, sexual abuse of" in *Gyn/Ecology* are to a discussion of child brides in India (119–125) and a critique of Freud's interpretation of Dora case. Although Dora's age (14) at the time of the traumatic kiss from Herr K is mentioned in the discussion, it does not frame Daly's retelling or interpretation.

Chapter 2

1. There were at least a handful of other similar groups, including Christopher Street in Minneapolis, and a Vermont group.

2. Other activity around incest in Boston prior to 1980 included feminist clinicians and researchers, including Judith Herman.

3. Before IR, Karen founded a similar organization, INSIST.

4. Grant Request to Women in Crisis Committee, Episcopal Diocese of Massachusetts, from Incest Resources, July 31, 1981. Files of Incest Resources, private collection of author.

5. Minutes of IR meetings, 1981, private collection of author.

6. Grant request to Women in Crisis Committee, Episcopal Diocese of Massachusetts, from Incest Resources, 1989. Files of Incest Resources, private collection of author.

7. Grant request to Women in Crisis Committee, 1981, pp. 2–3.

8. Grant proposal to Women in Crisis Committee, 1989, p. 1.

9. Andrea, for example, brought an activist from Connecticut to speak in Boston.

10. This included opposition to the anti-gay Briggs Initiative in 1980, and ongoing organizing against violence against women and lesbians and gay men, including: Lesbians Against Police Violence, organized in response to a 1979 police raid on the lesbian bar Amelia's, and Women Against Violence and Pornography.

11. Other activists worked on child sexual abuse in San Francisco at this time, including Diana Russell, who reportedly came briefly to Pleiades, but remained centered in her own networks; the writer Jean Swallow; and others. There were several other support groups, a fledgling abuse-prevention program in the schools, and family service agencies dealing with incest. Letter from Maggie Jochild, January 25, 1982. Private collection of author.

12. Letter to We Want the Music Collective, from San Francisco Support Group for Survivors of Childhood Sexual Abuse, July 17, 1981. Private collection of author.

13. Ibid.

14. Maggie Jochild estimated attendance at 150. Untitled document, notated "Planning notes for 2nd West Coast Women's Music Festival events by Pleiades ca. September 1981." Private collection of author.

15. Untitled document. Private collection of author, notated "Notes from a Pleiades planning session—after MWMF [Michigan Women's Music Festival]—possibly for Old Wives' Tale event." Likely early fall, 1981.

16. The workshop occurred shortly after the demise of the Pleiades, but the organizers and presenters were members of the Pleiades. Letter from Maggie Jochild, March 3, 1982, p.1. Private collection of author.

17. The Vermont group met biweekly and in early 1982 consisted of six women. Letter and flyer sent to Maggie Jochild, February 24, 1982. Private collection of author.

18. The Pleiades did meet organizers from the Child Assault Prevention Project at their Michigan workshop.

19. Letter from Karen, Incest Resources, to Cambridge Women's Center, December 30, 1980, p. 2. Files of Incest Resources, private collection of author.

20. Grant request to Women in Crisis Committee, 1981.

21. Incest Resources Brochure, n.d., early 1980s. Private collection of author.

22. Letter from Maggie Jochild to—, March 3, 1982. Private collection of author.

23. Ibid.

24. Some facilitators were studying to become counselors, and the majority of participants in the group had sought professional psychotherapy. Research based on a sample from IR found that 98 percent had been in professional therapy, ranging from 8 months to 15 years, with a mean time in therapy of 6.4 years. 95 percent in had been in individual therapy, 65 percent in group therapy, and 63 percent in both (Westerlund 1992: 31–33).

25. M— [Maggie Jochild], USA, "The Long Struggle Out of Incest Distress." *Present Time* 59: April 1985, p. 29. For more information about RC, see Kaufmann (2004). RC was controversial for many reasons, including accusations of authoritarianism and sexual misconduct by leaders. These issues had relatively little effect on the local work within RC on child sexual abuse, however, until the 1990s.

26. Respondents reported participating in mixed-sex RC support groups on both coasts; a 1982 workshop for survivors of child sexual abuse in Los Angeles led by Cheryl Bain, which two Pleiades members attended, and which Maggie Jochild reported drew many men and heterosexuals; and

workshops on "early sexual memories." Joan Karp, who coordinated work on early sexual memories in RC, led numerous such workshops at least into the 1990s. Despite this activity, most respondents who were involved with RC did not find it a supportive place to counsel about their experiences of child sexual abuse.

27. M—[Maggie Jochild], USA, "The Long Struggle Out of Incest Distress."

28. As far as I can determine, this internal group largely disbanded after the purge of an influential leader and a ban by national RC leaders on workshops or support groups focused on incest or child sexual abuse in the early 1990s.

29. After the first Bass workshop, for example, attendees founded "For Crying Out Loud," a newsletter for survivors.

30. M—, USA [Maggie Jochild], "The Long Struggle Out of Incest Distress."

31. Letter from Maggie Jochild, December 31, 1981, p. 1. Private collection of author.

32. Respondents from both IR and Pleiades noted discussion in support groups of some participants' sexual arousal during abusive experiences. "Sexual feelings for children" was one possible topic mentioned in Pleiades' planning notes for a 1981 workshop. Untitled document. Private collection of author, notated "Notes from a Pleiades planning session—after MWMF [Michigan Women's Music Festival]—possibly for Old Wives' Tale event." Likely early fall, 1981.

33. Letter from Maggie Jochild, January 12, 1982, p. 1; Letter from Maggie Jochild, January 1, 1982, p. 2. Private collection of author.

34. E.g., letter from Karen, Incest Resources, to Andrea, Cambridge Women's Center, Dec. 30, 1980, p. 2. Files of Incest Resources, private collection of author.

35. There is also considerable feminist theory on standpoint and epistemology. For feminist theorizing on the significance of experience and daily life, see Smith 1987. On standpoint and epistemology, see Hartsock 1998; Collins 1990. For discussion of debates over experience as related to trauma, see Doane and Hodges 2001; Champagne 1996; Kilby 2007.

36. Letter from Maggie Jochild, October 12, 1981. Private collection of author.

37. Letter and flyer sent to Maggie Jochild, February 24, 1982. Private collection of author.

38. Letter from Maggie Jochild, March 3, 1982, p. 2. Private collection of author.

39. A section of the APA focusing on women formed in 1973 and fostered a network for feminist psychologists (Society for the Psychology of Women, "Division 35." Retrieved June 10, 2008 (www.apa.org/divisions/div35/).

40. Transcript of tape of Kathy Morrissey's 1982 Address to the American Psychiatric Association. Tape, private collection of author.

Chapter 3

1. Or postmodern, depending on the theorist (Nolan 1998; Giddens 1991).

2. For example, Nolan (1998: 15) contrasts modern societies with premodern ones where suffering was not a cause for complaint about

victimization, but was viewed as a divinely determined part of life and as preparation for salvation: "With the devaluing of these older moral orders and the greater cultural emphasis on the self and on individual rights, Americans today are more inclined to blame someone or something else for whatever difficulties they face."

3. All discussion of NCCAN grants is based on my own analysis.

4. See chapter 5. Densen-Gerber later was the target of investigations and outrage over misuse of Odyssey House funds for personal expenses and other problems within the Odyssey Houses; she remained controversial for years afterwards (Tanne 2003).

5. The federal Bureau of Family Services was founded at this time and oversaw such efforts.

6. In practice, the states' responses to the 1962 amendments fell short of their mandate. The states manipulated the reimbursement formula to receive the higher rate without providing the services required, while the services that were provided often "bore no relation to the model of therapeutic intervention" (Polsky 1991: 166).

7. Administration for Children and Families. "Social Services Block Grant, Program Overview." Available at http://www.acf.hhs.gov/programs/ocs/ssbg/docs/overv.htm (accessed September 28, 2005).

8. Ibid.

9. In constant 2007 dollars, it disbursed $149,695,760 in 1975 and $98,162,646 in 1978. Calculations are based on grants listed in NCCAN Clearinghouse Compendium of Discretionary Grants, Fiscal Years 1975–1995. Published September 1996, by NCCAN (henceforth cited as "NCCAN Compendium"). Figures are rounded. Grant amounts of individually cited grants are not adjusted for inflation.

10. NCCAN Compendium, p. 47. The Parents' United grant was for $90,000; the others ranged between $351,730 and $382,800. In addition, a grant to the Odyssey House, a New York City-based nonprofit, in the "adolescent treatment" priority area focused on service delivery for "treating adolescent sexual exploitation." NCCAN Compendium, p. 49.

11. Ibid, p. 89.

12. Administration for Children and Families, "Social Services Block Grant, Program Overview." Funding went from $8.166 billion in 1979 to $5.044 billion in 1982; by 1988, funding stood at $4.586 billion (in constant 2007 dollars).

13. Russell received NCCAN funding for additional research and analysis focusing on abuse within the family in 1980. NCCAN Compendium, p. 96.

14. Ibid.

15. Ibid., pp. 93–94. The institutes were the Joseph J. Peters Institute (Philadelphia), the Knoxville Institute for Sexual Abuse Treatment (Knoxville, Tenn.), the Child Abuse Unit for Studies Education, and Services (CAUSES) (Chicago), and the Sexual Assault Center at the Harborview Medical Center (Seattle) (Kinnear 1995: 105). Earlier grants had funded the centers in Chicago and Knoxville, as well as similar programs in Minneapolis and Albuquerque (Marks 1980).

16. Ibid., pp. 97–98.

17. Ibid., p. 100.

18. "Public Law 97–193: National Child Abuse Prevention Week." (1982). Text from: United States Public Laws. Available from Congressional Universe (Online Service), Bethesda, Md.: Congressional Information Service. "Public Law 98–7: National Child Abuse Prevention Month." (1983). Text from: United States Public Laws. Available from Congressional Universe (Online Service), Bethesda, Md.: Congressional Information Service.

19. NCCAN Compendium, pp. 155–156.

20. In 1986, Congress amended the Act further, renamed it the Child Abuse and Pornography Act, and again modifying penalties for child pornography, and prohibiting its production. "Public Law 98–292: Child Protection Act" (1984). Text from: United States Public Laws. Available from Congressional Universe (Online Service), Bethesda, Md.: Congressional Information Service. "Public Law 99–628: Child Sexual Abuse and Pornography Act" (1986). Text from: United States Public Laws. Available from Congressional Universe (Online Service), Bethesda, Md.: Congressional Information Service.

21. The study was funded by NCCAN and based on data from 1987 and 1988 on custody-visitation disputes in 12 states.

22. The National Committee for the Prevention of Child Abuse, a nonprofit with chapters in several locations, received grants to its Rhode Island and Chicago chapters. The Chicago grant also supported planning for the Seventh National Conference on Child Abuse and Neglect. Organized by a variety of groups over the years including the American Humane Association, these biannual conferences were organized by the federal Children's Bureau in HHS by 2005. (Administration for Children and Families, National Clearinghouse on Child Abuse and Neglect Information, "Fifteenth National Conference on Child Abuse and Neglect." Available at http://nccanch.acf.hhs.gov/profess/conferences/index.cfm (accessed February 4, 2006). NCPCA information from Family Resource Coalition, "Family Support Programs and the Prevention of Child Abuse." Available at www.fww.org/articles/misc/frc.htm (accessed October 4, 2005).

23. NCCAN Compendium, p. 185.

24. Ibid., pp. 185–188.

25. Ibid., pp. 211–218, 281–290.

26. Ibid., p. 360. Information on NCAC from The National Children's Advocacy Center, available at http://www.nationalcac.org/ncac/history.html (accessed October 13, 2005).

27. Eleven grants were made in 1985 under the priority area "coordination and handling of reported cases of child sexual abuse by child protective services, police agencies, and the justice system;" and six under "coordination among social service and law enforcement and improvement of response to reports of abuse. Four of these focused directly on multidisciplinary support, aiming to "provide adequate advanced training for personnel other than child protective services workers to assist those workers in the identification, prevention, and/or the treatment of child abuse, including sexual abuse." (Ibid., pp. 206–210, 230–232.)

28. Ibid.

29. Ibid.

30. Ibid., pp. 220–230, 239–240.

31. At the time of this writing, an excerpt was available online at http://www.youtube.com/watch?v=agK2uZBNbnU (accessed June 10, 2008).
32. NCCAN Compendium, pp. 278–81, 297–298, 299–300, 302.
33. Ibid., pp. 270–271.
34. Ibid., pp. 321–322, 331–333, 341–342, 344, 351–352, 358, 363, 369–371.
35. Ibid., p. 375.
36. Figures are based on my own count and analysis of these cases. Of 18 other multiple-offender cases examined, 14 ended in convictions of at least one of the principal defendants; eight of these had been overturned by early 2002, usually based on problems with the questioning or testimony of child witnesses. A vast amount of literature documents these cases from various points of view. By reading multiple sources one can get a fairly accurate accounting of the known facts. (These rarely include any clear indication of what actually happened to the children in question.) For a range of approaches, see Cheit 2007; Crewdson 1988; DeYoung 2007; Hechler 1988; Nathan and Scott 2001; Snedeker 1995; Wright 1994.
37. See Chapter 5.
38. U.S. Department of Health and Human Services, January, 1985. "Model Child Care Standards Act—Guidance to States to Prevent Child Abuse in Day Care Facilities." P. iii. HHS guidelines followed those put forward earlier by other sources.

Chapter 4

1. Voices in Action, ""History." Available at http://www.voices-action.org/about.html (accessed April 19, 2002).
2. Interview, Mary.
3. ISRNI, "More Detailed Description of ISRNI." Available at www.zianet.com/ISRNI/Doc-six.html. (accessed July 16, 1998).
4. Ibid.
5. ISRNI, "A Beginning List of Groups/Programs/Newsletters Outside North America Founded and Operated by Survivors of Childhood Sexual Abuse." Private collection of author.
6. These moved to the Internet in the late 1990s.
7. I have insufficient data on inclusion of gay men or bisexuals.
8. The organizations did not maintain lists of members that contained data on race, class, sexuality, religion, or political viewpoint. Comments are based on my observation of conferences and organizational newsletters.
9. SIA modified AA's twelve steps more than ISA, and barred current perpetrators of abuse from its meetings. ISA was open to supporters of survivors. The groups differed somewhat in their language, with SIA using more gender-neutral language and referring to a Higher Power more often than to God, while ISA used the term God; SIA used more language from the broader self-help movement, such as the "inner child." Information on SIA from: www.siawso.org; on ISA from: www.lafn.org/medical/isa/home.html. Thanks to Lindsey Dawson for comparison of the groups.

Chapter 5

1. One other article included a personal disclosure of abuse from a principal, Frank Osanka, active against child pornography (Bridge 1978: 69), but it was only mentioned in passing.
2. The artistic director of the Minneapolis Children's Theater Company was charged with sexually abusing several children in the company (Olson 1984).
3. These were Joyce N. Thomas, director of the Division of Child Protection at Children's Hospital National Medical Center in Washington, D.C., and Dr. Gerald Foster, director of the Hampton University Center for Social Research.
4. She and others sued the Fresh Air Fund, winning a settlement and changes in screening practices (Hechler 1985, 1988).
5. One person charged was not indicted; convictions of two others were overturned (Associated Press, 1989).
6. Charges against five of the seven McMartin defendants were dropped in 1986; one of the remaining defendants was acquitted in 1990; the other was acquitted of most charges. The jury was deadlocked in the remaining charges, as was a subsequent jury on retrial, after which the charges were dismissed (DeYoung 2007: 11).
7. The 1984 edition listed a small number of books under other categories.
8. I included books from headings other than "On Healing" only if their focus was clearly on healing and/or self-help; I excluded first-person narratives, scholarly or political analyses, or other general books, and those that did not focus specifically on child sexual abuse.
9. These included 14 listed under other categories.

Chapter 6

1. This chapter is based on analysis of the FMSF newsletter between its founding year of 1992 and 2005. I coded every third issue of the newsletter, which was published 6 to 10 times per year. In addition, I selectively coded other issues when important items were referenced in the issues I coded in full. In citing from the FMSF Newsletters, I cite year, volume, and number. I cite title and author when available, but many items appeared without title or attribution. I used the electronic edition of the newsletter (available at fmsfonline.org; accessed July, 2006); no page numbers are available. In addition, I have drawn on the scant secondary sources on the countermovement (Champagne 1996; Davis 2005, 2000), and published writings by proponents and opponents of the FMSF position.
2. Meyer and Staggenborg refer to pairs of opposing movements, rather than movements and countermovements. I refer to the FMSF and its allies as a "countermovement" for ease of use.
3. For various perspectives on the debate over recovered memories, see Jim Hopper's comprehensive website, http://www.jimhopper.com; J. Freyd

and DePrince 2001; McNally 2003; Ross Cheit's Recovered Memory Project's documentation of cases at http://www.brown.edu/Departments/Taubman_Center/Recovmem/; and the website and materials of the False Memory Syndrome Foundation at www.fmsfonline.org.

4. The Recovered Memory Project, op. cit.

5. According to the FMSF's surveys in 1993 and 1997, "about 18 percent of accusations [against members] involved allegations of satanic ritual abuse." "Family Survey Update," *FMS Foundation Newsletter* 1997, 6(4) (henceforth cited as *Newsletter*).

6. See VOCAL of Missouri, "Fall 2004 State of the Family Report." Available at. www.vocalofmo.org/home.htm (accessed April 19, 2006).

7. *Newsletter* 1992, 1(8).

8. Information about IPT and Wakefield and Underwager comes from the Institute for Psychological Therapies, "Our Staff"; "Publications.". Available at http://www.ipt-forensics.com (accessed March 18, 2003). For publications prior to the establishment of the FMSF, see Wakefield, H., and Underwager, R., 1988, 1990, and 1992.

9. *Newsletter*, 1992, 1(8). Freyd saw them as indispensable, writing, "We would not exist without them," *Newsletter* 1992, 1(5).

10. Wakefield and Underwager became controversial after giving an interview to the pro-pedophilia publication *Paidika*, appearing to advocate pedophilia as a potentially responsible choice that could be beneficial to children, and suggesting what advocates ought to do to make pedophilia more socially acceptable. They denied these implications, but the interview circulated widely among survivors' groups and was used to discredit them as expert witnesses in child sexual abuse trials. Underwager resigned from the FMSF advisory board under pressure; Wakefield remained a member. For the interview, see *Paidika: The Journal of Pedophilia* 3(1):9 (June, 1993); for the FMSF response, see Lawrence 1993; for Underwager and Wakefield's somewhat dissembling response, see Underwager and Wakefield 1994.

11. *Newsletter* 1992, 1(3), 1992 1(8).

12. Ibid., 1(8).

13. "Who Are the Volunteers," ibid.

14. Ibid., 1(1).

15. Ibid., 1(8).

16. Pamela Freyd, "Dear Friends," *Newsletter* 1992, 1(8).

17. Ibid., 1(9).

18. Pamela Freyd, "Dear Friends," Ibid., 2(1).

19. *Newsletter* 1993, 2 (1).

20. Founded two years earlier by a woman who had retracted her accusation of abuse (*Newsletter* 1994, 3[7]), the newsletter was again published autonomously by retractors a year later (Diana Anderson, "A Newsletter of Our Own," *Newsletter* 1995, 4[3]).

21. *Newsletter* 1992, 1(1), 1(8); and 2006, 15(2).

22. *Newsletter* 1992, 1(8).

23. The chair was Charles Caviness, "a vice president and financial consultant with a major brokerage house" and active in other philanthropic work. "Fund-Raising," *Newsletter* 1994, 3(1).

24. "Great News—Matching Offer Surpassed!" *Newsletter* 1995, 4(3).

25. "How FMSF Money Is Spent," *Newsletter* 1995, 4(3). Percentages were for the period from March 1993 to February 1994. "FMSF Expenses March 1996–February 1997," *Newsletter* 1997, 6(7). "Financial Update," *Newsletter* 1999, 8(7) (FY 1998/99).

26. "FMS is in the language," *Newsletter* 2001, 10(2).

27. Pamela Freyd, "Dear Friends," *Newsletter* 2003, 12(5). The opinion was written by Justice Breyer in *Stogner v. California*, U.S. Supreme Court, 6/26/03.

28. *Newsletter* 1997, 6(4).

29. Pamela Freyd, "Dear Friends," *Newsletter* 2000, 9(5).

30. *Newsletter* 2001, 10(5).

31. Pamela Freyd, "Dear Friends," *Newsletter* 1999, 8(1).

32. *Newsletter* 1999, 8(1).

33. A Dad, *Newsletter* 1993, 2(6).

34. A Mom, *Newsletter* 1993, 2(6).

35. *Newsletter* 1993, 2(6).

36. *Newsletter* 1997, 6(4).

37. "Cult-Like Experience," *Newsletter* 1999, 8(1).

38. Pamela Freyd, "Dear Friends," *Newsletter* 1(2).

39. "Domains of Recovered Memories," *Newsletter* 1992, 1(6).

40. "American Psychiatric Association," *Newsletter* 1993, 2(6).

41. Review of "Progress and Controversy in the Study of Post-Traumatic Stress Disorders," by Richard J. McNally, which appeared in *Annual Review of Psychology*, 2003, vol. 54, pp. 229–252. *Newsletter* 2003, 12(2).

42. "Questions Raised by These Two Columns," *Newsletter* 1993, 2(1).

43. "American Psychiatric Association Convention," *Newsletter* 1993, 2(6).

44. Advisory board members also published books anthologizing newsletter commentaries. E.g., Harrison G. Pope, Jr., M.D. *Psychology Astray: Fallacies in Studies of 'Repressed Memory' and Childhood Trauma*. Upton Books. *Newsletter* 1998, 7(5).

45. "Evidence that is cited to show that recovered memories are true," *Newsletter*," 1993, 2(3). The study was Herman and Schatzow, 1987, "Recovery and Verification of Memories of Sexual Trauma," in *Psychoanalytic Psychology* 4(1), 1–14.

46. The primary critique, a legitimate one, was that subjects were in treatment and thus not representative, and the study failed to use a matched comparison group. The proposed alternative was to "do a community survey of several hundred random subjects, then select those who reported a history of childhood sexual abuse, regardless of whether they displayed any current psychopathology... [and] obtain a matched control group from the same community sample, comprised of individuals who reported similar rates of psychiatric disorder in their family trees and similar rates of adverse experiences in their childhood, but who had never been sexually abused." "Focus on Science," *Newsletter* 1996, 5(2).

47. Harrison Pope, M.D., "The Emperor's Tailoring," *Newsletter* 1997, 6(1).

48. See, e.g., Alan Feld, "Can Myths Be Created in Therapy?" *Newsletter* 2000, 9(2).

49. Pamela Freyd, "Dear Friends," *Newsletter* 1996, 5(8).

50. "What do we know about therapists?" *Newsletter* 1992, 1(9).
51. Pamela Freyd, "Dear Friends," *Newsletter* 1999, 8(1).
52. Mom of a Retractor, "Reconciliation with Your Daughter: Excerpts from the Indiana Conference," *Newsletter* 1996, 5(8).
53. *Newsletter* 2003, 12(2).
54. Pamela Freyd, "Dear Friends," *Newsletter* 1994, 3(1).
55. "Focus on Science," *Newsletter* 1996, (5).
56. Pamela Freyd, "Dear Friends," *Newsletter* 2002, 11(1). (Results were also reported over successive newsletters.)
57. Pamela Freyd, "Dear Friends," *Newsletter* 2004, 14(6).
58. E.g., "Notices," 2000, 9(5).
59. *Newsletter* 1993, 2(1).
60. Mother and Father, *Newsletter* 1993, 2(3).
61. A Dad, *Newsletter* 1994, 3(7).
62. "Wills," *Newsletter* 1999, 8(4).
63. A not-so-grieving father. *Newsletter* 2004, 1(5).
64. "Common Sense and Statistics of Sexual Abuse," *Newsletter* 1992, 1(7).
65. "Excerpts from Child Maltreatment 2002," *Newsletter* 2004, 13(4).
66. Howard Fishman, "Commentary on Child Maltreatment Data: The Numbers Tell the Tale...Or Do They? *Newsletter* 2004, 13(4).
67. *Newsletter* 1995, 4(6).
68. Pamela Freyd, "Dear Friends," *Newsletter* 1994, 3(1).
69. "My Prayers," *Newsletter* 2000, 9(5).
70. Pamela Freyd, "Dear Friends," *Newsletter* 1993, 2(1).
71. "Researcher Request," *Newsletter* 1993, 2(1).
72. E.g., see Pamela Freyd, "Dear Friends," *Newsletter* 1993, 2(1).
73. Statistical significance was irrelevant to the surveys, which used nonrandom samples of families who had contacted the FMSF. Nevertheless, the use of "p-values," that is, scientific language, provided an impression of scientific validity. See, e.g., Pamela Freyd, "Dear Friends," *Newsletter* 2002, 11(2).
74. "Make a Difference," *Newsletter* 1999, 8(4).
75. "Publicity," *Newsletter* 1992, 1(8).
76. "Make a Difference," *Newsletter* 1995, 4(9).
77. E.g. "California," *Newsletter* 1996, 5(8); "Texas," *Newsletter* 1997, 6(1).
78. "Free Library Displays," *Newsletter* 1996, 5(5).
79. "Make a Difference," *Newsletter* 1997, 6(7).
80. "Make a Difference," *Newsletter* 1998, 7(8).
81. "Make a Difference," *Newsletter* 1995, 4(6).
82. Pamela Freyd, "Dear Friends," *Newsletter* 1995, 4(3). Noah's affiliation with the FMSF is unclear; one target of his pickets, David Calof (1998), reported that the FMSF sent Noah's contact information as the Seattle-area "volunteer coordinator." Noah's reported behavior during these demonstrations included shouting obscenities, racial and sexual insults, and placards with slogans accusing targets of being "femi-nazis" (Calof 1998).
83. "What Can Families Do?" *Newsletter* 1992, 1(9); "Seattle Families Picket Therapist's Office," *Newsletter* 1994, 3(4).

84. Pickets of Ellen Bass reported in Wisconsin ("Wisconsin," *Newsletter* 1997, 6[1]), the VOICES in Action Conference in Illinois in 1998 ("Protesting a Conference," *Newsletter* 1998, 7(8) and Field notes, VOICES in Action Conference; "Frustrated Families," *Newsletter* 1998, 7[7]), and the 1999 Incest Awareness Foundation conference (Field notes, IAF Conference). Picket of Judith Herman described in "Grannies Take a Stand," *Newsletter* 1999, 8(1). Picket of Laura Davis's 2002 appearance at the Midwest Conference on Child Sexual Abuse in Madison, Wisconsin, described in Nadeen Cool, "Accountability," *Newsletter* 2002, 11(5). FMSF members also protested to the hosts of Herman's speeches, the University of Wisconsin in Madison and Northwestern University. PR Newswire Association, July 5, 1995, *Mental Health Law Reporter*, April 1995.

85. See Calof 1998 for citation of trial transcripts.

86. "Mistaken Claims"; quote is from "Editor's Note, "Protesting a Conference," *Newsletter* 1998, 7(5). According to Calof (1998), posters used by Noah in demonstrations provided a backdrop to Pamela Freyd's public talks on two occasions.

87. "Legal Information," *Newsletter* 1992, 1(8).

88. "Legal Corner," *Newsletter* 1994, 3(4).

89. "Legal Articles Available," *Newsletter* 1996, 5(8).

90. For example, see the program for "Expert Testimony" and "Justice Gone Astray: Trauma, Memory, and Child Sexual Abuse," which qualified as continuing education for "psychologists, counselors, social workers, attorneys, and law enforcement personnel." "Notices," *Newsletter* 2002, 11(5).

91. "An Interesting Decision," *Newsletter* 1994, 3(1). *Daubert* superseded the 1923 *Frye* ruling that required the court "to determine whether the expert's methodology was generally accepted in the relevant scientific community." *Daubert* required hearings about the scientific validity of the evidence, rather than whether it was broadly accepted, as under *Frye*. The FMSF newsletter, however in summarizing *Daubert*, focused on the question of "general acceptance," which actually was a feature of the *Frye* ruling. This was consistent with the FMSF's attempts to portray therapists using recovered-memory techniques as marginal to the field. However, FMSF families had greater success excluding evidence from recovered memory under *Daubert*, since expert witnesses could use various forms of evidence to debunk recovered memory therapy (Walsh 1999). Because of the nature of the U.S. Supreme Court's ruling in *Daubert* (which was not a constitutional ruling, but rather focused on interpreting federal rules of evidence), it is not binding on states, some of which have adopted *Daubert* rules (through their own appeals courts) and others of which continue to use *Frye* to determine whether to admit scientific testimony (Dixon and Gill 2002).

92. R. Christopher Barden, "Commentary: The Real Truth About Science-Intensive Litigation Against Negligent Psychotherapists," *Newsletter* 2002, 11(2).

93. Ibid.

94. "Illinois Considers Limit on Sex Suits," *New York Times*, March 27, 1994. Quoted in "News Notes," *Newsletter* 1994, 3(4).

95. "Legislative Initiatives," *Newsletter* 1996, 5(2).

96. "Statutes of Limitations," *Newsletter* 1996, 5(5).

97. Pamela Freyd, "Dear Friends," *Newsletter* 2003, 12(2).

98. "Kansas Appeals Court Tolls Time Limits in Retractor Case," "Wisconsin Supreme Court Decides Mental Illness Tolls Statute of Limitations," *Newsletter* 2003, 12(5).

99. Pamela Freyd, "Dear Friends," *Newsletter* 1995, 4(3). The article was by John Backus, Sc.D., and Barbara Una Stannard, Ph.D., "Your Memories Are Not False: A Reply to the False Memory Syndrome Foundation" [published in *Healing Woman*, 1994]. The claim was about Pamela and Peter Freyd's contacts with members of their daughter Jennifer Freyd's academic department as she was about to be reviewed for promotion.

100. *Freyd v. Whitfield*, 972 F. Supp. 940 (Maryland Federal District Court, 1997). Thanks to Ross Cheit for pointing out this case.

101. Pamela Freyd, "Dear Friends," *Newsletter* 1994, 3(4).

102. There are no data on the overall number of lawsuits by children against their parents or parents against their children or therapists, nor on the overall pattern of wins and losses. All parties agreed that the overwhelming number of rulings after the mid-1990s went in favor of accused parents.

103. "What Can Parents Do?" *Newsletter* 1992, 1(9); A Mom, "How to Locate the Therapist," *Newsletter* 1993, 2(6).

104. "What Can Families Do?" *Newsletter* 1992, 1(9).

105. Pamela Freyd, "Dear Friends," *Newsletter* 1993, 2(6).

106. Pamela Freyd, "Dear Friends," *Newsletter* 1994, 3(4), citing Bill Scanlon, "Therapists Under Fire." *Rocky Mountain News*, March 10, 1994.

107. "Make a Difference; Missouri," *Newsletter* 1996, 5(8).

108. Jim Simmons, with comments from the FMSF staff. "Analysis of the Ramona Case, Part II," *Newsletter* 1994, 3(7).

109. Pamela Freyd, "Dear Friends, " and "FMSF Files Amicus Brief in Alabama Case," *Newsletter* 1995, 4(6).

110. "Notices," *Newsletter* 2001, 10(5).

111. Pamela Freyd, "Dear Friends," *Newsletter* 1997, 6(1).

112. "Examples of Charges in a Legal Situation," *Newsletter* 1996, 5(2).

113. "$2.5 Million Jury Award to Retractor," *Newsletter* 1996, 5(2); the case was *E. Carlson v. Dr. Diane Humanansky*. Other awards included a $7.5 million settlement in 2004 against Bennett Braun, M.D.; Roberta Sachs, M.D.; Corydon Hammond, Ph.D.; and Chicago's Rush-Presbyterian-St. Luke's Medical Center (Pamela Freyd, "Dear Friends," *Newsletter* 2004, 13[2]) and a 2006 award of $330,000 in Lancaster, Pennsylvania (Pamela Freyd, "Dear Friends," *Newsletter* 2006, 15[2]).

114. Pamela Freyd, "Editor's Note," *Newsletter* 1995, 4(9).

115. Pamela Freyd, "Dear Friends," *Newsletter* 1996, 5(2); and Pamela Freyd, "Dear Friends," *Newsletter* 2002, 11(2).

116. "Continuing Education," *Newsletter* 1996, 5(5); "October in Chicago," *Newsletter* 1996, 5(8); "What's New in the Memory Wars?" *Newsletter* 1997, 6(1).

117. Pamela Freyd, "Dear Friends," *Newsletter* 1999, 8(1).

118. "Bill Hits Unproven Mental Health Treatments," *Newsletter* 1995, 4(3); Pamela Freyd, "Dear Friends," *Newsletter* 1995, 4(3).

119. "Legislative Initiatives," *Newsletter* 1996, 5(2).

120. "Informed Consent Bill Passed in Indiana Senate," *Newsletter* 1996, 5(5).

121. Alan Feld, "More on Informed Consent," *Newsletter* 1999, 8(7).

122. "Our Critics," *Newsletter* 1992, 1(9). The therapist was Susan Asher of Provo; the report was in the *Utah Daily Herald,* Sept. 5, 1992.

123. Pamela Freyd, "Dear Friends," *Newsletter* 1993, 2(9).

124. "More Evidence of Changed Climate," *Newsletter* 1993, 2(8).

125. See discussion in a special issue of *Psychotherapy Networker* (Miller 2003; Simon 2003).

126. The case was dismissed on First Amendment grounds.

127. For overviews, see Freyd, 1996; Freyd et al. 2007, 2005.

128. "Worried About the FMS Foundation," *Newsletter* 1992, 1(8).

129. "Our Critics," *Newsletter* 1993, 2(1).

130. For example, see the review of "Suggestibility, Reliability, and the Legal Process," *Robert Rosenthal Developmental Review* 22 (2002) 334–369 in *Newsletter* 2003, 12(2).

131. "Overturned Convictions Suggest Changes in Standards for Investigating Sex Abuse Involving Young Children," *Newsletter* 1995 4(9).

132. Jeffrey Victor, review of Nathan and Snedeker (1995), *Newsletter* 1996, 5(2).

133. Victor, op. cit.

134. Pamela Freyd, "Dear Friends," *Newsletter* 1995, 4(9).

135. Pamela Freyd, "Dear Friends," *Newsletter* 1999, 8(1).

136. Pamela Freyd, "Dear Friends," *Newsletter* 2002, 11(2).

137. Pamela Freyd, "Dear Friends," *Newsletter* 2004, 13(4).

138. *Newsletter* 2001, 10(5). Another conference publicized in the FMSF newsletter was titled "Child Abuse Allegations: Science vs. Suspicion" and included sessions on DNA, defending juvenile offenders, shaken-baby syndrome, false confessions, and "Differentiating Between Real and Computer-Generated Porn," *Newsletter* 2003, 12(2).

139. Thanks to Ross Cheit for emphasizing the importance of "Witchhunt."

140. VOCAL of Missouri, "About VOCAL." Available at www.vocalofmo.org/about.htm. The same statement was posted on the websites for other state chapters, e.g., VOCAL Michigan. Available at www.geocities.com/vocalmi (both accessed 4/19/2006.)

141. "Our Critics," *Newsletter* 1993, 2(1); Response to "Dear FMSF Editor," *Newsletter* 1993, 2(3). This position was similar to that of other conservative "feminists," who claimed to be the real feminists, criticized discussion of women's oppression as victimhood, and argued that the heterosexual family and child-rearing were the best sources of women's happiness, yet had been undermined by the women's movement (Faludi 1995; Roiphe 1993; Sommers 1994).

142. "Our Critics: Their Semantics," *Newsletter* 1993, 2(6).

143. Howard Fishman, "Highly Recommended Book Distinguishes Scientifically Supported Practices from 'Junk Science' in Clinical Psychology," *Newsletter* 2003, 12(5).

144. "Legal Actions Against Parents," *Newsletter* 1(6). Freyd wrote that others had "suggested" that professionals encouraged suits for these reasons, rather than suggesting this herself, but offered no alternate explanations.

Chapter 7

1. Many also participated in professional therapy.

2. Toylee Green, "Self Help Groups: How to Develop and Conduct." At "Unlock the Voice...Free the Spirit," 16th VOICES in Action, Inc., Conference, Evanston, Ill., July 24, 1998. Quotes are close paraphrases based on my field notes. The NBWHP facilitated self-help groups focused on health issues for African-American women in many cities and combined encouragement for individuals with advocacy for social change.

3. The Healing Woman Foundation flier, collected at the VOICES in Action, Inc., Conference, Evanston, Ill., July 24–26, 1998. Personal collection of author.

4. Field notes, VOICES in Action, Inc., Conference, Evanston, Ill. July 24–26, 1998.

5. Field notes, 16th VOICES in Action, Inc., Conference, Evanston, Ill., July 24, 1998. Robin Moulds, Introduction to Ellen Bass talk.

6. Holly Broach-Sowels, "Take Control and Stand Triumphantly as a Conqueror." Field notes, 16th VOICES in Action, Inc., Conference, Evanston, Ill., July 24, 1998.

7. "Write to Congress!" *The Healing Woman*, 1994, 2(10): 6; Lynn, "An Open Letter to Survivors," *The Healing Woman*, 1994, 2(10): 6; Margot Silk Forrest, "Survivors in 25 States Join Forces 'To Tell the Truth,'" *The Healing Woman*, 1993, 2(5): 3.

8. Field notes, 16th VOICES in Action, Inc., Conference, Evanston, Ill., July 24–26, 1998; VOICES in Action 2006 Conference presenters list. Available at http://www.voices-action.org/conf2006presenters.html (accessed May 17, 2006).

9. To Tell the Truth conference flier and field notes, New York City, January 30–31, 1999.

10. Field notes, 16th VOICES in Action, Inc., Conference, Evanston, Ill., July 24–26, 1998 and To Tell the Truth Conference, New York City, January 30–31, 1999.

11. Field notes, 16th VOICES in Action, Inc., Conference, Evanston, Ill., July 24–26, 1998.

12. Margot Silk Forrest, "Survivors in 25 States Join Forces 'To Tell the Truth,.'" *The Healing Woman*, 1993, 2(5): 3. Coordination of To Tell the Truth was taken over by ISRNI in the early 1990s, and passed to Survivor Connections in 1998. "To Tell the Truth." Available at http://members.cox.net/totellthetruth/index.html (accessed May 19, 2006).

13. "To Tell the Truth," loc. cit.

14. Donna Jensen, "People of Fire Grant Proposal," June, 1999; private collection of author.

15. Survivors Healing Center (Santa Cruz). "Services." Available at http://www.survivorshealingcenter.org/services.html (accessed May 5, 2006).

16. Kilby (2007) provides an excellent discussion of these debates on experience.

Chapter 8

1. VOCAL was notorious for making this critique.

2. A VAWA-mandated study of the prevalence of violence against women found that, of women who reported being raped, 22 percent had been raped under the age of 12, and 32 percent between ages 12 and 17 (Laney and Siskin 2003).

3. Calculated from figures provided in table 1, "Violence Against Women Funding, FY 1995 through FY 2001." Available at www.unsinfo.state.gov/usa/women/violence/rl30871.pdf (accessed July 7, 2006). (These programs cover all forms of child abuse. Spending on programs that cover both adult and child victims is excluded. These are rural domestic violence and child abuse enforcement; training programs for probation and parole officers who work with released sex offenders; and the national domestic violence hotline.)

4. Interview, anonymous. VAWA's office became a potential center for such work (Laney and Siskin 2003).

5. NCCAN Compendium Supplement, FY 1997, p. 461.

6. Theresa Reid, 1995. "Speech to the Child Abuse Prevention Symposium." University of Minnesota, November 30. Available at http://www.cyfc.umn.edu/family/research/tr_kn.htm (accessed July 17, 2006).

7. Herman Ohme's "It felt something like the WTC Towers 9/11 attack." *Ohio Association of Responsible Mental Health Practices*, March 2002. Available at The Memory Debate Archives, "Viewpoints" (www.tmdarchives.org) (accessed June 28, 2007). In addition to decommissioning NCCAN, changes to CAPTA consistent with countermovement goals included new "procedures for appealing and responding to appeals of substantiated reports of abuse and neglect" and "provisions requiring...the prompt expungement of any records that are accessible to the general public or are used for purposes of employment or other background checks in cases determined to be unsubstantiated or false." NCCAN, March 12, 1997. U.S. Department of Health and Human Services Administration for Children and Families, "Availability of Fiscal Year (FY) 1997 State Grant Funds Under the Child Abuse Prevention and Treatment Act." Available at http://www.acf.hhs.gov/programs/cb/laws_policies/policy/pi/capi9701.htm (accessed May 29, 2008). (Recency quotation from Reid, 1995. "Speech to the Child Abuse Prevention Symposium.")

8. NCCAN Compendium Supplement, FY 1997, p. 462; Compendium Supplement, FY 1998, pp. 79–88; Compendium Supplement, FY 2000, p. 286. Parents Anonymous is distinct from Parents United, the organization sponsored by the Giarretto Institute in San Jose, California. It was previously a peer-led self-help network analogous to Alcoholics Anonymous.

9. Parents Anonymous, "Parent and Shared Leadership," "Parents' Anonymous Programs," "Research Results." Available at http://www.parentsanonymous.org/paIndex10.html (accessed July 14, 2006).

10. RAINN, "About Us." Available at http://www.rainn.org/about/index.html (accessed July 14, 2006).

11. The National Domestic Violence Hotline, "History." Available at http://www.ndvh.org/tenth/history.html (accessed July 14, 2006).

12. For example, a New York City conference sponsored by the short-lived Incest Awareness Foundation offered workshops for continuing education credit. Field notes, IAF conference, NYC 1999.

13. "Uniform Victims of Crime Act," p. 1.

14. 48.5 percent goes to victim compensation, 48.5 percent to victim assistance, and 3 percent is for discretionary grants. VOCA provides block grants to states, which states must supplement (Department of Justice 2001: 27161).

15. National Criminal Justice Reference Service, Victim Services. "What Is Victim Assistance?" Available at http://www.ncjrs.gov/App/QA/Detail.aspx?Id=568&context=11 (accessed July 17, 2006).

16. Claimants under VOCA are generally required make claims between one and three years after the crime (or after they reach the age of 18 if the crime occurred when they were children), and to cooperate with law enforcement by making a police report or a report to the appropriate agency, such as Child Protective Services. The federal statute encourages states to consider reasons that reporting or cooperating with law enforcement might be difficult for some groups, such as children, also noting that "embarrassment, shame, and psychological trauma may delay the reporting of sexual assault" (Department of Justice 2001: 27159, 27162.)

17. State of Colorado, "Victims of Crime Act." Available at http://dcj.state.co.us/ovp/voca.htm (accessed July 17, 2006). CAPTA amended VOCA in 2001 to require an increase in funds for child abuse victims in years when the funds took in increased amounts of money (Department of Justice 2001: 27159).

18. Massachusetts Victim and Witness Assistance Board, 2001. "Victims of Crime Act, Victim Assistance Grant Program, Massachusetts State Wide Assistance Report," p.1. 35,715 grants to individuals were made in 2001. Available at www.ojp.usdoj.gov/ovc/fund/sbsmap/ovcpfma1.htm (accessed July 17, 2006).

19. Massachusetts Victim and Witness Assistance Board, 2001, op. cit., p. 10.

20. State of Colorado, "Victims of Crime Act," op cit.

21. State of Colorado, "2000 Colorado VOCA Assistance Funding Awards." Available at http://dcj.state.co.us/ovp/voca.htm (accessed July 17, 2006).

22. State of Colorado, "2000 Colorado VOCA Assistance Funding Awards."

23. The VCAD was part of the office of Family and Community Crimes Bureau.

24. Disability rights activists transform the identity of being disabled into a source of advocacy. Thus claiming to be disabled is not a clear-cut statement of powerlessness, but can have multiple meanings depending on context and interaction.

25. Incarceration rates for child sexual abuse varied between 45 percent and 78 percent, depending on the study.

26. Finkelhor and Ormrod (2001) show that there has been a sharp increase in the number of offenders incarcerated, based on a survey of state correctional facilities: 19,900 in 1986, 43,500 in 1991, and 60,700 in 1997.

27. One Voice was tax exempt; ACAA was a lobbying group.

28. "One Voice Merges with Justice for Children," *Justice for Children Newsletter* October 2000. Available at http://www.jfcadvocacy.org/news/October2000.pdf (accessed Sept. 8, 2008). "Justice for Children received VOCA funding: Organizational Update" *Justice for Children Newsletter* March 2000. Available at http://www.jfcadvocacy.org/news/March2000.pdf (accessed Sept. 8, 2008).

29. Modifications of these measures, particularly how information about registered sex offenders could be released to the public, proceeded throughout the 2000s. Not only violent sex offenders were required to register, but anyone convicted of a sex crime, including sometimes consensual sex between different-aged teenagers or public sex between gay men. However, community notification was almost always limited to Level 3 sex offenders: those convicted of serious crimes and deemed at high risk for re-offense.

30. Bureau of Justice statistics showed a 3.3 percent re-arrest rate within three years for sex offenders against children, lower than the re-arrest rate for sex offenders as a whole (Bureau of Justice Statistics, 2007. "Criminal Offenders Statistics." Available at http://www.ojp.usdoj.gov/bjs/crimoff.htm#child (accessed May 30. 2009).

31. Stop the Silence, "Stop Child Sexual Abuse annual race." Available at http://www.stopcsa.org/sponsors.cfm. Mothers Against Sexual Abuse, "Home." Available at http://www.againstsexualabuse.org. Both accessed May 31, 2006.

32. Stop It Now, "Child Abuse: A Public Health Epidemic." Available at http://www.stopitnow.org/asit_epidemic.html (accessed May 31, 2006).

33. Stop It Now allied itself with professional associations for sex offender treatment and presented statistics about the effectiveness of treatment. Stop It Now, "The Key Premises of Our Work," available at http://www.stopitnow.org/asit_premises.html_; and "Child Abuse: A Public Health Epidemic," available at http://www.stopitnow.org/asit_epidemic.html (both accessed May 20, 2006).

34. Stop It Now, "The Key Premises of Our Work."

35., Stop It Now, "How Our Programs Work." Available at http://www.stopitnow.org/asit_howwework.html (accessed May 20. 2006).

36. Annie Lee. "Letter from the President." *Newsletter* April 2006, p. 2. Available at http://www.darkness2light.org/docs/newsletter_2006_04.pdf; "Stewards of Children Now in Full Release," *Newsletter*, April 2005, p. 1. Available at http://www.darkness2light.org/docs/newsletter_2005_04.pdf;

"Media Campaigns." Available at http://www.darkness2light.org/AboutUs/media_campaign.asp. All accessed May 31, 2006.

37. Darkness to Light, "Media Campaigns."

38. "Darkness to Light Launches New Corporate Identity During Child Abuse Prevention Month." Available at http://www.darkness2light.org/news/archives/news_04_01_04.asp (accessed May 31, 2006).

39. Gen5 also discusses "mental health" and "human rights" approaches, presenting strengths and weaknesses of both; while both approaches are evident in its discourse, its primary focus is on framing child sexual abuse in terms of public health and family violence. Generation Five, "Defining the Problem." Available at http://www.generationfive.org/defining.html (accessed May 31, 2006). Its history shaped its linkage of child sexual abuse to other issues. It grew from the activist survivor group Run Riot, which initiated a series of foundation-funded meetings between activists on child sexual abuse from diverse ethnic communities, which in turn led to Generation Five.

40. The online prevention program was funded by a $461,208 U.S. Department of Commerce Technologies Opportunity Program grant and a $250,000 Department of Justice Grant. "Darkness to Light Awarded Federal TOP Grant;" "Office of Juvenile Justice Grant to Aid Stewards Program." *Newsletter*, April, 2005, p. 3. Available at http://www.darkness2light.org/docs/newsletter_2005_04.pdf (accessed May 31, 2006).

41. Generation Five, "Q&A: The Community Response Project 2003."
Available at http://www.generationfive.org/crpQ_and_A.html (accessed May 31, 2006). Projects described are from the 2002 Bay Area project.

42. The retreat was held in March 2002. Gen5 received *Ms.* Foundation funding and, with Stop It Now, helped organize the retreat. See Murphy 2002 and Generation Five, "Our Supporters." Available at http://www.generationfive.org/aboutUs.html (accessed May 31, 2006).

43. All three organizations were founded by survivors of child sexual abuse, and all three incorporated the voices and ideas of survivors through focus groups, quotes, and vignettes in publicity.

44. Fran Henry, "Where Is Will Shakespeare When We Need Him? Preventing the Sexual Abuse of Children." Presentation to the 16th Annual meeting of the San Diego Conference on Child and family Maltreatment, San Diego, California, Jan. 25, 2002. Available at http://www.stopitnow.com/downloads/fh_sandiego_speech.pdf (accessed June 2, 2008).

45. See Henry, ibid., and Fran Henry, "A Prescription for Change on Child Sexual Abuse," Presentation to National Advisory Council on Violence and Abuse, American Medical Association, Chicago, Illinois, November 1, 2001. Available at http://www.stopitnow.com/downloads/fh_ama_speech.pdf (accessed June 2, 2008).

References

"A Senator Recalls a Wrong." 1984. *Time* 123 (2, May 7): 27.
Alcoholics Anonymous. 2002. "What Are the 'Twelve Steps'?" http://www.alcoholics-anonymous.org/english/E_Pamphlets/P–2_dl.htm.
Angel, Sherry. 1978. "Don't Be Afraid to Say No!" *Redbook Magazine* 151 (July): 40 et seq.
Apostolidis, Paul. 2008. "Feminist Theory, Immigrant Workers' Stories, and Counterhegemony in the United States Today." *Signs* 33(3): 545–568.
Armstrong, Louise. 1978. *Kiss Daddy Goodnight*. New York: Hawthorn Books.
———. 1986. *Kiss Daddy Goodnight: Ten Years Later*. New York: Pocket Books.
———. 1990. The Personal Is Apolitical." *Women's Review of Books* (March): 1–44.
———. 1994. *Rocking the Cradle of Sexual Politics*. Reading, Mass.: Addison-Wesley.
Ascher, Barbara. 1978. "L.A. Cop Lloyd Martin Fights a Grimy War Against 'Chicken Hawks' and Other Child Molesters." *People Weekly* 10 (Oct. 9): 99–100.
Associated Press. 1989. "Prosecutor Won't Seek New Abuse Charges: *New York Times*, Sept 21.
Barasko, Maryann. 2004. *Governing NOW*. Ithaca, NY: Cornell University Press.
Bass, Ellen, and Laura Davis. 1988. *The Courage to Heal: A Guide for Women Survivors of Child Sexual Abuse*. New York: Harper and Row. Second edition, 1994.

Bass, Ellen, and Louise Thornton. 1991. *I Never Told Anyone: Writings by Women Survivors of Child Sexual Abuse.* New York: Harper Perennial. (First edition published 1983, Harper Colophon).
Baye, Betty, and Jill Nelson-Ricks. 1984. "In the Matter of Incest." *Essence* 15 (June): 74–76, 143–144.
Beck, Melinda, and Tessa Namuth. 1974. "An Epidemic of Child Abuse." *Newsweek* 104 (August 20): 44.
Beckett, K. 1996. "Culture and the Politics of Signification: The Case of Child Sexual Abuse." *Social Problems* 43(1): 57–76.
Bell, Vicki. 1993. *Interrogating Incest: Feminism, Foucault, and the Law.* London: Routledge.
Bellah, Robert, et al. 1985. *Habits of the Heart: Individualism and Commitment in Public Life.* Berkeley: University of California Press.
Benedict, Helen. 1984. "Molesters Beware: What Kids Must Know." *Ladies Home Journal* 101 (July): 48–54, 162.
Benford, Robert D. 1997. "An Insider's Critique of the Social Movement Framing Perspective." *Sociological Inquiry* 67(4): 409–430.
Benford, Robert D., and David Snow. 2000. "Framing Processes and Social Movements: An Overview and Assessment." *Annual Review of Sociology* 26:611–639.
Benski, Tova. 2005. "Breaching Events and the Emotional Reactions of the Public: Women in Black in Israel." In Helena Flam and Debra King, eds., *Emotions and Social Movements.* London: Routledge.
Besharov, Douglas. 1981. "The Third International Conference on Child Abuse and Neglect: Conference Highlights." *Children Today* 10:12–15, 36.
Best, Joel. 1990. *Threatened Children.* Chicago: University of Chicago Press.
Blessing, Shana Rowen. 1992. "How to Be a Political Dyke and an Incest Survivor at the Same Time, or, Why Are All the Dykes I Know Reading *The Courage to Heal*?" *Lesbian Ethics*, 4 (3): 122–128.
Blume, E. Sue. 1989. *Secret Survivors: Uncovering Incest and Its Aftereffects in Women.* New York: John Wiley and Sons.
Bolen, Rebecca. 2001. *Child Sexual Abuse.* New York: Kluwer Academic/Plenum.
Bolen, Rebecca, and Maria Scannapieco. 1999. "Prevalence of Child Sexual Abuse." *Social Service Review* 73(3): 281–313.
Boles, Janet. 1989. "A Policy of Our Own: Local Feminist Networks and Social Services for Women and Children." *Policy Studies Review* 8(3, Spring): 638–647.
Bowen, Ezra. 1984. "Facing Up to Sex Abuse." *Time* 124 (November 12): 91–92.
Breines, Wini. 2006. *The Trouble Between Us.* New York: Oxford.
Bridge, Peter. 1978. "What Parents Should Know and Do About 'Kiddie Porn'." *Parents Magazine* 53: 42–43, 69.
Broadhurst, Diane D. 1975. "A School Program to Combat Child Abuse." *Education Digest* 41 (October): 20–23. [Condensed from *Children Today.*]
Brown, Wendy. 1995. *States of Injury.* Princeton, N.J.: Princeton University Press.

———. 2005. *Edgework*. Princeton, N.J.: Princeton University Press.
Brownmiller, Susan. 1975. *Against Our Will: Men, Women, and Rape*. New York: Simon and Schuster.
Buechler, Steven M. 1995. "New Social Movement Theories." *Sociological Quarterly* 36(3): 441–464.
Burstein, Paul, Rachel Einwohner, and Jocelyn Hollander. 1995. "The Success of Political Movements: A Bargaining Perspective" (pp. 275–295) in J. Craig Jenkins and Bert Klandermans, eds., *The Politics of Protest*. Minneapolis: University of Minnesota Press.
Butler, Judith. 1990. *Gender Trouble*. New York: Routledge.
Butler, Sandra. 1985. *Conspiracy of Silence: The Trauma of Incest*. San Francisco: New Glide Publications.
Calof, David L. 1988. "Notes from a Practice Under Siege: Harassment, Defamation, and Intimidation in the Name of Science." *Ethics and Behavior* 8(2): 141–161.
Castelli, Jim. 1993. "Crisis of Faith: The Crime of Priest Pedophilia." *U.S. Catholic* (Sept.): 7–15.
Champagne, Rosaria. 1996. *The Politics of Survivorship*. New York: New York University Press.
Chaze, William L. (with the magazine's domestic bureaus). 1984. "Now, Nationwide Drive to Curb Child Abuse." *U.S. News and World Report* 97 (Nov. 2): 73–74.
Cheit, Ross E., and Erica B. Goldschmidt. 1997. "Child Molesters in the Criminal Justice System: A Comprehensive Case-Flow Analysis of the Rhode Island Docket (1985–1993)." *Criminal and Civil Confinement* 23: 267–301.
Cheit, Ross. 2007. "Myths about the Country Walk Case." *Journal of Child Sexual Abuse* 16(3): 95–116.
Chetin, Helen. 1977. *Frances Ann Speaks Out: My Father Raped Me*. Berkeley: New Seed Press.
Clarke, Lee. 2002. "Panic: Myth or Reality?" *Contexts* 1(3): 21–6.
Cleary, Chris. 1984. "Incest Survivor Sues Father." *Ms.* 13 (Dec.): 25.
Clinton, William J. 1995. "Remarks in Observance of National Domestic Violence Awareness Month." Weekly Compilation of Presidential Documents; 10/9/95, 1 (40): 1750.
Coburn, Judith. 1979. "Trafficking in Innocence: The Child as Sex Object." *New Times* 12 (Jan. 8): 70–71.
Cohen, Jean. 1985. "Strategy or Identity." *Social Research* 52: 663–716.
Collins, Patricia Hill. 1990. *Black Feminist Thought*. Boston: Unwin Hyman.
Collings, S. J. (1995). "The long-term effects of contact and noncontact forms of child sexual abuse in a sample of university men." *Child Abuse and Neglect* 19: 1–6.
Combahee River Collective. [1977](1983). "The Combahee River Collective Statement" (pp. 272–282). In *Home Girls: A Black Feminist Anthology*, edited by Barbara Smith. New York: Kitchen Table Women of Color Press.
Courtois, Christine A. 1988. *Healing the Incest Wound: Adult Survivors in Therapy*. New York: WW. Norton and Co.

Coy, Patrick G., and Lynne M. Woehrle. 1996. "Constructing Identity and Oppositional Knowledge: The Framing Practices of Peace Movement Organizations during the Gulf War." *Sociological Spectrum* 16: 287–327.

Crawford, Christina. 1981. "Conspiracy of Silence." *Ladies' Home Journal* 98 (Nov.): 69 et seq.

Crenshaw, Kimberlé. 1991. "Mapping the Margins: Intersectionality, Identity Politics, and Violence against Women of Color." *Stanford Law Review* 1241.

Crewdson, John. 1988. *By Silence Betrayed*. Boston: Little, Brown.

Cross, Theodore, Wendy Walsh, Monique Simone, and Lisa Jones. 2003. "Prosecution of Child Abuse." *Trauma, Violence, and Abuse* 4(4): 323–340.

Cullen, Bernard, Peg Smith, Jeanne Funk, and Robert Haaf. 2000. "A Matched Cohort Comparison of a Criminal Justice System's Response to Child Sexual Abuse." *Child Abuse and Neglect* 24(4): 569–577.

Currie, Dawn H. 1990. "Battered Women and the State: From a Failure of Theory to a Theory of Failure." *Journal of Human Justice* 1(2): 77–96.

Darnton, Nina. 1991. "The Pain of the Last Taboo." *Newsweek* October 7: 70–72.

Daly, Mary. 1978. *Gyn/Ecology: The Metaethics of Radical Feminism*. Boston: Beacon.

Day of the Child. 2000. "Dear Mr. Jesus." Available at http://www.dayofthechild.org/dc98/dmj.htm (accessed July 28, 2006).

Davis, Joseph. 2005. *Accounts of Innocence*. Chicago: University of Chicago Press.

———. 2000. "Accounts of False Memory Syndrome: Parents, 'Retractors,' and the Role of Institutions in Account Making." *Qualitative Sociology* 23(1): 29–56.

"Dear Mr. Jesus." 1987. *Time*, 130 (25, Jan. 21.).

Densen-Gerber, Judianne. 1977. "What Pornographers Are Doing to Children: A Shocking Report." *Redbook* 149(August): 86 et seq.

Department of Justice, Office for Victims of Crime. 2001. "Victims of Crime Act Victim Compensation Grant Programs." *Federal Register* 66(95, Wednesday, May 16): 27158–27166.

DeRose, Denise M. 1985. "Adult Incest Survivors and the Statute of Limitations: The Delayed Discovery Rule and Long-Term Damages." *Santa Clara Law Review* 25(1): 191–225.

DeYoung, Mary. 2007. "Two Decades After McMartin: A Follow-up of 22 Convicted Day Care Employees." *Journal of Sociology and Social Welfare*, 34(4): 9–33.

Doane, Janice, and Devon Hodges. 2001. *Telling Incest: Women's Narratives of Dangerous Remembering from Stein to Sapphire*. Ann Arbor: University of Michigan Press.

Downs, Susan Whitelaw, Lela B. Costin, and Emily Jean McFadden. 1996. *Child Welfare and Family Services: Policies and Practice*. White Plains, N.Y.: Longman Publishers.

Dudar, Helen. 1977. "America Discovers Child Pornography." *Ms.* 6 (August): 45–47, 80.

Dworkin, Andrea. 1988. "Feminism: An Agenda" (pp. 133–152), in *Letters from a War Zone*. New York: E. P. Dutton.

Echols, Alice. 1990. *Daring to Be Bad*. Minneapolis: University of Minnesota Press.

Eisenstein, Hester. 1991. *Gender Shock*. Boston: Beacon Press.

Elshtain, Jean Bethke. 1985. "Invasion of the Child Savers: How We Succumb to Hype and Hysteria." *The Progressive* (Sept.): 23–26.

Epstein, Steven. 1996. *Impure Science: AIDS, Activism, and the Politics of Knowledge*. Berkeley: University of California Press.

Estrin, Eric. 1984. "*Amelia*'s Psychologist, Stan Katz, Advises Families Faced with Incest." *People Weekly* 21 (Jan. 16): 91.

Farragher, Thomas, Matt Carroll, and *Boston Globe* Staff. 2003. "Boston Church Review Board Dismissed Accusations by Females." *Boston Globe*, February 7.

Ferree, Myra Marx, and Beth Hess. 1994. *Controversy and Coalition: The New Feminist Movement Across Three Decades of Change*. New York: Twayne.

Ferree, Myra Marx, and Patricia Yancey Martin. 1995. *Feminist Organizations: Harvest of the Women's Movement*. Philadelphia: Temple University Press.

Ferree, Myra Marx, William A. Gamson, Jürgen Gerhards, and Dieter Rucht. 2002. *Abortion Discourse: Democracy and the Public Sphere in Germany and the United States*. New York: Cambridge University Press.

Fine, Gary. 1995. "Public Narration and Group Culture: Discerning Discourse in Social Movements." In *Social Movements and Culture*, ed. Hank Johnston and Bert Klandermans, pp. 127–143.

Finkelhor, David. 1979. *Sexually Victimized Children*. New York: Free Press.

Finkelhor, David, G. Hotaling, I. Lewis, and C. Smith. 1990. "Sexual Abuse in a National Survey of Adult Men and Women." *Child Abuse and Neglect* 14: 19–28.

Finkelhor, David, and Lisa Jones. 2004. "Explanations for the Decline in Child Sexual Abuse Cases." *Juvenile Justice Bulletin* No. NC199298.Washington, D.C.: Office of Juvenile Justice and Delinquency Prevention.

Finkelhor, David, and Richard Ormrod. 2001. "Offenders Incarcerated for Crimes Against Juveniles." *Juvenile Justice Bulletin* No. NCJ191028. Washington, D.C.: United States Department of Justice, Office of Juvenile Justice and Delinquency Prevention.

Firestone, Shulamith. 1970. *The Dialectic of Sex*. William Morrow.

Forward, Susan, and Craig Buck. 1978. *Betrayal of Innocence: Incest and Its Devastation*. New York: St. Martin's Press.

Fox, Tom. "What They Knew in 1985." *National Catholic Reporter*, May 17, 2002.

Frame, Randy. 1985. "Child Abuse: The Church's Best Kept Secret?" *Christianity Today*, Feb. 15: 32–34.

Fraser, Nancy. 1989. "Women, Welfare, and the Politics of Need Interpretation." In *Unruly Practices: Power, Discourse, and Gender in Contemporary Social Theory*. Minneapolis: University of Minnesota Press.

Freeman, Jo. 1972/3. "The Tyranny of Structurelessness." *Berkeley Journal of Sociology* 17: 151–165.

Freyd, Jennifer. 1993. "Theoretical and Personal Perspectives on the Delayed Memory Debate." Paper presented at the Center for Mental Health at Foode Hospital's Continuing Education Conference: Controversies around recovered memories of incest and ritualistic abuse. August, Ann Arbor, Michigan.

———. 1996. *Betrayal Trauma: The Logic of Forgetting Childhood Abuse*. Cambridge, Mass.: Harvard University Press.

———. 1998. "Science in the Memory Debate." *Ethics and Behavior* 8(2): 101–113.

Freyd, Jennifer, and Anne P. DePrince, eds. 2001. *Trauma and Cognitive Science*. Binghamton, N.Y.: Haworth Press.

Gamson, William. 1990. *The Strategy of Social Protest*, 2nd ed. Belmont, Calif.: Wadsworth.

———. 2004. "Bystanders, Public Opinion, and the Media" (pp. 242–261), in David Snow, Sarah Soule, and Hanspieter Kriesi, eds., *Blackwell Companion to Social Movements*. Malden, Mass.: Blackwell Publishing.

Gest, Ted. 1985. "The Other Victims of Child Abuse." *U.S. News and World Report* April 1: 66.

Giddens, Anthony. 1991. *Modernity and Self Identity*. Stanford, Calif.: Stanford University Press.

Goldsmith, Barbara. 1987. "We Are Survivors." *Ms.* July/August: 88–89.

Goode, Erich, and Nachman Ben-Yehuda (1994): *Moral Panics: The Social Construction of Deviance*. Oxford: Blackwell.

Goodman, Gail, and Jodi Quas. 1997. "Children's Religious Knowledge: Implications for Understanding Satanic Ritual Abuse Allegations." *Child Abuse and Neglect* 21(11): 1111–1130.

Gordon, Linda. 1988. "The Politics of Child Sexual Abuse: Notes from American History." *Feminist Review* No. 28, January: 56–64.

Gornick, Janet C., and David S. Meyer. 1998. "Changing Political Opportunity: The Anti-Rape Movement and Public Policy." *Journal of Policy History* 10 (4): 367–398.

Habermas, Jurgen. 1979. *Communication and the Evolution of Society*. Boston: Beacon Press.

Hacking, Ian. 1991. "The Making and Molding of Child Abuse." *Critical Inquiry* 17 (Winter): 253–288.

Hall, Stuart, Charles Critcher, Tony Jefferson, John Clarke, and Brian Robert. 1978. *Policing the Crisis* (London: Macmillan).

Hartsock, Nancy. 1998. *The Feminist Standpoint Revisited and Other Essays*. Boulder, Colo.: Westview.

Hechler, David. 1985. "My Child Was Sexually Molested." *Essence*, July: 118.

———. 1988. *The Battle and the Backlash: The Child Abuse War*. Lexington, Mass.: Lexington Books.

Helfer, Mary Edna, Ruth S. Kempe, and Richard D. Krugman. 1997. *The Battered Child*, 5th ed. Chicago: University of Chicago Press.

Hendershott, Anne. 2002. "A Perfect Panic." *San Diego Union-Tribune*, March 20: B7.

Herman, Judith. 1981. *Father-Daughter Incest*. Cambridge: Harvard University Press.

———. 1992. *Trauma and Recovery*. New York: Basic Books.
hooks, bell. 1993. *Sisters of the Yam: Black Women and Self-Recovery*. Boston: South End Press.
———. 2003. *Rock My Soul: Black People and Self-Esteem*. New York: Atria Books.
Hopkins, Nancy Myer, and Mark Laaser. 1995. *Restoring the Soul of a Church: Healing Congregations Wounded by Clergy Sexual Misconduct*. Princeton, N.J.: Liturgical Press.
Horn, Miriam. 1993. "Memories Lost and Found." *U.S. News and World Report*, November 29: 52–63.
Hyde, Cheryl. 1992. "The Ideational System of Social Movement Agencies." In *Human Services as Complex Organizations*, ed. Y. Hasenfeld. Newbury Park, Calif.: Sage.
———. 1995. "Feminist Social Movement Organizations Survive the New Right." In *Feminist Organizations* (pp. 306–322), ed. Myra Marx Ferree and Patricia Yancey Martin. Philadelphia: Temple.
Investigative Staff of the *Boston Globe*. 2002. *Betrayal: The Crisis in the Catholic Church*. Boston: Little, Brown and Company.
Irvine, Janice. 2002. *Talk About Sex*. Oxford University Press.
Jacoby, Susan. 1981. "Nothing Really Happened." *McCall's* 109 (Nov.): 74, 79–84, 197–198.
Jasper, James. 1997. *The Art of Moral Protest*. Chicago: University of Chicago.
Jenkins, Philip. 1998. *Moral Panic: Changing Concepts of the Child Molester in Modern America*. New Haven: Yale University Press.
———. 2001. *Pedophiles and Priests: Anatomy of a Contemporary Crisis*. New York: Oxford University Press.
John Jay College of Criminal Justice. 2004. *The Nature and Scope of the Problem of Sexual Abuse and Minors by Catholic Priests and Deacons in the United States*. Washington, DC: United States Conference of Catholic Bishops. Available at http://www.usccb.org/nrb/johnjaystudy/ (accessed March 16, 2009).
Johnston, Josee, and Judith Taylor. 2008. "Feminist Consumerism and Fat Activists: A Comparative Study of Grassroots Activism and the Dove 'Real Beauty' Campaign." *Signs* 33 (4): 941–966.
Justice, Blair, and Rita Justice. 1979. *The Broken Taboo: Sex in the Family*. New York: Human Sciences Press.
Kaminer, Wendy. 1992. *I'm Dysfunctional, You're Dysfunctional: The Recovery Movement and Other Self-Help Fashions*. Reading, Mass.: Addison-Wesley.
Katzenstein, Mary. 1998. *Faithful and Fearless*. Princeton, NJ: Princeton University Press.
Kaufmann, Katie, and Caroline New. 2004. *Co-Counselling: The Theory and Practice of Re-Evaluation Counselling*. New York: Brunner-Routledge.
Kempe, C. Henry, Frederic N. Silverman, Brandt F. Steele, William Droegemuller, Henry K. Silver. 1962. "The Battered Child Syndrome." *Journal of the American Medical Association* 181: 17–24.
Keslow, Sally Platkin. 1981. "Incest: The Ultimate Family Secret." *Glamour* 79 (Nov.): 154–160.

Kilby, Jane. 2007. *Violence and the Cultural Politics of Trauma*. Edinburgh: Edinburgh University Press.

Kinnear, Karen L. 1995. *Childhood Sexual Abuse: A Reference Handbook*. Denver: ABC-CLIO.

Kirschenbaum, Carol. 1987. "Was I Molested? The Gray Area of Sexual Abuse." *Mademoiselle* 93 (March): 188 et seq.

Kleinmann, Leanne. 1984. "Keep Your Child Safe from Sexual Abuse." *McCall's* 111 (Aug.): 20.

Koopmans, Ruud. 2004. "Movements and Media: Selection Processes and Evolutionary Dynamics in the Public Sphere." *Theory and Society* 33: 367–391.

Koopmans, Ruud, and Paul Statham. 1999. "Ethnic and Civic Conceptions of Nationhood and the Differential Success of the Extreme Right in Germany and Italy." In Marco Giugni, Doug McAdam, and Charles Tilly, eds., *How Social Movements Matter*, pp. 225–251. Minneapolis: University of Minnesota Press.

Krouse, Mary Elizabeth. 1993. "Gift-Giving and Social Transformation: The AIDS Memorial Quilt as Social Movement Culture." Unpublished dissertation, Ohio State University.

Kuhn, Thomas. 1996. *The Structure of Scientific Revolutions*, 3rd ed. Chicago: University of Chicago Press.

Laney, Garrine P. and Alison Siskin. "Violence Against Women Act: History, Federal Funding, and Reauthorizing Legislation." Report for Congress. Available at http://kohl.senate.gove/pdf/VAWA.pdf (accessed July 17, 2006).

Lasch, Christopher. 1978. *The Culture of Narcissism*. New York: W.W. Norton and Co.

Lawrence, Lana R. 1993. "FMS Foundation Asks Underwager and Wakefield to Resign from Advisory Board, Then Changes Position," *Moving Forward* 2(4): 12–13.

Leiby, James. 1978. *A History of Social Welfare and Social Work in the United States*. New York: Columbia University Press.

Lindner, Eileen W. 1985. "Child Carelessness: Sexual Abuse in Day Care." *The Christian Century* (March) 270–272.

Loftus, Elizabeth. 1994. *The Myth of Repressed Memory*. New York: St. Martin's Press.

Low, Alice M. 1979. "Reporting Child Abuse." *American Education* 15:20.

Lynn, Morgan. 2001. "(In)Visible Privilege." Unpublished senior honors thesis, Smith College.

Mahany, Barbara. 1990. "Can Childhood Nightmares Ever Be Put to Rest?" *U.S. Catholic* (June) 34–39.

Maney, Gregory M., Lynne M. Woehrle, and Patrick G. Coy. 2005. "Harnessing and Challenging Hegemony: The U.S. Peace Movement after 9/11." *Sociological Perspectives* 38(3).

Mann, Mary Beth. 1989. "Victims of Abuse: Paying the Price for the Sins of Others." *U.S. Catholic* (July) 36–39.

Marks, Jane. 1987. "We Have a Problem." *Parents* (May) 70–75.

Martin, Patricia Yancey. 2005. *Rape Work*. New York: Routledge.

Masson, Jeffrey Moussaieff. 1984. *The Assault on Truth: Freud's Suppression of the Seduction Theory*. New York: Farrar, Straus, and Giroux.

Mathewes-Green, Frederica. 2000. "Ask the Victims." *Citizen*. Available at http://www.family.org/cforum/citizenmag/features/a0013078 (accessed June 10, 2005).

Matthews, Martha A. 1999. "The Impact of Federal and State Laws on Children Exposed to Domestic Violence." *The Future of Children*, special issue on domestic violence. 9(3): 50–66.

Matthews, Nancy. 1994. *Confronting Rape: The Feminist Anti-Rape Movement and the State*. London: Routledge.

McAdam, Doug. 1988. *Freedom Summer*. New York: Oxford University Press.

McAdam, Doug, John McCarthy, and Mayer N. Zald, eds. 1996. *Comparative Perspectives on Social Movements: Political Opportunities, Mobilizing Structures, and Cultural Framings*. Cambridge: Cambridge University Press.

McFarlane, Kee. 1981. "'Jolly K' Dies; Maureen Barton Lifton, 1940–1980." *Children Today* 10 (Jan.–Feb.): 31.

McGee, Micki. 2005. *Self-Help, Inc.* New York: Oxford University Press.

McIntosh, Peggy. 1988. "White Privilege and Male Privilege: A Personal Account of Coming to See Correspondences Through Work in Women's Studies." Reprinted in Verta Taylor, Nancy Whittier, and Leila J. Rupp, eds., *Feminist Frontiers*, 7th ed. New York: McGraw Hill, 2006.

McKuen, Rod. 1982. "A Poet Finds Neither Rhyme Nor Reason in a Cruel Childhood Rape." *People Weekly* 17 (March 15): 41–42.

McNally, Richard. 2001. *Remembering Trauma*. Cambridge, Mass.: Belknap Press of Harvard University Press.

McNaron, Toni A. H., and Yarrow Morgan, eds. 1982. *Voices in the Night: Women Speaking About Incest*. Minneapolis: Cleis Press.

McRobbie, Angela, and Sarah L. Thornton. 1995. "Rethinking 'Moral Panic' for Multi-Mediated Social Worlds." *The British Journal of Sociology* 46 (4): 559–574.

Meiselman, Karin C. 1978. *Incest: A Psychological Study of Causes and Effects with Treatment Recommendations*. San Francisco: Jossey-Bass.

Melucci, Alberto. 1989. *Nomads of the Present*. Philadelphia: Temple University Press.

Meyer, David S. 2006. *The Politics of Protest*. New York: Oxford University Press.

Meyer, David S., and Debra Minkoff. 2004. "Conceptualizing Political Opportunity." *Social Forces* 82(4): 1457–1492.

Meyer, David S., and Suzanne Staggenborg. 1996. "Movements, Countermovements, and the Structure of Political Opportunity." *American Journal of Sociology* 101:1628–1660.

Meyer, David S., and Nancy Whittier. 1994. "Social Movement Spillover." *Social Problems* 41(2): 277–298.

Meyer-Emrick, Nancy. 2001. *The Violence Against Women Act of 1994*. Westport, Conn.: Praeger.

Miller, Dusty. 2003. "The End of Innocence." *Psychotherapy Networker* 27(4): 24–33.

Miller, Leslie. 1992. "Sexual Abuse Survivors Find Strength to Speak in Numbers." *USA Today* August 27, 1992.

Minkoff, Debra. 2002. "The Emergence of Hybrid Organizational Forms: Combining Identity-Based Service Provision and Political Action." *Nonprofit and Voluntary Sector Quarterly* 31(3): 377–401.

Minow, Martha. 1997. *Not Only for Myself: Identity, Politics, and the Law.* New York: New Press.

Mitchell, Timothy. 1991. "The Limits of the State." *American Political Science Review* 85(1): 77–97.

Mithers, Carol. 1984. "Incest: The Crime That's All in the Family." *Mademoiselle* 90 (June): 125–127, 216.

Moore, Jamie M. 1986. "Civil Remedies for Incest Survivors." *Response* 9(2): 11–16.

Morgen, Sandra. 2002. *Into Our Own Hands.* New Brunswick, N.J.: Rutgers.

Mouton, F. Ray, and Thomas P. Doyle. *The Problem of Sexual Molestation by Roman Catholic Clergy.* Available at http://www.natcath.com/NCR_Online/documents/part1.pdf (accessed March 23, 2009).

Murphy, Gillian. 2002. *Beyond Surviving: Toward a Movement to Prevent Child Sexual Abuse.* New York: Ms. Foundation for Women.

Naples, Nancy. 2002. "Materialist Feminist Discourse Analysis and Social Movement Research: Mapping the Changing Context for 'Community Control.'" In Nancy Whittier, Belinda Robnett, and David S. Meyer, eds., *Social Movements: Identity, Culture, and the State.* New York: Oxford University Press, 226–246.

Nathan, Debbie, and Michael Snedeker. 1995. *Satan's Silence: Ritual Abuse and the Making of a Modern Witch Hunt.* New York: Basic Books.

Nelson, Barbara J. 1984. *Making an Issue of Child Abuse.* Chicago: University of Chicago Press.

Nepstad, Sharon Erickson. 2001."Creating Transnational Solidarity: The Use of Narrative in the U.S.–Central America Peace Movement." *Mobilization* 6(1): 21–36.

Nolan, James, Jr. 1998. *The Therapeutic State: Justifying Government at Century's End.* New York: New York University Press.

Ofshe, Richard, and Ethan Watters. 1994. *Making Monsters: False Memory, Psychotherapy, and Sexual Hysteria.* New York: Charles Scribner's.

O'Hare, Janet, and Katy Taylor. 1983. "The Reality of Incest." *Women and Therapy* 2(2/3): 215–229.

Olson, Lynne. 1984. "The Scandal That Shocked the Nation." *Working Woman* 9 (2, Aug.): 67–68, 70.

O'Neill, Katie. 1984. "My Father Abused Me Sexually." *Glamour* 82 (June): 264–265, 286–288.

"Painful Secrets." 1985. *Time,* July 1: 51.

Piven, Frances Fox, and Richard Cloward. 1979. *Poor People's Movements: Why They Succeed, How They Fail.* New York: Vintage.

Polletta, Francesca. 2002. *Freedom Is an Endless Meeting: Democracy in American Social Movements.* Chicago: University of Chicago Press.

Polletta, Francesca, and James M. Jasper. 2000. "Collective Identity and Social Movements." *Annual Review of Sociology* 27:283–305.

Polsky, Andrew J. 1991. *The Rise of the Therapeutic State*. Princeton, N.J.: Princeton University Press.

Press, Aric. 1985. "The Youngest Witnesses." *Newsweek* (Feb. 18): 72–75.

Proffitt, Norma Jean. 2000. *Women Survivors, Psychological Trauma, and the Politics of Resistance*. Binghamton, N.Y.: Haworth Press.

Quarantelli, E. L. 2001. "Sociology of Panic." In *International Encyclopedia of the Social and Behavioral Sciences*. Oxford, U.K.: Pergamon Press.

Rapping, Elaine. 1996. *The Culture of Recovery: Making Sense of the Self-Help Movement in Women's Lives*. Boston: Beacon Press.

Ray, Raka. 1998. "Women's Movements and Political Fields: A Comparison of Two Indian Cities." *Social Problems* 45(1): 21–36.

"Readers' Response." 1986. *The Christian Century* (Feb. 19): 440.

Reed, Thomas J. 1978. Letter to the Editor. *The Progressive* 42 (December): 62–3.

Reinelt, Clare. 1995. "Moving Onto the Terrain of the State: The Battered Women's Movement and the Politics of Engagement." In *Feminist Organizations*, pp. 84–104. Myra Marx Ferree and Patricia Yancey Martin, eds. Philadelphia: Temple,

Reger, Jo. 2005. *Different Wavelengths*. New York: Routledge.

Rochon, Thomas R. 1998. *Culture Moves*. Princeton, N.J.: Princeton University Press.

Roiphe, Katie. 1993. *The Morning After: Sex, Fear, and Feminism on Campus*. Boston: Little, Brown.

Rondon, Nayda. 1986. "Kid-Ability: Taking Action Against Child Sexual Abuse." *Children Today* July-August: 22–25.

Rose, Nikolas. 1990. *Governing the Soul: The Shaping of the Private Self*. London: Routledge.

———. 1999. *Powers of Freedom*. New York: Cambridge University Press.

Rossi, Alice. 1982. *Feminists in Politics*. New York: Academic Press, 1982.

Roth, Benita. 2004. *Separate Roads to Feminism*. Cambridge: Cambridge University Press.

Rupp, Leila J., and Verta Taylor. 2003. *Drag Queens at the 801 Cabaret*. Chicago: University of Chicago Press.

Rush, Florence. 1974. "The Sexual Abuse of Children: A Feminist Point of View," pp. 64–75 in Noreen Connell and Cassandra Wilson, eds., *Rape: The First Sourcebook for Women*. New York: American Library.

Rush, Florence. 1977. "Freud and the Sexual Abuse of Children." *Chrysalis* 1(1).

———. 1980. *The Best-Kept Secret: Sexual Abuse of Children*. New York: McGraw-Hill.

Russell, Diana E. H. 1986. *The Secret Trauma: Incest in the Lives of Girls and Women*. New York: Basic Books.

Russell, Diana E. H., and Bolen, Rebecca M. 2000. *The Epidemic of Rape and Child Sexual Abuse in the United States*. Thousand Oaks, Calif.: Sage.

Russell, Diana E. H., and Nicole Van de Ven, eds. 1976. *The Proceedings of the International Tribunal on Crimes Against Women*. Millbrae, Calif.: Les Femmes.

Ryan, Charlotte. 1991. *Prime-Time Activism*. Boston: South End Press.

Sacco, Lynn 2002. "Sanitized for Your Protection." *Journal of Women's History* 14(3): 80–105.
Salter, Anna C. 1998. "Confessions of a Whistle-Blower: Lessons Learned." *Ethics and Behavior* 8(2): 115–125.
Schmitt, Barton D. 1976. "What Teachers Need to Know About Child Abuse and Neglect." *Education Digest* 41(March): 19–21.
Schultz, Dodi. 1977. "The Terror of Child Molestation." *Parents Magazine* 52:44–45, et seq.
Scott, Jeffery Warren. 1986. "Confidentiality and Child Abuse: Church and State Collide." *The Christian Century* (Feb. 9) 174–175.
Scott, Sara. 2001. *The Politics and Experience of Ritual Abuse*. London: Open University Press.
Scourfield, Jonathan, and Ian Welsh. 2003. "Risk, Reflexivity and Social Control in Child Protection." *Critical Social Policy* 23(3): 398–420.
Sedlak, Andrea, Howard Doueck, Peter Lyons, Susan Wells, Dana Schultz, and Francis Gragg. 2005. "Child Maltreatment and the Justice System." *Research on Social Work Practice* 15(5): 389–403.
"Sexual Abuse by Clergy: A Moral Panic." Religioustolerance.org website. Available at www.religioustolerance.org/clergy_sex1.htm (accessed July 14, 2008).
Shalala, Donna. 1994. "Domestic Terrorism: An Unacknowledged Epidemic." Delivered before the Mass. Conference on Family Violence, Washington, D.C., March 11. *Vital Speeches of the Day*, 0042–742X, May 15, 1994. Vol. 60 (15).
"Sick Fathers." 1984. *The Nation* 238 (2, Jan. 21): 35–36.
Simonds, Wendy. 1992. *Women and Self-Help Culture*. New Brunswick, N.J.: Rutgers University Press.
Skrentny, John D. 2002. *The Minority Rights Revolution*. Cambridge, Mass.: The Belknap Press of Harvard University Press.
Smith, Christian. 1996. *Resisting Reagan*. Chicago: University of Chicago Press.
Smith, Dorothy. 1987. *The Everyday World as Problematic*. Toronto: University of Toronto Press.
Snow, David A. 2004. "Framing Processes, Ideology, and Discursive Fields." In David A. Snow, Sarah A. Soule, and Hanspeter Kriesi, eds., *The Blackwell Companion to Social Movements*, pp. 380–412. New York: Blackwell.
Snow, David A., and Robert D. Benford. 1992. "Master Frames and Cycles of Protest." In Aldon Morris and Carol Mueller, eds., *Frontiers of Social Movement Theory*, pp. 133–35. New Haven: Yale University Press.
Snow, David A., R. Burke Rochford Jr., Steven K. Worden, and Robert D. Benford. 1986. "Frame Alignment Processes, Micromobilization, and Movement Participation." *American Sociological Review* 51: 464–81.
Sommers, Christina Hoff, and Sally Satel. 2005. One Nation Under Therapy: *How the Helping Culture Is Eroding Self-Reliance*. New York: St. Martin's Press.
Specht, Harry, and Mark E. Courtney. 1994. *Unfaithful Angels: How Social Work Has Abandoned Its Mission*. New York: The Free Press.

Springer, Kimberly. 2005. *Living for the Revolution*. Durham, N.C.: Duke University Press.

Staggenborg, Suzanne. 1988. "The Consequences of Professionalization and Formalization in the Pro-Choice Movement." *American Sociological Review* 53: 585–605.

———. 1989. "Stability and Innovation in the Pro-Choice Movement: A Comparison of Two Movement Organizations." *Social Problems* 36: 75–92.

Stark, Elizabeth. 1984. "The Unspeakable Family Secret." *Psychology Today* 18 (May): 38–39, 42, 44–46.

Steinberg, Marc. 2002. "Toward a More Dialogic Analysis of Social Movement Culture." In Nancy Whittier, Belinda Robnett, and David S. Meyer, *Social Movements: Identity, Culture, and the State*. New York: Oxford University Press.

———. 1999. "The Talk and Back Talk of Collective Action." *American Journal of Sociology* 105: 736–80.

Stewart, Deborah. 1992. "Sexually Transmitted Disease." In *Evaluation of the Sexually Abused Child: A Medical Textbook and Photographic Atlas*, edited by Astrid Heger and S. Jean Emans, pp. 145–6. New York: Oxford University Press.

Stout, Linda. 1996. *Bridging the Class Divide and Other Lessons for Grassroots Organizing*. Boston: Beacon Press.

Stroud, Delores, Sonja Martens, and Julia Barker. 2000. "Criminal Investigation of Child Sexual Abuse." *Child Abuse and Neglect* 24(5): 689–700.

Stucker, Jan. 1977. "I Tried to Fantasize That All Fathers Had Intercourse with Their Daughters: The Story of Mary C." *Ms.* 5 (10, April): 65–67, 105.

Swidler, Ann, and Jorge Arditi. 1994. "The New Sociology of Knowledge." *Annual Review of Sociology* 20: 305–29.

Sykes, Charles. 1992. *A Nation of Victims: The Decay of the American Character*. New York: St. Martin's Press.

Szasz, Thomas. 1961. *The Myth of Mental Illness*. New York: Paul B. Hoeber.

Tanne, Janice Hopkins. 2003. "Obituary, Judianne Densen-Gerber." *BMJ* 326 (1216, 31 May). Available at http://bmj.bmjjournals.com/cgi/content/full/326/7400/1216 (accessed October 24, 2005).

Tarrow, Sidney. 1994. *Power in Movement*, 2nd ed. Cambridge University Press.

Tavris, Carol. 1993. "Beware the Incest-Survivor Machine." *New York Times Book Review*, 1, Jan. 3: 16–17.

Taylor, Verta. 1996. *Rock-a-bye Baby: Feminism, Self-Help, and Postpartum Depression*. New York: Routledge.

Taylor, Verta, and Nancy Whittier. 1992. "Collective Identity and Lesbian Feminist Mobilization." In *Frontiers of Social Movement Theory*, edited by Aldon Morris and Carol Mueller. New Haven: Yale University Press.

Tewksbury, Richard, and Matthew Lees. 2006. "Perceptions of Sex Offender Registration." *Sociological Spectrum* 26(3): 309–344.

Thoennes, Nancy. 1988. "Child Sexual Abuse: Whom Should the Judge Believe?" *The Judges Journal* 27(Summer): 14–18.

Thompson, Dianne. 1987. "Our 'Nice' Neighbor Was Sexually Abusing Our Daughter." *McCall's* (Feb.): 93–94.

Tunley, Roul. 1981. "Incest: Facing the Ultimate Taboo." *Readers Digest* 118 (Jan.): 137–146.

Underwager, Ralph, and Hollida Wakefield. 1994. "Misinterpretation of a Primary Prevention Effort," *Issues in Child Abuse Accusations*, 6(2), 96–107.

Victor, Jeffrey S. 1993. *Satanic Panic: The Creation of a Contemporary Legend.* Chicago: Open Court Publishing Company.

———. 1994. "Fundamentalist Religion and the Moral Crusade Against Satanism." *Deviant Behavior* 15: 305–334.

———. 1998. "Moral Panics and the Social Construction of Deviant Behavior: A Theory and Application to the Case of Ritual Child Abuse." *Sociological Perspectives* 41(3): 541–565.

Wakefield, H., and Underwager, R. 1988. *Accusations of Child Sexual Abuse* (Springfield, Ill.: Charles C. Thomas)

———. 1990. "Effective Use of a Mental Health Expert in Child Sexual Abuse Cases." *The Champion* (Aug.): 21–25.

———. 1992. "Recovered Memories of Alleged Sexual Abuse: Lawsuits Against Parents." *Behavioral Sciences and the Law*, 10: 483–508.

Walker, Gillian. 1990. *Family Violence and the Women's Movement: The Conceptual Politics of Struggle.* Toronto: University of Toronto Press.

Weber, Ellen. 1977. "Incest—Sexual Abuse Begins at Home." *Ms.* 5 (10, April): 64–67.

Weed, Frank J. 1995. *Certainty of Justice: Reform in the Crime Victim Movement.* New York: Aldine de Gruyter.

Weigand, Kate. 2001. *Red Feminism.* Baltimore, Md.: Johns Hopkins University Press.

Westerlund, Elaine. 1992. *Women's Sexuality After Childhood Incest.* New York: W.W. Norton.

Wexler, Richard. 1985. "Invasion of the Child Savers: No One Is Safe in the War Against Abuse." *The Progressive*, September: 19–22.

Whalen, Jack, and Richard Flacks. 1989. *Beyond the Barricades: The Sixties Generation Grows Up.* Philadelphia: Temple University Press.

"What to Do About Child Abuse." 1985. *Ebony* 40 (May): 158–164.

Whittier, Nancy. 1995. *Feminist Generations: The Persistence of a Radical Women's Movement.* Philadelphia: Temple University Press.

———. 2001. "Emotional Strategies: The Collective Reconstruction and Display of Oppositional Emotions in the Movement Against Child Sexual Abuse." In Francesca Polletta, Jeff Goodwin, and James Jasper, eds., *Political Passions: Emotions and Social Movements.* Chicago: University of Chicago Press.

———. 2002. "Meaning and Structure in Social Movements." In David S. Meyer, Nancy Whittier, and Belinda Robnett, eds., *Social Movements: Identity, Culture, and the State*, pp. 289–307. New York: Oxford University Press.

Williams, Rhys. 2004. "The Cultural Contexts of Collective Action: Constraints, Opportunities, and the Symbolic Life of Social Movements." In David Snow, Sarah Soule, and Hanspieter Kriesi, eds., *Blackwell*

Companion to Social Movements, pp. 91–115. Malden, Mass.: Blackwell Publishing.

———. 1995. "Constructing the Public Good: Social Movements and Cultural Resources." *Social Problems* 42(1): 124–144.

Williams, Rhys, and Timothy J. Kubal. 1999. "Movement Frames and the Cultural Environment: Resonance, Failure, and the Boundaries of the Legitimate." *Research in Social Movements, Conflict, and Change* 21: 225–48.

Wilson, Melba. 1994. *Crossing the Boundary: Black Women Survive Incest.* Seattle: Seal Press.

Wright, Lawrence. 1994. *Remembering Satan.* New York: Knopf.

Wuthnow, Robert. 1985. "State Structures and Ideological Outcomes." *American Sociological Review* 50 (Dec.): 799–821.

Yudkin, Marcia. 1981. "Breaking the Incest Taboo: Those Who Crusade for Family 'Love' Forget the Balance of Family Power." *The Progressive* 45(May): 26–28.

Zegart, Dan. 1989. "Solomon's Choice." *Ms.*, June: 78–83.

Zeldin, Lea. 1978. "The Road to Hell..." *The Progressive* 42 (Sept.): 11.

Zerilli, Linda. 2005. *Feminism and the Abyss of Freedom.* Chicago: University of Chicago Press.

Index

ACT-UP, 41, 168, 202
African-Americans
 black power movement, 62
 and child sexual abuse 3–4, 60–61, 119
 status of, 62
Against Our Will, 23, 36, 58
Aid to Families with Dependent Children (AFDC), 78
Alcoholics Anonymous, 102, 107–108
American Coalition for Abuse Awareness, 198
American Humane Association, Children's Division, 37, 75
American Medical Association, 200, 205
American Professional Society on the Abuse of Children (APSAC), 100
American Psychiatric Association (APA), 49, 50, 51, 56, 65
American Society for the Prevention of Cruelty to Children, 107
Americans with Disabilities Act, 194, 235 n. 24
anti-feminism, 30
anti-rape movement. *See also* rape
 history of, 22–28
 influence on survivors' movement, 22–27, 32–38, 175
 funding of, 39, 189–190
 professionalization of, 25, 54, 189–190
 strategies of, 22–27, 32

Armstrong, Louise, 35, 37–38, 41, 98
art, activist, 175, 178–179
Association for the Treatment of Sexual Abusers, 205
Attorney General's Task Force on Family Violence, 86

Barden, Christopher, 151–152
Bass, Ellen, 52, 150, 157, 163, 171, 229 n. 84
Batts, Sharon, 107
Berkeley Women's Center, 45
Bernardin, Cardinal, 152, 209
Besharov, Douglas, 83, 124
The Best Kept Secret, 58, 118, 127
Betrayal Trauma (J. Freyd), 159
Brady, Kate, 98
Brown, Laura, 150
Brown, Wendy, 41
Brownmiller, Susan, 23, 33, 35–38, 116, 123
Burgess, Ann, 65
Bush, George W., 187
Butler, Sandra, 27, 38

Comprehensive Employment and Training Act of 1973 (CETA), 39
Calof, David, 150
Cambridge Women's Center, 43, 44, 46
Carson, Diana, 97–98
Catholic Church, 5

Catholic Church, (*continued*)
  clergy abuse, 10, 17, 105–107, 125, 195, 209–210
Cheit, Ross, 130, 137
child abuse, physical, 21
Child Abuse Prevention and Treatment Act/Child Abuse Prevention and Treatment and Adoption Reform Act (CAPTA/CAPTARA), 30, 76–77, 80–83, 86, 94, 188–189, 207, 223 n. 20
Child Assault Prevention Project (CAP), 28, 32–35
  controversy about, 34
  funding of, 39
  national influence of, 34, 85, 89, 118
child care, 91–92
Childhelp, 126
child pornography, 76–77, 86, 91, 114, 115, 118
child protective movement, 7, 37, 96, 105
Child Protective Services (CPS), 17, 37, 41, 70–71, 76, 188
  critique of, 90, 124, 138, 162, 186
  multidisciplinary connections, and, 84–85, 87, 96
  See also child sexual abuse, investigations of, legal
child neglect, 30, 70, 74, 76, 83, 90, 119, 124, 147
child sexual abuse
  allegations of, false, 91, 123–125
  awareness about, public, 5, 8, 93–94, 119
  coalitions in opposition to, 92–93 (*see also* coalitions)
  daycare centers, in, 86, 90–93, 120, 124
  definitions of, 10, 23–24, 56, 76, 85
  effects of, 53, 54, 56–58, 118
  and gender, 20
  healing, individual, 128
  history of, 5, 7–10, 17
  and homophobia, 210
  investigations of, legal, 86–87, 90, 91–93 (*see also* child protective services)
  and law-enforcement, 71, 85, 86–88, 90, 196–199
  legislation regarding, 75–78, 82–83, 86–87 (*see also* United States Congress)
  and litigation, civil, 195–196
  of males, 60, 89, 100, 109, 177–178, 209–210
  mandated reporting, 171–172, 188
  media attention to, 9, 20, 76, 93–94, 99, 111–132 (*see also* media)
  organizing against, non-feminist, 84–90, 95–110
  penalties for, 86, 90, 196–199, 205
  perspectives on
    Christian, 82, 92, 93, 105–106, 1–7, 120, 164, 171
    conservative, 6, 82, 92–93, 106, 123, 124, 162, 171
    criminal, 9, 11, 86–87, 211
    feminist, 5–6, 7–8, 27–39, 55, 69, 84, 114–115, 123, 197, 209–210
    government, 85–90
    left, 123
    medical, 9, 11, 75, 199–206, 211
    single-issue, 8, 20, 95–110, 211
    sociological, 17–18
    See also frames; discourse
  prevalence of, 24–25, 55, 83, 215–216 n. 1
  prevention of, 32–35, 85, 88–90, 115–116, 191, 197, 200–207
  prosecutions of
    frequency, 196–199
    high profile 90–93
    opposition to, 93
    See also child sexual abuse, and law enforcement
  and public health, 199–207, 212, 236 n. 38
  and public policy, 9, 20, 86–87, 182–207
  public view of, 4, 9, 54, 90, 212
  and psychotherapy, 6, 8, 54
  recovery from, 93–94
  reporting of, 83–84
  scholarly debates about, 11, 16–18
  and sensationalism, 93
  stigma about, 46, 111, 157, 205, 209
  statute of limitations for, 108, 152–153, 195, 197–198, 234 n. 16
  symptoms of, 66, 144
  trauma model, 57
  treatment of, 65–67, 84–86, 118, 122, 125
  victims, gender of, 20, 216 n. 2, 220 n. 26,
  visibility, 3–4, 5, 29–30, 48, 50, 53, 83, 95, 116
  women, by 89, 109
Children's Bureau, United States, 75, 81, 115, 188
Children's Institute International, 88, 91
Children's Justice Act of 1986, 86
Christian Century, 106
Christian Coalition, 164
Christian fundamentalism 92–93
Christian, Meg, 44
Christianity Today, 105
Chrysalis, 36
Civil rights movement, 62, 78, 176
Clinton, (Bill) administration, 187
Clothesline Project, 178
collective identity, 13–14, 48, 214, 217 n. 4
  and selection processes, 16, 194, 196
  survivor, 42, 46, 58, 60, 96, 98, 104, 108, 168 (*see also* racial identity)

Colorado Mental Health Grievance Board, 153
Colorado National Center for the Prevention and Treatment of Child Abuse and Neglect, 116
co-counseling, 49, 51–52, 63
Cohn, Anne, 121
Columbus, Ohio, 32–33
Combahee River Collective, 59, 62, 64
Coming out. *See also* collective identity; False Memory Syndrome Foundation, coming out; visibility, politics of
 as lesbian/gay/bisexual/transgendered, 167–169
 as survivor of child sexual abuse, 2–4, 10, 29–30, 48, 50, 53, 60, 61, 116–118, 125, 167–169, 175–181, 200, 209
Community Mental Health Centers (CMHC), 79–80
consciousness raising, 22, 29, 33, 35, 57, 62
Conspiracy of Silence, 58, 127
Cooper, Sally, 118
Counter Abuse, Inc., 105
countermovements. *See also* False Memory Syndrome Foundation
 activities of, 9, 139–140, 149–160, 191, 211–212
 survivors' movement, effects on, 167, 169–174, 198, 200, 205–207
The Courage to Heal, 52, 127–129, 145, 157, 163, 171
Courtois, Christine, 25, 35

Daly, Mary, 37
Danson, Ted, 120
Darkness to Light (D2L), 201, 202–206
Daubert ruling of 1994, 151, 229 n. 91
Davis, Joseph, 54
Davis, Laura, 150, 157, 163
"Dear Mr. Jesus," 107
Densen-Gerber, Judianne, 76–77, 115
discourse. *See also* child sexual abuse, perspectives on; frames
 criminal, 82, 194–195
 mainstream, about child sexual abuse, 110–112
 medical, 10, 37, 194–195
 patriarchy, 57
 and political opportunities, 15
 public health, 200–201
 scientific, 133, 146, 164–165
 and selection processes, 126, 131, 183–184, 196, 203
 state, therapeutic, 10, 12, 13, 71, 73, 208
 therapeutic, use by movement, 13–14, 71, 73, 94
 twelve-step, 108, 160

"women-and-children," 28, 38
dissociative identity disorder, 154
domestic violence, 46, 82, 187–88, 190–92, 198, 200, 201, 203, 204, 211
Dworkin, Andrea, 22

Ebony magazine, 119
Echols, Alice, 41
Economic Opportunity Act of 1964, 79–80
Elders, Joycelyn, 171–172
emotions
 and politics, 6, 40, 46
 role in social change, 47–48, 68–69, 169–170
 transformation of, 46, 175
Episcopal Diocese of Massachusetts, 43
Essence magazine, 119

False Memory Syndrome Foundation (FSMF), 3, 9, 225 n. 1
 activities of, 9, 139–140, 149–, 191
 child sexual abuse, views on, 9, 147–148
 coalitions of, 9, 10, 20, 137, 160–164
 and coming out, 150
 constituencies of, 9, 138–139
 as countermovement, 9, 20, 133–135, 137, 148–166
 feminism, views on, 141, 162–164, 165
 founding of, 133, 138–139
 frame extensions, 143
 frames, memory science, 141–146, 165
 funding of, 139–140
 and gender, 161
 goals of, 9, 134, 146–148
 and government, 188–189
 as hybrid organization, 134
 and the left, 10, 163–164
 professionals, response to, 158–160
 public opinion, impact on, 9, 140, 146, 157, 165–166, 211–212
 public policy, impact on, 135, 140, 146, 166, 211–212, 233 n. 7
 and recovered memories, 9, 134, 141–146, 154–155, 162, 209
 and science, 141, 143–146, 149, 155, 164–165
 strategies and tactics of, 137–138, 140–160, 229 n. 84,
 survivors' movement, confrontations with, 155–160, 174, 209
 therapy, impact on, 153–155, 157, 159–160
 "Witchhunt," 162
 See also countermovements
Father-Daughter Incest (Herman), 58, 127
Federal Uniform Crime Victims Reparations Act of 1973, 192

Index

Feld, Alan, 154
feminism.
  See also child sexual abuse, perspectives on, feminist; feminist movement; frames, feminist
  black, 58, 177
  critiques of, 93
  and self-defense, 26
  and speak outs, 29, 175
  psychotherapy, approaches to, 11, 16, 35–36
Feminist Karate Union, 26
feminist health movement, 48
feminist movement, 27–28
  decline of, 40
  gains of, 10, 62, 125, 199, 226 n.10
  influence on survivors' movement, 39, 95–96, 210
  institutions of, cultural, 27
  outcomes, 6
  therapeutic turn in, 12–16, 41–42
  views on survivors' movement, 61
  See also feminism
Finkelhor, David, 83–84, 127
Firestone, Shulamith, 22
Fitzpatrick, Frank, 158
Focus on the Family, 106
Foucault, Michel, 41
Frames, 6, 217 n. 4
  civil liberties, 92, 115, 137, 161, 163–164, 211
  conservative, 6, 82, 92–3, 106, 123, 124, 162, 171
  criminal, 86, 112, 183, 192–197
  cult, 141–143
  feminist, 22–28, 112, 116–117, 123
  government, 90
  master, 109–110
  medical, 10, 119, 121, 126, 183, 197
  policy-making, 112
  psychological, 118
  rights, 110
  self-help, 116
  treatment, 37, 116
  See also child sexual abuse, perspectives on; discourse
Frances Ann Speaks Out: My Father Raped Me, 36–37
Fresh Air Fund, 119
Freud, Sigmund, 24, 36
Freyd, Jennifer, 138, 159
Freyd, Pamela, 138, 139–140, 145–148, 152, 154, 156, 159, 161
Freyd, Peter, 138, 159
Funding
  crime victims compensation funds, 10, 192–196
  federal, 8, 77–90, 93–94, 187–192, 207 (*see also* NCCAN)
  foundation, 182
  social service block grants (SSBGs), 80–82
  state, 8, 80–81, 182, 192–196
Flintstones, 89
The Furies, 62

Gardner, Richard, M.D., 188
gay liberation, 62
Gay Liberation Front, 62
Generation Five, 201, 203–206, 236 n. 39
Giaretto, Hank, 37
Giaretto Institute, 81, 120, 125
Girls Clubs of America, 34, 89
Glamour magazine, 117

Harrington, Michael, 78
Hartley, Mariette, 89
Harvard Medical School, 122
Hawkins, Paula, 117
Healing Woman Foundation, 170
Heaven's Gate cult, 142
Henry, Fran, 30
Herman, Judith, 43, 54, 65, 122, 123, 127, 150, 159
Hopkins, Carol, 188
Huskey, Alice, 105
hybrid organizations
  definitions of, 40–41
  functions of, 14, 46–47, 212–213
  missions of, 105

identity politics, 58–60, 61, 98, 180
Illusion Theater, Minneapolis, 89
incest
  and abortion, 106
  advocacy of, 114–
  definitions of, 22–27, 35, 39, 40, 104, 173
  emotional, 101
  emphasis on, in survivors' movement, 35–38, 42–49, 55–57, 60, 99–101 104, 114, 118, 120, 129–130, 209, 218 n. 11
  myths about, 35, 37, 122
  prevalence of, 31, 216 n. 1
Incest Awareness Foundation (IAF), 171, 172
Incest Resources, 42–44, 45, 49–51, 55
  child protection agencies, relationship to, 84
  goals of, 47, 99
  and internalized oppression, 62–64
  services provided by, 47, 121, 122, 169
  causes of incest, analysis of 55–56
  diversity in, 60–61
  effects of incest, analysis of 56–58
  psychotherapy, influence on, 64–67
Incest Survivors Anonymous, 107–108. *See also* self-help, twelve-step groups

Incest Survivors' Resource Network International (ISRNI), 96–103, 105, 121, 122, 169. *See also* self-help, incest
I Never Told Anyone, 52–53, 127
Institute of Psychological Therapies, 139
Internalization. *See* oppression, internalized
International Congress on Child Abuse and Neglect, 83
International Society for Traumatic Stress Studies (ISTSS), 100
International Tribunal on Crimes Against Women, 28–30, 83
International Women's Year, 28, 30–31

Jackson, Michael, 119
Jenkins, Philip, 120
Jet magazine, 119
Johnson, Virginia, 114
Jones, Jim, 142
Justice for Children, 198

Kaminer, Wendy, 41
Kempe, Henry, 21, 83
Kempe National Center, C. Henry, 88
Kirschenbaum, Carol, 125
Kiss Daddy Goodnight, 127
knowledge
  experiential, 42, 54–58, 61, 101, 118, 149–150, 159, 191, 204, 209, 221 n. 35
  expert, 54, 69, 101, 191
  production of, 5, 40, 42, 53, 54–58, 134–137, 141–156, 164–166, 212 (*see also* False Memory Syndrome Foundation)
  social movements' contributions to, 135, 136, 208
  sociology of, 9
Koresh, David, 142

Ladies' Home Journal, 118
Landor Associates, 202
Lauper, Cyndi, 202
the left, 41, 61, 79
lesbian feminism, 42
lesbians, in survivors' movement, 44, 46
liberalism, 41
Loftus, Elizabeth, 144–145
Los Angeles Police Department, 37
Low, Alice, 116
Lucy Parsons Women's Coalition, 31

MacFarlane, Kee, 91
Madamoiselle magazine, 117, 123
Manhattan Inter-Hospital Sub-committee on Child Sexual Abuse, 98
Massachusetts General Hospital Boston Area Sexual Assault Coalition, 65
Rape Victims Advocates Group, 44
Masson, Jeffrey, 24
Masters, William, 114
McCalls magazine, 118
McKuen, Rod, 117
McMartin Preschool, 117, 120
Media
  and feminism, 116–117, 128–132
  government, federal, influence on, 116
  journalism, 114–120, 121–126
  publishing, 8–9, 126–129 (*see also* self-help, books)
  selection processes, 112–114, 123, 126, 206
  sexual abuse, coverage of, 20, 111–132, 200–206
  Survivor activists', influence on, 8, 126, 129–132, 183, 200–206, 211
  television, 121, 200–206
Mental Retardation Facilities and Mental Health Centers Construction Act, 79
Michigan Women's Music Festival, 45, 50, 63
Minneapolis Children's Theater Company, 117
Model Child Care Standards Act of 1985, 92
Moral Majority, 82, 92
moral panic, 11–12, 16–18, 120, 125, 129–130, 217 n. 4–9
Morrissey, Kathy, 49, 50, 51, 65–66
Mothers Against Drunk Driving, 200
Mothers Against Sexual Abuse, 200
Ms. Foundation for Women, 4, 204
Ms. magazine, 27, 37, 115, 123, 124, 126
multiple personality disorder. *See* dissociative identity disorder

The Nation, 163
National Assault Prevention Center, 187
National Black Women's Health Project, 170
National Catholic Reporter, 125
National Center on Child Abuse and Neglect (NCCAN). *See also* funding
  establishment of, 76
  funding by, 19, 74, 80–85, 87–90, 115, 117, 188–192, 198, 222 n. 9,
  priorities of, 84–85, 87–90, 93–94, 233 n. 7,
  programs, sponsored by, 118–119, 188
  publications, 115
  and survivors' movement, 84–90, 93–94, 116, 188
National Center for Missing and Exploited Children, 126
National Centers for Disease Control and Prevention (CDC), 4, 200, 205–206

National Child Abuse Defense and Resource Council, 162
National Committee for the Prevention of Child Abuse, 117, 121, 223 n. 22
National Conference on Sexual Victimization of Children, 117
National Institutes of Mental Health (NIMH), 32, 39, 79
National Network of Child Advocacy Centers, 198
National Organization on Child Abuse and Neglect conference, 99
National Organization for Victim's Assistance, 125
National Organization for Women, 27, 31
Native Americans, 85
Nelson, Barbara, 76
New Haven Women's Liberation, 27
New Orleans Southern Female Rights Union, 26
Newsweek magazine, 120, 124
New Times, 114
New York City Advisory Task Force on Sexual Assault, 97
New York Radical Feminists, 22, 23, 27, 35
New York Times, 139
New York Women Against Rape (NY-WAR), 35–36, 98
Nixon, Richard, 76
Noah, Chuck, 150, 157
Nolan, James, 73
Norwood, Robin, 129

Odyssey drug treatment centers, 76
O'sHare, Janet, 35–36
Old Wives' Tales bookstore, 45
On Our Way, 26
offenders, sexual
  detention of, indefinite, 9
  female, 101, 109, 211
  incarceration of, 9, 74, 196, 199, 205, 235 n. 25
  juvenile, 101–102
  registries and community notification laws, 9, 198–199, 235 n. 29
  treatment of, 10, 101–102, 125, 199, 226 n.10
Ofshe, Richard, 162
Ohme, Herman, 188–189
One Voice, 198
oppression, internalized
  and African-Americans, 62
  definition of, 8, 40
  social change, relationship to, 8, 42, 51, 62, 95
  theorizing about, 62–64, 210
Osanka, Franklin, 76–77
The Other America: Poverty in the United States, 78

Pandora, 25, 26
Paramount Home Video, 89
Parents Anonymous, 81, 85, 89, 189, 192, 207
Parents magazine, 115, 125
Parents United, Inc., 81, 85, 101, 117, 122, 125, 126, 129
pedophilia, 10, 125, 197, 199, 226 n. 10
Pendergrast, Mark, 157
People of Fire, 178
People magazine, 115
People Weekly, 118
Pleiades, 44–46, 50–51, 55
  causes of incest, views on 56
  child protection agencies, relationship to, 84
  diversity in, 60–61
  incest, analysis of effects of, 56–58
  and internalized oppression, 62–64
  media, contacts with, 122
  psychotherapy, influence on, 66–67
  political opportunities, 70–71, 74–77, 90–94, 182–186, 192–199, 209–213
Polsky, Andrew, 93
Pope, Harrison, 145
pornography, 30
post-traumatic stress disorder, 143, 194
Proffitt, Norma Jean, 183
The Progressive, 115, 124
prostitution, 91, 115
Protection of Children Against Sexual Exploitation Act of 1977, 77, 86
psychotherapy
  Christian, 92
  and family systems theory, 56
  feminist, 35–39, 64, 67, 221 n. 39
  sexual abuse, dominant discourse about, 48, 125
  survivors' movement, critiques of, 56, 64–69
  survivors' movement's influence on, 64–69, 169–174, 210
public policy
  survivors' movement, relationship to, 70–71, 79–94, 182–207
Puerto Rican Association for Community Affairs daycare center, 120
Puerto Rico, 90

Quakers, 98–99, 102, 105
Queer Nation, 168

race
  media coverage, 119
  prosecution, disparities in, 199
  public health campaigns, 203–204
  and survivors' movement, 172, 177, 199, 232 n. 2

racial identity
    survivors movement, in 3–4, 60–61
racism, 3
Radical Faeries, 62
Radicalesbians, 62
Ramona, Gary, 153, 158
Rape, 24–27, 35. *See also* child sexual abuse
Rape, Abuse, and Incest National Network (RAINN), 190
Rape crisis centers, 35–36, 46
Raphael, Sally Jesse, 139
Rapping, Elaine, 41
Reagan, Ronald administration, 82–84, 90
recovered-memory therapy. *See* False Memory Syndrome Foundation
Redbook magazine, 114, 118
Republican National Committee, 188
Republican Party, 86, 188
ritual abuse, 17, 90–93, 120, 129–130, 154, 163
Re-evaluation counseling (RC). *See* co-counseling
Ritter, John, 89
Rochon, Thomas, 64, 111, 212
Roiphe, Katie, 41
Roman Catholic Church. *See* Catholic Church
Rose, Nikolas, 72
Run Riot, 3, 157, 176
Rush, Florence, 23–24, 27, 33, 35–38, 98, 115, 118, 119, 125
Russell, Diana, 29, 83, 122, 127
Ryan, Jim, 171

Salter, Anna, 150, 153
Santa Clara Child Sexual Abuse Treatment Program, 37, 81
Sarrel, Lorna and Philip, 118
satanic abuse. *See* ritual abuse
"Scared Silent," 121
Schactow, Emily, 65
Schmitt, Barton, 116
schools, 10, 125, 199, 226 n.10
    and child abuse prevention, 32, 85, 89–90
The Secret Trauma (Russell), 127
selection processes, 11–12, 71, 93–94, 126, 183–186, 192, 199, 211–213
self, 10, 125, 199, 226 n.10
    definitions of, 46
    versus social structure, 41, 109, 168
self-help, 7–8, 40–42, 46, 48–51
    books, 126–129, 169 (*see also* media, publishing)
    Christian, 105–107, 171
    and education, 104, 109
    and feminism, 97–98, 101, 103, 108–110
    feminist, 7, 40–42, 95–96, 126, 210–211
    and lesbians, 98, 104, 171
    New Age, 171
    organizations, Twelve-step 46, 107–108, 169
    politicized forms of, 68–69, 97
    and politics, 96, 108–110, 131–132, 172–181
    and professionals, mental health, 104, 131–132, 169–170, 172
    and public policy, 99, 102, 104, 109–110,
    techniques of, 49
    traditions, twelve-step 102, 107, 108, 224 n. 9
    See also Incest Survivors' Resource Network International; VOICES in Action)
service provision
    social movements, by, 14, 81–82, 84–85, 87–90, 102–103, 182–183, 186–196
    state, by, 77, 80–90
sexual abuse. *See* child sexual abuse
Sexually Victimized Children (Finkelhor), 127
smurfs, 89
social movements
    changing forms of, 4, 5, 13–14, 212–213
    culture of, 12
    and cultural change, 4, 11, 15, 112–114, 129–132, 208, 212
    influence of, 15, 18
    and institutional change, 4, 213
    outcomes, 6, 10, 11–12, 15, 20, 73, 136–137, 182–186, 196, 207, 210, 213, 214
    of the 1960s, 6, 38, 41, 73, 79
    and political opportunities, 15
    professionalization, 190–192, 206
    and selection processes, 15–16, 112–114, 208, 211
    social programs, effects on, 79–80
    and the state, 8, 13, 41
    tactics and strategies, 5, 11, 13
Social Security Act, 78
Social Service Block Grants (SSBGs). *See* funding; NCCAN
Social work, government influence on, 77–79, 93
"Something About Amelia," 99, 120
speaking out. *See* coming out; visibility, politics of
Spiderman, 118
Steinem, Gloria, 31
Stop It Now!, 4, 30, 201–206
Stop the Silence, 200

"Strong Kids, Safe Kids," 89
Stuart, Robbie, 35
Survivor Connections, 158
Survivors of Incest Anonymous (SIA), 100, 107–108. *See also* self-help, twelve-step organizations
Survivors' movement. *See also* self-help; Incest Resources; Incest Survivors' Resource Network
International; Pleiades; Voices in Action
   coalitions in, 6, 10, 20, 198
   diversity in, 3–4, 5–6, 15, 18
   outcomes of, 16, 20, 186, 196, 214 (*see also* selection processes)
   phases of, 7–10
     feminist, 7, 19, 66, 95–96, 108–110, 209–211
     feminist self-help, 7–8, 19, 42–69
     single issue, 20, 95–110, 211
     See also child sexual abuse, and public health; discourse, public health; visibility, politics of

Tarrow, Sidney, 13
Tavris, Carol, 41
Taylor, Katy, 35–36
therapeutic politics, 11, 12–14, 39, 42, 213
   feminist critiques of, 41–42, 67–68, 109–110
   as structural challenge, 6–7, 13–14, 68–69, 208, 213–214
therapeutic state
   individual subjectivity, effects on, 11, 12, 68, 72, 213–214
   feminists in, 186–189
   quasi-governmental organizations, 189–192, 212 (*see also* Parents Anonymous; Rape; Abuse and Incest National Network; VAWA; Voices in Action; and Survivors' movement, quasi-governmental organizations)
   resistance to, 6, 13–14, 71, 81, 109–110, 206, 208, 213–214
   social control by, 11–12, 71–75, 82, 200, 206, 208, 213–214
   and social movements, 13–14, 72–73, 109–110, 196, 212–214
   strategies, 5, 6, 11
   survivor activists' participation in, 20, 74–75, 80, 109–110, 182–207, 211
   theories of, 71–75
Therapeutic turn. *See* therapeutic politics
Time magazine, 89, 115
True Memory Foundation, 158
twelve-step organizations. *See* self-help, twelve step organizations

Underwager, Ralph, 139, 153, 161, 226 n. 10,
United Nations, 28, 30
U.S. News and World Report, 115, 124
United States Congress, 76, 83, 188
United States Department of Health, Education and Welfare (HEW), 76, 83, 92
United States, Department of Justice, 205
United States, Office of the Surgeon General, 200

Voice of the Faithful, 209
victimization, 73
Victims of Child Abuse Act of 1990, 86
Victims of Crime Act (VOCA), 192–196, 234 n. 16
Victims of Child Abuse Laws (VOCAL), 124, 137, 162–163
Victims of Memory (Pendergrast), 157
Violence Against Women Act (VAWA), 187–190, 198, 207
visibility, politics of, 5, 10, 20, 167–169, 179–181, 200, 205–206, 210. *See also* child sexual
   abuse, visibility of
VOICES in Action (VOICES), 96–97, 98–99, 103–105, 107, 108, 121, 126, 169, 170–172, 182, 190–91. *See also* self-help

Wakefield, Hollida, 139, 153, 181, 226 n. 10,
War on Poverty, 77–80
Washington, D.C., Rape Crisis Center, 26
welfare rights movement, 79
welfare state, 41
West Coast Women's Music Festival, 44, 45
Williams, Rhys, 112
Winfrey, Oprah, 121
Wings Foundation, 193
Winkler, Henry, 89
Women Against Rape (WAR), 32–33
Women and Therapy, 36
Women in Black, 179
Women's Action Alliance, 27
Women's Action Collective, 32
Women's Mental Health Collective of Somerville, MA, 122
Women's movement. *See* feminist movement
Women's rights, 30
Women Who Love Too Much (Norwood), 129
Working Woman magazine, 120
writing workshops, 52–53

Young and Rubicam, Inc., 202

Made in the USA
Lexington, KY
21 April 2013